Women's International Thought: A New History is the first cross-disciplinary history of women's international thought. Bringing together some of the foremost historians and scholars of international relations working today, this book recovers and analyzes the path-breaking work of eighteen leading thinkers of international politics from the early to mid-twentieth century. Recovering and analyzing this important work, the essays offer revisionist accounts of IR's intellectual and disciplinary history and expand the locations, genres, and practices of international thinking. Systematically structured, and focusing in particular on Black diasporic, Anglo-American, and European historical women, it does more than "add women" to the existing intellectual and disciplinary histories from which they were erased. Instead, it raises fundamental questions about which kinds of subjects and what kind of thinking constitutes international thought, opening new vistas to scholars and students of international history and theory, intellectual history and women's and gender studies.

PATRICIA OWENS is Professor of International Relations and Fellow of Somerville College at the University of Oxford. Her previous publications include *Economy of Force* (2015), winner of BISA's Susan Strange Prize, *Between War and Politics* (2007) and co-editor of *The Globalization of World Politics* (2020). She is a former fellow of the Radcliffe Institute for Advanced Study and Proctor Fellow at Princeton University.

KATHARINA RIETZLER is Lecturer in American History at the University of Sussex. She is currently completing a book on American philanthropy, International Relations and the problem of the public, 1913–1954. Her work has appeared in journals such as *Modern Intellectual History*, *Diplomatic History*, and the *Journal of Global History*. She is a former Mellon Fellow in American History at the University of Cambridge.

Women's International Thought: A New History

Edited by

Patricia Owens
University of Oxford

Katharina Rietzler
University of Sussex

CAMBRIDGE
UNIVERSITY PRESS

University Printing House, Cambridge CB2 8BS, United Kingdom

One Liberty Plaza, 20th Floor, New York, NY 10006, USA

477 Williamstown Road, Port Melbourne, VIC 3207, Australia

314–321, 3rd Floor, Plot 3, Splendor Forum, Jasola District Centre, New Delhi – 110025, India

79 Anson Road, #06–04/06, Singapore 079906

Cambridge University Press is part of the University of Cambridge.

It furthers the University's mission by disseminating knowledge in the pursuit of education, learning, and research at the highest international levels of excellence.

www.cambridge.org
Information on this title: www.cambridge.org/9781108494694
DOI: 10.1017/9781108859684

© Patricia Owens and Katharina Rietzler 2021

First published 2021

A catalogue record for this publication is available from the British Library.

Library of Congress Cataloging-in-Publication Data
Names: Owens, Patricia, 1975– editor, writer of introduction. | Rietzler, Katharina, 1978– editor, writer of introduction.
Title: Women's international thought : a new history / edited by Patricia Owens, University of Oxford, Katharina Rietzler, University of Sussex.
Description: First edition. | New York : Cambridge University Press, 2021. | Includes bibliographical references and index.
Identifiers: LCCN 2020022748 (print) | LCCN 2020022749 (ebook) | ISBN 9781108494694 (hardback) | ISBN 9781108796873 (paperback) | ISBN 9781108859684 (epub)
Subjects: LCSH: International relations–History–20th century | Women–Political activity. | Women–Intellectual life. | Feminism–History–20th century. | Internationalism–History–20th century.
Classification: LCC JZ1253.2 .W68 2021 (print) | LCC JZ1253.2 (ebook) | DDC 327.101–dc23
LC record available at https://lccn.loc.gov/2020022748
LC ebook record available at https://lccn.loc.gov/2020022749

ISBN 978-1-108-49469-4 Hardback
ISBN 978-1-108-79687-3 Paperback

Contents

List of Illustrations

Contributors

LUCIAN M. ASHWORTH is a Professor in the Department of Political Science at the Memorial University of Newfoundland

KEISHA N. BLAIN is an Associate Professor of History at the University of Pittsburgh

CATIA C. CONFORTINI is Associate Professor and Co-Director of the Peace and Justice Studies Program at Wellesley College

GEOFFREY FIELD is Emeritus Professor of History at Purchase College, State University of New York, where he was Doris and Karl Kempner Distinguished Professor

KIMBERLY HUTCHINGS is Professor of Politics and International Relations at Queen Mary University of London

ANDREW JEWETT is a Visiting Associate Professor of History at Boston College

HELEN M. KINSELLA is an Associate Professor of Political Science at the University of Minnesota

VIVIAN M. MAY is Director of the Humanities Center and Professor of Women's and Gender Studies at Syracuse University

PATRICIA OWENS is Professor of International Relations and Fellow of Somerville College at the University of Oxford

TAMSON PIETSCH is Associate Professor and Director of the Australian Centre for Public History at the University of Technology Sydney

KATHARINA RIETZLER is a Lecturer (Assistant Professor) in the History Department at the University of Sussex

OR ROSENBOIM is a Lecturer (Assistant Professor) in Modern History at City University of London

BARBARA D. SAVAGE is Geraldine R. Segal Professor of American Social Thought at the University of Pennsylvania

GLENDA SLUGA is Professor of International History at the European University Institute/University of Sydney

ROBBIE SHILLIAM is Professor in the Department of Political Science at Johns Hopkins University

IMAOBONG UMOREN is Assistant Professor of International History of Gender at the London School of Economics

NATASHA WHEATLEY is Assistant Professor of History at Princeton University

Preface and Acknowledgments

The subtitle of this volume refers to a "new history" of women's international thought. Two caveats are in order. First, a new history is not the last word. We are conscious that this volume is merely a beginning, that we ourselves are guilty of omissions, and that there will likely be further selective readings, myopias, and appropriations down the line. Yet, it was important to us to capture the sense of openness and possibility that the category of "women's international thought" had to offer, and this is the spirit in which we have approached our work as editors. Second, we wish to acknowledge the many labors of others that went into making this book. We have incurred multiple debts, intellectual, material, institutional and historiographical, and we wish to acknowledge them here.

This is the first major publication of our interdisciplinary research project Women and the History of International Thought (2018–2022), generously funded by the Leverhulme Trust (grant number RPG-2017-319). We are hugely grateful to the Trust for its commitment to recovering and evaluating historical women's international thought in a genuinely interdisciplinary context. We would also like to thank our co-investigator Kimberly Hutchings for her steadfast commitment to the project and for making each iteration of the grant application and subsequent work immeasurably better. Many colleagues at Sussex and beyond helped to shape our initial ideas into a coherent and (we hope) achievable research program. We are grateful to Duncan Bell, Lene Hansen, Andrew Hurrell, Helen M. Kinsella, Helen McCarthy, Iain McDaniel, Susan Pedersen, Jan Selby, Glenda Sluga, and Rorden Wilkinson for valuable feedback, support, and encouragement. We also thank David Armitage, Robert Vitalis, and Penny Weiss, who serve as the Advisors on the Leverhulme project.

The idea for this volume was sparked at a small workshop in 2015, co-organized by Valeska Huber, Tamson Pietsch, and Katharina Rietzler, and funded by the German Historical Institute, London and the Consortium of the Humanities and the Arts South-East England. The event was originally conceived as a meeting of historians interested in how to write the intellectual history of twentieth-century internationalist women, inspired by approaches to women's intellectual history that American historians such as Mia Bay, Farah J. Griffin, Martha S. Jones, Barbara D. Savage, and Linda Kerber have developed.[1] The workshop organizers also sought to draw in expertise from the discipline of International Relations (IR), and Patricia Owens, author of the only IR monograph on an historical woman thinker, happily joined the discussion.[2] In the course of the day's conversations, the idea for a collaborative and genuinely interdisciplinary project across History and IR gradually took shape.

Our collaboration received initial financial support from the Radcliffe Institute for Advanced Study at Harvard University and the British International Studies Association, which enabled us to convene two further workshops where we initially brought together several of the authors in this volume. Kimberly Hutchings joined us to co-sponsor a British International Studies Association pre-conference workshop in Brighton in June 2017, while, in March 2018, David Armitage co-sponsored a Radcliffe Exploratory Seminar for which Patricia was eligible to apply as a former Fellow of the Radcliffe Institute. We are extremely grateful to both institutions and their staff for facilitating these productive intellectual encounters, as well as to the participants at both workshops who have been generous with their time, knowledge, and good cheer. There were moments of gravity when the historiographical lineages were invoked: over dinner in Cambridge, MA, Linda K. Kerber and Glenda Sluga reminded us of the distinct but overlapping stages of recovery and analysis that must underpin women's international intellectual history. And there were moments of levity: David Armitage captured the spirit of what we hope is a creative re-imagining of what the history of international thought might become by introducing us all to "Martina Wight" at the start of the Radcliffe Seminar.

But most of all, we want to acknowledge the hard work and great patience of all our contributors as the essays went through multiple revisions. Every single contributor has been a pleasure to work with and we have learned so much from each of them. At Sussex, we thank Sharon Krummel, Morgan Williams, and Michael Hamilton for their administrative assistance. For incisive comments and suggestions on

---

[1] Mia Bay, Farah J. Griffin, Martha S. Jones, and Barbara D. Savage (eds.), *Toward an Intellectual History of Black Women* (Chapel Hill: University of North Carolina Press, 2015); Linda K. Kerber, *Toward an Intellectual History of Women: Essays* (Chapel Hill: University of North Carolina Press, 1997).

[2] Patricia Owens, *Between War and Politics: International Relations and the Thought of Hannah Arendt* (Oxford University Press, 2007).

earlier drafts of the introduction we thank Kimberly Hutchings, Helen M. Kinsella, Paul Kirby, Joanne Paul, Louiza Odysseos, Vanessa Ogle, Glenda Sluga, and Joanna Wood. As we came closer to producing a draft of the full manuscript, we found a very enthusiastic supporter in Liz Friend-Smith and Atifa Jiwa at Cambridge University Press (CUP). We are grateful for their commitment to this book and to our anthology, *Women's International Thought: Towards a New Canon*, which is a teaching companion to this volume, co-edited with Kimberly Hutchings and Sarah C. Dunstan. We are also grateful to Natasha Whelan who has expertly guided the book to publication, Joanna North for her copy-editing work, and the three anonymous reviewers for the Press. We have been fortunate to be able to access and reprint rare images of the thinkers in this volume, often taken from archival material. The inspiration for our front cover came from the papers of F. Melian Stawell, whose obituary in the Newnham College Roll pointed mourners "who did not know her in youth" to the central figure in Giovanni Bellini's *Fortune or Melancholy* (c.1490), an allegorical portrait of a woman with a globe on her knees. We are grateful to the Gallerie dell'Accademia di Venezia for permission to reprint. Here we also acknowledge permission from Newnham College, Cambridge, Western Michigan University Archives and Regional History Collections, Julian Brigstocke, the Women's Library at the London School of Economics, McMaster University/the Vera Brittain Estate, the University of Southern California Libraries Special Collections, Wellesley College, Oberlin College Archives and Schlesinger Library, Radcliffe Institute, Harvard University to reprint images of F. Melian Stawell, Merze Tate, Elizabeth Wiskemann, Helena Swanwick, Vera Brittain, Elizabeth McQueen, Emily Greene Balch, Anna Julia Cooper, and Barbara Sutro's portrait of Vera Micheles Dean.

Linda K. Kerber once argued that the locus of women's intellectual life "has rarely been institutional" and that historians ought to direct their attentions to "wherever women gathered to argue."[3] Yet, where they exist, institutions – and their histories – matter. Through their distinct contributions and ethos, two institutions have shaped the production of this volume. Of course, the first of these, as we've already mentioned, is the Radcliffe Institute for Advanced Study at Harvard University, which was founded in 1999 when Radcliffe College and Harvard merged. Established in 1879, then Radcliffe College played a distinct role in institutionalizing women's research in international politics. After white women in the United States gained the vote in 1920, the

---

[3] Kerber, *Toward an Intellectual History*, 227–28.

Harvard/Radcliffe Bureau of International Research began as a feminist project to "equip qualified women with the information and training which will enable them to become teachers and interpreters in the field of international affairs."[4] Ada Comstock, then president of Radcliffe College, approached powerful institutional backers to "show the interest of women in the field of international research," and to promote her most promising students whom she expected to "achieve results of considerable value."[5] Some of these scholars completed benchmark studies under the auspices of the Bureau, including two figures in this book: Merze Tate and Vera Micheles Dean, the latter offered (but declined) the presidency of Radcliffe in 1943. Although the feminist identity of the Harvard/Radcliffe Bureau was swiftly diluted and appropriated, women international thinkers found an institutional welcome there. Comstock put her faith in the relevance of women's international thought, a faith without which Tate, Dean, and many others would not have completed their work.

We would also like to acknowledge the University of Sussex, both of our academic homes when our collaboration began and where we worked on this book. The Heads of School and Research Directors and Development Officers of Sussex's Schools of Global Studies and History, Art History and Philosophy have been extremely supportive of the Leverhulme Project. But apart from the material and moral support we received, we were also buoyed by distinct institutional legacies in our respective departments. Sussex was the first university in Britain to establish degree programs and academic posts specifically in the field of intellectual history. Since the 1970s and 1980s, intellectual historians at Sussex have developed an approach to intellectual history that embraced methodological and terminological eclecticism, paid close attention to the idiosyncrasies of voices from the past, was open to a range of genres and welcomed intellectual endeavors that sat between and across disciplinary boundaries.[6] This vision would have attracted Elizabeth Wiskemann, one of the figures in this volume, who taught modern and international history at Sussex between 1961 and 1964.

[4] Katharina Rietzler, "Experts for Peace: Structure and Motivations of Philanthropic Internationalism in the Interwar Years," in Daniel Laqua (ed.), *Internationalism Reconfigured: Transnational Ideas and Movements between the World Wars* (London: I. B. Tauris, 2011), 47.

[5] Ada Comstock to Beardsley Ruml, May 6, 1923, Rockefeller Archive Center, Tarrytown, NY, Laura Spelman Rockefeller Memorial Archives, Series III.6, box 54, folder 573.

[6] Stefan Collini, "General Introduction," in Stefan Collini, Richard Whatmore, and Brian Young (eds.), *Economy, Polity, and Society: British Intellectual History 1750–1950* (Cambridge University Press, 2000), 1–21.

The idea that the intellectual history of international thought should be broader than a specialist history of one subject matter suited us better than a more conventional approach to writing international intellectual history as the disciplinary history of International Relations would have done, not least because of the exclusions based on gender, race, class, and ideology that have shaped this discipline, arguably more than others. Yet, we are fortunate to have benefited from the intellectual openness of the Department of International Relations at Sussex, at the forefront of so much theoretical innovation within the discipline. That said, we were also very wary of anachronistically assimilating women into an existing disciplinary history of International Relations, which would have obscured many roads not taken and "what-might-have-beens." While we hope to build on Sussex's tradition of openness to discovery in our work, we are also mindful that genuine dialogue between the disciplines is hard, and dismissals of the things that other scholars care about not uncommon. Our academic home when this book was conceived made it possible for us to talk to and to learn from each other, and for that benign influence of the "Sussex spirit" we are truly grateful.

Our final words of thanks go to our partners and extended families for supporting our academic work and for sharing all the other work that goes into maintaining family lives and the kind of home most of us need outside of academe. We'd like to dedicate this volume to our children, Maggie, Edith, Cali, and Myla.

Patricia Owens and Katharina Rietzler

Introduction: Toward a History of Women's International Thought

Patricia Owens and Katharina Rietzler

In the early 1970s, historian Linda K. Kerber observed that "when women are absent from the narrative history of ideas, it is not because they are truly absent, but because the historian did not seek energetically enough to find them."[1] What was true of the historical profession in the early 1970s is even more so now for cross-disciplinary work on the history of international thought. Intellectual history as a subfield has long marginalized gender.[2] While *international* intellectual history and the history of the academic discipline of International Relations (IR) are flourishing, there is a serious lack of engagement with historical women by both historians and IR scholars.[3] Neither have investigated women's foundational role in the emerging intellectual field of international relations in the early twentieth century or the later post-World War II academic discipline of IR. Even scholarship within social and political theory dedicated to retrieving and evaluating women's thought has

---

[1] Linda K. Kerber, *Toward an Intellectual History of Women: Essays* (Chapel Hill: University of North Carolina Press, 1997), 19.

[2] See Richard Whatmore, *What is Intellectual History?* (Cambridge: Polity Press, 2015). Cf. Hilda L. Smith, "Women's History as Intellectual History: A Perspective on the *Journal of Women's History*," *Journal of Women's History* 20.1 (2008): 26–32; Rachel Foxley, "Gender and Intellectual History," in Richard Whatmore and Brian Young (eds.), *Palgrave Advances in Intellectual History* (Basingstoke: Palgrave Macmillan, 2006), 189–209.

[3] David Armitage, "The International Turn in Intellectual History," in D. M. McMahon and S. Moyn (eds.), *Rethinking Modern European Intellectual History* (Oxford University Press, 2014), 232–52; Samuel Moyn and Andrew Sartori (eds.), *Global Intellectual History* (New York: Columbia University Press, 2013); Robert Vitalis, *White World Order, Black Power Politics: The Birth of American International Relations* (Ithaca, NY: Cornell University Press, 2015); Ian Hall, "The History of International Thought and International Relations Theory: From Context to Interpretation," *International Relations* 31.3 (2017): 241–60; Duncan Bell, "Writing the World (Remix)," in Brian C. Schmidt and Nicolas Guilhot (eds.), *Historiographical Investigations in International Relations* (London: Palgrave Macmillan, 2019), 15–50. In addition to this book, we point readers to the anthology Patricia Owens, Katharina Rietzler, Kimberly Hutchings, and Sarah C. Dunstan (eds.), *Women's International Thought: Towards a New Canon* (Cambridge University Press, forthcoming).

neglected distinctly international questions. Although gender studies and feminism are well established in IR, there is no substantial body of scholarship remedying women's erasure from IR's canon of intellectual "greats" or its disciplinary history.[4]

The erasure of women from existing histories of international thought is striking. This is obviously not due to the lack of women as "leaders of world thought," to use Amy Ashwood Garvey's term.[5] The very use of the term "international thought" can be traced to the 1929 publication of Florence Melian Stawell's *The Growth of International Thought*, but the first close reading of this work appears only now, in an essay for this volume.[6] Especially from the late nineteenth and early twentieth centuries, women were central to and often defined emerging discourses about international relations. They were acute observers of the first truly "global" international order in multiple locations both inside and outside academe. Public intellectuals, thinker-practitioners, and "street-scholars" thought deeply about world politics in and through a variety of genres. Inside academe, women founded or co-founded some of the earliest teaching and research centres dedicated to the study of international relations and were among the first cohort of scholars appointed in the earliest academic departments specializing in this subject. They wrote some of the first and most influential textbooks on and surveys of international relations.[7]

Women defined and transformed the study of international relations, generating a multiplicity of forms of international thought. There is a stark contrast between the central presence of historical women in the multiple forms and sites of international thought and their erasure from the relevant intellectual and disciplinary histories. How can we think systematically about this important but forgotten history? What assumptions about these categories – women, international, and thought – should we make? It is high time to begin confronting these questions, retrieving and analyzing women's international thinking, and broadening

---

[4] We do not believe that this constitutes a "failure" of feminist IR, as some have claimed. Jan Stöckmann, "Women, Wars, and World Affairs: Recovering Feminist International Relations, 1915–39," *Review of International Studies* 44.2 (2018), 2. It was the task of IR's disciplinary and intellectual historians to produce histories capable of reading and challenging the obviously gendered politics of their subject. See Kimberly Hutchings and Patricia Owens, "Women Thinkers and the Canon of International Thought," *American Political Science Review*, forthcoming.

[5] Rhoda Reddock, "The First Mrs Garvey: Pan-Africanism and Feminism in the Early 20th Century British Colonial Caribbean," *Feminist Africa* 19 (2014): 58–77.

[6] F. Melian Stawell, *The Growth of International Thought* (London: Butterworth, 1929).

[7] Glenda Sluga, "'Add Women and Stir': Gender and the History of International Politics," *Humanities Australia* 5 (2014): 65–72.

and deepening the currently accepted practices and locations of international thought.

A first, initial step in writing a new history of international thought has been suggested by historian Glenda Sluga: to engage in "recovery history," unearthing the foundational role of historical women who are missing from existing scholarship on the history of international thought. Such essential work, writes Sluga, "requires not merely the rereading of well-read texts, but the recovery of those texts, alongside others lost to their own time because of the bias against women publishing in 'masculine' genres, and the formulation of a context by virtue of which these recovered texts might be read into the larger story of an internationalised intellectual history – a sizeable task."[8] Our goal with this volume is to do more than "add women" to the existing record of international thought and its received historical and theoretical categories. But their omission makes it necessary in the first instance to bring together existing forays even as we ultimately seek to unsettle conventional assumptions.

We are certainly not the first to notice the absence and erasure of women in international intellectual and disciplinary history.[9] There is a small but growing number of journal articles and chapters on individual figures in both History and IR, though generally outside the mainstream of these fields.[10] There is also a literature on women and the practices of

[8] Glenda Sluga, "Turning International: *Foundations of Modern International Thought* and New Paradigms for Intellectual History," *History of European Ideas* 41.1 (2015), 112. There is a long tradition of "recovery work," for example, Dale Spender, *Women of Ideas (and What Men Have Done to Them)* (London: Ark, 1982). For an early and powerful analysis on the meanings of sexual difference beyond the recovery of forgotten women see several of the essays in Joan Wallach Scott (ed.), *Feminism and History* (Oxford University Press, 1996).

[9] Christine Sylvester, *Feminist International Relations: An Unfinished Journey* (Cambridge University Press, 2002), 11; Sluga, "Turning International"; Patricia Owens, "Women and the History of International Thought," *International Studies Quarterly* 62.3 (2018): 467–81; Valeska Huber, Tamson Pietsch, and Katharina Rietzler, "Women's International Thought and the New Professions, 1900–1940," *Modern Intellectual History*, First View (2019): 1–25.

[10] In History see Robert Shaffer, "Women and International Relations: Pearl S. Buck's Critique of the Cold War," *Journal of Women's History* 11.3 (1999): 151–75; Linda Schott, *Reconstructing Women's Thoughts: The Women's International League for Peace and Freedom before World War II* (Stanford University Press, 1997); Kristen E. Gwinn, *Emily Greene Balch: The Long Road to Internationalism* (Urbana, IL: University of Illinois Press, 2010); Or Rosenboim, "Barbara Wootton, Friedrich Hayek and the Debate on Democratic Federalism in the 1940s," *The International History Review* 36.5 (2014): 894–918; Barbara Savage, "Professor Merze Tate: Diplomatic Historian, Cosmopolitan Woman," in Mia Bay, Farah J. Griffin, Martha S. Jones, and Barbara D. Savage (eds.), *Toward an Intellectual History of Black Women* (Chapel Hill: University of North Carolina Press, 2015), 252–69. In IR see Patricia Owens, *Between War and Politics: International Relations and the Thought of Hannah Arendt* (Oxford University Press, 2007); Lucian M. Ashworth, "Feminism, War, and the Prospects for Peace:

international relations and diplomacy.[11] We build on this important work. However, we ask not only where are women in histories of international thought. We also ask which women are already where and why this is so. This allows us to both acknowledge the importance of the relatively few existing studies, but to not content ourselves with increasing the number of works on elite white women, the subjects of almost all the existing secondary literature. As discussed in more detail below, "women" is a deeply contested category which emerges through intersection with other identities and positions.[12]

Hence, there is an urgent need to put histories of international thought into conversation with the flourishing literature on Black women's intellectual history.[13] Given the systematic marginalization of Black scholars from the Anglo-American academic discipline of IR, but also its entanglements with European traditions of international thought, we focus on a selection of Black as well as white Anglophone and white European figures. We recognize the inadvisability of assuming a universal experience of raced positionality, and the contested nature of racial and ethnic categorizations. Thus, we have left it to the authors in this volume to determine the most appropriate terminology and they adopt a variety of terms, including white, black, Black, African American, and Jewish. To partially mitigate the near complete absence of people of color in existing histories of international thought we draw on Bay, Griffin, Jones, and Savage's "intellectual history 'black women style,'" which

Helena Swanwick (1864–1939) and the Lost Feminists of Interwar International Relations," *International Feminist Journal of Politics* 13.1 (2011): 25–43; Lene Hansen, "A Research Agenda on Feminist Texts and the Gendered Constitution of International Politics in Rebecca West's *Black Lamb and Grey Falcon*," *Millennium* 40.1 (2011): 109–28; Helen M. Kinsella, "Simone Weil: An Introduction," in Felix Rösch (ed.), *Émigré Scholars and the Genesis of American International Relations: A European Discipline in America?* (Basingstoke: Palgrave Macmillan, 2014), 176–97.

[11] Special Issue, "Women and International Relations," *Millennium: Journal of International Relations* 17.3 (1988); Craig Murphy, "Seeing Women, Recognizing Gender, Recasting International Relations," *International Organization* 50.3 (1996): 513–38; Ann E. Towns, *Women and States: Norms and Hierarchies in International Society* (Cambridge University Press, 2010); Glenda Sluga and Carolyn James (eds.), *Women, Diplomacy and International Politics since 1500* (London: Routledge, 2016); Karen Garner, *Women and Gender in International History* (London: Bloomsbury, 2018).

[12] Cynthia Enloe, *Bananas, Beaches and Bases: Making Feminist Sense of International Politics* (London: Pandora Books, 1989); Anne McClintock, *Imperial Leather: Race, Gender, and Sexuality in the Colonial Conquest* (New York: Routledge, 1995).

[13] Melinda Plastas, *A Band of Noble Women: Racial Politics in the Women's Peace Movement* (Syracuse University Press, 2011); Keisha N. Blain, *Set the World on Fire: Black Nationalist Women and the Global Struggle for Freedom* (Philadelphia: University of Pensylvania Press, 2018); Imaobong Umoren, *Race Women Internationalists: Activist-Intellectuals and Global Freedom Struggles* (Oakland: University of California Press, 2018).

emphasizes ideas in the context of lived experience "and always inflected by the social facts of race, class, and gender."[14] In the context of international relations, we consider nation, citizenship, and empire as additional factors that structured intellectual production.[15]

Inspired by this important earlier work, we seek to return to the foundational questions of which kinds of subjects and what kind of thinking constitutes international thought, which we define broadly as reflection on the relations between peoples, empires, and states. Our definition of *thought* is also, by necessity, capacious. Despite facing multiple axes of structural exclusion and discrimination, each of our subjects had the audacity to self-consciously make sense of international politics in a deep and sustained way. If we had adopted a narrow understanding of "thought" as dense theoretical treatise, disconnected from positionality, and excluded policy formulation, practice, and activism, then we could not have assembled this collection of essays.[16] Several of our subjects produced dense theoretical treatises, making explicit and obvious contributions to theorizing, conventionally understood. However, we do not subsume thought into theory. Bearing in mind the gendered and racialized manner in which conventional genres of theorizing were formed, we see theory in a wide range of genres and forms, and we invite readers to adopt a broader understanding of what it means to produce thought and theory than is often the case in intellectual history and contemporary IR. Of course, a capacious understanding of what constitutes "thought" has costs as well as benefits. A few of our figures received only scant recognition as thought leaders in their lifetime, and identifying their distinct intellectual contributions requires a high level of contextualization.

Together, the essays examine the substantive intellectual contributions of eighteen thinkers from the late nineteenth to the mid-twentieth century. We selected this period for two reasons. First, this was a

---

[14] Mia Bay, Farah J. Griffin, Martha S. Jones, and Barbara D. Savage, "Introduction: Toward an Intellectual History of Black Women," in Bay et al. (eds), *Toward an Intellectual History of Black Women*, 4. In a survey of sixty texts on the history of international thought, only four women of color are among the seventy-nine historical women identified: the African Americans Merze Tate (1905–96), Eslanda Robeson (1895–1965), Lorraine Hansberry (1930–65), and Pauli Murray (1910–85). All four were mentioned in a single text that focuses on IR's racist past. Vitalis, *White World Order*; Owens, "Women and the History of International Thought," 470.

[15] Blain, *Set the World on Fire*; Umoren, *Race Women Internationalists*.

[16] As Foxley has put it, "attention to gender may challenge some of our beliefs about the 'right' way to do intellectual history." "Gender and Intellectual History," 18. Also see the broad understanding of intellectual history practiced at the blog of the *Journal of the History of Ideas* (https://jhiblog.org/) (accessed June 24, 2019) and, on "vehicles" of thought, Bay et al., "Introduction," 5.

fundamental moment in the imagining of international relations as a distinct sphere but it was also deeply entangled with imperialism and the continuing aftermaths of slavery, world wars and genocides, stark racialized, class, and gendered conflicts, the emergence of new international organizations and conceptualizations of international law, decolonizing movements, and calls for global social democracy. Through the nineteenth century, Anglophone thinkers often engaged with empire, as imperialist discourse enabled elite white women to carve out positions of power in a domain structured by notions of racial superiority.[17] Intellectuals were beginning to imagine imperial *and* international relations as spheres that remained necessarily entangled and not always clearly distinguished. New international organizations such as the League of Nations consolidated, rather than undermined, the European empires.[18] In common with British liberal internationalist thought in the interwar years, race and empire were the foundation of Stawell's *The Growth of International Thought*, a Euro- and Christian-centric account of, among other things, the dilemmas of accessing natural resources in world regions "nominally in the possession of savage … races."[19] Several other figures examined wrote extensively on both international relations and imperialism from a variety of political positions. Indeed, we suggest that their focus on imperial relations is one of the reasons why so many women were subsequently marginalized in many later accounts of IR's intellectual and disciplinary history which erased imperialism and "race relations" from the history of the field.[20]

Second, we focus on the late nineteenth to early mid-twentieth century because these were formative years in the emergence of international relations as a distinct interdisciplinary field drawing on methods and approaches from History, Classics, Anthropology and Colonial Administration, Law, Economics, and Political Science. Thus we do not endorse IR's conventional periodization, either of itself or of international history. The multiple intellectual, racialized, class, and gendered conflicts

---

[17] Deirdre David, *Rule Britannia: Women, Empire, and Victorian Writing* (Ithaca, NY: Cornell University Press, 1995); Allison L. Sneider, *Suffragists in an Imperial Age: U.S. Expansion and the Woman Question, 1870–1929* (New York: Oxford University Press, 2008); Melinda Plastas, "A Different Burden: Race and the Social Thought of Emily Greene Balch," *Peace & Change* 33.4 (2008): 469–506 (478–79, 497).

[18] Susan Pedersen, *The Guardians: The League of Nations and the Crisis of Empire* (Oxford University Press, 2015); Daniel Gorman, *The Emergence of International Society in the 1920s* (New York: Cambridge University Press, 2012).

[19] Stawell, *Growth of International Thought*, 173–74; Jeanne Morefield, *Covenants without Swords: Idealist Liberalism and the Spirit of Empire* (Princeton University Press, 2005).

[20] For an analysis of the case of Lucy Philip Mair see Owens, "Women and the History of International Thought."

defining the late nineteenth to early mid-twentieth centuries have rarely been central to the telling of IR's intellectual and interdisciplinary history. In the decades after World War II, scholars in both Britain and the United States sought to define a new intellectual program for a separate and distinct academic discipline, which developed as a subdiscipline of Political Science in the United States from the 1950s and from the 1970s in Britain. In this process, the earlier interdisciplinary field of international relations debate and scholarship was widely presented as emerging out of the desire to understand the causes of World War I and the conditions of peace, a seemingly noble lineage.[21] This retrospective version of disciplinary history, eventually framed around a mythical series of gladiatorial "great debates" between different "isms" and ahistorical "traditions", erased earlier women intellectuals and scholars of international relations. To counter some aspects of this flawed conventional narrative, more recent studies have rightly focused on early twentieth-century imperialism, colonial administration, and "race development" as central to the establishment of academic IR as "white man's IR."[22] IR was not unique among academic disciplines in marginalizing women. Yet IR still lacks an account of both the early years of "white women's IR";[23] an awareness of the myriad ways in which Black and other women of color responded to and wrote about the international politics of this era; and how the much later and gradual carving out of a distinct IR "discipline" and, more widely, a tradition of "international thought" was itself highly gendered as well as racialized, a process that has been obscured by the existing historiography.

The disciplinary history of academic IR is not the sole, or even primary, focus of this volume and the gendered history of the discipline is the subject of ongoing research. Here we are less interested in bringing our subjects into the mainstream of contemporary IR or assimilating them into disciplinary history or ways of organizing IR theory. This would be naïve about the effects of advocating for "inclusion." But we

---

[21] Brian Porter (ed.), *The Aberystwyth Papers, 1919–1969* (Oxford University Press, 1972); William C. Olson and A. J. R. Groom, *International Relations Then and Now: Origins and Trends in Interpretation* (London: Unwin Hyman, 1991). For a summary and critique see Lucian Ashworth, *A History of International Thought: From the Origins of the Modern State to Academic International Relations* (London: Routledge, 2014).

[22] David Lake, "White Man's IR: An Intellectual Confession," *Perspectives on Politics* 14.4 (2016): 1112–22; Brian C. Schmidt, *The Political Discourse of Anarchy: A Disciplinary History of International Relations* (Albany, NY: State University of New York Press, 1998), 123–49; David Long and Brian Schmidt (eds.), *Imperialism and Internationalism in the Discipline of International Relations* (Albany, NY: State University of New York Press, 2005); Vitalis, *White World Order*.

[23] Owens, "Women and the History of International Thought," 467.

do seek to initiate and contribute to further revisionist accounts which pay due attention to racism, colonialism, class, *and* gender in the writing of disciplinary and intellectual history. For example, women's focus on imperialism is not the only source of their later exclusion from IR historiography. The *historical* character of much women's scholarship contributed to their marginalization in a post-World War II discipline in which the previously central role of diplomatic history was weakened and caricatured in order to attain the coveted status of a policy "science" and abstract "theory" of the international "system." In contrast, some men who produced historical scholarship, such as Arnold Toynbee or Felix Gilbert, suffered no such disadvantage when articulating historicist visions for IR realism.[24]

Recent accounts of the relatively late emergence of "IR theory" do not mention, let alone center, gender. However, the search for an abstract theory of IR can be seen, in part, as a reaction not just to traditional forms of diplomatic history or behavioral social science but also against genres of international thought in which women excelled.[25] A great deal of early to mid-twentieth-century international relations scholarship centered on the problem of mass democracy, whether and how foreign policy ought to be responsive to "the people," and how knowledge on international politics should be popularized. Much of this work was written in the genre of popular writing, for instance in the Foreign Policy Association's *Headline* series. IR's disciplinary and often intellectual insecurity, including the ongoing debate on whether IR can be more than commentary on current affairs, can be read in this context. Similarly, feminists, Black and white, were among the earliest and, at the time, central protagonists in early twentieth-century Anglo-American debates about the problems and possibilities of international order.[26] As Ashworth explains in this volume, as a result, erstwhile intellectual "insiders" became post-hoc "outsiders" in a discipline that conventionally dates the advent of feminist IR to the 1980s.

---

[24] Nicolas Guilhot, "Portrait of the Realist as a Historian: On Anti-Whiggism in the History of International Relations," *European Journal of International Relations* 21.1 (2015): 3–26.

[25] Nicolas Guilhot (ed.), *The Invention of International Relations Theory: Realism, the Rockefeller Foundation, and the 1954 Conference on Theory* (New York: Columbia University Press, 2011).

[26] Helen McCarthy, *The British People and the League of Nations: Democracy, Citizenship and Internationalism, c.1918–45* (Manchester University Press, 2011), 182–211; Julie Gottlieb, *'Guilty Women': Foreign Policy, and Appeasement in Inter-War Britain* (Basingstoke: Palgrave Macmillan, 2015); J. Ann Tickner and Jacqui True, "A Century of International Relations Feminism: From World War One Women's Peace Pragmatism to the Women, Peace and Security Agenda," *International Studies Quarterly* 62.2 (2018): 221–33; Stöckmann, "Women, Wars, and World Affairs."

Analyzing women's international thought raises new questions about the timing, location, and politics of the belated privileging of "theory," at least in certain, very narrow forms, in the history of academic IR.[27] It also raises questions about which fields and which approaches have been considered as relevant to the formation of a separate IR discipline, and the gendered politics of these inclusions and exclusions. Enormous investments appear to have been made to preserve the white and homosocial character of international thought and disciplinary history, that is, as a conversation "between men."[28] Thus in addition to recovery and analysis of women thinkers we are interested in the politics of IR's "not knowing," of "patterned forms" or "epistemologies of ignorance."[29] IR's willful and unconscious/patterned ignorance of women's intellectual labors is as significant and complex as what the field claims to know about its own intellectual genealogy. Thus, some contributors to this volume examine a number of the practices that led to historical women's constitutive exclusion, ranging from sexist and patriarchal discourses and ideologies, to everyday practices of sexism and racism in their relations with academic mentors, the production and politics of multiple forms of ignorance, and the gendered politics of disciplinary formation.

Examining the intellectual biographies of the scholars and thinkers in this volume and the patterns of inclusion/exclusion therein, is a first step in the intellectual project of writing a new history of international thought. A second, interconnected step is not essentializing or romanticizing women as a category of analysis. Certainly, one of the most obvious ways in which the gender binary has shaped intellectual production is through the reception of work understood to be carried out by "women." Indeed, one of the mechanisms in which women have been excluded is through a form of "pseudo-inclusion," when a small number

---

[27] IR has long viewed itself as dominated by "theory," conceived in terms of "isms." A recent account is Richard Devetak, *Critical International Theory: An Intellectual History* (Oxford University Press, 2018), which contains very little on the gendered and raced manner in which "the *critical* intellectual persona" is produced.

[28] Eve Kosofsky Sedgwick, *Between Men: English Literature and Male Homosocial Desire* (New York: Columbia University Press, 1985).

[29] Paul Gilroy, "Race and Racism in 'The Age of Obama,'" The Tenth Annual Eccles Centre for American Studies Plenary Lecture given at the British Association for American Studies Annual Conference, 2013 (www.bl.uk/britishlibrary/~/media/bl/global/eccles%20centre/ec%20plenaries/baas-2013-gilroy.pdf) (accessed June 26, 2019); Shannon Sullivan and Nancy Tuana (eds.), *Race and Epistemologies of Ignorance* (State University of New York Press, 2007); Priya Satia, "Inter-War Agnotology: Empire, Democracy and the Production of Ignorance," in Laura Beers and Geraint Thomas (eds.), *Brave New World: Imperial and Democratic Nation-Building in Britain between the Wars* (London: Institute of Historical Research, 2011), 209–25. Thanks to Paul Kirby for suggesting the relevance of this concept.

of feminists come to represent all women and women's intellectual interests are limited to a focus on gender narrowly understood.[30] However, our analysis does not assume the stability of the category of "women" and we reject the intellectual closures that shut out non-normative gender identities. To investigate historical women's international thought we need only assume that the operations of gender, the discursive organization and interpretation of sexual difference, shaped the conditions, content, and reception of international thought.[31] The historical construct of the gender binary produced the identities of women and men, which profoundly shaped the intellectual production we wish to investigate. Hence, we adopt the category of *historical* women to indicate the discursive and produced character of our main object of study and to acknowledge the manifold ways in which historical actors have strategically deployed, professed indifference to, or indeed rejected prevailing gender norms. At least one of the figures in this volume, Simone Weil, was gender non-conforming.[32]

We can take seriously both the mutually constitutive relationship between gender and intellectual history but also the ideas and experiences of historical women. Despite or indeed because of the historical construct of gendered and racialized identities we are nonetheless able to examine the international thought and imaginaries of these subjects and assess whether they developed recognizably distinctive ways of conceiving international relations. However, to take seriously this international thought is not to endorse or necessarily evaluate as positive all that these newly recovered figures thought or did. As to be expected, there are logical inconsistencies and errors of judgment in some of the thought analyzed in his volume, and there is a fine balance between critique, appreciation, and the open-mindedness that is necessary for the work of recovery. For some of our authors this is a question of historical justice given their subject's exclusion from intellectual canons and privileged sites of knowledge production. The authors assembled have taken different positions in this regard; we view this diversity as a strength, fit for a

---

[30] Beverly Thiele, "Vanishing Acts in Social and Political Thought: Tricks of the Trade," in Carol Pateman and Elizabeth Gross (eds.), *Feminist Challenges: Social and Political Theory* (Boston, MA: Northeastern University Press, 1986), 30–34.

[31] Joan Wallach Scott, *Gender and the Politics of History* (revised edition) (New York: Columbia University Press, 1999).

[32] Weil's gendered understanding of war and conflict is worthy of further exploration, for instance her idea of a nurses' unit in World War II, charged with "mothering" soldiers in the battlefield. Weil insisted that none of these nurses should have children themselves. Simone Pétrement, *Simone Weil: A Life* (New York: Schocken, 1976), 27–29, 476; Simone Weil to Maurice Schumann, July 30, 1942, encl., in Richard Rees (ed.), *Simone Weil: Seventy Letters* (Eugene, OR: Wipf & Stock, 2015), 145–53.

heterogeneous cast of thinkers, ranging from those who received the academic imprimatur to those whose intellectual ambitions failed, sometimes for good reasons.

The figures analyzed encompass a variety of intellectual positions and diverse political projects that might be characterized as conservative, imperialist, liberal internationalist, socialist, feminist, or committed to black Atlantic and Afro-Asian internationalisms, and there are many more that we have not been able to incorporate in one volume. It was important to us to highlight this range, if only to counter still-prevalent assumptions about the content of women's intellectual production. Yet while it is appropriate to use a particular term or "label" to capture certain ideas emergent from the analysis of a subject's writing, for example McQueen's "techno-optimist internationalism," we have consciously sought not to reduce thinkers to the "isms" still commonly used to organize the history of international thought especially in IR: realism, liberalism, Marxism, and so on. Indeed, many of our figures would remain out of place if we did so, even those trained within IR's leading centers of teaching and research in its early years. For example, while Merze Tate, who studied with liberal imperialist Alfred Zimmern at Geneva and Oxford, can be described as a small r "realist," she clearly lacked the blinkers of many 1950s realists when it came to race and empire. We may speculate what a more sophisticated realism might have looked like had African American thinkers such as Tate not been systematically marginalized from the academic discipline of IR.[33]

The contributors to this volume have been careful to analyze historical women on their own terms, whether feminist or not. Certainly, some thinkers, such as Eslanda Robeson and Emily Greene Balch, made gender hierarchies central to their international thought and participated in explicitly feminist networks and projects. But many resisted a strong identification with a gendered identity or with feminist movements, for instance Rosa Luxemburg, Simone Weil, and Elizabeth Wiskemann. Yet, even when figures are not themselves straightforwardly feminist, we argue that the recovery and analysis of their work is a fundamentally feminist project.[34] Indeed, just as intellectual historians can benefit from engagement with themes developed by feminist IR scholars, including the contested character of gender, so feminist IR continues to gain

---

[33] Vitalis, *White World Order.*

[34] As Foxley has written, "Feminist scholars do not pretend that they can abstract themselves from the present and their own beliefs in interpreting the texts of the past. Arguably, this self-consciousness about engagement in the material studied may be more helpful in avoiding inappropriate anachronism and value judgement than a naïve belief in neutrality." "Gender and Intellectual History," 200–201.

from historical approaches to thinking about women and international thought.[35]

Several essays in this volume examine thinking inside the academy. F. Melian Stawell, Emily Greene Balch, Merze Tate, Krystyna Marek, Barbara Wootton, and Vera Micheles Dean operated in the spaces closest to existing histories of international thought and academic IR, even when working in branches of the humanities and social sciences that would become less evident as pathways to theorizing international relations during the post-1950s phase of disciplinary consolidation. Contributors also examine the international thought of a number of figures that are canonical in their respective traditions. We use this terminology for Anna Julia Cooper, Rosa Luxemburg, Simone Weil, and Eslanda Robeson not because we seek to inscribe them into existing hierarchies in the canon of international thought but to acknowledge the degree of recognition that they have already received.[36]

Yet, we are not conflating the categories of "canonical" and "serious" thinker. An exclusive focus on the academy or on canonical thinkers risks omitting figures in a range of different sites of knowledge production. Positionality matters to international intellectual history not just in terms of race, gender, class, and nation but also profession, genre, and audience, especially in early twentieth-century Europe and the United States, as women's employment opportunities significantly expanded.[37] Taking this shift into account, we multiply the sites where we look for intellectual labor, thereby disrupting current conventional understandings of the boundaries, genres and audiences of international relations expertise as well as canonical status. As already suggested, we wish for our readers to consider serious international thought outside the canon, an invitation that may be more familiar to historians than to IR scholars.[38] In this volume, we open with canonical thinkers, as is common in international intellectual history and international theory. But we propose figures that

---

[35] Christine Sylvester, "The Early Field of IR: Musings, Assertions, Debates, and (Now) Feminist Interruptions," in *Feminist Theory and International Relations in a Postmodern Era* (Cambridge University Press, 1994), ch. 2; J. Ann Tickner, "Retelling IR's Foundational Stories," in *A Feminist Voyage through International Relations* (Oxford University Press, 2014), ch. 11; Catia Cecilia Confortini, *Intelligent Compassion: Feminist Critical Methodology in the Women's International League for Peace and Freedom* (Oxford University Press, 2012).

[36] Of these, only Rosa Luxemburg has anything close to partial recognition as a significant thinker in the existing histories of international thought. Owens, "Women and the History of International Thought," 477.

[37] Huber et al., "Women's International Thought and the New Professions."

[38] Edward Keene, "International Intellectual History and International Relations: Contexts, Canons and Mediocrities," *International Relations* 31.3 (2017): 341–56.

are not usually regarded as canonical in international thought.[39] We then take a radical step change away from thinking through familiar canonical figures.

A great deal of intellectual production on international relations was written by thinkers positioned outside or on the margins of the academy, as social workers, educators, journalists, and members of the anti-colonial liberation, Pan-African, and women's suffrage movements.[40] As historians increasingly argue, many women in the early and mid-twentieth century developed their international thinking in congenial professional contexts such as social work, teaching, journalism, librarian-ship, and information management.[41] These were women-dominated "new professions" which offered paid employment and an intellectual home. They were important alternative settings for especially middle-class women's international thought. They also offered a platform for international ideas developed for the general population, rather than simply academics. Cooper, Stawell, Weil, Luxemburg, Wiskemann, Robeson, Gordon, McQueen, Dean, and Balch all wrote for popular or educational as well as or instead of scholarly purposes.

The existing historiography on internationalist organizations and net-works shows that encounters across the boundaries of race and nation allowed women to fuse internationalist practice with new ways of theor-izing.[42] Such encounters played a part in the production of the gendered, racialized, and classed subjectivities of specific thinkers and the politics of feminist and internationalist organizations such as the Women's Inter-national League for Peace and Freedom. Several of the figures in the volume are located in specific international networks and organizations and these were fundamental contexts as well as subjects of international thought. These essays demonstrate that participation in and deep reflection on organizations and networks are not mutually exclusive.

---

[39] For a study of the problem with canons in IR see Hutchings and Owens, "Women Thinkers and the Canon of International Thought."

[40] Cheryl Higashida, *Black International Feminism: Women Writers of the Black Left, 1945–1995* (Urbana, IL: University of Illinois Press, 2011); Hansen, "A Research Agenda on Feminist Texts."

[41] Huber et al., "Women's International Thought and the New Professions"; Merze Tate, "Teaching of International Relations in Negro Colleges," *The Quarterly Review of Higher Education among Negroes* 15 (1947): 149–53.

[42] Schott, *Reconstructing Women's Thoughts*; Erik S. McDuffie, *Sojourning for Freedom: Black Women, American Communism, and the Making of Black Left Feminism* (Durham, NC: Duke University Press, 2011); Christine von Oertzen, *Science, Gender, and Internationalism: Women's Academic Networks, 1917–1955* (New York: Palgrave Macmillan, 2014); Christine von Oertzen, Maria Rentetzi, and Elizabeth Watkins (eds.), *Beyond the Academy: Histories of Gender and Knowledge* (New York: Wiley, 2013).

However, moving beyond networks and the new professions, we also include more radically alternative sites of intellectual production and genres.[43]

For example, Black working-class intellectual Mittie Maude Lena Gordon theorized the connections between peoples of African and Asian descent in parks and street corners in front of large numbers of followers, practicing what Ula Taylor described as "street scholarship" and "street strolling" as a means to generate and disseminate international theory.[44] Such approaches to theorizing, and the importance of orality as well as oratory, may not be readily obvious to conventional and even many so-called critical international theorists, given the white androcentrism built into assumptions about the nature and form of "theory." Here again we also point to the diverse approaches of our contributors, not only in the level of critique and use of racial categories, but also regarding the level of historical contextualization and theoretical development and analysis. Several of the essays do not just expound the views of their subjects but, to borrow the title of one of our essays, "theorize with" them. Sometimes this difference is a product of the level of recovery of individual thinkers, the biographical information already available, or the scarcity of sources. Indeed, not only genre and audience but the organization and accessibility of documents, "the archive," is deeply racialized, classed, and gendered.[45] The contributions on Cooper and Ashwood Garvey return to the methodological challenges that have long preoccupied feminist and postcolonial historians when confronted with lost papers, letters, speeches, and book manuscripts and the alternative interpretive strategies needed to reconstruct international thought from fragments. Such work is indispensable if we are to capture women's intellectual labors on themes ranging from the world economy, race, and empire, to the building of inter- and transnational community, international relations, and spirituality, intellectual resources for addressing pressing issues in contemporary international politics and international theory today.

---

[43] There has been a great deal of recent attention given to "scholar-activism" in IR. However, it is important to recall that in Britain the academic field of IR was established in and through what Sluga in this volume calls "the web of Oxbridge internationalist networks, melding scholarly endeavors and political activism" by figures such as Arnold Toynbee, Alfred Zimmern, and Gilbert Murray.

[44] Ula Taylor, "Street Strollers: Grounding the Theory of Black Women Intellectuals," *Afro-Americans in New York Life and History* 30.2 (2006): 153–71; Blain, *Set the World on Fire*.

[45] Shiera S. el-Malik and Isaac A. Kamola (eds.), *Politics of African Anticolonial Archive* (London: Rowman & Littlefield, 2017).

Outline of the Book

The first four essays of the book re-situate already canonical thinkers in twentieth-century international thought. Two of them, Anna Julia Cooper and Eslanda Robeson, are African Americans whose own diasporic experiences had a profound influence on their thought and their epistemological commitments. The others, Rosa Luxemburg and Simone Weil, both Jewish, were deeply enmeshed in the radical politics and imperial entanglements of continental Europe in the first half of the twentieth century. Strikingly, all four analyzed the international politics of racialization, and all of them reflected on the importance of one's positionality when making claims to knowledge.

Vivian M. May frames her essay on Anna Julia Cooper's analysis of imperialism and colonialism in the Age of Revolutions within an explicit reflection on the politics and practices of recovery. Cooper's thought is a rich resource when countering the active erasure of Black women's writings on international relations, and as in the case of Amy Ashwood Garvey, readers are invited to theorize *with* the committed educationalist Cooper, not just about her. Confronting the absences and enforced silences she encountered when working in French colonial archives in the 1920s, Cooper developed a methodology for recovering the voices of marginalized people of color in the French Empire.

Cooper's identity, that of a Black American woman in interwar France, a former slave who argued with white supremacist exponents of the "Nordic vogue," was central to her writing. She was an outsider, marginalized by gender, race, class, age, and nationality, who dared to criticize the greats of French sociology while she completed her doctoral work in Paris. As did other intellectuals in this volume, Cooper had a complex relationship with her male academic mentors, not least her doctoral examiner Célestin Bouglé who became an ideological and methodological opponent. Challenging Bouglé's claims to racial superiority, Cooper tested her analytical tools in a scholarly confrontation that was always also a political act of insubordination.

Kimberly Hutchings' re-reading of Rosa Luxemburg's international thought reintroduces us to a canonical thinker whose contributions have not yet received the recognition they deserve in histories of international thought. Instead, Luxemburg has been infantilized by both Marxist and liberal traditions, traditions that she challenged for their exalting of national self-determination. Her most important contribution, however, relates to capitalism's reliance on tapping into non-capitalist modes of production and exchange. This was central to her sophisticated understanding of imperialism. In a world in which capitalism continues to feed on non-capitalist forms of labor, Luxemburg represents a thinker to be reckoned with. As Hutchings explains, to Luxemburg it would have been unsurprising that the world economy today continues to rely on bonded labor.

But Luxemburg's positionality as an international thinker is also relevant to histories of international thought. Hers was a life steeped in political activism within the imperialist core, and her analysis of international politics contended with the religious, class, ethnic, and racial hierarchies of the land-based empires of pre-World War I Eastern and Central Europe. Luxemburg strategically invoked her gender when she used affective experience in her analysis of the evils of colonialism but, fully aware of her own marginalization as a woman, Pole, and Jew, she ultimately regarded herself as a member of the universal class.

Simone Weil was an unsettled thinker intent on disturbing preconceived categories and thinking in opposites. Helen M. Kinsella's essay on Weil invites us to re-read this compulsive outsider both for her theoretical contributions and for the ways in which she challenged conventional notions of what it meant to be an intellectual. It was her asceticism, her androgyny, and her complex religious identity, abandoning Judaism, becoming a Christian mystic, that made her a "lonely" figure and prefigured her erasure as an international thinker.

Kinsella roots Weil's political philosophy, commonly understood as concerned with the use of force and rights, in a penetrating analysis of colonialism. Weil recognized the 1930s as the apogee of French colonialism which lay at the origin of the crisis of modern international politics. When Germany applied the method of colonial conquest and domination to the European continent, occupied France reaped the reward for its expansionist hubris, which degraded both the colonized and the colonizer in a frenzied search for power. To Weil, the despoliation of human beings and their environment lay at the core of colonialism. Its end could not be brought about by political means but on grounds that transcended politics and comprised an empathetic understanding of the degradation of people and land under colonial conditions, an understanding she sought to achieve through the attempt to obliterate any collective identities in her person. Reading Weil thus prompts readers to rethink the connection between international relations, empire, and the spiritual.

Imaobong Umoren's essay discusses a canonical thinker within Black internationalism, Eslanda Robeson. Earlier accounts of Robeson have tended to focus on her stage-managing her husband Paul Robeson's career, minimizing her decision to go to Africa as an outcome of the breakdown of their marriage. And yet, after the 1945 publication of

African Journey Robeson became a household name among African American intellectuals, famous for her shrewd analyses of race and empire in a world structured by the emerging Cold War. Building on recent work on the history of Black international thought that has taken Robeson seriously as a public intellectual, Umoren's essay foregrounds her journalistic writings and her involvement in internationalist and Pan-African networks, often centered on the United Nations.[46]

Robeson was an activist-intellectual whose international thought centered on the struggle for women's participation in and the significance of the so-called Third World to international politics. She astutely observed the limits of action imposed by international organizations, even if her optimistic politics of solidarity at times obscured class hierarchies and privilege *within* Black and Third World internationalisms. Committed to promoting women as political actors, Robeson nonetheless remained wedded to maternalist thinking that essentialized pacifism as "a woman's job." Yet, her widely read writings offered new representations of global politics and its actors to her readership, and Umoren rightly highlights Robeson's pedagogical commitment.

The second part of the book recovers and evaluates international thinkers, who, due to multiple forms of discrimination and sometimes simply out of choice, remained outside, or on the margins of, the academic centers of IR. As Geoffrey Field notes in his chapter, three of the top four best books on international affairs in 1938, according to *The Times*, were by women without established university positions: Wiskemann, Shiela Grant Duff, and Elizabeth Monroe. Reading diverse thinker-outsiders challenges our understanding of genre but also of the relevant sites for intellectual production in international thought: are they academic studies, lecture halls, and seminar rooms, or do they extend to union locales, public parks, the streets of Harlem, or a religious shrine in Southern California?

Tamson Pietsch's essay on Elizabeth Lippincott McQueen analyses the ways in which gender intersected with international thought-as-spirituality. McQueen can hardly be regarded as a conventional intellectual: she was a charismatic entrepreneur thriving on a localized form of techno-optimist internationalism in 1930s Southern California. However, it was her religious formation as a Christian Scientist that enabled her to promote and *experience* thinking as a process of change.

---

[46] Maureen Mahon, "Eslanda Goode Robeson's African Journey: The Politics of Identification and Representation in the African Diaspora," *Souls* 8.3 (2006): 101–18; Barbara Ransby, *Eslanda: The Large and Unconventional Life of Mrs Paul Robeson* (New Haven, CT: Yale University Press, 2013).

In Christian Science, a religion founded by a woman and that explicitly conferred spiritual authority onto women, the human body could be changed through the power of thought. McQueen's conversion-like encounter with aviation prompted her to transfer a spiritual model to a political project, the promotion of world peace and Anglo-American liberal empire through aviation.

McQueen's gender positioning was crucial. Not only did she strategically draw on gendered notions of sociability and spirituality, she also developed her gospel of aviation during a time when women were integral to the rise of a new technology. In the interwar period, the aviation industry relied on celebrity women aviators such as Amelia Earhart to advance and commercialize aviation. Gender stereotypes were used to manipulate emotions: women flyers would make aviation *feel* safe for the American public. Once commercial aviation was securely established in part through the labor of women, women were relegated to service tasks, a move that eerily resembles the formation of IR as a discipline. In a time of a resurgent post-liberal subjectivity, when thinking, knowing, and feeling can no longer be separated, McQueen's millenarian international thought may be more relevant than ever.

Lucian M. Ashworth's chapter focuses on the role of international institutions in shaping women's international thought. Ashworth analyses the thought of four women intellectuals and activists in the Women's International League for Peace and Freedom (WILPF) during a time when interwar norms of international governance in the shape of the League of Nations were tested by fascist aggression. In the 1930s, Emily Greene Balch, Helena Swanwick, Vera Brittain, and Mary Agnes Hamilton all held roles in or were close to WILPF and advanced a feminist approach to international relations, "even if their policy prescriptions were often shared by non-feminists who had come to the same conclusions by different routes," writes Ashworth. These women were public intellectuals, with a stake in the concrete policy debates of their time, which revolved around the questions of collective security and appeasement. Balch and Swanwick opposed collective security and embraced a pacifist position, while Hamilton and, to some extent, Brittain supported it.

The WILPF women strategically invoked their gender, based on the intellectual traditions of suffragism and feminist pacifism that countered masculinist discourses about international relations. Swanwick, Balch, Brittain, and Hamilton "turned an earlier misogynistic tradition on its head," by making a claim on representing "women's perspectives" on international politics, even if their disagreements showed that there certainly was no unanimity among them. Ashworth reads their conclusions against Merze Tate's work on collective security in the 1940s, which avoided gender-based claims to authority in an intellectual context that would have mocked them. The contribution of WILPF thinkers to the academic debate on collective security was vital in its time. Yet, in the end, it was written out of IR's intellectual history.

Robbie Shilliam's chapter on Amy Ashwood Garvey returns to the foundational questions of what it means to produce international thought: who is a thinker? What makes their thought international? What are the markers of recognition, in terms of location and genre, for international thought? Such questions are vital in order to avoid reducing Black international thought to "lived experience," thereby missing its theoretical contributions. Certainly, Garvey was a race woman, a "street-strolling" Pan-Africanist and leader of the Universal Negro Improvement Association (UNIA).[47] For this gifted conversationalist, public orator, and rhetorician, political praxis and organizing were a way of theorizing. And although her political activism spanned the Black Atlantic, it was partly due to her commitment to localized "women's work" that she understood the limits of a patriarchal and monolithic Pan-Africanism.[48]

Shilliam characterizes Garvey's theoretical approach to Pan-Africanism as "fractal," rooted in the understanding that the dynamics of liberation struggles are endlessly repeated on different scales. Rather than positing a unitary Blackness, Garvey critically analyzed the intersections of race, class, sex, gender, and nation in community-level struggles for self-determination. Viewed through such a lens, Black patriarchy did not suppress but politicize Black women. Understanding Garvey's theorizing as fractal, accommodating struggle within struggle, resolves some of the seeming contradictions in Garvey's thought. At its core, these contradictions centered on the paradoxical pursuit of both women's respectability and liberation. Although Garvey playfully subverted Black male sexual and political entitlement, she also extolled the benefits of Black patriarchy, expecting women to conform to middle-class norms of respectability. If we theorize *with* Amy Ashwood Garvey, we may have to entertain a critical re-evaluation of respectability politics and accept that a thinker of liberation adopted a mode of theorizing that was also radically conservative.

In Keisha Blain's chapter on Mittie Maude Lena Gordon, the founder and president of the Peace Movement of Ethiopia (PME) in Chicago, we

---

[47] Umoren, *Race Women Internationalists*.

[48] Paul Gilroy, *The Black Atlantic: Modernity and Double Consciousness* (Cambridge, MA: Harvard University Press, 1993).

encounter a triple outsider. Although Gordon drew on a long tradition of Black internationalism, notably that of the UNIA, her pursuit of an African American alliance with Japan in the years leading up to World War II ran counter to the ideas of mainstream Black leaders. Gordon also lacked the formal education that middle-class Black intellectuals such as Eslanda Robeson relied upon to communicate with their audience. Gordon was another "street-scholar" who wrote pamphlets and letters that were read aloud at weekly meetings because her organization did not have enough funds to publish a regular newspaper for her working-class audience.

Her ideas on Afro-Asian solidarity extolled common strategies of resistance and evoked historical connections between peoples of African and Asian descent. Black nationalist women like Gordon were the most ardent supporters of recruiting Japan as a viable ally in the Black freedom struggle but, in their search for strategies to bring white empire to an end, many African American intellectuals shared a blind spot regarding Japanese imperialism. Black intellectuals disagreed on the concrete political projects that should underpin Afro-Asian solidarity. Gordon, for instance, opposed African American migration to Japan's conquered territory of Manchuria, believing that only a "return to Africa" would serve the cause of liberation. In sum, Gordon was an organic intellectual with a distinct class position, who searched for concrete ways for people of color to challenge racism and colonial rule.

Elizabeth Wiskemann's international thought was also forged in the international politics of the 1930s. Geoffrey Field's chapter on this scholar-journalist, a prolific writer with a staggering breadth of expertise, spans the worlds of anti-fascist activism, diplomacy, and academe. Although Wiskemann took the Montague Burton Chair in International Relations at the University of Edinburgh in 1958, this post was primarily intended to further public education in international affairs, and Wiskemann, with her roster of serious but non-academic books on contemporary politics and history, was a fitting candidate. Wiskemann had originally set out to become an academic after achieving a first class degree in History at Newnham College, Cambridge, but was thwarted by her mentor, the influential diplomatic historian H. W. V. Temperley, who prevented her from being awarded a doctorate. Nonetheless, she made a successful career specializing on Central Europe, as the lead Berlin correspondent for *The New Statesman* from 1932, a researcher for the think tank Chatham House, and in government service in World War II as an intelligence officer, only the second British woman to be awarded full diplomatic status.

Wiskemann's international thought emerged from her cutting-edge journalism and her anti-fascist and anti-appeasement activism (in 1936, she was briefly held by the Gestapo). Her writing was often empiricist and focused on power politics and diplomacy. This, however, was in line with much of British writing on international relations before the 1960s and the tilt toward the social sciences. Wiskemann deplored this development and, toward the end of her career, described herself as a contemporary historian. Her trajectory underlines the importance of incorporating history and public education into intellectual and disciplinary histories of IR, as well as a consistent practice orientation that sprung from a reluctance to engage in purely abstract thinking.

In the final part of the book we turn to women thinking in the academy. They often overcame considerable odds to secure permanent employment and even when they did so, continued to experience marginalization. Several themes come to the fore in these chapters: the complex and often exploitative relationships between women thinkers and their academic mentors; the frequent repositioning in different academic disciplines and discourses; and a concern with translating theory into practical proposals accessible to a broader audience for the benefit of individuals and groups.

Glenda Sluga's essay on F. Melian Stawell makes a case for including more popular writings in histories of international thought, work that had a primarily pedagogic rather than scholarly function, even when written by outstanding scholars. Like several other interwar liberal internationalists, Stawell was a classicist by training, set for an illustrious career at Cambridge working simultaneously on the ancient Greeks and contemporary world order. Even her name denoted her vocation: Melian, after the ill-fated inhabitants of Melos, whose failed attempt to negotiate with Athens is taught to every current first term, first year student of IR.

In existing histories, Stawell is best known as the author of *The Growth of International Thought*, a book increasingly cited, if not read, as the first to use the term "international thought." Sluga reveals a gendered irony in Stawell's albeit fleeting and very recent position in this regard. Stawell was asked to write *The Growth of International Thought* due to an intellectual theft. Her mentor, Gilbert Murray, the influential Oxford liberal internationalist and founder of the League of Nations Union, purloined for himself Stawell's original idea for a book on the League of Nations, a book which he never wrote. Sluga offers the first close reading of the text itself and of its major influences and context, challenging the (gendered) distinction between international and international*ist* thought. She powerfully reminds international theorists working today that it was interwar *internationalist* international thought that "inspired so many academics to bring their scholarship into the public domain, and women to engage international politics."

Emily Balch is a familiar figure to historians of the transnational women's movement of the early twentieth century, not least because of her central role in the WILPF. Balch was one of WILPF's pillars – but did she assume this role because she was marginalized from academic locations and discourses on international relations? Catia C. Confortini's chapter considers Balch as a scholar focusing on the time before she was fired from her job at Wellesley College in 1919 due to her pacifism during World War I.

There is no doubt that Balch was a thinker engaged in conversations now recognized as squarely belonging to the history of international thought. These include debates on race and immigration, economic interdependence, the reform of colonialism, and visions for a world society based on a common consciousness. There were limits and contradictions within Balch's thought but her commitment to empirical research and a skepticism regarding abstraction enabled her to challenge some of the racist stereotypes within American international relations discourse in the 1910s and 1920s. Balch was never interested in separating the domestic from the international. Her starting point remained her "fellow citizens" and the concrete contexts that shaped their lives, whether these were the messy ethnographic realities of East-Central Europe or the impact of the United States' occupation of Haiti.

Merze Tate was by all accounts an unusual woman academic. A graduate of both Oxford and Harvard, she was one of the few African American women who secured a full professorship at an American university before the 1960s. Barbara D. Savage's chapter analyses Tate's intellectual trajectory that immersed her in the world of interwar Anglo-American academic internationalism – the circle of Stawell, Murray, and first British professor of International Relations, Alfred Zimmern – and took her to Howard University where she became involved with but never quite immersed in the so-called "Howard School" of African American IR scholars.[49] Tate shared a commitment to the analysis of American racism and colonialism with her contemporaries, developing what Savage describes as a distinctive "anti-racist geopolitics." But she also regarded herself first and foremost as a diplomatic historian, with a realist bent. Her books on international disarmament and diplomacy in the Pacific remain classics.

---

[49] Vitalis, *White World Order*, 11–14.

Tate's career was facilitated by her academic mentors, especially at Oxford. Yet she broke with many of their analytical assumptions, not least on the centrality of public opinion as a category in international thought. This did not mean that Tate embraced a restrictive view on the public's say in foreign policy formation, particularly when this public was African American. But Tate insisted that in order to hold power to account, one had to understand what power was, especially as it was wielded internationally by the United States. Like Balch, Tate was a fierce critic of American empire, but she remained much more skeptical when it came to building world community.

Or Rosenboim's chapter on Barbara Wootton analyzes an international thinker who neither placed herself within the academic discipline of IR, nor consistently analyzed international questions alone. Instead, for two decades, international thought became a medium for Wootton to explore her concerns for social and economic justice, concerns which she argued had to be viewed through a lens attuned to both global and domestic forces. A graduate of Girton College, Cambridge, Wootton became Professor of Sociology at Bedford College, London, the first higher education college for women in Britain.

Wootton has previously been positioned in the context of federalism and the thought collective around the British organization Federal Union. Writing briefing papers and pamphlets for both Federal Union and the think tank Chatham House, Wootton proposed practical solutions and policies for a wide, non-academic readership, and opposed "abstract thinking" on principle. Wootton's views on the purpose of the social sciences resonated with the academic ethos of Bedford College, which specialized in social work, but it marginalized her in academic debate. Nonetheless, her federalist proposals of the 1940s are worth recovering and analyzing. They fused liberal and socialist analyses and should be put into context with the intellectual history of European integration and proto-welfarism. Implicitly, Wootton argued for Britain to sever relations with its imperial possessions in a "turn to Europe." However, she did so without analyzing how the injustices and inequalities of empire could be undone. This unresolved tension in her thought makes her newly relevant in an era of imperial nostalgia and profound disillusionment with the European project.

Andrew Jewett's chapter on Vera Micheles Dean analyzes another thinker concerned with international economic organization, but through the lens of economic security. And, unlike Wootton, Dean acknowledged the centrality of the non-Western world in the Cold War, an analytical move taken decades before Cold War historians and IR scholars began to "decenter" the United States and the Soviet Union in their accounts. An expert on Soviet Russia, Dean argued for a policy of mutual understanding, advocating collective forms of economic organization and the pooling of sovereignty. Ideologically, she was committed to global social democracy, anti-racism, and, importantly, a holistic understanding of security that encompassed psychological aspects.

Dean was a Radcliffe woman. This is where she acquired her PhD in International Law and International Relations in 1928, before launching a long career that took her from the Foreign Policy Association to the University of Rochester in 1954 and then to New York University. Unlike many of the thinkers in this volume, Dean actually taught in IR centers and departments. Although she remained distant from the dominant theoretical approaches of her time, it is possible to classify her stance as realist with a thorough grounding in social psychology.[50] Yet hers was not the paternalistic and anti-democratic realism of foreign policy experts and defense intellectuals. Despite her academic grounding, she was a public intellectual, embracing a "common-sense cosmopolitanism" that sought to make the world relatable to ordinary citizens.

Natasha Wheatley's essay charts the co-implication of "the personal and the intellectual" in the work of international legal thinker Krystyna Marek. This Polish exile wrote in the context of the dissolution of the Austro-Hungarian, Nazi, and the Soviet Empires in Eastern Europe. Though she worked for the Polish government-in-exile in World War II, rising to Embassy Attaché in London, and for international organizations during her doctoral research, rising to Professor of International Law, Marek's authority was regularly questioned. Yet she wrote the first international legal monograph on statehood as such, reflecting a crucial historical moment in which the structure of international legal reasoning shifted from an exclusive focus on states to one grappling with the birth and death of states. How and through what means might a state's legal identity survive decades, even a century, of imperial administration? How would observers know if a state's international personality was extinguished?

In Wheatley's essay, Marek is read not as an international thinker in the straightforward sense of writing about international subjects, though she did, but in responding to these questions by raising the international to an epistemological and "juridical-methodological premise." To offer a legal answer to the question of the birth and death of states one must first

---

[50] Dean, however, does not fit the story of the elective affinity between IR realism and psychology as told in Nicolas Guilhot, "Imperial Realism: Post-War IR Theory and Decolonisation," *The International History Review* 36.4 (2014): 698–720.

ask, from where does international law think? In posing this question, and answering "from *outside* states," Marek's 1954 book *The Identity and Continuity of States in Public International Law* "quietly ushered in a tectonic shift in the history of legal knowledge about sovereignty." States themselves were unable to *think* their own non-existence. The vantage point (or legal fiction) of international law was that it existed both before and after states, a radical and now foundational claim initiated by a "now-forgotten book by a now-forgotten Polish exile."

While collectively cohering by grouping, period, and themes, our multidisciplinary authors adopt a variety of approaches to histories of women's international thought, a multivalency that is part of the field of intellectual history itself.[51] Contributors are interested in a wide range of forms of thought ranging from that produced by canonical thinkers to marginalized "thinker-outsiders" and those inside the academy, as well as the circumstances and reception of their ideas. Together, the essays expand the locations and genres of international thought as they examine numerous substantive ideas in light of their historical context but also with an eye toward contemporary concerns. Of course, a new history is not a finished history. We do not suggest that the figures analyzed here are the only women to take seriously as international thinkers, even in our narrow period or location; on the contrary. There are many more we could have selected, such as Bertha von Sutter, Ellen Churchill Semple, Jane Addams, Hannah Arendt, and Claudia Jones to name just a very few of the most prominent. Even more importantly, the indispensable project of a history of a more "Global IR," which necessarily includes global intellectual history, will be severely limited in its depth and range if it reproduces gendered exclusions. There is a serious need for larger, multilingual, projects shaped in conversation with colleagues who work on international thought from around the world. We hope such a project can be taken up in future research.

---

[51] Stefan Collini, "What is Intellectual History?" *History Today* 35.10 (1985): 46–54 (46–48); Joel Isaac, James T. Kloppenberg, Michael O'Brien, and Jennifer Ratner-Rosenhagen (eds.), *The Worlds of American Intellectual History* (Oxford University Press, 2016).

Part I

Canonical Thinkers

1   Anna Julia Cooper on Slavery's Afterlife: Can International Thought "Hear" Her "Muffled" Voice and Ideas?

Vivian M. May

Anna Julia Cooper (c. 1858–1964), an important early Black feminist scholar, educator, and activist, powerfully contested hegemonic mind-sets, systems, and practices.[1] Anticipating intersectional, transatlantic analyses of power and inequality, she pinpointed how diverse forms of dominance interrelate and questioned reductive approaches to identity and power in collective freedom efforts. For instance, Cooper condemned white supremacist thinking on the part of (white) feminists, decried misogyny on the part of Black male colleagues engaged in freedom struggles for "the race," and denounced internalized racism and classism by *gens de couleur* in Saint-Domingue (Haiti), during the Age of Revolution.[2] And, though rarely recognized for it, she played a part in the larger project of mapping out a history and understanding of global humanism that approach slavery as a central, if often denied, underpinning of modernity.

Cooper's ability to read omissions, disrupted silences, and trace inter-connected dimensions of slavery's afterlife should be of interest to

---

[1] On Cooper's life's work pursuing a more just world, see: Louise Daniel Hutchinson, *Anna J. Cooper: A Voice from the South* (Washington, DC: Smithsonian Press, 1981); Charles Lemert and Esme Bhan (eds.), *The Voice of Anna Julia Cooper* (Lanham, MD: Rowman & Littlefield, 1998); Vivian M. May, *Anna Julia Cooper, Visionary Black Feminist* (New York: Routledge, 2007); Vivian M. May, "Anna Julia Cooper (1858–1964): Black Feminist Scholar, Educator, and Activist," in Michele Gillespie and Sally McMillen (eds.), *North Carolina Women: Their Lives and Times* (Athens, GA: University of Georgia Press, 2014), 192–212; Mary Helen Washington, "Introduction," in Anna Julia Cooper, *A Voice from the South by a Black Woman of the South* (New York: Oxford University Press, 1988), xxvii–liv.

[2] Cooper emphasizes *gens de couleur* were interested in limited political and social change: as free landowners and slaveholders, they first sought civil and legal equality with white *colons*. Anna Julia Cooper, *Slavery and the French and Haitian Revolutionists*, ed. Frances Richardson (Lanham, MD: Rowman & Littlefield, 2006), 79.

international thought. As a writer, orator, and educator, she exposed numerous historical absences, refused sustained attempts to silence Black women's ideas, and unpacked political contradictions that undermined democracy's possibilities. Cooper named ongoing legacies of slavery and settler colonialism and underscored the fundamentally interlocking nature of misogyny, white supremacy, economic exploitation, and imperialism. She is a foundational Black feminist thinker and important early contributor to Black Atlantic thought.

Yet, despite over forty years of careful recovery efforts and interdisciplinary scholarship on Cooper, her works often remain overlooked in fields where they could be taken up, including in international thought and theory. This is certainly the case with her 1925 Sorbonne dissertation, *L'Attitude de la France à l'égard de l'esclavage pendant la Révolution* (Cooper was the first Black woman to earn a PhD at the Sorbonne, and the fourth in the United States to earn one).[3] Here, Cooper focused on the transatlantic interplay of French and Haitian politics, and highlighted slavery's role in the rise of capitalism, shifting established historical approaches to the Age of Revolution. She argued that resistance from *gens de couleur* and slaves in Saint-Domingue impacted France's nascent democracy and that France's colonial expansion, dedication to slavery, and reliance on exploitation undermined its egalitarian ideals.

But even her more widely recognized *A Voice from the South by a Black Woman of the South* (1892), the first volume of Black feminist thought in the United States, remains frequently sidelined or superficially treated. In this book, Cooper astutely analysed how structural exploitation, combined with racist, sexist, and xenophobic ideas, lies at the center of how the law and the state operate and infuse daily life – including cultural production, religious and theological practices, schooling, the family, and our interior lives, as part of what today we might characterize as the psychological components of oppression. Cooper focused on willful ignorance, crafted an ability to read the world differently – against the bias of prevailing logics – and unearthed sites of agency that had been overlooked or robustly denied.

As scholars of international thought craft more inclusive histories to account for a broader range of thinkers, issues, and sources, Cooper's

---

[3] For Frances Richardson Keller's English translation, see: Cooper, *Slavery and the French and Haitian Revolutionists*. Cooper's dissertation, other writings, and ephemera are digitized at Howard University, thanks to Shirley Moody-Turner's collaboration with the Moorland-Spingarn Research Center: http://dh.howard.edu/ajcooper/.

ideas should be looked to. However, if the field's normative genealogies, methods, and histories have been implicitly if not explicitly biased, and marked by prevailing race, gender, and class assumptions about what "counts" as international thought, these problems cannot be remediated by folding heretofore excluded thinkers, concepts, and issues into extant frames and histories. Such change requires confronting how power imbues interpretive norms (and ensures archival absences), and transforming knowledge practices more broadly to be both equitable and just.

Can Recovery Suffice?

Cooper's work is relevant for scholars of international thought interested in addressing interlocking questions of race, gender, and empire; for scholars of Black Atlantic thought; and for researchers engaged in mapping out "a larger genealogy of race women internationalists who have been committed to ... challenging inequalities within global freedom struggles."[4] But again, if international thought has, in its genealogies or methods, overlooked Black women's contributions more broadly, and Cooper's ideas specifically, I have doubts as to whether uncovering (or recovering) her work, highlighting its merits, and advocating for its inclusion will suffice to address such omissions or intervene in the epistemological practices that led to them.

Certainly, many Cooper scholars have focused on recovery as a tactic and devoted energies to close reading as an accompanying interventionist method. A debt is owed to such labors driven by a robust critique of Black women's exclusion.[5] Thankfully, a dearth of information about Cooper is no longer an issue, nor is lack of access to her writing. However, despite this recovery work, and multipronged efforts by scholars across disciplines to have her ideas be taken more seriously, the body of extant Cooper scholarship, combined with ready access to her published and archived works, has *not* yet resulted in Cooper having

---

[4] Imaobong D. Umoren, *Race Women Internationalists: Activist-Intellectuals and Global Freedom Struggles* (Oakland, CA: University of California Press, 2018), 122.
[5] Much of my own work about Cooper has also been driven by this impetus. Nearly all the early scholarship on Cooper, up to and including much contemporary work, has sought to make her extant works available, and advocated that her ideas be taken up meaningfully across the disciplines, including literature, history, rhetoric, religion, education, and sociology, and in the inter-disciplines, including feminist/women's studies, African American/Black studies and American Studies.

the "hearing at the bar of the nation" she tried, repeatedly, to claim as her due.[6] Of course, Cooper is not unique in this regard – the endemic silencing of Black women's ideas continues more broadly, despite recovery efforts, painstaking archival work, and much careful scholarship.

Given such enduring silences, many scholars working on Black feminist knowledges and intellectual histories have come to question the effectiveness of recovery and inclusion strategies alone,[7] without concomitant, concerted efforts to examine broader knowledge politics, reflect upon our fields' exclusionary legacies and biased foundations, and confront evidence of a kind of willful, sustained ignorance about Black women's intellectual and political contributions. When it comes to Cooper, a twofold, reflexive approach seems apt: one that attends to her work and seeks to recover any remaining fragments, while also accounting for normative knowledge paradigms and structural inequities that may shape interpretive assumptions.

I am not suggesting that recovery efforts have been for naught. Rather, to underscore how Cooper's ideas are germane to international thought and its histories, I want to emphasize Cooper's innovative and strategic methods, but also the need to engage with absence as a normative force. Just as Cooper did, we must approach gaps in our fields as sites of meaning. Contemporary scholars might do well, in other words, to employ some of Cooper's analytic techniques as part of our own methodological transformation (rather than simply enfold her ideas into prevailing frames in our fields).

Cooper developed a variety of interpretive tactics and narrative strategies useful for analyzing silences and absences (a task that scholars of

---

[6] Anna Julia Cooper, "The Intellectual Progress of the Colored Women in the United States since the Emancipation Proclamation: A Response to Fannie Barrier Williams," in Lemert and Bhan (eds.), The Voice of Anna Julia Cooper, 202.

[7] For example, see Brittney Cooper, *Beyond Respectability: The Intellectual Thought of Race Women* (Urbana, IL: University of Illinois Press, 2017); Kristie Dotson, "Theorizing Jane Crow, Theorizing Unknowability," *Social Epistemology* 31.5 (2017): 417–30; Ann duCille, "The Occult of True Black Womanhood: Critical Demeanor and Black Feminist Studies," *Signs* 19.3 (1994): 591–629; P. Gabrielle Foreman, "A Riff, A Call, and A Response: Reframing the Problem That Led to Our Being Tokens in Ethnic and Gender Studies; or, Where Are We Going Anyway and with Whom Will We Travel?" *Legacy* 30.2 (2013): 306–22; Marisa J. Fuentes, *Dispossessed Lives: Enslaved Women, Violence, and the Archive* (Philadelphia: University of Pennsylvania Press, 2016); Jennifer Morgan, "Archives and Histories of Racial Capitalism," *Social Text* 33.4 (2015): 153–61; Andréa Williams, "Recovering Black Women Writers in Periodical Archives," *American Periodicals* 27.1 (2017): 25–28.

Black feminist intellectual-political history inevitably undertake). These include: naming and combating the politics of absence; reading materials/archives/ideas against the grain; and raising doubts about prevailing social imaginaries and accepted paradigms that reinforce the status quo (e.g., by shifting historical timeframes, or refusing to accept that enslaved persons had no agency, or personhood, despite such biases built into the archives). Cooper also exposed contradictions, particularly those that seem studiously ignored or smoothed over (e.g., how both French and US republics proclaimed democracy but were invested in slavery from the start) and considered questions of power, positionality, and responsibility vis-à-vis Black women's ideas and histories – so as better to listen to (and not "muffle") the ideas at hand.

To address troubling absences in international thought, as part of a larger set of critical recovery practices, scholars thus need to confront an enduring political and interpretive conundrum Cooper was all too familiar with. By this I mean scholars of international thought must recognize a core predicament which has long faced Black women knowers more broadly: the interpretive catch-22 of being wholly ignored no matter how much one protests or raises one's ideas, or, alternatively, being engaged with in ways that violate and, in the end, still fundamentally silence what one has to say. As Cooper famously asserted, "the colored woman ... is confronted by both a woman question and a race problem, and is as yet an unknown or unacknowledged factor in both."[8]

Despite the title of her first volume, *A Voice from the South by a Black Woman of the South*, Cooper knew that raising her "voice" might not suffice – since, as she also argued, endemic "pathetic misapprehension" of Black women is a pivotal means by which dominance solidifies and is perpetuated.[9] Cooper skillfully negotiated historical absences, grappled with opacities, listened to silences, and refuted prevailing logics, while, simultaneously, anticipating being doubted or misunderstood due to her positionality (and ideas forged) as a Black woman knower. Even when shared, she argued, Black women's ideas often have no reception, and remain an "uncomprehended cadenza."[10]

---

[8] Cooper, *A Voice from the South*, 134.
[9] Cooper, *A Voice from the South*, ii.
[10] Cooper, *A Voice from the South*, i.

Anna Julia Haywood Cooper

H. M. PLATT, Mrs. Geo. A.C. Cooper, Oberlin, O.

1.1 Anna Julia Cooper, Oberlin College Class of 1884.
Courtesy of the Oberlin College Archives

Navigating Absences

When it comes to considering Cooper's contributions to international thought, one inevitably confronts literal absences: this requires pausing to think about the meaning of different losses, including her missing personal papers, writings refused publication,[11] projects denied

---

[11] Late in life, in 1951, Cooper privately published her two-volume set, *The Life and Writings of the Grimké Family* and *Personal Recollections of the Grimké Family*, after unsuccessfully asking W. E. B. Du Bois to do so. At age one hundred, still hoping to

support,[12] speeches not saved, and more. Given that we have several archival gaps to confront, and since her life's work focused intensely on historical absences and enforced silences as sites of meaning and signs of power's workings, when examining her work, it is essential to remember what's missing, attend to the scraps of evidence available, and use interpretive strategies like inference or piecing fragments (as in a quilt) to get at a larger picture.

Archival holes inevitably shape our understanding of Cooper's legacy and these can require a different interpretive approach – reading between the lines, maneuvering across her available texts, archival snippets, and gaping absences. For instance, we know Cooper was one of two African American women invited to speak at the first Pan-African Congress in London, in 1900. Cooper found it intensely ironic that, once abroad, her US passport afforded her protections as a citizen which, at home, she could not enjoy (because, on US soil, she did not have the full rights and protections of the state as a Black woman).[13] Unfortunately, we have neither her paper, "The Negro Problem in America," nor that of her colleague, Anna H. Jones, who discussed "The Preservation of Race Individuality":[14] ideas presented by the only two African American women invited to speak at the Congress seem to be gone.[15]

In addition to her international scholarly reputation, Cooper was admired at home and abroad for her contributions across more than seven decades of teaching and school leadership. Tracing more inclusive

---

publish her speech "The Ethics of the Negro Question" (1902) and essay "The Negro's Dialect" (1930s?), she deposited funds for this purpose in an account (both now appear in Lemert and Bhan (eds.), *The Voice of Anna Julia Cooper*). Cooper also confronted bias when trying to distribute and copyright, in the United States, her translation (from medieval to modern French) of the eleventh-century epic, *The Pilgrimage of Charlemagne*. Despite demand for her 1925 Paris edition, she could not secure a US distributor or even donate her 500 copies to Oberlin, her alma mater, due to racist backlash. Katherine Shilton, "'This Scholarly and Colored Alumna': Anna Julia Cooper's Troubled Relationship with Oberlin College": www.oberlin.edu/external/EOG/History322/AnnaJuliaCooper/AnnaJuliaCooper.htm.

[12] In the 1930s, the Brookings Institution and American University "raised the color bar," rejecting Cooper's proposals to write a history of Black Americans in Washington, DC. See Cooper in Leona C. Gabel, *From Slavery to the Sorbonne and Beyond: The Life and Writings of Anna J. Cooper* (Northampton, MA: Smith College Department of History, 1982), 82.

[13] Arlette Frund, "Emancipation through Mobility: Phillis Wheatley, Anna Julia Cooper and the Black Atlantic Diaspora," *Revue Française d'études Américaines* 149.4 (2016), 44.

[14] Hutchinson, *Anna J. Cooper: A Voice from the South*, 110–11.

[15] Subsequent Congresses were held during the school year, which Cooper complained about to W. E. B. Du Bois because "working people" (teachers like herself) were unable to attend. The prohibitive cost was another obstacle: sarcastically, she wrote she would tell her "*wealthy friends*" about it (italics original). W. E. B. Du Bois Papers (MS 312) Special Collections and University Archives, University of Massachusetts Amherst Libraries.

histories of international thought may require looking to broader contexts (e.g., not only at published books) for relevant materials and contributions. For instance, in the late nineteenth century and early twentieth century, many Black women intellectuals in the United States were employed in Black public schools. Crafting more comprehensive histories of international thought, and identifying how Black women also helped shape Black international analytics, might require looking to their high school teaching, leadership, and curriculum contributions as pivotal. Likewise, Black women's community work, political organizing, and labor politics more broadly are also relevant sites of knowledge production.

In Cooper's case, broadening the scope leads to some additional materials to consider, but often in the form of fragments or gaps. Where we should have reams of content to draw upon, to flesh out how her work as an educator linked to her contributions to international thought as a scholar and orator, we again confront lack – and, once more, need interpretive strategies to counter it. The task at hand is to read the traces, and plumb the silences, for meaning and insight.

For instance, we know Cooper's pedagogical renown was national and international. The French scholar Félix Klein, after touring American schools, described her skillful pedagogy as unrivaled – a controversial claim since, at the invitation of the US president, Klein had visited both white and Black US schools. In the end, he lavished praise on Cooper and the "M Street" high school[16] in his 1905 book about American education (rather than showcase white educators, leaders, and students).[17] We also know that Cooper's liberal arts philosophy was inclusive, one in which all students, no matter their race, sex, age, or class, should be educated as whole people. Critical of Jim Crow's oppressive educational mandates and norms, and troubled by sexist curricula that expected nothing much of girls, intellectually, Cooper was skeptical about what integration would mean for Black teachers and students.

Rather than simply rely on hand-me-down racist textbooks selected by the white school board, Cooper called on Black teachers to carefully design curricula that could foster critical consciousness and that would include content focused on inequality, combating structural oppression, and introducing a global approach to Black history. Unfortunately, as with many other areas of Cooper's work, there is a paucity of her teaching and leadership materials from M Street/Dunbar and Frelinghuysen

---

[16] Cooper taught at M Street from 1887 to 1906 and again from 1910–30, decisively shaping the curriculum and direction of the school.

[17] Félix Klein, *Au pays de 'La vie intense'* (4th edition) (Paris: Plon-Nourrit, 1905).

University (where she founded the Hannah Stanley Opportunity School, a division of Frelinghuysen focused on adult literacy and named after Cooper's mother).

And, in addition to her educational philosophy, there are some scraps of curricular information to look to when considering Cooper's contributions to international thought. For instance, she translated her Sorbonne doctoral exams into English and used them as part of the history curriculum at Frelinghuysen. Her treatise "Equality of Races and the Democratic Movement" was a searing critique of her examiner, Célestin Bouglé, and his claims for Nordics' superior capacities for civilization, enlightenment, and equality.[18] Her other exam, "Legislative Measures Concerning Slavery in the United States: 1787–1850," began the country's history with slave trade ships arriving in Jamestown in 1619, tracing the nation's origins directly to slavery and illustrating how this origin continues to be denied or suppressed.[19] This tidbit offers some clues about her pedagogical vision, particularly since we know, via another fragment from her career at M Street/Dunbar High School, that Georgiana Simpson (the first Black woman to earn a PhD in the United States), her colleague in languages, edited and annotated Thomas Gragnon-Lacoste's biography of Toussaint Louverture for use in Dunbar's French curriculum, suggesting the Haitian Revolution (and a global approach to Black history) was core to Frelinghuysen's languages/linguistics curriculum, too.[20]

With little to go on, we can piece together slivers of information and deduce that Cooper helped develop innovative language curricula shaped by an internationalist approach to Black culture and history, one that attended to legacies of anti-Blackness and underscored a global history of collective resistance and critical consciousness. Knowing she translated her Sorbonne exams for use at Frelinghuysen, we can infer that a Black Atlantic internationalist approach shaped that school's curriculum.[21]

---

[18] Anna Julia Cooper, "Equality of Races and the Democratic Movement," in Lemert and Bhan (eds.), *The Voice of Anna Julia Cooper*, 291–98.

[19] Anna Julia Cooper, "Legislative Measures Concerning Slavery in the United States: 1787–1850," in Lemert and Bhan (eds.), The Voice of Anna Julia Cooper, 299–304.

[20] Thomas Gragnon-Lacoste, *Toussaint Louverture (surnommé le premier des noirs)* (Haiti: Associated Publishers, 1924).

[21] On international aspects of Cooper's educational contributions, see: Lemah Bonnick, "'In the Service of Neglected People': Anna Julia Cooper, Ontology, and Education," *Philosophical Studies in Education* 38 (2007): 179–97; Stephanie Evans, "African American Women Scholars and International Research: Dr. Anna Julia Cooper's Legacy of Study Abroad," *Frontiers* 18 (2009): 77–100; David H. W. Pellow, "Anna Julia Cooper: The International Dimensions," in Dolan Hubbard (ed.), *Recovered Writers/Recovered Texts: Race, Class, and Gender in Black Women's Literature* (Knoxville: University of Tennessee Press, 1997), 60–74. Bonnick underscores how Cooper

I point to these fragments and archival gaps as an invitation for experts in international thought and international relations to consider Black educational history and curriculum strategies, and to delineate how these overlooked sites of knowledge production might shift key frames and perspectives in IR.

Listening to Muffled Sounds

How unequal power relations shape knowledge – what can be told, heard, and documented – is an asymmetry marked by race and gender that Cooper identified as a persistent legacy of slavery. She opens *A Voice* by underscoring how Black women's voices, collectively, have been "muffled,"[22] even as *A Voice* is also about the power of raising one's voice and fostering collective vocalization. Cooper's choice of muffling suggests active attempts to silence Black women's words while signaling, simultaneously, their longstanding (if unnoticed) resistance to such oppression. Muffled voices still emit sound, despite efforts to stifle – sometimes, some people can hear these sounds.

Using a double-voiced strategy, Cooper highlighted epistemological violence and worked against it. Even as she opened by sharing doubts about whether readers would be able to hear her ideas, she forged ahead: though consigned to the margins, Cooper carved out space for her own insights about how power infuses knowledge production and disrupts liberation politics, resulting in ongoing ignorance, erasure, and epistemic distortion. Notably, this ability to name oppression, and identify resistance to it, is a twofold method Cooper used across her oeuvre, including in *A Voice*, speeches and essays, and her dissertation.

For instance, she described how, like Abraham in the biblical parable about Lazarus and the rich man, though she knows of what she speaks, she doubts she will be heard.[23] Cooper also pointed to instances of nearly indiscernible resistance (e.g., how African Americans kept alive an "unwritten history").[24] At the World Congress of Representative Women, Cooper underscored there has been "no word from the Black Woman,"

"refused to construct black people as problems and instead focused on the problems they faced" (185) and also Cooper's critiques of Western modernity to connect to contemporary issues in Afro-Caribbean educational debates in the United Kingdom. Pellow highlights how "Cooper provides us with a unique analysis of diasporean discourse in general and Haiti as a new world narrative of containment in particular" (61), and traces Cooper's transnational approach to Black history to her educational pathway, beginning at St. Augustine's in Raleigh, NC, after emancipation.

[22] Cooper, *A Voice from the South*, vii.   [23] Cooper, *A Voice from the South*, 24.
[24] Cooper, *A Voice from the South*, 101.

though not for lack of trying: Black women's stories *could* "furnish material for epics" if they could be heard.[25]

In 1902, Cooper returned to this issue, emphasizing "White America" sought to consign African Americans to *"terra incognita,"* a place of un-knowability and un-hearability from which "a voice of a truth" seemingly cannot be uttered.[26] Building on her earlier analyses in *A Voice* about the dangers of maintaining an "apotheosis of greed and cruelty,"[27] Cooper linked practices of silencing with white supremacy and violence in the age of American empire. She remarked, "The American conscience would like a rest from the black man's ghost. It was always an unpalatable subject but preeminently now in the era of good feeling, and self-complacency, of commercial omnipotence and military glorification."[28]

Rather than ignore inequities in the name of "good feeling," Cooper called for remembering the past differently, to realize a more just future. In *A Voice*, she wrote, "the memory of past oppression and the fact of present attempted repression only serve to gather momentum for [the race's] irrepressible powers."[29] Here, we find an early example of the type of historiography Cooper later employed in her dissertation and in her curriculum and school leadership work. She emphasized the *"Singing Something"* of the enslaved, in Saint-Domingue and the United States, pointing to an internal force that "never is wholly smothered or stamped out,"[30] even if nobody else at the time (or since) noticed their "song."

Though much has changed, many of the material obstacles and know-ledge politics Cooper navigated *live on*. Slavery's raced-gendered afterlife continues to aid in the perversion of, or ignorance about, Cooper's ideas, and remains a barrier to her work (and to Black women's intellectual production more broadly). She exposed it, while modeling ways to read/teach/speak/write against the grain. In referencing muffling, unknowabil-ity, un-hearability, as well as the "ghosts" and "skeletons" of slavery[31] that haunt the nation's origins, beginning with the Constitution[32] and living on in the present, Cooper asked that we recognize how such epistemological issues have deep roots and a tenacious grip – and con-tinue to affect our lives. She also urged reflexivity about our work and

---

[25] Cooper, "The Intellectual Progress of the Colored Women in the United States," 202.
[26] Anna Julia Cooper, "The Ethics of the Negro Question," in Lemert and Bhan (eds.), *The Voice of Anna Julia Cooper*, 209.
[27] Cooper, *A Voice from the South*, 51.
[28] Cooper, "The Ethics of the Negro Question," 209.
[29] Cooper, *A Voice from the South*, 145.   [30] Cooper, "Equality of Races," 293.
[31] Anna Julia Cooper, "Sketches from a Teacher's Notebook: Loss of Speech through Isolation," in Lemert and Bhan (eds.), *The Voice of Anna Julia Cooper*, 301.
[32] Cooper, "The Ethics of the Negro Question," 207.

wider responsibilities: "We look within that we may gather together once more our forces, and ... address ourselves to the tasks before us."[33]

Delineating Slavery's Afterlife

Cooper placed slavery, and its afterlife, at the center of national and international issues. Throughout *A Voice*, she illustrated how power asymmetries and pernicious forms of racism-sexism stemming from slavery permeate contemporary life: impacting plausibility, narrowing the shape of our imaginations, and shaping everyday institutional and material realities. Cooper's earlier writings, focused more explicitly on race and gender politics within the United States, laid the ground for her Sorbonne dissertation, in which she exposed how slavery, "founded on the abuse of power ... and maintained by violence,"[34] intertwined with the rise of capitalism and colonialism. Cooper also juxtaposed racial subjugation with professed enlightenment ideals, historically and in the present, and, perhaps most unthinkably (to her committee and to history as a field, at the time), approached the enslaved as agents of history.[35]

To execute her analyses, Cooper used a variety of techniques, including humor, flipping the question, exposing contradictions, and homing in on pieces of evidence dominant groups assiduously denied. In her 1902 speech, "The Ethics of the Negro Question," Cooper quickly turned from (dominant) logics posing Blackness as a problem, to argue, instead, that racial diversity is the nation's greatest promise. Make no mistake, she argued, the United States *does* have a "race problem": white supremacy.

Reminding her audience that "the Negro was transplanted to this continent in order to produce chattels and beasts of burden for a 'Nation conceived in liberty and dedicated to the proposition that all men are created equal,'"[36] she emphasized how the nation's founding violations in slavery live on. They shape-shifted into legally- and socially-sanctioned mob violence, including lynching, used by whites to threaten and attempt to extinguish Black communities: "Ku Klux beatings with re-enslaving

---

[33] Cooper, *A Voice from the South*, 27.

[34] Cooper, *Slavery and the French and Haitian Revolutionists*, 31.

[35] May, *Anna Julia Cooper, Visionary Black Feminist*; Vivian M. May, "'It Is Never a Question of the Slaves': Anna Julia Cooper's Challenge to History's Silences in Her 1925 Sorbonne Thesis." *Callaloo* 31.1 (2008): 903–18. See also Gurminder K. Bhambra, "Undoing the Epistemic Disavowal of the Haitian Revolution: A Contribution to Global Social Thought," *Journal of Intercultural Studies* 37.1 (2016): 1–16; Nathifa Greene, "Anna Julia Cooper's Analysis of the Haitian Revolution," *The CLR James Journal*, 2017, https://doi.org/10.5840/clrjames201712445.

[36] Here, Cooper riffs on President Lincoln's words in his 1863 Gettysburg Address.

black codes became the sorry substitute for the overseer's lash and the auction block" during Reconstruction.[37]

Across her writings, Cooper also called for coalitional, intersectional approaches to liberation (including her astute critique in *A Voice* of "Eye vs. Foot" thinking, where she highlighted the futility of either/or race versus gender models of freedom that reinforce hierarchy and undermine justice for all in the name of feminism).[38] Such thinking likewise informed her dissertation, where she traced how race and class intertwined, in France and Saint-Domingue, during the French and Haitian revolutions. Cooper's dissertation analysis of how France repeatedly chased profit over egalitarianism/*égalité*, exploit over liberty/*liberté*, and slavery over brotherhood/*fraternité* echo her earlier critiques of US slavery and capitalism, where, she argues, the "desire for quick returns and large profits tempts capital ofttimes into … inhuman investments."[39]

In her dissertation exams, Cooper maintained that "Law, in the abstract founded on the unalienable Rights of Man and the indestructible value of Humanity makes sheer mockery of Equality."[40] She contended that human hierarchies are socially created and maintained, not innate and immutable, for "the democratic sense is an inborn human endowment."[41] Drawing on her lived experience, Cooper worked from within her archival materials to show how "the divine Spark is capable of awakening at the most unexpected moment." Since this "Spark" or "urge-cell"[42] can *never* be fully extinguished, domination is rarely totalizing: the capacity to resist may be ignited at any time, even in extreme states of subjection.

Cooper also illustrated how those in power (in the period, but also, we may surmise, members of her Sorbonne committee as well as many of her contemporaries in the discipline of History) could not understand this. France had created "a plutocracy incapable of perceiving, in Saint-Domingue, anything other than a source of exploitation,"[43] she argued. Cooper illustrated that slavery has both a material and epistemological afterlife – and the incapacity to perceive, or willful ignorance, is one of those legacies.

Cooper clarified that accepting human exploitation in the name of profit was not a shortcoming unique to France: this rationalization had

[37] Cooper, "The Ethics of the Negro Question," 207, 210–11.
[38] Cooper, *A Voice from the South*, 118–23.   [39] Cooper, *A Voice from the South*, 130.
[40] Cooper, "Legislative Measures Concerning Slavery," 294.
[41] Cooper, "Equality of Races," 293.   [42] Cooper, "Equality of Races," 293.
[43] Anna Julia Cooper, *L'attitude de La France à l'égard de l'esclavage Pendant La Révolution* (Paris: impr. de la cour d'appel, L. Maretheux, 1925), 126 ("une plutocratie incapable de voir autre chose, dans Saint Domingue, qu'une source d'exploitation").

not bothered the "big consciences" of George Washington and Thomas Jefferson in the "birthplace" of political independence, the United States.[44] Here, as elsewhere, Cooper used humor and analogy to make her point indirectly, rather than via overt claims. To appreciate her critiques of how France and the United States undermined their democratic visions we must follow Cooper's sarcastic asides, note her use of analogy and juxtaposition, and discern the signs and symbols of resistance Cooper asked us to appreciate.

Cooper's dissertation prefigured contemporary scholarship on the Black diaspora as a transnational historical configuration, and anticipated by more than a decade C. L. R. James' renowned volume, *The Black Jacobins*. Cooper showed how the *noirs* (free and enslaved) were repeatedly overlooked by politicians in France and by *colons* in Saint-Domingue. She finds this ironic, in that the *noirs* would come to play a significant political role in French politics, at home and abroad, and "would not fail to be an active element of the insurrection."[45]

Likewise, Cooper argued, the *noirs* were underestimated by the *philosophes* of the period, and by most scholars and historians of the era . In other words, she anticipated Saidiya Hartman's keen insight: that "the genealogy of freedom ... discloses the intimacy of liberty, domination, and subjection."[46] Such inconsistencies not only undermine democracy, argued Cooper: these axiomatic problems were readily accepted by most whites in the period, and since. Black agency and subjectivity, inconceivable to those in power, were palpable and obvious to Cooper.

Another interpretive tactic used by Cooper was to alter conventional timeframes. She began her dissertation by shifting the Age of Revolution's periodization to trace a longer history linking the rise of slavery, settler colonialism, and capitalism. Cooper opened by discussing Spain and Portugal's conquests in the Americas and their unbridled exploitation under the aegis of "Discovery": she decried the heinous rise of racial slavery to accommodate rapacious European empires after the genocide of Native populations. Tracing the roots of the Haitian Revolution to Portugal's commencing the slave trade in West Africa in the fifteenth century and to Columbus' arrival on Hispaniola, Cooper intervened in prevailing timelines of resistance and did not follow conventional approaches to the Age of Revolution.

---

[44] Cooper, *L'attitude de La France*, 57.

[45] Cooper, *L'attitude de La France*, 22–23 ("ils n'allaient pas manquer d'être un élément actif d'insurrection").

[46] Saidiya Hartman, *Scenes of Subjection: Terror, Slavery and Self-Making in Nineteenth-Century America* (Oxford University Press, 1997), 123.

By emphasizing an interactive rather than mimetic relationship between France and Saint-Domingue,[47] Cooper introduced a Black Atlantic framework and resisted a triumphal account of French history. She stretched the bounds of what constituted the French nation beyond the metropole and altered parameters of who should be considered historical agents. Even if they have been ignored, discounted, or treated as anomalous, Cooper showed that the actions of the slaves, the *affranchis* (free Blacks), and *gens de couleur* (free, often propertied, frequently slave-owning, people of color) are politically relevant and historically significant.

Cooper also homed in on what Hartman has named "incidental death." In her own archival work, Hartman came to realize how "all this death had been incidental to the acquisition of profit and to the rise of capitalism. … Death wasn't a goal of its own but just a by-product of commerce, which has had the lasting effect of making negligible all the millions of lives lost. Incidental death occurs when life has no normative value, when no humans are involved, when the population is, in effect, seen as already dead."[48] In this light, we can better appreciate Cooper's attention to slaves' excessive mortality rates – nearly triple the birth rate. For every slave brought to the colonies, Cooper documented, four would die.[49]

Cooper pointed to assertions by *colons* and French merchants, that the "dependence in which [the slaves] live is a hundred times easier than that in which live a great portion of French individuals."[50] In contrast, she highlighted intensely cruel working conditions[51] and extremely high slave mortality rates tied to capitalist profit and national greed. The countless dead point to the truth (9). She also emphasized how whites and *gens de couleur* used the law as well as torture and cruelty to try to keep the enslaved subjected (23), suggesting that if slavery were so easy, "sweet," or "natural," such brutal enforcement would be unnecessary.

Cooper noted how whites in Saint-Domingue and France spent a lot of energy maintaining an ostensibly "natural" state of Black subjection.

---

[47] Cooper, *L'attitude de La France*, 66. "Or, de même que les événements de France réagissaient sur Saint-Domingue, ceux de Saint-Domingue réagissaient sur l'opinion française et sur l'Assemblée Constituante" (While the events of France had an effect on Saint-Domingue, those of Saint-Domingue had an effect on French public opinion and the Constituent Assembly).

[48] Saidiya Hartman, *Lose Your Mother: A Journey Along the Atlantic Slave Route* (New York: Farrar, Straus & Giroux, 2007), 31.

[49] Cooper, *L'attitude de La France*, 9.

[50] Cooper, *Slavery and the French and Haitian Revolutionists*, 119. Although Keller (trans.), uses the term "easier," "douce" also means "sweeter."

[51] Cooper, *L'attitude de La France*, 24.

Whites imposed an artificial race supremacy, then deluded themselves into believing it was "natural."[52] This self-delusion was so imbued that, once the Haitian Revolution was well under way, the French continued to see the enslaved as inclined to "submission" and the King proclaimed nothing had changed in slaves' "obedience" to their "masters."[53] Letters from the period contain patently false statements, such as "'I do not believe that there is any insurrection of the Negroes'" in Saint-Domingue, even as signs of revolt and evidence of collective resistance were everywhere.[54]

Repeatedly, Cooper emphasized whites' inability to understand that *noirs* sought freedom and never *had* "agreed" to be enslaved. Even after several successful and large-scale slave revolts had taken place, she wrote: "people thought, superficially enough, that an alliance of the whites and the mulattoes would be sufficient to put down the revolt of the blacks."[55] While the settler colonial system based on slavery was untenable,[56] repeated slave uprisings continued to be seen as anomalous: their larger meaning was unfathomable.

Raising Doubts, (Re)reading the Archive

In different genres, contexts, and periods, Cooper read lacunae and unpacked their possibilities. In her dissertation, she approached the Age of Revolution from her particular standpoint and time period to read French political and military archives against the grain and to navigate a discipline and an academic context that were not necessarily open to questions about the roots of France's celebrated republican democracy.

Cooper shifted analytic focus toward the enslaved, free Blacks, and *gens de couleur*, rejecting the usual historiographic frames that glorify France and erase Saint-Domingue/Haiti. She suggested that ignorance, not reason, structured Enlightenment theorizing and pinpointed deep contradictions between the *philosophes'* democratic ideals and France's actual political practices. Cooper underscored French refusal to think through the meaning of enslavement for French republicanism and to recognize the agency (and humanity) of the enslaved.

---

[52] Cooper, *L'attitude de La France*, 43.   [53] Cooper, *L'attitude de La France*, 82 fn. 3.

[54] Letter from an inhabitant of Nantes, November 28, 1789 in Cooper, *Slavery and the French and Haitian Revolutionists*, 121.

[55] Cooper, *Slavery and the French and Haitian Revolutionists*, 87.

[56] Cooper, *L'attitude de La France*, 55.

One important way Cooper intervened was by reading absences in her primary and secondary sources as full of meaning. She noted the "unsuspected power" of slaves and free Blacks, who were "endowed with remarkable qualities of intelligence and dignity," even though, in the historical record, "they are never thought of at all." Regarding debates in the French Assembly about race and rights, Cooper underscored that repeatedly the Assembly acted "without ever giving a thought to the condition of the slaves."[57] Cooper paralleled such willful ignorance and exploitation at the heart of French republican democracy with similar dynamics in US history. She compared French and American republican practices and showed them to be linked by lofty aspirations but also by shared fundamental contradictions and investments in slavery and exploitation.

She argued, for example, "In drawing up the Constitution ... the words 'Slave,' 'Slavery' and 'Slave Trade' were carefully avoided although evidently present in the conscious minds of all."[58] Cooper added, "*the fact* of slavery as a skeleton at the feast had already become an embarrassment ... requiring and exacting many compromises, much confusion in trying to reconcile the convenience of the moment with those principles elaborated in the Declaration of Independence."[59] As Jane Gordon suggests, Cooper repeatedly showed how "the language of independence itself was premised upon multiple and fundamental forms of ruthless trampling and greedy devouring. Exploitation ... marked the origins of the United States as a nation."[60]

In addition to revealing the mental contortions, sizable resources, and extreme violence deployed in attempting to maintain slavery and uphold racial supremacy, Cooper underscored a profound economic reliance on human exploitation in both US and French contexts. In France, she highlighted the deep "gulf" or "gap" between celebrated democratic *theories* of universal reason and republican rights and extensive evidence of the widespread abusive *practices* of violently expansionist, capitalist empire dependent on slave and colonial labor.[61] Cooper also took on specious ideas about slavery's "humanizing" or "civilizing" capacity to expose its utter brutality. Presuming the subjectivity (and resistant capacity) of the enslaved (which neither her committee nor her materials

---

[57] Cooper, *Slavery and the French and Haitian Revolutionists*, 45, 50, 94.

[58] Cooper, "Legislative Measures Concerning Slavery," 300.

[59] Cooper, "Legislative Measures Concerning Slavery," 301.

[60] Jane Anna Gordon, "Unmasking the Big Bluff of Legitimate Governance and So-Called Independence: Creolizing Rousseau through the Reflections of Anna Julia Cooper," *Critical Philosophy of Race* 6.1 (2018), 10.

[61] Cooper, *Slavery and the French and Haitian Revolutionists*, 70.

account for), she mapped out a different history that highlighted the deep impact of slaves' insurgent freedom struggles on French democracy.

Though the Haitian Revolution is often portrayed via a mimesis framework, Cooper delineated mutually constitutive, transatlantic networks of power between Haiti and France. And, while French state and military archival materials tended to glorify the nation, celebrate settler colonialism, slavery, and war, and operate as reservoirs of history for propertied, white male citizen-subjects, Cooper read these materials differently. She illuminated how her sources exalted a narrow, white, Eurocentric, propertied notion of citizenship and rights, despite claims to universal freedom and personhood.

Cooper unmasked the preposterous nature of whites' desire for assurance that the colonial social order was viable and that slaves were content. She turned to contradicting evidence from the archives that dates, chronologically, from long before the full-blown Haitian Revolution and declaration of independence. Thus, two pages after Cooper described how the slaves are confidently reported to be as obedient as ever, she focused on other reports in the National Assembly about the Artibonite revolts[62] and on correspondence about other massive uprisings by both *noirs* (free and enslaved) and *gens de couleur*.[63] She adroitly characterized the *noirs* as "surexcités" (74), meaning a state of both political agitation (protest) and exaltation (joy, exhilaration).[64] The *noirs*' "surexcitation" suggests Black discontent with domination and slavery, despite the *colons*', king's, and merchants' delusions.

Cooper also approached her materials with a healthy skepticism. Several pamphlets were, she stated, "shaded by inevitable prejudice"[65] and many reports written "from a point-of-view as favorable as possible to the white colonists."[66] She described how "Many papers, letters and memoranda from the Massaic Institute tend[67] to prove that the Negroes are not unhappy, that they have not asked for ... liberty... [and] that the [slave] trade ... is preferable to the fate which awaits them in Africa"[68] – something Cooper found illogical and untrue, given reference, in the same materials, to work stoppages on multiple plantations[69] and large-scale

---

[62] Cooper, *Slavery and the French and Haitian Revolutionists*, 67.

[63] Cooper, *Slavery and the French and Haitian Revolutionists*, 71–72.

[64] See Paul Robert's *Le Petit Robert 1: Dictionnaire de la Langue Française*. Rédaction dirigée par A. Rey et J. Rey-Debove (Paris: Le Robert, 1990).

[65] Cooper, *Slavery and the French and Haitian Revolutionists*, 48.

[66] Cooper, *Slavery and the French and Haitian Revolutionists*, 75–76.

[67] Cooper, *L'attitude de La France*, 146. Here, Keller translates "tendent à prouver que" as "tend to prove that," but, given the arc of Cooper's argument, I would prefer "predisposed," as in they "are predisposed toward proving that."

[68] Cooper, *L'attitude de La France*, 128.   [69] Cooper, *L'attitude de La France*, 104.

slave and maroon uprisings over several decades.[70] To further her argument about willful ignorance, Cooper paused to mention some scholars from the period, particularly Jean-Philippe Garran de Coulon.[71] She also took on contemporary international thinkers like T. Lothrop Stoddard,[72] who, given his eugenicist standpoint, found many of Garran de Coulon's reflections spurious: Cooper thus advised "caution" when reading Stoddard, highlighting his "constantly obvious prejudice against the mulattoes and the blacks."[73]

Warnings about "Arbitrary Preconceptions"

In addition to navigating biased archival materials, while taking on prevailing historiographic frameworks that discounted the humanity and agency of enslaved peoples, Cooper had to contend with a doctoral committee led by "civilizationist" sociologist Célestin Bouglé. He had publicly suggested that Cooper would inherently be biased toward the slaves in Haiti because she herself had been enslaved. Rather than be cowed by his assertions, just as in *A Voice*, where she had observed that "the man who is dominated by the sentiment of race prejudice" is, by definition, "impervious to reason,"[74] in her Sorbonne oral defense and exams, Cooper daringly suggested that those who reap the benefits of domination are more prone to dangerous arrogance and bias (i.e., Bouglé).

Boldly, she cautioned, "it is necessary in every case to beware of arbitrary preconceptions, and especially it is necessary to *note well the importance of every exception* which may vitiate the argument or falsify the conclusion."[75] Here, Cooper indirectly distinguished between the concerted mental focus needed to contest oppression, read against the grain, and combat prevailing ways of thinking (her method/approach), and the types of self-serving bias and unreflexive "arbitrary perception" that

---

[70] Cooper, *L'attitude de La France*, 22.

[71] Cooper, *Slavery and the French and Haitian Revolutionists*, 149, fn. 139. *An Inquiry into the Causes of the Insurrection of the Negroes in the Island of St. Domingo to which are added Observations by M. Garran-Coulon on the Same Subject, Read in His Absence by M. Guadet, before the National Assembly, 29 February 1792* (London, 1792).

[72] T. Lothrop Stoddard, *The French Revolution in San Domingo* (Boston: Houghton Mifflin, 1914). In 1920, Stoddard had published an anti-immigration book about the threat of "surplus" colored humanity, *The Rising Tide of Color Against White World-Supremacy.*

[73] Cooper, *L'attitude de La France*, 147 fn. 102. For IR scholars, Cooper's brief engagements with Stoddard and Coulon would be useful to take up in the context of Robert Vitalis, *White World Order, Black Power Politics: The Birth of American International Relations* (Ithaca, NY: Cornell University Press, 2015) and Matthew Pratt Guterl, *The Color of Race in America, 1900–1940* (Cambridge, MA: Harvard University Press, 2002).

[74] Cooper, *A Voice from the South*, 232.   [75] Cooper, "Equality of Races," 291.

collude with oppression and are pivotal to wielding privilege and maintaining hierarchy (i.e., Bouglé's views and the frames used in French historiography more broadly).

Cooper began with the (seemingly) more innocuous past and showed that an endemic bias toward white supremacy (and against Black humanity) made key French thinkers and leaders during the Age of Revolution unable to perceive resistance by the enslaved (and eventually, *gens de couleur*) in Saint-Domingue. This is why, even when the Haitian Revolution was well under way, nobody in positions of privilege could see the reality in front of them.[76] This short-sighted thinking, she argued, held France back from achieving its fullest democratic vision.

Then, Cooper turned from this historical conundrum to discuss Bouglé's volume,[77] which he had assigned for her exams. Addressing Bouglé, who claimed "Nordic" people were superior, she declared: "To assume that the ideas inherent in social progress descend by divine favor upon the Nordic people, a Superior Race chosen to dominate the Earth, assuredly pampers the pride of those believing themselves the Elect of God. But one may as well anticipate Surprises" (i.e., present-day uprisings of oppressed peoples in China, Russia, Turkey, Egypt, and India – none of whom were Nordic, despite their clear ability to rise up and fight for collective equality on their own terms).[78]

Bouglé presumed Cooper's work would inherently be skewed, but never considered this could be true of his work. Dominant groups rarely perceive their own biases and privileges – yet often deploy (or project) charges of bias to maintain power and ward off critique. On one level, Bouglé was correct – Cooper *was* biased toward the enslaved, though not in the harmful way he implied. Unlike Bouglé, she was wary of "arbitrary preconceptions," approached all "exceptions" as significant, and noted realities that blatantly contradicted prevailing arguments.

Cooper successfully developed an epistemological orientation, a critical bias toward marginalized lives and suppressed voices, necessary for thinking against the grain of prevailing mindsets.[79] She forged an alternative historiographic approach by using epistemic defiance. Cooper was

---

[76] Cooper, *Slavery and the French and Haitian Revolutionists*, 23, 55–58.

[77] *Les idées égalitaires; étude sociologique* (Paris: F. Alcan, 1899).

[78] Cooper, "Equality of Races," 293. Note also, here, Cooper's sardonic use of capitalization (which would not have been heard in an oral exam) to emphasize and ridicule Bouglé's bias – "Elect of God," "Superior Race," etc.

[79] For more on bias as an epistemological skill for contesting dominant ideas, see Susan E. Babbitt, "Objectivity and the Role of Bias," in Nancy Tuana and Sandra Morgen (eds.), *Engendering Rationalities* (Albany, NY: SUNY, 2001), 297–314; Maria Lugones, "From within Germinative Stasis: Creating Active Subjectivity, Resistant Agency," in AnaLouise Keating (ed.), *Entremundos/Among Worlds: New Perspectives on Gloria*

rightly and necessarily concerned with what and who is missing from the record. She zoomed in on contradictions as pregnant with meaning, rather than as anomalies, outliers, inconsistencies, or minutiae to be brushed aside. Rather than undermining knowledge, Cooper's "bias" fostered greater understanding. Sustained bias against dominant mind-sets was (and remains) a requisite tactic for fighting the pull of prevailing frameworks and assumptions: it offers a way to work from within history's cracks, silences, or undersides, a means to fill lacunae or flesh out "muffled" voices, past and present.

In turn, Cooper was right about Bouglé: like the host of archival materials and established historiographic frameworks she contended with, he, too, was narrow-minded (though *this* type of bias, which flourishes in centers of power, usually remains unmarked and goes unremarked). Bouglé's text was skewed toward dominance, predisposed toward status quo power and whiteness, and oriented toward the widely accepted (and carefully archived) story of French history and the Age of Revolution that was waiting to be told. But, Cooper had a different standpoint, and a different history to tell.

Conclusion

Across her oeuvre, Cooper adroitly attended to intermeshed structures of race, gender, and class on an international scale. She exposed forms of violence that pervade social life and impact lived bodies and pivoted away from dominance. Showing how structural inequality has a global history, and how interlinked questions of race, class, and gender inequality are fundamental to modernity, Cooper analyzed centers of power and hegemony, but also looked to, and thought from within, the margins. Both are sites of critical engagement for her work and both are loci, she argued, where oppressive forms of power can play out.

Offering an approach to global humanism which highlights how enslavement has been, and remains, a deeply suppressed subtext of modernity, Cooper offered a profound critique of capitalism, patriarchy, racism, and violence in *A Voice* and *L'Attitude*. She focused on fragments of information and pinpointed textual, analytical, and archival incongruities (between theory and action, philosophical vision and lived reality, and historical proclamations versus archival content) to reveal obscured facts, listen to silenced voices, and remember forgotten lives. Today, we should model these same techniques when delving into the archives,

---

Anzaldúa (New York: Palgrave Macmillan, 2005), 85–100; Vivian M. May, *Pursuing Intersectionality, Unsettling Dominant Imaginaries* (New York: Routledge, 2015), ch. 5.

tracing intellectual histories, and when reading Cooper, and other Black women thinkers, in pursuit of more inclusive and accurate political genealogies.

When considering Cooper's contributions to international thought, it is imperative to appreciate how she refused to acquiesce to prevailing logics. Ever the teacher, she models how to trace residues, unpack normative assumptions, expose gaps, and reveal agency by presuming subjectivity where those in power cannot expect it because they assume its impossibility. Certainly, Cooper should be more recognized for her dissertation, in which she demonstrated how whites in Saint-Domingue and France exerted unbelievable energies and capital trying to preserve white supremacy and to protect the tremendous profits gained from slavery and exploited labor (capitalism and slavery are intimately bound together in her analysis).

Cooper carefully documented how whites went to extremes to delude themselves into believing an (artificial) racial hierarchy to be an inherent state of being, not a constructed (and changeable) historical condition.[80] Furthermore, she adeptly read French archival materials and standard histories of the period against the grain to argue that, though overlooked at the time, and studiously erased since, the actions of the slaves, the *affranchis* (free Blacks), and the *gens de couleur* were politically and historically significant. Cooper's noting of mass resistance by slaves and free Blacks was pivotal, as was her focus on entrenched denial on the part of (propertied) whites in France and the colonies. This twofold approach allowed Cooper to underscore capacities for resistance on the part of those who had been silenced or ignored and to highlight Black political agency and transatlantic flows of power in original and groundbreaking ways.

Much remains to be learned from Cooper – particularly her ability to read multiple sites of power at once, listen to "muffled" ideas, approach the ignored, unwritten, and unspeakable as sites of meaning, and perceive an internal "Spark."[81] While mapping signs of resistance, she unpacked dominance, analyzed oppression's intricate workings, contested prevailing points of view, and combated accepted versions of history. In her scholarship, community engagement, and lifelong work as a teacher, Cooper refused to support any form of oppression in the name of (partial) liberation and rejected lofty theories of equality that could not meaningfully dismantle multiple forms of brutality and exploitation.

---

[80] Cooper, *L'attitude de La France*, 43.   [81] Cooper, "Equality of Races," 293.

Cooper's contributions have been lauded previously: but, robust scholarly efforts focused on recovery work on Cooper, over more than four decades, have not yet sufficiently transformed intellectual geneal- ogies and feminist methods across the academy. The task before histor- ians of international thought is (deceivingly) simple: pause to listen more carefully to Cooper's voice, just as *she* attended to those "muffled" voices before her; ask *where* her work is overlooked; and, beyond simply "including" her ideas, make every effort to transform the methods and frameworks that led to Cooper being absent(ed) and excluded in the first place.

Perhaps sustained dedication and careful attention to the contribu- tions of Black women thinkers, combined with vigilance about resisting the pull of prevailing ways of thinking, might just do the trick, to trans- form the politics of knowledge and to better map out and understand genealogies of resistance. However, there is no guarantee. After all, it is Cooper herself who reminded us that "rhetoric," on its own, can never "annihilate" inequality.[82]

---

[82] Cooper, *A Voice from the South*, 232.

2   Revolutionary Thinking: Luxemburg's Socialist International Theory

Kimberly Hutchings

The name Rosa Luxemburg (1871–1919), unlike that of many of the women contributing to the study of international politics in the early part of the twentieth century, is well-known, even if the details of her thought are not. Nevertheless, with the partial exception of some work in International Political Economy[1] there is very little sustained engagement with her work in the field of International Relations (IR). Does this matter? At least in the case of Luxemburg one can hardly complain that she is a neglected figure in general, so in what sense would reinstating her specifically as part of the IR canon open up new pathways for international thought in the present, or add to our understanding of disciplinary history?

In this chapter, I will argue that the reasons to return to Luxemburg are: first, even if we do not follow Luxemburg all the way in her analytical and political claims and actions, her work and activism prefigure what remain core questions and concerns, in particular for critical traditions of international theory today.[2] Second, in terms of the history of international thought, I argue that returning to Luxemburg sharpens our understanding of the conditions within which theorizations of the international took shape in the late nineteenth and early twentieth centuries in Europe. These were conditions of political activism and engagement within the imperialist core and from the vantage point of the imperialist core, and of intense argument about a range of international issues that were not yet settled in the terms set by Versailles.[3] Luxemburg's theory

---

[1] Riccardo Bellofiore (ed.), *Rosa Luxemburg and the Critique of Political Economy* (London: Routledge, 2009); Andreas Bieler, Sümercan Bozkurt, Max Crook, Peter S. Cruttenden, Ertan Erol, Adam D. Morton, Cemal B. Tansel, and Elif Uzgören, "The Enduring Relevance of Rosa Luxemburg's *The Accumulation of Capital*," *Journal of International Relations and Development* 19 (2016): 420–47.

[2] Owen Worth, "Accumulating the Critical Spirit," *International Politics* 49.2 (2012): 136–53.

[3] Erez Manela, *The Wilsonian Moment: Self-Determination and the International Origins of Anticolonial Nationalism* (Oxford University Press, 2007); Deborah Whitehall, "A Rival

and practice sharpen our understanding because, even as she conforms to Eurocentric assumptions about the direction and leadership of historical progress, shared by liberal and socialist "progressives" in her day, she also challenges those assumptions.

The chapter is in four sections: first, sketching the context of Luxemburg's work and its reception; second, outlining key elements of Luxemburg's international theory on imperialism, capitalism, and nationalism; third, examining Luxemburg's novel understanding of revolutionary practice; fourth, outlining the ongoing relevance of Luxemburg's thought for international theory, and how her thought connects to the concerns of contemporary critical and feminist IR. It will be argued that what distinguishes Luxemburg's international thought from others of her contemporary liberal and socialist internationalisms is the way she unsettles the progressive, Eurocentric reading of history on which she simultaneously relies.

Luxemburg's Context: Life and Afterlife

Luxemburg came from a middle-class, assimilated Polish-Jewish family. Born in 1871, she was educated in Warsaw, which was then part of the Russian Empire, and became an active revolutionary as a student. At the age of eighteen she went into exile in Switzerland, enrolling at Zurich University. She gained her PhD with a thesis on the process of industrialization in Poland in 1897. She then moved to Germany, where she became a leading member of the Social Democratic Party (SPD) and developed a career as a Marxist theoretician, teacher, and activist. She was active in revolutionary politics in Germany, Poland, and Russia, even during periods of imprisonment. She broke with the SPD over their support for Germany in World War I and founded the German Communist Party (KPD). She was murdered in January 1919. Much has been written about Luxemburg's life,[4] and her relation to her family and to her Jewishness, especially the latter, have been the subject of controversy.[5] Although the evidence is clear that she remained close to her family, she rejected their bourgeois mores. She married only as a convenience to

History of Self-Determination," *European Journal of International Law* 27.3 (2016): 719–43.

[4] John P. Nettl, *Rosa Luxemburg* (Oxford University Press, 1969); Elzbieta Ettinger, *Rosa Luxemburg: A Life* (Boston: Beacon Press, 1987).

[5] Rory Castle, "'You alone will make our family's name famous': Rosa Luxemburg, Her Family and the Origins of Her Polish-Jewish Identity," *Praktyka Teoretyczna* 6 (2012): 93–125; Robert S. Wistrich, "Rosa Luxemburg: The Polish-German-Jewish Identities of a Revolutionary Internationalist," *Leo Baeck Institute Year Book* 57 (2012): 239–66.

gain German citizenship and did not marry the men with whom she had longstanding relationships. She was firmly opposed to Zionism and has been accused of despising Yiddish-speaking Eastern European Jews, and of not grasping the significance of anti-Semitism, even though she was frequently the object of anti-Semitic attack.[6] In all of her work and in her letters, Luxemburg was resistant to identifying herself with what she saw as exclusive identities: woman, Polish, Jewish. For her the only identity that mattered was identification with the working class, which was the universal class because it would bring about the revolution abolishing gendered, national, racial as well as economic hierarchies.

Luxemburg's theoretical reflections, her activism, and her lived identity were tightly intertwined. All three dimensions of her existence were marked by movement, across geographical borders, across languages, and, temporally, in the way in which her ideas shifted over time. A focus on Luxemburg highlights the *existential* as well as *political* stakes of internationalism. On the one hand, she belongs nowhere, on the other, she belongs everywhere.

What do you want with this particular suffering of the Jews? The poor victims on the rubber plantations in Putumayo, the Negroes in Africa with whose bodies the Europeans play a game of catch, are just as near to me. Do you remember the words written on the work of the Great General Staff about Trotha's campaign in the Kalahari desert? "And the death-rattles, the mad cries of those dying of thirst, faded away into the sublime silence of eternity." Oh, this "sublime silence of eternity" in which so many screams have faded away unheard. It rings within me so strongly that I have no special corner of my heart reserved for the ghetto: I am at home wherever in the world there are clouds, birds and human tears.[7]

Luxemburg developed her theoretical arguments in the rich and complicated context of European Marxist internationalist debates, in which theory was designed to serve the purposes of revolutionary practice. This situation embodied lived tensions between nationalism and internationalism within a broader imperial context. This was not simply a matter of competing views about theory, strategy, and tactics. It concerned how these Marxist intellectuals and activists understood their own identity and location, spatially (in terms of their positioning within German, Austro-Hungarian, or Russian empires and the various nationalities they subordinated) and temporally (their reading of the world-historical relation between national and class struggle).

---

[6] Wistrich, "Rosa Luxemburg."
[7] Rosa Luxemburg, "Letter to Emmanuel and Mathilde Wurm, February 1917," in Peter Hudis and Kevin B. Anderson (eds.), *The Rosa Luxemburg Reader* (New York: Monthly Review Press, 2004), 389.

The debates between "revisionist" and "revolutionary" interpretations of Marx reflected a continuum of positions within historically progressive (liberal and socialist) interpretations of international relations. Amongst these thinkers the limits of liberal internationalism were being continually contested, most fundamentally by Luxemburg herself, who refused to contemplate commitments to national self-determination even as a stage on the way to a genuine overturning of existing class relationships. As a woman revolutionary who went beyond subordinate roles and relegation to a focus on the "woman question," Luxemburg was fundamentally disturbing. As a foreigner in the world of German social democracy, she disrupted faith in the highly successful SPD organization and its parliamentary successes. As a Polish woman, schooled in Tsarism, she built on her experience of the 1905 Russian Revolution to challenge Leninist arguments for how the revolutionary vanguard and party should operate. And she was amongst the minority who regarded the SPD endorsement of Germany's war in 1914 as the ultimate betrayal of the universal politics of socialism.

During her lifetime, Luxemburg was recognized as a significant interlocutor by those in the movement with whom she disagreed. Most Marxist readers disagreed with her interpretation of Marx in *The Accumulation of Capital*. In polemical exchanges it was common for her identity as a woman to be invoked in relation to her errors about Marxism, her inability to be "scientific," and her tendency to get overemotional about the victims of capitalism.[8] However, this was in a context in which her status as a revolutionary thinker and activist was clear, and in which she used as well as was the object of racialized and gendered polemical language.[9] Since her death, the reception of her work has continued to be highly politicized, as well as being marked by an increased focus on her life as opposed to her work. This is in part due to the deliberate vilification and suppression of her ideas. In the wake of the failure of the German Communist uprisings in 1919, the European left, dominated by the USSR, was obliged to denigrate Luxemburg's critiques of aspects of the Bolshevik revolution, to the extent that her reflections on it were omitted from published versions of her work.[10] As well as being politically contentious for Marxism, Luxemburg's legacy is also highly

---

[8] Alexandra Kemmerer, "Editing Rosa: Luxemburg, the Revolution, and the Politics of Infantilization," *European Journal of International Law* 27.3 (2016): 853–64; Daniel Gaido and Manuel Quiroga, "The Early Reception of Rosa Luxemburg's Theory of Imperialism," *Capital and Class* 37.3 (2013): 437–55.

[9] Wistrich, "Rosa Luxemburg"; Eric Blanc, "The Rosa Luxemburg Myth: A Critique of Luxemburg's Politics in Poland (1893–1919)," *Historical Materialism* 25.4 (2017): 3–36.

[10] Kemmerer, "Editing Rosa."

controversial in relation to its arguments about nationalism and race, in particular in the contexts of Poland and Zionism, leading her to be decried as a traitor to the cause of Polish self-determination and a self-hating Jew.[11]

As Kemmerer has pointed out, the standard Soviet line on Luxemburg for most of the twentieth century, was that although her heart was in the right place, she was guilty of major errors in her Marxist theory. This reading was enabled through the feminization and romanticization of her as a person and activist, along with a belittling of her as a thinker. To a large extent this pattern of feminization and romanticization has also marked more positive receptions of Luxemburg's work. In contrast to her male contemporaries, her work has often been read through the prism of her personal life and loves.[12] Her commitments to free sexual relations, along with her terrible death at the hands of proto-fascist forces fed into a myth of Rosa as romantic heroine, who died for the love of revolution. This is the myth that is celebrated not only in biographical works, but also in many fictionalized accounts of Luxemburg's life as "Red Rosa" in films and novels, most recently a graphic novel.[13]

Nevertheless, at various points over the past century there have been revivals of positive interest in Luxemburg's *work* as well as her life, despite its active suppression and marginalization by her political opponents.[14] There is a considerable body of secondary literature surrounding her Marxist theories of capital accumulation, nationalism, imperialism, militarism, and revolution. In addition, she has been identified as an important influence on later thinkers, most notably Hannah Arendt.[15] Her current status as a Marxist thinker in Anglophone contexts is confirmed by the recent and ongoing publication of her complete works in English translation.[16]

---

[11] Wistrich, "Rosa Luxemburg"; Blanc, "The Rosa Luxemburg Myth."

[12] Maria Tamboukou, "Love, Naratives, Politics: Encounters between Hannah Arendt and Rosa Luxemburg," *Theory, Culture & Society* 30.1 (2013): 35–56; Maria Tamboukou, "Imagining and Living the Revolution: An Arendtian Reading of Rosa Luxemburg's Letters and Writings," *Feminist Review* 106 (2014): 27–42.

[13] Kate Evans, *Red Rosa: A Graphic Biography of Rosa Luxemburg* (London: Verso, 2015).

[14] Nettl, *Rosa Luxemburg.*

[15] Hannah Arendt, "A Heroine of Revolution," *New York Review of Books*, October 6, 1966; Sidonia Blattler, Irene M. Marti, and Senem Saner, "Rosa Luxemburg and Hannah Arendt: Against the Destruction of Political Spheres of Freedom," *Hypatia* 20.2 (2005): 88–101; Tamboukou, "Imagining and Living the Revolution."

[16] Peter Hudis (ed.), *The Complete Works of Rosa Luxemburg, Volume I: Economic Writings I* (London: Verso, Kindle Edition, 2013); Peter Hudis and Paul Le Blanc (eds.), *The Complete Works of Rosa Luxemburg, Volume II: Economic Writings II* (London: Verso, Kindle Edition, 2015); see also Stefanie Ehmsen and Albert Scharenberg (eds.), *Rosa Remix* (New York: Rosa Luxemburg Stiftung, 2016).

Within this context, it is interesting to speculate as to why, within the field of IR, even in work that does focus on Marxism, Luxemburg rates only passing mention compared to figures of her contemporaries, such as Lenin, Bukharin, Hilferding, and the Austro-Marxists.[17] The Marxist or Marxist-inspired theorists that have contributed to IR over the past thirty years are much more likely to reference Gramsci, Trotsky, or members of the Frankfurt School than Luxemburg – even when these thinkers are echoing aspects of her ideas. In one of the few existing IR texts that deals specifically with the history of Marxist thought on the international, Linklater's *Beyond Realism and Marxism* (1990), Luxemburg merits only a mention. I suggest that there are two different reasons for the relative neglect of Luxemburg's work in IR: first, a historical reason relating to the Cold War context (1950s–1970s) in which IR organized the production of teaching of IR knowledge in terms of three key "isms": realism, liberalism, and Marxism. At this time, IR scholars sympathetic to Marxist ideas would be dealing with a tradition that had largely suppressed Luxemburg's legacy as an independent Marxist thinker, and which had yet to take the role of women as either actors or theorists of international politics seriously. Second, a theoretical reason: in spite of her commitment to Marxist orthodoxy in many respects, as we will see, Luxemburg's international theory, and her approach to theorizing itself, are not easily captured as a static "ism."

Luxemburg's International Theory

Marx had quite a lot to say about imperialism in his occasional writings and journalism, and acknowledged the role of imperialism and colonialism in early capitalist accumulation in Europe. However, he never produced a fully-fledged theory of imperialism. Within IR, Lenin's pamphlet, *Imperialism: The Highest Stage of Capitalism* is most often taken to exemplify a Marxist position on imperialism in the early twentieth century.[18] For Lenin, imperialism was a response to, and outcome of, a variety of problems in mature capitalist economies. The competition of great powers for control over the earth's people and resources, and the rise of militarism and the drive toward world war, were outcomes of the logic of capitalist development, once it had got beyond a certain stage. Luxemburg gives a different account of the causes of imperialism and the

---

[17] Patricia Owens, "Women and the History of International Thought," *International Studies Quarterly* 62.3 (2018): 467–81.
[18] Vladimir I. Lenin, *Imperialism: The Highest Stage of Capitalism* (Moscow: Progress Publishers, 1963 [1916]).

extent to which imperialism was necessarily or contingently connected to capitalism. For Luxemburg, imperialism (and the militarism by which it is always accompanied) could not be understood either as a technique of primitive accumulation at the dawn of the capitalist world order, or as a by-product of late capitalism. For her, imperialism was crucial to the accumulation of capital throughout capitalism's history. Her argument for this drew on her knowledge of the development of industrial capitalism in Poland (which was the subject of her doctoral thesis), and was fully articulated in her major work in political economy *The Accumulation of Capital: A Contribution to the Economic Theory of Imperialism*.[19] Her argument was articulated again in the lengthy *Anti-Critique*, in which she addressed critics of her argument in *The Accumulation of Capital*.[20]

Luxemburg's claims about capitalism and imperialism rested on a famous disagreement with Marx's account of capitalist accumulation, in which Luxemburg claimed to have proved that such accumulation, on which capitalism relied in order to exist at all, was not possible within a Marxist account of purely capitalist economic and social relations. Luxemburg's argument is highly technical and draws heavily on the assumptions and concepts of Marxist political economy. Put simply, she claims that only through tapping into the resources of non-capitalist modes of production and exchange – natural or simple commodity economies – could sufficient surplus value be generated to enable the accumulation of capital. This link between capitalism and non-capitalist social forms could be seen in the predatory relation of capitalism to peasant and handicraft economies at home and abroad from its inception, and explained the growth of empires within the capitalist core, in Europe, as much as the successive land grabs of the European powers in America, Africa, Asia, and Australasia.

In Europe itself capitalism's first grand gesture is the revolutionary overthrow of feudalism's natural economy. In lands across the seas its first action in the subjugation and ruination of the traditional communal system.[21]

For Luxemburg, late nineteenth-century imperialism was essentially a continuation of an ongoing feature of the capitalist social form, but

---

[19] Rosa Luxemburg, "The Accumulation of Capital: A Contribution to the Economic Theory of Imperialism," in Hudis and Le Blanc (eds.), *The Complete Works, Volume I*.

[20] The *Anti-Critique* was written in 1915, while Luxemburg was in prison, but not published until after her death in 1921; it is reproduced in full in the 2015 Verso Volume II of her *Complete Works*.

[21] Rosa Luxemburg, "The Accumulation of Capital, Or, What the Epigones Have Made Out of Marx's Theory: An Anti-Critique" [1915/1921], in Hudis and Le Blanc (eds.), *The Complete Works Volume II*, 320.

taking on a particular urgency as capitalist states struggled to grab the remaining non-capitalist parts of the globe. The key problem for capitalism was that once it had transformed all parts of the world in its own image, it would become impossible to sustain, as it could no longer accumulate the capital needed to fuel the growth it needed in order to survive. Late nineteenth-century imperialism was therefore distinctive only in the sense that it would bring capitalism to crisis, in a way that had not happened as long as there was a non-capitalist milieu to draw upon. This is the point at which the capitalist core begins to experience fully the kinds of militarism and violence that have been the political technologies of imperialism:[22]

After the expansion of capital over four centuries had sacrificed the existence and culture of all the noncapitalist peoples of Asia, Africa, America and Australia, subjecting them to ceaseless convulsions and violence, causing their decline and fall on a massive scale, in the same way now the expansion of capitalism plunges the cultured people of Europe itself into a series of catastrophes that are bound to have as their final result either the destruction of all culture or a transition to the socialist mode of production.[23]

One of the most striking aspects of Luxemburg's political economy from the contemporary point of view is the consistency of her analysis as a class analysis. For Luxemburg, the key category for understanding international political economy is the category of class. Capitalism and imperialism are the work of the bourgeois class, following its material interests. The key effect of capitalism and imperialism is the construction of the proletarian class, which becomes the only available agent for revolutionary, progressive change. From this follows her views on the state, on bourgeois democracy, and, most famously, on national self-determination. For Luxemburg, the modern state is in the service of the bourgeois class, and modern imperialism follows from the interests of the bourgeois class. In this context, she takes a great deal from the history of Poland's shifting political existence, as a state and as an imperial possession in the context of intensive capitalist development.[24] Capitalist states become empires, and capitalist empires subsume their imperial possessions under capitalism.

---

[22] Luxemburg, "The Accumulation of Capital," 235–342; Rosa Luxemburg, "The Junius Pamphlet: The Crisis of Social Democracy" [1916], in Hudis and Anderson (eds.), *The Rosa Luxemburg Reader*, 327.

[23] Luxemburg, "The Accumulation of Capital," 446–47.

[24] Rosa Luxemburg, "The Industrial Development of Poland" [1898], in Hudis and Le Blanc (eds.), *The Complete Works, Volume I*; Rosa Luxemburg, "The National Question" [1909], in Horace B. Davis (ed.), *The National Question: Selected Writings by Rosa Luxemburg* (New York: Monthly Review Press, 1976).

Within this history principles of democracy and national self-determination are respected only insofar as they support the power of the bourgeois class. Luxemburg was highly suspicious of the argument that there was any *necessary* connection between capitalism or the bourgeois class and democracy. In her view, this was a fallacy that could only be held by those who mistakenly identified capitalism with the organization of some states in the capitalist core. She argued that capitalism could happily coexist with a variety of political orderings, and pointed to the lack of democracy characteristic of the imperial possessions of supposedly democratic capitalist states. In her view, bourgeois democracy, to the extent that it existed in countries such as Britain or Germany would always be instantly traded off against the interests of capital. She made this claim in 1899 and saw it vindicated in the increasing suppression of democracy in the run up to and during the 1914–18 war.

Two factors dominate the political life of contemporary states: *world politics* and the labour movement. –

If it is true that world politics and militarism represent a *rising* tendency in the present phase, then bourgeois democracy must logically move in a *descending* line.[25]

As we saw in the previous section, Luxemburg's views on capitalism and democracy were reflected also in her persistent objection to the idea that national self-determination could be considered a progressive ideal from a socialist point of view.[26] Her position on this point set her against liberal and socialist arguments, and remained a key point of contention between her, Austro-Marxism, and Lenin's bolshevism. For Luxemburg, the identification of the principle of self-determination with that of self-determination of a people fell into a variety of traps. First, it failed to grasp that the modern state was characterized by national multiplicity, so that nationalism would always become a pretext for secession or irredentism. Second, it pushed against the movement of capitalism toward larger and larger political structures, mirroring and managing the expansion of capitalist social and economic forms. Third, to the extent nationalism had ever been about liberation it had only ever been about the liberation of the bourgeois class to run the state in its own interests. Fourth, nationalism ran directly counter to the internationalism of the working class. Luxemburg acknowledged that national cultures were important, both as sources of particular cultural riches in poetry and music, and also

---

[25] Rosa Luxemburg, "Social Reform or Revolution?" [1899], in Hudis and Anderson (eds.), *The Rosa Luxemburg Reader*, 153–54.

[26] Luxemburg, "The National Question" [1915], in Hudis and Anderson (eds.), *The Rosa Luxemburg Reader*, 327.

as providing the milieu within which workers could be educated, but she entirely rejected the view that they needed to be reflected in any political arrangement. For Luxemburg class not nationality had to be the principle on which a future socialist order was organized, and any notion of national self-determination as a stage on the way, as opposed to a hindrance, to such an order was mistaken.

Luxemburg's theories of political economy, imperialism, militarism, and nationalism are written in the language of Marxist orthodoxy, and firmly located in a reading of history as moving toward the development of the first, genuinely universal class. Her criticisms of the idea of "national economies," her insistence on the centrality of imperialism to capitalism, and her dismissal of nationalism are all part of an internationalist narrative, in which a worldwide socialist revolution will become possible. Nevertheless, this is by no means the whole story of her international theory. Even as she relies on Marxist categories, suggests diffusionist accounts of the spread of capitalism from a European core, and affirms capitalism as a progressive force in the overall story of world history, some of Luxemburg's analysis disturbs that overall story. One of the reasons why her accounts of the accumulation of capital and the regressive nature of nationalism were so strongly objected to by her Marxist peers, was the way in which she made her case. When it came to both capital accumulation and nationalism, she argued first, that one needed to analyze capitalism as an actual social formation and not as an analytical abstraction; second, that historical contexts changed and that this meant that theoretical and political judgments must change also.

Marx had not witnessed the aggressive acceleration of imperialism in the latter part of the nineteenth century, neither had he witnessed how Poland's industrialization, sponsored by the Russian Empire, had shifted the ground on which progressive revolutionary action was possible, from the bourgeois revolutions of 1848 to potential proletarian revolution in the early twentieth century. Polish and Russian workers now had identical interests in the overthrow of capitalism, nationalist sentiment had become a distraction rather than a force for progress. At the same time, therefore, as using the language of Marxist science, Luxemburg was practicing a mode of theorizing that required her not to take the direction of history for granted, and to have her analysis led by ongoing historical research on her current context. In her current context, as we see in her analysis of what happens when capitalism uses up the entirety of its non-capitalist milieu, she is by no means certain that history will actually deliver the outcome to which she is committed. Yes, the conditions for the triumph of the universal class are in place, but it is also quite possible that history will end in catastrophe and "barbarism" as capitalism implodes.

A characteristic of Luxemburg's theoretical work is that her arguments are full of empirical examples and interpretation of historical events, and they frequently evoke affective experience. She does not simply point to the ways in which capitalism displaces peasants and indigenous peoples as if capitalism were an impersonal force, but evokes the political agency of those doing the despoiling, and describes the resistance, the suffering, but also the cultural as well as personal losses involved for those who are despoiled. One of the ways in which her work on capitalist accumulation was criticized was that it spent too much time weeping over the losses of ways of life that Marxist orthodoxy knew to be backward and that needed to be swept away for an eventual socialist victory to be assured. At the same time as utilizing and relying on the story of history as that of the emergence of the universal class, Luxemburg also renders that story full of unredeemable pain, and always contingent. Here, we have to make the connection between Luxemburg as an international theorist and as a practicing revolutionary.

Luxemburg on Revolutionary Practice

Luxemburg's writings on revolutionary practice are explicit about the limits of "science" and the importance of practice and situation for knowledge. Her own views shifted in the light, in particular, of the experience of the 1905 Revolution, which in her eyes demonstrated that education in revolutionary action came through experience of that action. But even before that, in her critique of Bernstein, she was sharply critical of a "scientific" theory that set in stone the point at which the acquisition of political power by the proletariat could be appropriate. This undermined taken-for-granted positions in German social democracy at the time, which were committed to the view that only a proletariat schooled in capitalist oppression and organized to resist it over a long time would be capable of bringing about a socialist revolution, and to the view that the proletarian class needed to be led by the party. It also led to Luxemburg's disagreement with the Leninist policy of democratic centralism within Russian social democracy.

the idea of a 'premature' conquest of political power by the labouring classes appears to be a political absurdity, derived from a mechanical conception of social development and positing for the victory of the class struggle a *time* fixed *outside* and *independent* of the class struggle.[27]

---

[27] Luxemburg, "Social Reform or Revolution?," 159.

The mistakes that are made by a truly revolutionary workers' movement are, historically speaking, immeasurably more fruitful and more valuable than the infallibility of the best possible 'Central Committee'.[28]

After the 1905 Revolution, this theme in Luxemburg's work became the mark of her distinction from reformism and parliamentarianism, but also from Bolshevik vanguardism, pointing to a deep continuity between her response to Lenin's "What is to Be Done?," her experience of 1905, and her later response to the ways in which Lenin abolished the organs of democracy in the aftermath of the October Revolution in 1917.[29] Luxemburg's argument for the mass strike, and her ongoing celebration of the proletariat's capacity to learn from its own mistakes was more than part of a debate over tactics between her and Kautsky, or between her and Lenin. Rather, it was an argument for the production of knowledge through action, experience, and experiment, which necessarily required not only the most extensive democratization possible, but also that the party and the theoretician develop: "the most adroit adaptability to the given situation, and the closest possible contact with the mood of the masses."[30]

The more democratic the institutions, the livelier and stronger the pulse-beat of the political life of the masses, the more direct and complete is their influence.
The remedy which Trotsky and Lenin have found, the elimination of democracy as such, is worse than the disease it is supposed to cure.[31]

Luxemburg is most well known for her argument in relation to the mass strike, and has been vilified and celebrated as a proponent of "spontaneity" in revolutionary action. But, as many later commentators have pointed out, this is a caricature of her position, which was as clear in its critique of anarchism as of reformism and democratic centralism. Her focus was rather on how political action itself cultivated political consciousness, and on the idea that if the rule of the people was to have any meaning then it could not involve a small minority ruling on the people's behalf. This is a kind of democratic pedagogy, embracing a degree of prefigurative thinking, but also a strong sense that mistakes are both inevitable and identifiable in the revolutionary struggle, though it is only in retrospect that those mistakes can be understood and identified by

---

[28] Rosa Luxemburg, "Organizational Questions of Russian Social Democracy" [1904], in Hudis and Anderson (eds.), *The Rosa Luxemburg Reader*, 265.
[29] Rosa Luxemburg, "The Mass Strike, the Political Party, and the Trade Unions" [1906], in Hudis and Anderson (eds.), *The Rosa Luxemburg Reader*, 198.
[30] Luxemburg, "The Mass Strike," 198.
[31] Rosa Luxemburg, "The Russian Revolution" [1918], in Hudis and Anderson (eds.), *The Rosa Luxemburg Reader*, 302.

political actors themselves. Extending the freedom to make mistakes is the only way forward, since political action cannot be dictated and controlled in advance:[32]

> Freedom is always and exclusively freedom for the one who thinks differently. Not because of any fanatical concept of 'justice' but because all that is instructive, wholesome and purifying in political freedom depends on this essential characteristic, and its effectiveness vanishes when 'freedom' becomes a special privilege.[33]

Luxemburg herself was, of course, one who thought "differently." In her dismissal of the politics of national self-determination, in her opposition to the endorsement of the war by German social democracy, and in her outspoken criticisms of aspects of the Bolshevik Revolution, she became an increasingly marginalized figure within the context of revolutionary politics and polemics in which she spent all of her adult life. After her murder in 1919, her work was suppressed and vilified by a revolutionary movement now dominated by Soviet communism. And the debates between revisionist and revolutionary Marxism transformed into a social democratic accommodation of the capitalist state on the one hand, and the possibility of "socialism in one country" on the other. In both cases, from Luxemburg's point of view, supposedly progressive politics had fallen into the most profound error of parochialism, and strengthened the risk of collapse into barbarism in the wake of capitalist, imperialist war.

Luxemburg's position of identification with the universal class is essentially an identification with humanity as such, since the universal class ultimately liberates all. For her, this identification necessarily precluded embracing the tools of nationalism or of inter-state war, since these were political technologies that broke up the universal class and served only the interests of the bourgeoisie. The universal class was internationalist by definition. There is, however, a tension between Luxemburg's identification with the universal class, and the contextualism, contingency, and learning from experience that characterizes her accounts of revolutionary practice, and her critiques of vanguardism and scientism. When it comes to the universal class, her position, in common with that of the revisionists and revolutionaries with whom she was arguing, rests on a confidence that her location, at the heart of capitalist imperialism, was the cockpit of world history. Within her revolutionary imagination, as within the internationalist imagination of

---

[32] Luxemburg, "The Mass Strike," 198.
[33] Luxemburg, "The Russian Revolution," 305.

other socialists of her time, the universal class was not represented by figures of the people dying in the Kalahari, or by the peasants in the Russian hinterland, but by the industrial working class. Indigenous peoples and peasants were victims of capitalist oppression, potential beneficiaries of proletarian revolution, but not agents of revolution themselves. This position rested on an acceptance of Marx's theory of revolutionary agency and a diffusionist account of the development of capitalism from Europe outwards to the rest of the world. And it illustrates again the paradox of Luxemburg's thinking in general, which embraces the language of Marxist science and a Eurocentric narrative of historical inevitability throughout her writings, whilst at the same time developing a distinctive revolutionary discourse in the language of spontaneity, self-education, and unexpected turns of history when it comes to the times and places of emancipation.

Reflections on Luxemburg and International Thought

Luxemburg's *The Accumulation of Capital* attracted, and continues to attract, wholesale criticism, and some defenses, from her fellow Marxists.[34] A great deal of scholarship within Marxism, at the time and subsequently, has been devoted to showing how and why she was wrong about Marx's theory of capital accumulation and therefore the possibility for capitalism to flourish when there is no longer a non-capitalist milieu. From the point of view of non-Marxist political economy, her work is even more easily dismissed. Nevertheless, setting aside debates over technical positions underlying her analysis of capitalism, Luxemburg's argument, and its contention that capitalism is never wholly complete in and of itself, opened up a range of trajectories for international thought. In a recent article Luxemburg is praised for presaging later dependency and world systems theories; for her recognition of the importance of war and militarism as a capitalist technology for opening up new possibilities for capitalist accumulation; and for her insights into the recursive logic of imperialism.[35]

In terms of her substantive theoretical claims, two in particular stand out as of continuing central importance in IR and in contemporary international politics, and not only in Marxist or Neo-Marxist debates. The first is the relation between capitalism and non-capitalist milieu; the second is her claim regarding the right of national self-determination. Luxemburg put forward the idea that geopolitical hierarchy, inequality,

---

[34] Bellofiore (ed.), *Rosa Luxemburg.*   [35] Bieler et al., "Enduring Relevance."

and difference in economic and social form were integral to capitalism as a worldwide phenomenon, and had been since its inception. In this respect she presaged not only the arguments of dependency and world systems theory, or of uneven and combined development, but any work that argues that imperialism rather than the system of states is the key to past and present world order, a debate we have seen revived over the past two decades. In addition, she draws attention to the relation between capitalist and non-capitalist social forms within predominantly capitalist social forms, which we continue to see at national and transnational levels, in the organization of agricultural work, textile industries, and domestic and sexual services. For Luxemburg it would be no surprise that issues of slavery and various kinds of bonded labour remain part of international political economy.

In her work on nationalism, Luxemburg challenged liberal and socialist arguments about the progressive implications of the principle of national self-determination, and demonstrated both the tensions between principles of nationality and the idea of the modern state and its ideological fueling of imperialism and militarism. Her argument is deeply troubling to the liberal international norms that underpin much of the architecture of the contemporary world order, and to claims that the nation-state provides a setting within which democracy and peace will be able to flourish.[36] Although critics pointed out that Polish independence, which she had dismissed as a possibility, was actually achieved before her untimely death, the fate of nationalism in the last century has done more to support than to undermine Luxemburg's distrust. Her contemporaries fighting for national independence outside of Europe received short shrift in the "Wilsonian moment" for precisely the reasons she had outlined.[37] And where states have gained or retained national independence, the claimed elective affinity between capitalism and democracy has repeatedly been shown to be fragile and contingent.

But Luxemburg also offers resources for thinking beyond the broad terms of a Marxist theory of history. At the same time as her narrative of capital accumulation retains the position of the universal class as the agent of history, it also opens up the ongoing importance of the effects of non-capitalist social forms on capitalism. In treating capitalism as inherently a hybrid social form, it becomes possible to challenge dominant spatial and temporal assumptions, central to liberal and Marxist theory – even if Luxemburg does not do so consistently. For Luxemburg, capitalism happens as much in the peasant village, or in the production of

[36] Whitehall, *A Rival History.*   [37] Manela, *The Wilsonian Moment.*

conditions of famine in India, as it does in the factories of Manchester, an argument that can be used to disturb straightforward core–periphery thinking. The non-capitalist not only *is* but *has to be* simultaneous with the capitalist, an argument that can be used to disturb fixed notions of a world-historical past and future. In addition, as we have seen, Luxemburg is explicitly resistant both to determinist accounts of world history that subordinate political action to material structures, and to a reading of history in redemptive terms. In ways that prefigure Benjamin's cryptic theses on the philosophy of history, she refuses to see the wounds inflicted by capital accumulation as somehow justified by a future that is not, in any case, certain.[38] This is not to suggest that Luxemburg herself was not convinced that the future of socialism lay in the hands of the European working class, or that she avoided Eurocentrism in her understanding of world history. Rather, it suggests that Luxemburg is a thinker who provides resources for thinking against herself on this as on other issues.

In this respect, Luxemburg's work exemplifies two different approaches to critique. On the one hand, she uses the framework of Marxism and her identification with the universal class as a reference point from which to demonstrate the failures of the arguments and actions of others. On the other, she uses her experience and knowledge of events, contexts, and actions to do the same thing. Whereas the first critical pathway depends on the assumption of a correct understanding of the trajectory of history, the second depends on questioning the certainties of others from the standpoint of change, contingency, democracy, and the possibility of learning from failure. Within Luxemburg's own work again we find the resources for self-criticism, the latter mode of critique undermines the former and points to its dangers both for knowledge and for action. If Luxemburg's theoretical work on capitalism, imperialism, and nationalism points us toward historic and contemporary liberal internationalist, Marxist or Neo-Marxist arguments in IR, then her writings on revolutionary practice resonate much more strongly with poststructuralist and decolonial perspectives. Here we find themes of the critique of scientism, the uncontrollability of the implications of action, the production of knowledge from resistant practice, capitalism as a condition of hybridity and uncertainty, and the acknowledgment of failure as an integral aspect of acting toward universal emancipation.

Paradoxically in a project about women in international thought, I have paid little attention to whether Luxemburg's identification as a

---

[38] Walter Benjamin, "Theses on the Philosophy of History," in *Illuminations, ed. Hannah Arendt* (London: Pimlico, 1999).

woman made a difference to her thinking, and how her thought is or is not connected to the concerns of contemporary feminist IR. Both critics and admirers of Luxemburg have claimed that the fact she was a woman affected her work, and it is certainly the case that the reception of Luxemburg's thought has been highly gendered (see above). For other commentators, including Arendt, it seems that the most significant implication of Luxemburg's being a woman for her international thought, is that her sex amplified her outsider status as an exiled Polish Jew in German social democracy.[39] As is well known, Luxemburg, though she supported various campaigns in relation to women's rights, was suspicious of feminism as a separate political struggle. Along with her close friend, socialist feminist Clara Zetkin, Luxemburg saw the oppression of women as part of the broader capitalist oppression, and identified struggles for the franchise or for changes in women's legal status as essentially bourgeois distractions.

As a bourgeois woman, the female is a parasite on society; her function consists in sharing in the consumption of the fruits of exploitation. As a petty-bourgeois women, she is a workhorse for the family. As a modern female proletarian, the woman becomes a human being for the first time, *since the [proletarian] struggle is the first to prepare human beings to make a contribution to culture, to the history of humanity.*[40]

The above quotation, from a speech given by Luxemburg on International Women's Day in 1914 takes us back to Luxemburg's identification of herself with the universal class, and of the universal class with humanity as such. One way of perceiving her resistance to identification in terms of her sex is as part of her response to the dislocations of given identities that she experienced throughout her life. If her sex made a difference to Luxemburg's international thought on this account, then it did so insofar as being a woman reinforced all the other ways in which Luxemburg could not be at home in her own time and place. This not-at-homeness then helped to sustain her understanding of the revolutionary project as essentially one of world-making, in which specific identities would be transcended through the agency of the universal class.

No feminist peace movement, claim to abortion rights, reform of the family, or protest against male aggression taps the "Plutonian" depths of economic relations between militarism, war, capital, international monetary systems and working lives that Luxemburg examined.[41]

---

[39] Arendt, "A Heroine of Revolution."

[40] Rosa Luxemburg, "The Proletarian Woman" [1914], in Hudis and Anderson (eds.), *The Rosa Luxemburg Reader*, 243.

[41] Andrea Nye, *Philosophia: The Thought of Rosa Luxemburg, Simone Weil, and Hannah Arendt* (New York: Routledge, 1994), 43.

The above brief survey of arguments about the significance of being a woman for Luxemburg suggests that her work is open to multiple interpretations from a feminist point of view and may also, as suggested in the quotation from Nye, be used as a stick with which to beat other strands of feminism. Substantively, her approach puts her closest to Marxist feminism and international political economy, in which the focus is on how women's labor is exploited under capitalism, and in which it is assumed that gender oppression is parasitic on class oppression. In this respect she prefigures a great deal of work in feminist IR that has demonstrated the centrality of gendered relations of power to the sustaining of capitalism, imperialism, and war. Although she does not make this step herself, it could also be argued that her account of capital accumulation as dependent on its capacity to tap into the resources generated through other social forms, also fits well with arguments in socialist and radical feminism about the dependence of "productive" labor in the traditional Marxist sense on unpaid reproductive labor.

However, there are also aspects of Luxemburg's analysis that would associate her more closely with an anti-militarist ethic of care, or with feminist standpoint accounts of the production of knowledge. For example, it has been argued that Luxemburg's empathetic approach to her research on the accumulation of capital reflected her gendered identity and positionality. This worked to strengthen her analysis and evaluation of capitalism, since it gave much more adequate weight to the violence and suffering involved in this process than more impersonal accounts, and made it more difficult to see such violence and suffering as essentially justifiable collateral damage on the route to a better future. On this account, the complaint made by her critics of Luxemburg's irrationalist weeping and wailing over the fate of colonized and indigenous peoples, should be revalorized as an example of how identification with femininity provided Luxemburg with constructive resources for thought. Ultimately, as with her relationship to Marxism, Luxemburg's work does not fit neatly into any feminist category, but it makes an interesting and fruitful interlocutor for a range of contemporary feminist perspectives within IR.

Conclusion

Looking at Luxemburg's work and life from the standpoint of the present, it is tempting to reduce her contribution to one of two dimensions: The dimension of the Marxist theoretician able to explain and predict the unfolding course of capitalism and world history, reliant on the science of historical materialism, right or wrong in her debates over capitalism, nationalism, and imperialism. Or, alternatively, the dimension of the proponent of the mass strike, the fundamentally democratic thinker for whom genuine revolution was in the hands of the oppressed as opposed to the party, and for whom the end of revolution remained an open question. In both dimensions, there are plenty of resonances of contemporary concerns within critical IR scholarship. However, as thinkers as diverse as Norman Geras and Gillian Rose have argued, to attempt to reduce Luxemburg to one of the sides of her internationalism would be misleading.[42] Her Marx may be the Marx of the *18th Brumaire* rather than of the *Communist Manifesto*[43] but it was only her confidence in Marx's analysis that made it possible for her to argue that revolution was about risk and failure. For Rose, we should instead read Luxemburg as exploring the difficulties haunting the ideal of revolutionary action in modernity, risking in full awareness of that risk the opening up of revolutionary action to all:

> What is implicitly recommended here is a more thorough-going anxiety which would not fix any path in advance of the daily struggle, but would cultivate a plasticity that is able to educate and assimilate 'the afflux of non-proletarian recruits to the party of the proletariat'. This deeper submission to uncertainty leads to a more inclusive activity – to cultivation of plasticity rather than culture of terror.[44]

For any contemporary reader of Luxemburg there will be many aspects of her arguments that illuminate familiar theoretical and political questions in IR. However, examining her work is not only useful from the point of view of its theoretical and meta-theoretical contribution to international thought. It is also useful for illuminating the characteristics of "progressive," internationalist thought in an era in which many of the key categories for theorizing international politics were being formed. As many readers of Luxemburg have noted, it is impossible to grasp her thought without situating it in her revolutionary activism and the perspective she derived from the combination of her Marxist theory and her activism. This was a situation of polemical engagement between different wings of revisionist and revolutionary progressive politics. But it is notable that even while revisionists and revolutionaries tore the arguments of each other to pieces, there were certain shared assumptions that were taken for granted about how contemporary international politics and its future should be understood. Specifically, all of Luxemburg's

---

[42] Norman Geras, *The Legacy of Rosa Luxemburg* (London: New Left Books, 1976); Gillian Rose, *The Broken Middle: Out of Our Ancient Society* (Oxford: Blackwell, 1992).

[43] Loralea Michaelis, "Rosa Luxemburg on Disappointment and the Politics of Commitment," *European Journal of Political Theory* 10.2 (2011): 202–24.

[44] Rose, "The Broken Middle," 207.

interlocutors took for granted that the driver of historical change, whether via national liberation or proletarian revolution, was located in the modern imperial states of industrialized Europe, and that the meaning inherent in progressive political struggles in industrialized Europe was of universal consequence. This opens up questions of location, identity, and perspective, and of how connections between nationalism and internationalism, imperialism and universalism are forged through theorists' own positionality.

These are not questions that admit of a straightforward answer, but Luxemburg's work is a particularly fruitful place from which to explore them. For the Austro-Marxists and Lenin, nationalism and internationalism were connected through the trajectory of history, in which national self-determination was a stage on the way toward a socialist future. Luxemburg refuted this historical complacency; she knew from direct experience that nationalism was an exclusionary and divisive force, whether in the form of a romantic throwback, anti-Semitism, or a tool for the bourgeois class to gain power. Instead, she committed herself to an identification with the universal class, which was constructed through imperialism. This view was deeply informed by her direct experience of the development of capitalism in Poland. This is not an attempt to reduce theoretical arguments to the effects of personal experience. Rather, it is to argue that it would be much more difficult to have forged the links between nationalism and internationalism or between imperialism and universalism for revolutionaries situated in a different place than that of Central Europe at the turn of the nineteenth and twentieth centuries. And however implausible those links may now look, they have cast a very long shadow on liberal and critical traditions of international theory over the past century.

However, although I have suggested that Luxemburg's location and identity shaped her internationalist perspective, and the tendency of both her and her interlocutors to read the time of industrialized Europe in world-historical terms, Luxemburg's thought does as much to open up as to close down the reading of world history. In contrast to her interlocutors, she developed tools for thinking that disturbed as much as they confirmed the project of the universal class. We see this in the historical detail and the empathy with which she exposes the meaning of capitalism as imperialism, and the impossibility of justifying or redeeming the violence and suffering imposed by the accumulation of capital. We see it also in her recognition of the incompleteness and hybridity of capitalism. Above all, we see it in her understanding that circumstances change, that history is not predictable, and that knowledge does not prescribe the direction of history but rather emerges out of practical engagement, experimentation, and the experience of failure.

3   Of Colonialism and Corpses: Simone Weil on Force

Helen M. Kinsella

In his acceptance speech for the 1957 Nobel prize in literature, Albert Camus, who was one of Simone Weil's first translators and her literary executor, described the "insane history" of a "time of catastrophe" marked by the World Wars. This catastrophic time, which Simone Weil (1909–43) described in 1939 as colored by a common and "predominant feeling of ... some danger," shaped all of Weil's writings as she sought to both address and respond to its definitive events.[1] Her writings, published at the time in primarily leftist and labor journals, were directed at specific communities in which she moved or had some intellectual affinity. She participated in syndicalist labor movements, joined an anarchist militia in the Spanish Civil War, became a member of the Free French in World War II, and drafted what became *The Need for Roots* which was intended as a blueprint for the reconstruction of France at the close of the war. The piece for which she is possibly best known, *The Iliad or the Poem of Force*, was published in 1940 as the Germans marched into Paris and began their occupation of France. Mary Dietz calls it a "lament upon the awful and immediate reality of war in her own time."[2]

Weil's analysis of war, power, and force did not begin in 1940. Indeed, she claimed that she had been preoccupied by war since 1914 when as a small child she donated to the relief efforts for soldiers at the front.[3] But, it was in the early 1930s that she began first to explore the use of force in her writings on colonialism. Like all of Weil's positions, her take was a "composition on a multiple plane."[4] She recounts that her consideration of colonialism began with the strange juxtaposition of reading reports on the French massacres in Indochina and, at the same time, witnessing the preparations for and subsequent holding of the 1931 Colonial Exhibition

[1] Simone Weil, *Selected Essays* (1962; repr., Oxford University Press, 2015), 178.
[2] Mary G. Dietz, *Between the Human and the Divine* (Totowa, NJ: Rowman & Littlefield, 1988), 86.
[3] Simone Weil, *Seventy Letters*, ed. Richard Rees (1965; repr., Oxford University Press, 2015), 171.
[4] Simone Weil, *The Need for Roots* (1952; repr., London: Routledge, 2002), 214.

in Paris. Weil wrote that it was at the Exhibition, the last which "feted the accomplishments of colonialism" where for the first time she "felt and understood the tragedy of colonization."[5]

In the scholarship on Simone Weil, her emphasis on colonialism is not fully integrated into analyses of the use of force and rights nor, more generally, as another source of her reflections on the concepts which adumbrate her work.[6] Processes which she identified as constitutive of colonialism's brutality – uprooting, loss of the past, degradation of labor, and the pursuit of unlimited profit and power – inform her thought. As Dietz points out, the hallmarks of Weil's concerns are "the meaning of individual freedom in the modern collectivity, the nature of community in the nation state, and the political and social possibilities for an end to the affliction and oppression of the human condition," each of which directly implicates colonialism and empire.[7] In this chapter, I propose to explore the relationship of colonization to her concept of power and her exposition of rights – to draw out the ways in which her argument that force turns "man into a thing" is born out of her earlier analysis of how in colonial wars "we first of all reduce whole populations to slavery, and then we use them as cannon fodder."[8]

I argue that this accomplishes three things. First, Weil provides an analysis of modernity and the rise of totalitarianism that specifically centers colonialism as fundamental to each and, consequently, to any analysis of international politics. Second, she develops her theories through her own political engagement and activism in the context of her time, negotiating and unsettling the governing intellectual, social, and political expectations – as articulated through gender, certainly, but also no less so through the complex intersections of class and religion. Accordingly, her politics and her scholarship continue to challenge a disciplinary post-1945 positioning of colonialism as peripheral to the development of international thought, and further confirm the significance of "historical women" in the field.[9] Third, Weil's own reckoning

---

[5] Patricia A. Morton, "National and Colonial: The Musée des Colonies at the Colonial Exposition, Paris, 1931," *Art Bulletin* 80.2 (1998): 357–77 (357); Simone Weil, *Simone Weil on Colonialism: An Ethic of the Other*, ed. J. P. Little (Lanham, MD: Rowman & Littlefield, 2003), 47.

[6] Thomas Nevin, *Simone Weil: Portrait of a Self-Exiled Jew* (Chapel Hill: University of North Carolina Press, 1991), 321.

[7] Dietz, *Between the Human and the Divine*, 31.

[8] Simone Weil, *Letter to a Priest* (New York: Routledge, 2014), 3; Weil, *On Colonialism*, 49.

[9] Lucian M. Ashworth, "Feminism, War, and the Prospects for Peace: Helena Stanwick (1864–1939) and the Lost Feminists of Interwar International Relations," *International Feminist Journal of Politics* 13.1 (2011): 25–43; Patricia Owens, "Women and the History of International Thought," *International Studies Quarterly* 62.3 (2018): 467–81; Robert

with the tumultuous politics of her time can animate contemporary analyses of power as understood and enacted in complex and critical ways.

Before directly taking up the role of colonialism in Weil's writings, I want to note that Weil's work suffers from general neglect in political thought. It remains so "despite thought provoking, masterful, even extraordinary work."[10] This neglect continues even though her work has been subject to engagement and criticism by other notable theorists, such as Iris Murdoch, Emmanuel Levinas (who reserves especial scorn for her critique of Judaism), Giorgio Agamben (who wrote his dissertation on her thought), and Roberto Esposito (who calls her "one of the most radical thinkers of the 20th century").[11] Although only de Beauvoir knew her personally, Hannah Arendt admired her shrewd analyses of labor, and both were impressed with the acuity of her thought. Indeed, all three women proudly identified as political thinkers offering sophisticated reckonings of and in "dark times."

There are surely reasons we can marshal to explain why Weil remains a "pariah" or a "lonely figure" for certain forms of political thought: the putative peculiarity of her personality combined with her stringent asceticism has overwhelmed attention to her thought, the explicit foregrounding in her later writings of her conversion from an agnostic Jew to Christian, the incomplete and idiosyncratic nature of her work, and the way in which her work was first circulated. And, yet, none of these are satisfactory. Indeed, the question of why Weil remains a "lonely figure" should itself motivate attention to Weil worthy of the complexity and contradictions which her work and life exemplified.

"I am tired of talking to you about myself, for it is a wretched subject"

Weil was adamant that her life embodied a "strict adherence to understanding and practicing her philosophy of being," which occasioned a way of being "excruciatingly identical with her ideas."[12] A prime example

---

Vitalis, *White World Order, Black Power Politics: The Birth of American International Relations* (Ithaca, NY: Cornell University Press, 2015).

[10] Dietz, *Between the Human and the Divine*, xiii.

[11] Roberto Esposito, *The Origin of the Political* (New York: Fordham University Press, 2017), xi. I am not arguing that because three prominent men are interested in her work, so too should we be. I am arguing that her influence on each of them is elided, ignored, and, at the worst, her thought subsumed as theirs.

[12] Susan Sontag, "Simone Weil," *New York Review of Books*, February 1963. The quotation above which opens this section comes from Simone Weil, *Waiting for God* (1951; repr., New York: Perennial Library, 2009), 4.

is her refusal to eat more than those whom she identified as the worst off, to the point of facilitating her own death, as is her theorization of affliction rooted in her own experiences of acute pain and suffering. The very notion of an ascetic with a conversion experience, much less one who straightforwardly accepts that "Christ came down and took possession of me," banishes her from certain definitions of political thought, while her brazen admission that she was really an "anti-Semite" during the rise of Nazism trouble convention and comprehension.[13] Weil's vitriol toward Judaism is well documented and distinctly disconcerting as she brooked no moderation in light of the growing persecution of Jews and, in fact, did not cease when forced to flee France with her family. Notably, she was equally damning of some of the protocol and history of Christianity at the same time, claiming that the "Thomist conception of faith implies a 'totalitarianism' as stifling as that of Hitler, if not more so."[14] Weil's criticism of both was rooted in her revulsion toward dogma and the blind celebration of collective belief, as well as any notion of a "chosen" people or rule by divine right. Nevertheless, her critique was vitiated by her startling disregard of historical context as her damnation of Christianity neither incited nor legitimated similarly horrific repercussions.

As a result, Simone Weil inspired equal parts awe and vitriol. Even one of her most ardent admirers and translators, the Polish poet Czesław Miłosz , wrote that she lived a life of "deliberate foolishness."[15] Others, such as T. S. Elliot, equally fascinated with her austerity and self-mortification in pursuit of God, believed her to be a Christian mystic – no less than a "new kind of saint."[16] In contrast, her strongest critics wrote that, at the very least, she was advocating a dangerously anti-political "rule by saints."[17] "[H]er ideas … so clearly without substance, mere vaporous and platitudinous musings," are made all the more "pernicious because, couched in an archetypal (or stereotypical) religious vocabulary, they cannot fail to exert a powerful appeal."[18] A "Holy Fool" she may well have been for some but "she deserves better of us than to be

[13] Weil, *Waiting for God*, 24; Simone Petrement, *Simone Weil: A Life* (New York: Schocken Books, 1988), 392.
[14] Weil, *Letter to a Priest*, 23.
[15] Czesław Miłosz, *To Begin Where I Am: Selected Essays* (New York: Farrar, Straus & Giroux, 2001), 51.
[16] Simone Weil, *Gravity and Grace* (1952; repr., London: Routledge, 2002), viii.
[17] Connor Cruise O'Brien, "The Anti-Politics of Simone Weil," *New York Review of Books*, May 12, 1977.
[18] Joyce C. Oates, *The Profane Art* (New York: Dutton, 1983).

made into a Patron Saint of symposiums on literature and religion in the little magazine."[19] More critically, her work demands it.[20]

First, Weil herself refused to think or write in these sorts of dualisms. Even as the sheer power of her personality is unmistakable throughout her writings, and her own experiences ground her thought, it was her desire to abstract and impersonalize the body and the person, not to foreground them. It is no small irony that the Christian mystic preferred androgyny, answered to Simon, and repudiated her identity as a Jew all in an effort to impersonalize, deracinate and de-emphasize the body and the self. It is our *impersonal* characteristics held in common which were to be the source of our obligation and alliances, not those which were distinct to individuals.

Second, the characterization of Weil as either a spiritual or a political thinker ignores her own claim that her thought was "indivisible."[21] Such a characterization institutes an opposition not only into her writings, but also into the very concepts – political and spiritual – which Weil saw as fundamentally and necessarily integrated in any effort to think through "the dilemma of worldliness."[22] Weil was excruciatingly careful to underline the liminality of words and was exacting in her critique of how "words adorned with capital letters" miscue and misrepresent the complexity of the world.[23] She held that "by the power of words we always mean their power of illusion and error," thus we must guard against their ability to "stupefy the mind."[24] The wariness with which Weil approached "words adorned with capital letters" influenced her analysis of the success of totalitarianism. As did Arendt, Weil identified how the spread of propaganda and reliance on slogans induced a "terrible fatality" through the promulgation of "the big lie": itself an abstraction made possible by the stupefied mind and the "sullen complicity" of the majority.[25] Weil was adamant. Words cannot function as abstraction, they must lose their adornments so that we may attend to what they reveal, not conceal.[26] Accordingly, what Weil offers is a different valuation of the relation of the political and the spiritual, forcing a reworking of each such that neither is seen as the other's "complementary antagonist."[27]

---

[19] Isaac Rosenfield, "Simone Weil as Saint," *Partisan Review* 18.6 (1951): 712–15 (713).

[20] Helen M. Kinsella, "Simone Weil: An Introduction," in Felix Rösch (ed.), *Émigré Scholars and the Genesis of American International Relations: A European Discipline in America?* (Basingstoke: Palgrave Macmillan, 2014), 176–94.

[21] Weil, *Seventy Letters*, 196.   [22] Dietz, *Between the Human and the Divine*, 79.

[23] Weil, *Selected Essays*, 156.   [24] Weil, *Selected Essays*, 33, 170.

[25] Weil, *Selected Essays*, 102; Nevin, *Portrait of a Self-Exiled Jew*, 377.

[26] Weil, *Selected Essays*, 237.   [27] Weil, *Selected Essays*, 156.

Relatedly, it is important to remember that Weil died at the age of thirty-four with, comparatively speaking, very little of her writings published. Her early death resulted in a disorderly distribution of her writing, beyond those found in the labor/leftist journals of her time. Two of her most systematic works, *Oppression and Liberty* and *The Need for Roots*, were not published till after her death, respectively, 1955 and 1949 in France, and 1958 and 1952 in the United States, some twenty years after she wrote them. She was not able to account for the true extent of Nazi atrocities and the fall of imperialism, which would have surely affected her initial thinking on the perils of totalitarianism, the inequities of power and force, and the legacy of colonialism and its effect upon political thought and action. Her first longer translated works were guided by her family, a Dominican priest, and a Christian philosopher. Consequently, her writing was introduced into wider circulation as if it were naturally divided into two set categories and two set time frames; namely, spiritual (e.g., *Gravity and Grace*) or political (e.g., *The Need for Roots*) and before and after conversion. Her death prevented her from challenging such distinctions, much less completing any unfinished pieces. This left most of her work to be distributed "piecemeal" in form and substance, a consequence she had feared.[28]

Thus, third, when reading Weil we do well to remember that we are reading nascent and evolving articulations of her thought which is itself, as many have noted, disorienting in its singularity and its form. Maurice Blanchot captured it as "thought often strangely surprised."[29] Nonetheless, it made an impact. Mary McCarthy recalls that her translation of Weil's *The Iliad or the Poem of Force* ended her thinking in opposites.[30] Weil herself describes her thought as proceeding through contradictions. "Contradiction and analogy" compose the world and our understandings of it as is made most evident in "the knots of necessity and impossibility" which make up our existence.[31] Thus, while "everything" may be related, it is not that "everything" is coherent, symmetrical, or unified. Rather, "contradiction alone is the proof that we are not everything."[32] She thought to the edges of aporia – that is, "neither this nor that" but "both this and that" – while never ceasing to

[28] Weil, *Seventy Letters*, 196.

[29] Maurice Blanchot, *Infinite Conversation* (1969, repr., Minneapolis: University of Minnesota Press, 1993), 106.

[30] Deborah Nelson, *Tough Enough: Arbus, Arendt, Didion, McCarthy* (University of Chicago Press, 2017), 15.

[31] Simone Weil, *First and Last Notebooks* (1970; repr., Oxford University Press, 2015), 45–46.

[32] Weil, *Gravity and Grace*, 95.

answer what she identified as her abiding question: what are the causes of social oppression? Iris Murdoch, who was deeply influenced by Weil, held that consideration of Weil both required and effected the breakdown of "political categories."[33] Weil too was clear – her thought, and she herself, did not fit.

"To consent to being anonymous, to being human material (Eucharist); to renounce prestige, public esteem – that is to bear witness to the truth, namely, that one is composed of human material, that one has no rights. It is to cast aside all ornament, to put up with one's nakedness. But how is this compatible with social life and its labels?"[34]

Her own self-fashioning and her scholarly capaciousness are, as these highly charged assessments suggest, deeply unsettling. Weil's rejections and reworkings of the certainties of binary oppositions (e.g., Simon or Simone) and taken for granted categorizations (e.g., Jewish or Christian) illuminate her own recognition of her lack of "fit," while equally reflecting her deeply held philosophical conviction that the imposition of and reliance on preconstituted categories did more to conceal than to reveal a world produced and held in common. Her method takes the form of ceaseless questioning of received wisdom or conventions of thought – holding both "all this might not be true" and "all this might be true" simultaneously. This mitigates the desire for absolutes in either regard for they risk blind belief or an arrogant self-deception. Thus, to read Weil is to take seriously her own notation that to "receive" her work "calls for an effort," one which "consists of suspending *our* thought, leaving it detached, empty, and ready," and a willingness, "on pain of sinking into confusion or apathy ... [to] ... call everything into question again."[35]

In what follows, I seek to render Weil's arguments in their full complexity, without erasing their contradictions or shaping them into a more palatable or conventional form – as much as we might wish for such a concordance. Weil's brief against colonialism and the harms it demands amplifies in sharp terms both the destruction it wreaks and, potentially, the limits of politics. For insofar as she is able to argue politically for a progressive emancipation for those colonies, she ultimately grounded her argument in a source of obligation which is external and transcendent to politics itself.

---

[33] Iris Murdoch and Peter Conradi, *Existentialists and Mystics: Writings on Philosophy and Literature* (New York: Allen Lane, 1998), 159.

[34] Weil, *First and Last Notebooks*, 217.

[35] Weil, *Seventy Letters*, 196; Simone Weil, *Oppression and Liberty* (1958; repr., Amherst: University of Massachusetts Press, 1973), 36.

"The civilization we are so proud of has done everything it could to conceal the fact. ... we cannot be guiltless of a single one of Hitler's crimes"

In her last piece of writing, *The Need for Roots*, Weil identified France's 1871 defeat in the Franco-Prussian war as the moment France renounced its aspiration to more than bellicosity and "conquering."[36] Instead, France began "thinking only of carving out for herself black or yellow human flesh and gaining the hegemony of Europe."[37] Weil refers to this as a self-inflicted "moral injury" the effects of which, she argues, are clearly seen in France's concession to Hitler in 1940. Abandoning its revolutionary claim to "liberty, equality, fraternity," and further soiling the very meaning of such concepts in its turn toward conquest, France had corrupted its own soul, relinquished its own unique vocation and, thus, the one true source of strength from which to challenge Hitler.[38] The result as she acerbically noted, is that "a number of Frenchmen, having found it perfectly natural to talk about collaboration of the oppressed natives of the French colonies, went on making use of this word without any trouble in talking with their German masters."[39] Weil consistently called out the brazen hypocrisy of France's imperialism, asking "how many men have we deprived of a fatherland whom we now compel to die in order to preserve ours."[40] She also saw France's occupation as an example of the wisdom of karma.

Karma is significant here not as we commonly understand its use today, but as an "idea ... which is identical to the notion, sadly forgotten by us, of the Greek idea of nemesis, meaning the automatic punishment of *excess*."[41] Karma underlines and exposes the hubris inherent in believing that the search for power and the use of force can escape limits; that one is unlimited in all things. German occupation of France is karma in the simplest sense since Germany now applies "colonial methods of conquest and domination to the European continent."[42] It is also karma in a more complex sense. France's dedication to its imperial power in an unceasing search for more – more land, more resources, more rule, more influence – deforms power and force to an end unto itself. According to

---

[36] Weil, *The Need for Roots*, 195. The quotation above which opens this section comes from *The Need for Roots*, 282.

[37] Weil, *The Need for Roots*, 195.

[38] We see this charge in practice when, a decade or so later, publicizing France's violation of its own claim to represent liberty, equality, and fraternity became a major element in the strategies of Algeria's national liberation movement.

[39] Weil, *The Need for Roots*, 270.   [40] Weil, *On Colonialism*, 78.

[41] Weil, *On Colonialism*, 78.   [42] Weil, *Selected Essays*, 199.

Weil, power, like force, is properly understood as a "means of action" toward a desired end. Inherently unstable, comparative, and self-destructive, power itself can never be wholly obtained and, therefore, there is "never power, but only a race for power."[43] In the pursuit of empire and in its aftermath, France became the "plaything of the instruments of domination" it helped to manufacture, since those who "give themselves up to it ... must sacrifice" not only others, but also their own.[44] When power becomes an end unto itself in the hopeless attempt to make it absolute, the exaltation of war and of conquest and the justification of each becomes the leitmotif of politics. Yet, as Weil observes, it remains that within that system the "seed of death" is planted in the "necessarily limited character of the material bases of power and the necessarily unlimited character of the race for power."[45] She thought that eventually the finite material basis for power would cause the "series of massacres" to end, but until then, absent the dissolution of all states among other profound changes, it is ceaseless.[46]

Throughout her writing on colonialism, Weil details (as did Luxemburg and Arendt) how it is abetted by a fundamental belief that there is no limit to exploitation or consumption, human and material, in the pursuit of power. The materialist expansionism of colonialism *requires* an unmitigated use of force and the degradation of people into "living corpses" or "featureless human matter."[47] What ensures the initial success of colonization, on the one hand, is the ruthlessness of its practices, which include the literal and figurative uprooting of an entire people and the exploitation of both the land and the people as mere resources for imperial expansion and, on the other, the "lies" of Christianity and the propaganda of reactionary and quotidian ideas about inherent superiority. "Missionary zeal has not Christianized Africa, Asia, and Oceania, but has brought these territories under the cruel, cold, destructive domination of the white race, which has trodden down everything."[48] To tred down everything in pursuit of what she later calls "ersatz greatness," requires a particular synchronization of force and ideology – as exemplified by National Socialism but whose origins lie in imperialism.[49]

What stands out in Weil's writing is the culpability of the white race writ large for the extermination and enslavement of other races. She was clear. It is the "white man who has carried the disease," and has

---

[43] Weil, *Oppression and Liberty*, 67.   [44] Weil, *Oppression and Liberty*, 69.
[45] Weil, *Oppression and Liberty*, 75–76.
[46] Weil, *Selected Essays*, 140; Weil, *Oppression and Liberty*, 116–20.
[47] Weil, *Selected Essays*, 201.
[48] Weil, *Letter to a Priest*, 17; see also Weil, *The Need for Roots*, 287.
[49] Weil, *The Need for Roots*, 217, 97.

"everywhere destroyed."[50] Further, what is striking, especially for the time, is that she made no attempt to argue that colonization was in any case undertaken for the true benefit or protection of the colonized. To her that was an outright falsehood. If by chance any progress occurred, "it is not because of this frenzy" of colonization, but "in spite of it."[51] Moreover, the metrics of any such progress were arguably suspect as inevitably the destruction of culture leads to the destruction of a people and vice versa, so for whom is progress made? Damningly, she posited that if there were to be any consistency at all in this line of reasoning, then it would have to follow that "if Germany, thanks to Hitler and his successors, were to enslave the European nations and destroy most of the treasures of their past, future historians would certainly pronounce that she had civilized Europe."[52] Similarly, in her letter to the Minister of Propaganda in 1939, Weil calls him out for his claim made in a radio address that the colonies were committed to France by "ties other than those of subordination and exploitation."[53] Weil argued that there were no bonds of kinship or affection, and it was implausible to suggest otherwise for "we have murdered their culture," and tortured them for fighting for their freedom when, in fact, freedom which "lives in the soul of all men" is exactly what should be defended.[54] That France cannot identify its affinity with the colonial struggle for independence, but instead suppresses it precisely when fighting against Hitler is evidence of the corrosive and self-destructive effects of the race for empire. Although the blame lies with the white man and the white race, the effects extend beyond the colonized, reverberating upon all, and deforming the commitment to liberty. Colonization turns all individuals into a certain form of "inanimate chattel" in service to power.

Interestingly, both she and Arendt (who, like Weil, also used a distinctly non-Western concept, boomerang, to question the effects of colonialism and its redounding upon the metropole) refer to T. E. Lawrence's writings, his published letters and *Seven Pillars of Wisdom* to consider these claims. Both viewed them as tragic expositions of his actions and as attempts to disavow celebrations of his heroism. Each found evidence of the deformations of self which imperialism exacts. In his desolatory struggle to reconcile his exploits, "having used men as material ... to be grinded to his own ends" while simultaneously reckoning with his own role as "but a function," Lawrence exemplifies

---

[50] Weil, *The Need for Roots*, 50–51.   [51] Weil, *The Need for Roots*, 51.
[52] Weil, *Selected Essays*, 124.   [53] Weil, *On Colonialism*, 78.
[54] Weil, *On Colonialism*, 78.

the corruption of ends into means.[55] Thus, for Weil, he is the epitome of the "authentic hero" for he "knows the whole extent of the empire of might and at the same time despises it."[56] Moreover, he expresses how the particular practices of colonization threaten to ruin one of the ways in which power and force can be challenged; namely, through a rootedness (spiritual and material) in one's world.

One of the concepts that takes shape throughout Weil's writings is that of uprootedness which is the annihilation of forms of rootedness in one's world necessary for existence and resistance. Uprooting encompasses the extermination of people, encampment and forced removal, and the displacement from the land, all of which wreak utter desolation. The desolation derives from physical suffering and material loss, as well as what Weil identifies as loss of the past. Loss of the past has two effects which undermine the capacity for resistance and righting the world. First, uprooting violates a grasp of temporal limitations through its obliteration of the past which, in part, helps to buttress the belief in infinite future expansion necessary to maintain empire. As knowledge of the past helps to remind us, death is a limit beyond which one cannot go – an obstacle to the unceasing pursuit of more. Second, the past provides a reckoning of and rooting in a sense of continuation that is fundamental to the capacity to imagine oneself as both part of a collectivity and as possessing a future: "A human being has roots by virtue of his real, active, and natural life participation in the life of the community, which preserves in living shape certain particular treasures of the past and certain particular expectations for the future."[57] Destroying the past, uprooting, destroys the potential for recognition of oneself in a community which possesses a future and, thus, erases potential resources with which to confront colonialism. Colonialism and conquest bring "social death" which, as we shall see, is almost, but not quite, worse than death itself.[58]

Weil's views on colonialism evolved as she detailed her understanding of its effects on the colonies and France, but her first introduction to the hypocrisies and atrocities of the French colonial regime came in 1931 at the Colonial Exhibition in Paris. Nicknamed Lyauteville after one of the main organizers and its Commission General – the French counterinsurgent strategist, decorated hero of the war in Indochina, Proconsul of

---

[55] Weil quoted in: Louis Allen, "French Intellectuals and T. E. Lawrence," *The Durham University Journal* 60 (1976): 52–66; Hannah Arendt, *Origins of Totalitarianism* (New York; Harcourt, Brace, & Company, 1979), 221.

[56] Weil, *Seventy Letters*, 93.   [57] Weil, *The Need for Roots*, 43.

[58] Weil, *The Need for Roots*, 80.

Morocco, administrator in Madagascar Marshal Hubert Lyautey – it was everything such a nickname insinuates. She referred to this formative experience in her later writings and, specifically, Lyautey's letters from the French colony of Madagscar as unwittingly making explicit the analogies between "hitlerism and colonization."[59]

An unabashed celebration of French imperialism, the Exhibition was described by a contemporary report as a testament to "French genius and its manifestations across the World."[60] More accurately, colonies were vital economic, labor, and military resources for France both during World War I and, significantly, during the Great Depression. During World War I, some 100,000 colonial soldiers died while over 200,000 were drafted to work in France's factories to support the war effort. The colonies functioned as an imperial "fall back" supplying material, economic, military, and labor goods. Recognizing this, Lyautey organized the Exhibition to advertise the putative beneficence with which France had "civilized" its colonies, and to thus generate a greater sense of national pride in its colonial strategies and in its colonial possessions. The overall political goal, of which the Exhibition was just one part, was the acceptance and adoption of a notion of a fully unified French empire – with the express purpose to ensure continued investment in keeping the colonies as such. The Exhibition was also an effort to resituate colonial policy more broadly in response to what "the former Minister of Colonies Albert Sarraut called a 'moral crisis, crisis of domination, crisis of authority' of colonization, referring especially to the rise of nationalist movements."[61] Unsurprisingly, nowhere to be seen in the official exhibit was the violence, exploitation, or atrocities of colonization policies and practices. Instead, in the words of one glowing review at the time, it was a paean to "all the white men ... (who have shed) ... blood in jungles and on snow fields ... to conquer those outlandish beasts, and 15,000 assorted yellow, brown, and black barbarians."[62]

Although it is unknown whether Weil visited the Counter Exhibition mounted in protest or participated in the critiques launched by the "surrealists, socialists and communists," and expatriate "African, Maghrebian and Indochinese activists," she was shaken and shamed by her experience at the Exhibition.[63] Chastising those who were "mindlessly indifferent to the suffering caused by the regime thus symbolized," she

---

[59] Weil, *Selected Essays*, 202.   [60] Quoted in Morton, "National and Colonial," 357.
[61] Quoted in Benoît de L'estoile, "From the Colonial Exhibition to the Museum of Man," *Social Anthropology* 11.3 (2003): 341–61 (345).
[62] "Paris 1931: Colonies on Show," *Fortune* 3.5 (May 1931): 140.
[63] Weil, *On Colonialism*, 9.

questioned how they could ignore the hypocrisy of a regime which proudly claimed its civility and magnanimity while murdering and starving those over whom it ruled. Most specifically, she had in mind the 1930 Yen-Bay massacre in Indochina. Although only six French soldiers were killed when Communist-aligned Vietnamese troops in the French military mutinied, the manner of their death, by traditional swords, and what it demonstrated about French control of their troops, incited a severe response on the part of the French colonial administration. Two commissions sentenced fifty men to death and forty-six to hard labor, the latter of which a French minister in a public parliamentary hearing "characterized as a death sentence merely delayed." These sentences were delivered under a special commission's "exceptional jurisdiction ... circumventing native tribunals, civil courts, or any local appeals process," and were followed by generalized repression and unmitigated violence against the population.[64] For Weil, the violence, the scale of retribution, the denial of recognition of the suffering of the people, and of their right to rebel, was unsupportable. As she wrote repeatedly, France had no right of conquest. Equally, what troubled Weil was that to bring the French colonies into view in France – to "remind France" that the colonies existed and exacted an atrocious toll – it took blood "hitting the headlines" and even then it was not always assured.[65]

"Why am I being hurt?"

In 1934, seeing only the twin choices of dictatorship and a naïve socialist-communism, both of which she found suspect and oriented equally toward war, the latter "believing it to be for the sake of liberty, the proletariat etc.," she wrote to a student that "it was her firm decision to take no further part in any political or social activities, with two exceptions; anti-colonialism and the campaign against passive defence exercises."[66] Her concern at the time was that the rising fascism of Europe was being met with a dubious militarism and nationalism which were themselves integral to the success of fascism and, prior to that, to colonialism. She believed that both social and economic life were increasingly directed, controlled, and subordinated to preparation for

---

[64] Martin Thomas, "Fighting 'Communist Banditry' in French Vietnam: The Rhetoric of Repression after the Yen Bay Uprising, 1930–1932," *French Historical Studies* 34.44 (2011): 611–48 (628–29).

[65] Weil, *On Colonialism*, 41.

[66] Weil, *Seventy Letters*, 8. The quotation above which opens this section comes from Weil, *Selected Essays*, 30.

war which increased the power of the state and led toward a "totalitarian form of social organization."[67]

She did not hold true to this pledge in an absolute sense, as she actively backed workers' strikes and sit-ins, and was a fully fledged supporter, and occasional member, of the more radical syndicalist trade unions. She argued that war was premised on the continued exploitation of all workers, colonial or not. War promised no change and, in fact, threatened the possible gains made by the workers as the "craze" for money making and for weaponry were two sides of the same coin. Underlying Weil's critique was her continued frustration with the labor movement to think beyond the "lure of the pay packet" to more wholly address the conditions of labor.[68] She saw very clearly, and was often disappointed by this same lack of clarity in the labor movement, the link between colonial exploitation of labor to domestic factory work – "a difference in degree, not of nature."[69] In each, the worker is denied autonomous thought and action which is the foundation of liberty and is increasingly enslaved to the mass centralization of state and capital power. For Weil, the separation of domestic and international politics was artificial, designed to undermine solidarity and acute comprehension of the costs of capitalization and of war.

It was her own year of factory work, begun in 1934, which led Weil to question her original belief that "nothing on earth can stop man from feeling himself born for liberty" – for factory work indeed accomplished just that.[70] She conveyed the horror of "the bitterest and most unexpected" lessons of her time in the factory: "oppression, beyond a certain intensity, does not engender revolt but, on the contrary, an almost irresistible tendency to the most complete submission."[71] Factory work oppresses the body and obliterates the capacity to think. The inability to think or to act, itself a form of self-destruction, is further compounded by the seeming lack of attention or indifference on the part of those who know of or witness it. Not only is one made a "slave," with "body and soul in pieces," but one is rendered irrelevant. "One finally gets a clear idea of one's own importance. The class of those *who do not count* – in any situation – in anyone's eyes – and who will not count, ever, no matter what happens."[72]

---

[67] Weil, *Oppression and Liberty*, 116.   [68] Nevin, *Portrait of a Self-Exiled Jew*, 111.
[69] Weil, *On Colonialism*, 28.   [70] Weil, *Oppression and Liberty*, 226.
[71] Weil, *Seventy Letters*, 35.
[72] Simone Weil, *Formative Writings, 1929–1941*, ed. Dorothy Tuck McFarland and Wilhelmina van Ness (Amherst: University of Massachusetts Press, 1987), 225.

In 1937, Weil wrote an article excoriating the French public and the Popular Front, an alliance of socialists, communist, and labor movements, for ignoring the plight of workers in Tunisia until the murder of twenty striking mine workers. The article trenchantly outlines possible reasons for the ignorance and indifference displayed by the French – distance, racism, and minimization – concluding that the truth is that "the tragedy ... is not really very gripping" until there is blood.[73] The "pitiless severity" with which the colonial "oppressor" treats the colonies is of no real interest to the French or to the Popular Front not only because of these reasons, none of which she finds credible, but also because suffering, and what she is beginning to theorize more substantively as affliction, reduces one both to invisibility and to mute despair.[74] Crucially for Weil the communication and reception of suffering is one means to alleviate or to reduce it.

Thus, when the daily life of the majority – of factory workers and of the colonized – composed of "hopeless resignation, exhaustion, slow death" does not register, neither does the inexorable decay of their existence.[75] Indeed, as she continued in the article, to the degree that death without blood does not even "count: they are not real deaths."[76] The "most refined cruelty on a vast scale and the brutal manipulation of human beings as so much raw material" is commonplace and continues without comment unless, and only then, if the violence is so spectacular and bloody as to spark interest.[77] For Weil, the profound quotidian suffering experienced unseen and unvoiced not only resonated with her own experience of factory work (which she does not make equivalent to either the harms of colonial labor or colonization but saw as part of a whole), but also goes beyond suffering and becomes what she calls affliction.

Affliction is a complicated term in Weil's lexicon and like many of her concepts begins to take on multiple meanings as her thinking progresses. Affliction is defined as "the event that has seized and uprooted a life directly or indirectly in all its parts, social, psychological and physical ... there is not really affliction unless there is social degradation or the fear of it in some form or another."[78] The dimension of social degradation is what sets affliction apart from suffering, for social degradation exacerbates the isolation and humiliation of being set apart from the world. It is as an "attenuated form of death," the force of which can "turn something

---

[73] Weil, *On Colonialism*, 42.   [74] Weil, *On Colonialism*, 42.
[75] Weil, *On Colonialism*, 42.   [76] Weil, *On Colonialism*, 42.
[77] Weil, *Selected Essays*, 206.   [78] Weil, *Waiting for God*, 67–69.

yet alive into a thing."[79] Tracing the evolution of her analysis of coloni-alism through that of her own experience with factory work, the descrip-tions become more acute as she herself felt what she had previously only imagined. Marking this movement through her thought, we see how the social death of conquest and colonialism is the attenuated death of affliction, while the transformation of something "yet alive" into a thing echoes with her descriptions of individuals becoming mere matter under conditions of colonialism. In one of her more vivid descriptions she writes: "pulverizing the soul; the man who falls into it is like a workman who gets caught up in a machine. He is no longer a man but a torn and bloody rag on the teeth of a cog wheel."[80]

Affliction is different from suffering because it obliterates the person as such, robbing them of the capacity to speak and to be heard which, recursively, sinks them into "a state of dumb and unceasing lamenta-tion."[81] In her evocative renderings, the afflicted stutter, gasp for breath, and plead in vain in a court of law – as did those in the Yen-Bay uprising – "stammering before the magistrate," reduced to mute cries as if their "tongue has been cut out."[82] This description, of course, resonates with all of her writings on the experiences of colonialism and the reduction of the afflicted to non-beings not only in form, but in voice and deed. The communicability of suffering is put into question for Weil as a consequence of being both at another's full disposal and made non-being. Importantly, for Weil, it is not that the afflicted are a wholly absent voice, it is that the capacity to hear – and to make one's appeal audible – is deformed, and thus it is unregistered. And, while there are those able to rise up (as in the miners' strikes), this momentary interruption does not fully alter the prior conditions. And, it is here that one wonders what Weil would have made of the national liberation and decolonization movements which followed World War II.

"This obligation is an unconditional one"

Considering the full horrors of affliction, how does the transfiguration of things into human beings, and human beings as means into human beings as ends occur? [83] Although for Weil her full absorption into the state of affliction occurred most poignantly in her factory work, she does

---

[79] Weil, *Waiting for God*, 68; Simone Weil, *War and the Iliad*, ed. Rachel Bespaloff, trans. Mary McCarthy (1947; repr., New York Review of Books, 2005), 3.
[80] Weil, *Selected Essays*, 27.   [81] Weil, *Selected Essays*, 27, 11.
[82] Weil, *Selected Essays*, 25, 28.
[83] The quotation above which opens this section comes from Weil, *The Need for Roots*, 5.

not discard labor, as her careful study of it in *Need for Roots* evinces.[84] Instead, she carefully delineates how labor undertaken with consent, and with individual and collective recognition of the dignity of the self, "offers humans the opportunity to realize freedom in the confrontation with necessity and time."[85] The emphasis laid on necessity and time hearkens to her critique of colonialism, specifically power (which accepts no limitations) and uprootedness (which destroys a notion of chronological time in its obliteration of the past). Labor properly understood does not dominate but mediates the limits of the material world, while through its accordance with temporal rhythms – of seasons, of the day, of the body, and of life itself – labor literally roots one in the world in a consensual relationship. "Freedom derives in consenting spontaneously to that which necessity obliges."[86] In Weil's lexicon, labor reflects and produces "men and not things." Weaving her very pragmatic historical analysis of totalitarianism and its antecedents, Weil offers a plan to right human relationship with the world, to link labor to what she calls "reality, the truth, and the beauty of this universe and with the eternal wisdom which is order in it."[87] But what would prompt this transformation in labor which is, itself, an assurance of liberty? What facilitates the recognition of the dignity of self?

Her response? Complicated, as is her wont. She recognized the need for rights – which she describes as part of the "middle values" along with democracy and personality – but they are not enough. She saw rights as a pragmatic and necessary step in the emancipation of the colonies, and to possess citizenship is, in theory, to guarantee the right to consent, or not, to state actions.[88] However, rights are secondary to obligations. Rights are, in fact, "ludicrously inadequate" for most situations, and rights can be used for good or bad purposes whereas obligation is always good: "One has the right to choose whether to alleviate suffering, in the

---

[84] Nevin writes that Weil's unpublished reading notes demonstrate a debt to E. H. Carr's *Conditions of Peace* which was published in 1942. He tracks the lines of influence such as their shared belief in wars as moral as well as material catastrophes, and in the limitations of recourse to rights.

[85] Dietz, *Between the Human and the Divine*, 68.

[86] Esposito, *The Origin of the Political*, 2.   [87] Weil, *Selected Essays*, 17.

[88] Weil believes that France should relinquish the colonies. However, because of her critique of power and of her concern with the link between nations and war, she is less forceful in her advocacy for the colonies to become nations, which just draws them into the endless race for power. Rather her focus is that they feel and become free: Weil, *On Colonialism*, 117. Her earlier work in this regard is less than satisfying as she bends the question of independence to the strategic necessity of war against Germany and to the will of the French people.

language of rights. In the language of obligation, one must do so independent of conditions."[89]

To understand this, and to think through its implications for colonialism, it is first necessary to understand that for Weil in "all the crucial problems of human existence the only choice is between supernatural good on the one hand and evil on the other."[90] Rights, as a "middle value" are something which "hangs in the air" between supernatural good and evil, dependent as they are upon a "notion of exchange" or a "sharing out" and a "measured quantity."[91] Often subject to debate and, she claims, issued in a tone and a point of contestation (which rights for whom and when), rights have a "commercial flavor."[92] What this "bargaining spirit" of rights does is denigrate the individual as it predicates its delivery on the "social privilege" attached (e.g., middle class or wealthy) such that the full expression of rights relies on the degree of social privilege held. Indeed, the substance of human rights comes from those men who due to their social privilege and fluency with power have the "monopoly on language."[93] Those who experience the ravages of affliction through exploitation and degradation may issue a "cry of protest from the depth of the heart" but their cries are lost in the "shrill nagging of claims and counterclaims."[94]

If this is true, then those who are in most need of attention are the ones whose address is least likely to be voiced or heard, for it is precisely the cry from the heart which is almost impossible to hear, while to engage in claims and counterclaims presumes a valid, and thus audible, voice. When the assurance and protection of rights becomes an accounting problem, dependent upon hierarchies of privilege, it follows that those who do not "count" in either the sense of being identified as valuable or in being able to govern the count are by definition denied the rights needed the most. The social and political sorting of individuals according to whether they "count for something ... or count for nothing" is for Weil one of the sources of affliction which cannot be resolved by rights. Rights, the petition for and the delivery thereof, depend on personal attributes of the person – the political and social condition of their belonging to a community, as Hannah Arendt also argued.[95] As such they are useless to those whose very need results from their social degradation, exclusion, and silencing.

---

[89] Weil, *Selected Essays*, 21, 24.   [90] Weil, *Selected Essays*, 23.
[91] Weil, *Selected Essays*, 33, 18.   [92] Weil, *Selected Essays*, 18.
[93] Weil, *Selected Essays*, 21.   [94] Weil, *Selected Essays*, 21.
[95] Arendt, *Origins of Totalitarianism*.

For this reason, Weil introduces her notion of obligation. Obligation is prior to attributes for it is given through a transcendent faith in the "longing for good" which all of humanity shares.[96] Obligation is a form of compassion which is deeply inflected by a sense of a transcendental good – made explicit in the common love of justice – which allows for recognition and protection of the other's "human presence."[97] Obligation is not reducible to the particularity of the person; it is impersonal. If rights cannot respond to the derealization of the individual – because they are intimately linked to the specificity of that individual – obligation may. When the French public disregards the plight of the colonized, as exemplified by the 1930 Colonial Exhibition, the massacres in Indochina, and the repression in Tunisia, it is in essence stating "you do not interest me." As such, the French are "committing a cruelty and offending against justice" in the most profound sense of rejecting the obligation to find, in what at first is made to appear as "featureless human matter," the person to whom recognition and succor is owed.[98]

Obligation is equally the limit on the use of force; namely, that one does not exercise the power one has but, rather, quietly stills it in reference to the suffering of the other. Rights are an illusion, a form of consolation, that inure one from the true suffering of the other and of the "luck" by which we presume ourselves free of such pulverizing degrading forces. Obligation gains its strength in the humbling recognition that individual attributes, prestige, or being among the "counted" do not defend against affliction. As she wrote:

To acknowledge the reality of affliction means saying to oneself: I may lose at any moment, through the play of circumstance over which I have no control, anything whatsoever that I possess including those things which are so intimately mine that I consider them as being myself … it could happen at any moment that I might be abolished and replaced by anything whatsoever of the filthiest and most contemptible sort.[99]

In this, recognition of affliction does not succumb to the belief that those are miserable because, as she put (in reference to the French attitude toward colonial sufferings) they are "not of the same species" and in no way "like us."[100] Instead, it is precisely because the afflicted are potentially us at any and all times that requires recognition and response and, yet, may make it almost impossible. Obligation is unconditional and eternal. It is realized only with difficulty for it demands not only an openness to and affirmation of the vulnerability of the other, but also to

---

[96] Weil, *Oppression and Liberty*, 169.   [97] Weil, *First and Last Notebooks*, 324–29.
[98] Weil, *Selected Essays*, 9.   [99] Weil, *Selected Essays*, 27.
[100] Weil, *On Colonialism*, 43.

the presence of an eternal and transcendent love which Weil variously names as the Good and God. Obligation is "founded on something ... whatever it is ... that does not form part of our world."[101]

Conclusion

The rejuvenation of labor, taken together with the prioritization of obligation over rights, form the constellation of Weil's seemingly dissonant take on righting the world and preventing, if possible, the seemingly inevitable victories of the likes of National Socialism. As a whole, labor and obligation depend on a great host of related and involved concepts, such as attention, compassion, education, and one which is yet more difficult to grasp, decreation. Yet, as much as Weil's purchase on the plight of her contemporary condition, her diagnosis and her response, is striated by her encounter with the divine it is equally and firmly rooted, both in her sense of the word and of the world, in the most essential of human petitions: *why am I being harmed?* For her, reformation of labor and the introduction of obligation respond to this question when, properly undertaken and properly understood, they set the conditions for recognizing individuals as sacred unto themselves rather than commodities in a transactional exchange. While we may disagree with its source, we might abide by Weil's injunction that obligation is "always the human being as such," the adherence to which begins as a first step when no one suffers from hunger in any of its myriad manifestations.[102] Lest we dismiss this as merely spiritual, note that for Weil the provision of food to the hungry requires a complete revolution.

Weil's sense of the counted and uncounted prefigures Rancière, her critique of rights that of Arendt, Eyal Weizman, and Samuel Moyn, while her astute and unsparing analysis of race and power in the pursuit of colonialism sets her apart from most of her contemporaries. That she saw Hitler clearly as an effect of colonization and imperialism in spirit and practice, alone should suggest the value of her thought. Like Arendt who followed or Luxemburg who preceded, her grasp of the perils of colonialism unsettles and overturns not only the narratives of colonialism and nationalisms of her time, but it can also inform our own. Her insistence that there is an intrinsic link between domestic and international politics, as expressed through socio-material conditions of labor and exploitation resulting in affliction counters solely structural or state-based analyses of

---

[101] Weil, *The Need for Roots*, 4.   [102] Weil, *The Need for Roots*, 5.

power and of force.[103] That she was so bold and unconventional as to explore the role of spiritual belief in political practices challenges us all to rethink the distinction of the spiritual and political by which a certain version of political and international thought proceeds.

Certainly, if we accept a definition of political thought as that of a "critical practice ... commensurate with both the political desire that incites it and the world it describes and seeks to transform it," then Simone Weil should no longer be a lonely figure in the field of political thought and might take her place in international thought as well.[104]

---

[103] Weil would not recognize herself as feminist, even in the time in which she wrote; however, she did place what can be coarsely described as relational ontology at the heart of her theory.

[104] Robyn Wiegman, *Object Lessons* (Durham, NC: Durham University Press, 2012), 17.

4   Ideas in Action: Eslanda Robeson's International Thought after 1945

Imaobong D. Umoren

"International affairs are merely an extension of domestic affairs, which in turn are merely an extension of community affairs, family affairs and relations with the neighbors."[1] So said Eslanda Robeson in a 1957 interview for the Women's International Democratic Federation's (WIDF) magazine. By the 1950s, this anthropologist, activist, and journalist began to link race relations with "Human Relations, and International Relations."[2] In common with the work of predominantly male US-based international relations scholars in the early twentieth century, Robeson made race central to her international thinking.[3] Her assertions reflect her understanding of the significance of race and global politics as an extension of what has often been conceived as the "private sphere." Like the African American scholar and activist W. E. B. Du Bois, Robeson was deeply interested in understanding and challenging the twentieth-century global color line.[4] The importance that Robeson placed on race within an international sphere was grounded in and drew on a range of Black internationalist intellectual and activist movements that coalesced and thrived during the interwar period.

In the 1920s and 1930s, the Washington, DC born Robeson resided in London with her husband, the renowned artist-activist Paul Robeson and their son, Paul Jr.[5] Her experiences of interacting with Black Caribbean and West African activists in groups such as the West African Students Union (WASU) and of traveling to Paris where she met influential members of the city's Black population, such as the Martiniquan Paulette Nardal, influenced Robeson's thinking on Pan-Africanism,

---

[1] Eslanda Robeson, Interview: Women of the Whole World, December 1957, 3. Box 19 Eslanda G. Robeson Papers, Moorland-Spingarn Research Center, Howard University, hereafter EGR Papers.

[2] Robeson, Women of the Whole World, 3.

[3] Robert Vitalis, *White World Order, Black Power Politics: The Birth of American International Relations* (Ithaca, NY: Cornell University Press, 2015).

[4] W. E. B. DuBois, *The Souls of Black Folk* (Chicago, IL: A. C. McClurg, 1903).

[5] Martin B. Duberman, *Paul Robeson* (London: Bodley Head, 1989).

Negritude, and Garveyism.[6] While Robeson did not explicitly detail her thoughts on the latter two, she saw herself as a Black internationalist and Pan-Africanist, believing strongly in the shared cultural and historic links that tied African Americans to Africans and Black West Indians. In particular, Robeson worked hard to challenge negative notions of Africa and Blackness by stressing how much Blacks in the West had to learn from those on the continent, inversing what literary scholar Ifeoma Nwankwo has termed binaristic blackness, which was prevalent in Black diasporic politics.[7]

During her time in interwar London, Robeson befriended influential African activists like the Nigerian Ladipo Solanke who helped establish WASU. Through her studies at the London School of Economics and Political Science (LSE), Robeson developed close links with the Kenyan Jomo Kenyatta.[8] She and Paul Robeson also interacted with future Indian leaders like Krishna Menon and Jawaharlal Nehru . Robeson's experiences with WASU, at the LSE, and the inter-racial friendships she developed deepened her anti-colonial politics and interest in African cultures, which were further explored in her 1936 journey to the continent. This resulted in the 1945 publication of *African Journey*, based on the time she spent in Southern, Eastern, and Central Africa. It became a landmark text, described by her biographer as the result of "arduous research and fieldwork ... a richly detailed, insightful narrative that combined ethnography and travel memoir," later "recognized as an important early anthropological text on Africa ... and a treatise against colonialism."[9] It allowed her ideas about African politics and international affairs to reach a wider audience.[10]

Between 1945 and 1965, the United States and later the United Kingdom remained the couple's base, but Eslanda Robeson continuously traveled to countries in Africa, Asia, and the Caribbean. Robeson was involved in international organizations such as the Council on African Affairs (CAA) and the Sojourners for Truth and Justice (STJ).

---

[6] Jennifer Anne Boittin, *Colonial Metropolis: The Urban Grounds of Anti-Imperialism and Feminism in Interwar Paris* (Lincoln: University of Nebraska Press, 2010).

[7] Ifeoma Nwankwo, "Insider and Outsider, Black and American: Rethinking Zora Neale Hurston's Caribbean Ethnography," *Radical History Review* 87 (2003): 49–77.

[8] Hakim Adi, *West Africans in Britain: Nationalism, Pan-Africanism and Communism 1900–1960* (London: Lawrence & Wishart, 1998).

[9] Barbara Ransby, *Eslanda: The Large and Unconventional Life of Mrs. Paul Robeson* (New Haven, CT: Yale University Press, 2013), 153–54

[10] Maureen Mahon, "Eslanda Goode Robeson's African Journey: The Politics of Identification and Representation in the African Diaspora," in Manning Marable and Vanessa Agard-Jones (eds.), *Transnational Blackness: Navigating the Global Color Line* (New York: Palgrave Macmillan, 2008), 115–33.

In addition, she wrote for Black newspapers like the *Afro-American*, the radical *Freedom*, and the left-leaning *New World Review* where she was responsible for reporting on colonial issues and the United Nations (UN). These became critical spaces where she voiced her ideas on international politics, the UN, gender, race, freedom struggles, and peace.[11] In terms of religion, while Christianity did not explicitly shape Robeson's thought nor was it a theme in her writings, she recognized the importance of Black churches in the civil rights movement in 1950s America. Robeson's writings demonstrate her interest in reaching wide audiences, both White and Black, and her commitment to being a leading voice within leftist circles.

Robeson was one among a number of traveling Black women intellectuals in the early and mid-twentieth century.[12] These include Amy Ashwood Garvey, discussed elsewhere in this volume. It is likely that Robeson and Garvey interacted with each other in London and through the CAA. They shared similar views on Pan-Africanism but differed on the "Back to Africa" plank of the United Negro Improvement Association. Other women among Robeson's acquaintances were Una Marson and Constance Cummings-John, who were active in interwar London.[13] Other African American women involved in activism across borders that challenged racism, colonialism, and sexism included Esther Cooper-Jackson, Thyra Edwards, and Louise Thompson Patterson.[14] What made Robeson distinct, however, was the ways in which she used her frequent travels, friendships with notable African, African American, Afro-Caribbean, and Asian leaders and activists, and most importantly her journalism to carve out her ideas about not only the centrality of race but also the significance of the so-called Third World for fundamentally reshaping the dynamics of international relations, especially in the post-war era. In Robeson's opinion, "one of the most important issues in the future world is the quick progress of the colonial peoples."[15]

---

[11] Imaobong D. Umoren, "'We Americans Are Not Just American Citizens Anymore – We Are Also World Citizens': Eslanda Robeson, World Citizenship, and the New World Review in the 1950s," *Journal of Women's History* 34.4 (2018): 134–58.

[12] Imaobong D. Umoren, *Race Women Internationalists: Activist-Intellectuals and Global Freedom Struggles* (Oakland, CA: University of California Press, 2018).

[13] Tony Martin, *Amy Ashwood Garvey: Pan-Africanist, Feminist, and Mrs. Marcus Garvey No. 1 or a Tale of Two Amies* (Dover, MA: Majority Press, 2007); Minkah Makalani, *In the Cause of Freedom: Radical Black Internationalism from Harlem to London 1917–1939* (Chapel Hill: University of North Carolina Press, 2011); Marc Matera, *Black London: The Imperial Metropolis and Decolonization in the Twentieth Century* (Berkeley: University of California Press, 2015).

[14] Erik S. McDuffie, *Sojourning for Freedom: Black Women, American Communism, and the Making of Black Left Feminism* (Durham, NC: Duke University Press, 2011).

[15] Eslanda Robeson, "Congo Diary," 1946, 6. Box 11 EGR Papers.

After 1945, Robeson's participation in international conferences and journalism enabled her to focus on "some aspect of an issue, event, or discussion which has been (deliberately) overlooked by the organized press and radio."[16] This conscious choice enabled her to discuss "important and interesting facts about the new nations, the newly independent peoples, the peoples struggling to become independent."[17] Robeson's analysis of independence movements in former colonies intended to help equivalent movements in America gain a better understanding of changes within global politics. In her words, it would enable

the American people to recognize, understand, appreciate and respect these profound changes, and to learn how to adapt ourselves and our way-of-life to these changes as rapidly and as gracefully as possible, lest we become and remain isolated from the mainstream of world progress.[18]

Independence movements in former colonies would fundamentally upend Western hegemony. Those living in the global North would have to adjust to their new position in the world alongside those from the global South.

Robeson practiced what the co-editors of *Toward an Intellectual History of Black Women* call "intellectual history 'Black woman-style'" defined as "an approach that understands ideas as necessarily produced in dialogue with lived experience and always inflected by the social facts of race, class, and gender."[19] Although she did not refer to herself as a Black feminist, Robeson's ideas about race and gender were very much a part of a long tradition of Black feminist internationalism.[20] This chapter argues that two overlapping planks of Robeson's international thought consisted of an analysis of women's political participation and the connections between Third World and African American freedom struggles. Within these two areas, Robeson's thought centered on the links between US domestic racial and foreign policy, the impact of the Cold War on the civil rights movement, and the role of the United Nations. These features were shaped by Robeson's position as both an

---

[16] Eslanda Robeson, "Work for Peace in the United States," December 1954, 3. Box 13 EGR Papers.

[17] Robeson, "Work for Peace in the United States," 3.

[18] Robeson, "Work for Peace in the United States," 3.

[19] Mia E. Bay, Farah J. Griffin, Martha S. Jones, and Barbara Dianne Savage, "Introduction: Toward an Intellectual History of Black Women," in Bay et al. (eds.), *Toward An Intellectual History of Black Women* (Chapel Hill: University of North Carolina Press, 2015), 4.

[20] Cheryl Higashida, *Black Internationalist Feminism: Women Writers of the Black Left, 1945–1995* (Urbana, IL: University of Illinois Press, 2011).

insider and an outsider.[21] She was an insider in the sense that she was part of formal networks through her accreditation as a journalist and her friendships with key political and activist figures. But Robeson was also an outsider who did not fit within one organization or ideology. This allowed her the flexibility to travel, write, and attend conferences where she was able to thread together different aspects of her analysis of race and gender. Robeson's insider-outsider position further enabled her to put many of her ideas into practice. In this way, Robeson's international thought was inextricably tied to her activism, demonstrating the significance of her identity as an activist-intellectual and highlighting how "ideas-in-action" were a distinct and robust mode of her political thought.

Women's Political Engagement

Women's engagement with international politics was a central category in Robeson's thought. Robeson was firm in her belief that women's efficiency as mothers and workers within the home gave them valuable skills with which to engage with politics in public. Robeson was influenced by maternalist thinking, which is evident in the remarks she made about the position of women in the UN.

While female politicians and diplomats from across the world were involved in the UN from its inception, the power they had and the issues they were concerned with were not always front and center in the attention of Western media. Robeson noted that, "our general press pays too little attention to the activities, and important contributions, of the women at the United Nations."[22] Robeson used her position at *New World Review* to rectify this and informed her readers about the key role that women played in policy making. In 1954, she reported on the UN's eighth annual session of the Commission on the Status of Women. The commission consisted of women from the Dominican Republic, Byelorussia (Belorussia), Haiti, France, Cuba, USSR, UK, Poland, Iran, Venezuela, China/Formosa, Lebanon, Pakistan, Burma, and USA.[23] These delegates, Robeson wrote, represented "women throughout the world and they deal with vital matters."[24] At the UN, Robeson contacted a number of influential women and developed a particularly close

---

[21] For more on the insider-outsider perspective see Patricia Hill-Collins, *Black Feminist Thought: Knowledge, Consciousness, and the Politics of Empowerment* (London: Unwin Hyman, 1990).
[22] Eslanda Robeson, "Women in the United Nations," *New World Review*, July 1954, 7.
[23] Robeson, "Women in the United Nations," 7.
[24] Robeson, "Women in the United Nations," 7.

friendship with Indian diplomat Vijaya Lakshmi Pandit, Jawaharlal Nehru's sister. She also reached out to other women at the UN, including a delegate from Czechoslovakia, Helena Leflerova.[25] Yet, although women held influential positions at the UN, men still tended to dominate. Robeson reported that during discussions Britain's Patrick Atlee and Yugoslavia's Aleksander Bozovic "sometimes took the seat of the women delegates and expressed their views,"[26] although women did try to prevent them from interrupting debates. Overall, Robeson's stress on the critical role that women played at the UN as well as her emphasis on the importance of women from different nationalities working together, points to her vision for a strongly gendered international solidarity. Gender difference played a significant role in Robeson's thought. While she did not explicitly say so, Robeson subscribed to the view that there were innate differences between men and women, which is why collaboration between women was politically significant for her. The emphasis on women working in unison was a type of political act she herself engaged in through the group Sojourners for Truth and Justice.

In 1952, Robeson co-founded STJ, a Black women's organization that supported civil rights, anti-colonialism, and feminism.[27] The group sprang out of an event held in September 1951, when around a hundred African American women, as part of a STJ protest, traveled to Washington, DC to demand justice for victims of racial abuse.[28] Other radical Black women involved in STJ included the actress Beulah Richardson (Beah Richards), and activists Thompson Patterson, Yvonne Gregory, Claudia Jones, and Alice Childress.[29] The STJ were concerned with building transnational links which they did with South African women in the African National Congress Women's League.[30] Although the short-lived group was comprised of little over one hundred members, it influenced later groups like the Third World Women's Alliance.[31]

Working alongside Black women from across the African diaspora was a political practice Robeson continued in the late 1950s, upon her return to London. Alongside Trinidadian-born communist Claudia Jones, who had been active in the Communist Party in the United States in Harlem in the 1930s and who was editor of the influential *West Indian Gazette*,

[25] Robeson, "Women in the United Nations," 7.
[26] Robeson, "Women in the United Nations," 8.
[27] Dayo F. Gore, *Radicalism at the Crossroads: African American Women Activists in the Cold War* (New York University Press, 2011).
[28] Jacqueline Castledine, *Cold War Progressives: Women's Interracial Organizing for Peace and Freedom* (Urbana, IL: University of Illinois Press, 2012).
[29] McDuffie, *Sojourning for Freedom*; Gore, *Radicalism at the Crossroads.*
[30] Castledine, *Cold War Progressives.*   [31] McDuffie, *Sojourning for Freedom.*

and Ashwood Garvey, Robeson worked with the Afro-Women's Centre that supported the rights of women of African descent and had a meeting space in London.

The 1949 All-Asian women's meeting in Beijing also illustrates the importance Robeson placed on women's involvement in politics.[32] Robeson attended the meeting "as a reporter to gather first hand news from behind the Iron Curtain" and as a representative of the CAA, Congress of American Women (CAW), and the Progressive Party, the United States' third largest political party.[33] In China, Robeson "met, talked with, listened to, travelled with, and briefly lived with 165 delegates representing 14 Asian countries, and 33 observers representing Africa, Europe and the Americas – women delegates officially representing, in all, 500 million women."[34] The international make-up of the conference served as "an experience of a lifetime" for Robeson because it "gave us a new feeling about women, about the importance of the role we women have to play in this new and changing world."[35] It reinforced the maternalist strand in her thinking as she stressed that "We must, all of us, work and fight with our men first to preserve our lives, then for homes to live in, and then to preserve those homes so we can have a proper place in which to bring up our children."[36] Furthermore, Robeson emphasized essentialized notions of women and pacifism urging that "it is every woman's job to prevent war, and to work for peace. When they tell us that woman's place is in the home, we must answer: women dead in the war find their place in the grave; if women survive they must have a home before they can find a place in it."[37]

Yet, it was the friendship that Robeson developed with Madame Sun Yat-sen, also known as Soong Ching-ling, Vice President of the People's Republic of China, President of the Chinese People's Relief Administration that reflected her overriding belief in the significance of women working together on national and international issues at the highest levels of politics. The two women bonded during the conference. Robeson admired Soong Ching-ling, calling her "World Woman Number One" because of "her deep sense of being not only one of the 250 million

[32] Marc Gallichio, *The African American Encounter with China and Japan: Black Internationalism in Asia* (Chapel Hill: University of North Carolina Press, 2000); Vijay Prashad, *Everybody Was Kung Fu Fighting: Afro-Asian Connections and the Myth of Cultural Purity* (Boston, MA: Beacon Press, 2001); Heike Raphael-Hernandez and Shannon Steen (eds.), *AfroAsian Encounters: Culture, History, Politics* (New York: New York University Press, 2006).
[33] Eslanda Robeson, "Trip to China," 1950, 1. Box 12 EGR Papers.
[34] Eslanda Robeson, "China I," 1951, 1. Box 17 EGR Papers.
[35] Robeson, "China I," 1.   [36] Robeson, "China I," 1.   [37] Robeson, "China I," 2.

women of China, one of the 500 million people of China, but also one of and one with the billions of women and people of the world."[38] Robeson observed that Ching-ling "had much to tell, but much to ask, because her deep concern for her own people is bound up with a deep concern for the people of the world."[39] Soong Ching-ling's internationalist vision, incorporating international friendship and female solidarity, overlapped with Robeson's and the two women discussed world politics, gender relations, and civil rights in America.

Robeson, however, refrained from making (justified) criticisms of Soong Ching-ling and the state of women's rights in China. Robeson informed her audience that Soong Ching-ling "along with many other women of New China – helped to write ... equality into the Common Law, Article 6 which reads: The people's Republic of China abolishes the feudal system which holds women in bondage; woman shall enjoy equal rights with men in political, economic, cultural, educational life."[40] Rather than grappling with persistent disparities between middle- and working-class women, Robeson presented to the readers of her newspaper reports a prettified and utopian vision of women's rights in China. This was part of her repeated political efforts to craft a positive portrayal of Third World freedom fighters and struggles, a politics that she deployed to demand more rights for women, and specifically Black women, in the United States.

Practicing Colored Cosmopolitanism

Alongside advocating for the engagement of women within international politics and participating in transnational organizations, Robeson stressed the importance of Afro-Asian unity and promoting what historian Nico Slate has termed colored cosmopolitanism. According to Slate, the concept defines those Black activists such as Du Bois and Martin Luther King, Jr. as well as Asian activists who attempted to "forge a united front against racism, imperialism, and other forms of oppression" with White and non-White people across the world.[41] In common with Mittie Maude Lena Gordon, also discussed in this volume, Robeson practiced colored cosmopolitanism by stressing the similarities between African American, African, and Asian freedom struggles.

---

[38] Eslanda Robeson, "World Woman Number One," *New World Review*, July 1951, 1. Box 13 EGR Papers.

[39] Robeson, "World Woman Number One," 1.

[40] Robeson, "World Woman Number One," 2.

[41] Nico Slate, *Colored Cosmopolitans: The Shared Struggle for Freedom in India and the United States* (Cambridge, MA: Harvard University Press, 2012), 2.

In China, for instance, Robeson drew connections between Chinese and Black US freedom struggles. She argued that the changes in China had consequences for Black Americans. "Every Negro will be able to understand and appreciate what is going on in New China ... Every Negro who had faced discrimination that is."[42] Like the centuries-old Black American freedom struggle, Robeson wrote about the long Chinese freedom struggle and how Chinese men and women had won the fight to repossess their land and drive "the foreigners and the feudal lords off the mainland of China to Formosa, and set up their own Central Peoples Government."[43] According to Robeson:

in the New China the old familiar signs "Chinese AND DOGS NOT ALLOWED" have been torn down; the Chinese people now live in International Settlements and Concessions in their cities, which areas were formerly reserved for whites only, for the foreign government officials and businessmen.[44]

Robeson optimistically reported that these changes now meant that:

the Chinese people now walk freely everywhere in their land with dignity and confidence and with heads held high; they no longer say, in fear, Yes Sir and Yes Ma'am to the white colonial foreigners who ruled them and issued the orders.[45]

These descriptions highlight the positive changes taking place in the country, but their celebratory tone masks the ongoing tensions between different groups in China. In similarity with her views about the newly achieved rights of Chinese women, Robeson offered a sanguine representation of the political changes in China, in the hope that it would buoy African American freedom struggles. Yet she overlooked and minimized the persistent problems facing China in order to present a simplistic comparison.

Later that year, Robeson's interest in Asia shifted to US military action in Korea, where, again, she highlighted Afro-Asian connections. During the Korean War, the US Army remained segregated, despite President Truman's executive order 9981 demanding the desegregation of the army. Yet many African Americans enlisted for numerous reasons, including an escape from unemployment, with some choosing military service as a way to mitigate the economic challenges they experienced.[46] Historian Kimberly Phillips has stated that, "During the Korean War,

---

[42] Robeson, "China I," 2.   [43] Robeson, "China I," 2.   [44] Robeson, "China I," 4.
[45] Robeson, "China I," 4.
[46] Kimberly L. Phillips, *War! What Is It Good For? Black Freedom Struggles and the US Military from World War II to Iraq* (Chapel Hill: University of North Carolina Press, 2012), 124–27.

1.5 million men were inducted; nearly one-quarter of these new troops were African American (13.5% inducted; 13.4% enlisted)."[47] The irony of fighting against another foreign country made up of non-Whites who were the target of racist myths and propaganda spread by the army and the press while experiencing staunch resistance to ending Jim Crow was not lost on African American soldiers or activists. Robeson noticed that "A lot of Americans, especially Negro Americans, are very anxious to learn exactly what it is that Koreans have done to Americans and America, which makes us send our army all the way over there to make war against them."[48]

Robeson was one of many prominent African Americans to protest against the Korean War along with Du Bois, journalist Charlotta Bass, and Claudia Jones, amongst others.[49] Yet other activists such as Walter White argued that the Korean War was not a "race war" and was more about conflicting political ideologies between the communist Koreans and the democratic United States. White's stance should be read in the context of the National Association for the Advancement of Colored People's attempt to not be the target of a Cold War backlash against the civil rights movement.[50] For Robeson, her response to the conflict was based on her pacifism as well as the fact that the participation of Black American troops in conflict with non-White Third World peoples undermined Afro-Asian solidarity.

Robeson extrapolated her anti-war stance to a wider concern with the relationship between US political parties and Black voters. In trying to understand why Black Americans were caught up in a war against non-White people, she surmised that "It may be that the failure of our Government's Bi-Partisan Foreign Policy in Asia is, in the last analysis, partly the fault of Negro-American citizens."[51] She went on to stress that "We Colored Americans have not done our proper duty by the two major political parties which constitute our present government. We have not taught them RESPECT FOR THE RIGHTS OF COLORED PEOPLE. We have not taught them a basic fact of life – that people, no matter what their color, religion, background, all people are human beings, and cannot be denied their human rights indefinitely, if we are to have peace in the world."[52] Robeson argued that because both the Republican and Democratic parties still received votes from African Americans this led to the parties feeling confident of continued support

[47] Phillips, *War! What Is It Good For?*, 124.
[48] Eslanda Robeson, "Korea," July 26, 1950, 2. Box 12 EGR Papers.
[49] Phillips, *War! What Is It Good For?*, 133.   [50] Phillips, *War! What Is It Good For?*, 132.
[51] Robeson, "Korea," 2.   [52] Robeson, "Korea," 7–8.

"no matter how they treat us, no matter how long they deny us citizenship rights and our humanity."[53]

Although she reasoned that "We have made some protest here and there, we have resisted now and again" she argued that it was "not enough. They have come to feel that if fifteen million Colored People here in the United States cannot or will not insist upon their rights, cannot or will not resist denial of these rights, – then probably billions of Colored People in Asia and Africa also cannot or will not insist or resist. It turns out that in this they are mistaken."[54] She called upon African Americans to insist upon civil rights legislation immediately. Robeson's views about the racial politics informing the Korean War were based on her understanding of the entangled connections between US domestic racial and foreign policy. However, her criticism of African Americans and their relationship with the Democratic and Republican parties was also rooted in party-political motivations. Robeson was active in the Progressive Party, which she believed would present an alternative option for African American voters. With its broad left-wing policies, commitment to pacifism, support of civil rights, and its inclusion of a cadre of African American candidates, including Robeson, the Progressive Party's role as a third party was intended to not only challenge the two larger political parties but also re-align domestic and foreign policy away from the dominance of Cold War politics. The party, however, became mired in accusations of communism.[55]

While Robeson generally supported the UN, praising its efforts to represent the "world family" she levied some of her strongest criticism at the organization due to its role in the US–Korea War. "The United Nations has not only supported our intervention in the internal domestic affairs of Korea," she stated, "but has also sent its sacred flag of peace to sanctify this war, and has called upon other members of the UN to send troops to help the US Army ... In this matter of Korea, the United Nations has become an instrument for war, not for peace."[56] The UN's sanctioning of the war threatened the very core of its principles and demonstrated to Robeson the way in which the organization could become complicit in the victimization of peoples they sought to protect. Robeson was not the only activist to realize the limits of the UN. As scholar Carol Anderson has shown, initially many African American activists and groups like the NAACP hoped the UN would be an organization they could work with to demand human rights.[57] Yet, in the Cold

---

[53] Robeson, "Korea," 8.   [54] Robeson, "Korea," 8.
[55] Castledine, *Cold War Progressives.*   [56] Robeson, "Korea," 5.
[57] Carol Anderson, *Eyes Off the Prize: The United Nations and the African American Struggle for Human Rights, 1944–1955* (Cambridge University Press, 2003).

War climate, the overwhelming power of the American state curbed its influence which meant that the NAACP had to narrow its equality aims and focus on domestic civil rights. Robeson's criticism demonstrates her cautious optimism in the UN's ability to live up to its ideals, and but also her analysis of the shortcomings of liberal international organizations when it came to furthering Afro-Asian unity.

Documenting changing developments in emerging independent countries in Africa and Asia featured in Robeson's journalism, highlighting the salience of the Third World. In the spring of 1955 Robeson discussed the historic Bandung Conference. The host of the conference, the first president of Indonesia, Ahmed Sukarno, called the meeting "the first international conference of colored peoples in the history of mankind."[58] Robeson saw the conference as marking "a turning point in world affairs."[59] Bringing together representatives from Asia, Africa, and the Middle East, delegates met "to promote cooperation among the non-aligned nations of the Third World; to deliberate about such common problems as colonialism and racism; and to advocate world peace."[60]

For Robeson, the most important result of the Bandung Conference was the confidence participating countries had in the UN. She observed that "Seventeen of the twenty-nine nations represented there are members of the UN. In the resolution unanimously adopted, the seventeen pledged to reconstitute themselves as a consultative group to initiate and support all measures for peace, disarmament, self-determination, non-interference, human rights, friendly international relations and economic cooperation in the UN."[61] She believed that member states of the Bandung Conference could undermine the dominance of Western countries in the UN.

Robeson was also hopeful that African and Asian countries' presence at the UN could help to undermine racism. Seven months after Ghana gained independence from Britain, the Minister of Justice and chairman of Ghana's Delegation to the UN, Ako Adjei, gave a speech at the UN that Robeson believed would "be as sweet music to the ears of 16 million Negroes."[62] Robeson quoted parts of Adjei's speech in which he

---

[58] Richard Wright, *The Color Curtain: A Report on the Bandung Conference* (Cleveland, 1956), 117.

[59] Eslanda Robeson, "UN + Bandung = Peace," *New World Review*, June 1955, 10. Box 14 EGR Papers.

[60] Thomas Borstelmann, *The Cold War and the Color Line: American Race Relations in the Global Arena* (Cambridge, MA: Harvard University Press, 2001), 95.

[61] Eslanda Robeson, "Before and After Bandung," *New World Review*, July 1955, 29. Box 14 EGR Papers.

[62] Eslanda Robeson, "UN Assembly Rings with roar of Africa resurgent," 1957, 7. Box 14 EGR Papers.

underlined Ghana's commitment to Pan-Africanism calling upon "all Members of the United Nations to take note that the new State of Ghana is concerned with the freedom of all African peoples and also with the treatment that is meted out to all peoples of African descent, wherever they may be in any part of the world."[63] Adjei went on to talk about Ghana's relationship with the continent stating, "it is the hope of the Government of Ghana, that, by co-operation with the other independent States of Africa, an African personality in international affairs can be evolved."[64] According to historian Kevin Gaines, the African personality was "an ideology of African liberation reminiscent of Negritude but emphasizing the quest for political unity rather than Negritude's assertion, as formulated by Léopold Senghor, of the unity of African cultures."[65] Robeson praised Adjei's speech for its bold assertion of forging alliances with those of African descent within and outside of Africa, commenting that "we American Negroes can be very proud of our African descent on this day."[66] Her words reflect how after 1957, Ghana served as a symbol of hope for African Americans and West Indians, hundreds of whom were attracted by President Kwame Nkrumah's charismatic Pan-Africanism and moved to the country to offer their skills to the building of the new nation.[67]

While Robeson was forging new links in China and documenting the crisis in Korea, Paul Robeson came under attack from anti-communists in the United States. After giving a misquoted speech about African American and Soviet relations at the Congress of the World Partisans of Peace, a government investigation was launched. The State Department subsequently seized Paul and Eslanda Robeson's passports because they refused to sign an affidavit stating they were not communists.[68] It was in fact true that the Robesons were not communists but given their trips to the Soviet Union and their stable friendships with communists and communist sympathizers, they certainly supported communist values, believing that they helped to diminish inequality. For eight years, between 1950 and 1958, Paul and Eslanda Robeson could not leave the United States. Yet in 1958, when restrictions on Robeson's travels were lifted, she resumed advocating for and practicing "colored cosmopolitanism" through her travels to the multi-racial Caribbean.

---

[63] Robeson, "UN Assembly Rings," 7.   [64] Robeson, "UN Assembly Rings," 7.
[65] Kevin K. Gaines, *American Africans in Ghana: Black Expatriates and the Civil Rights Era* (Chapel Hill: University of North Carolina Press, 2006), 78.
[66] Robeson, "UN Assembly Rings," 7.   [67] Gaines, *American Africans in Ghana.*
[68] Ransby, *Eslanda*, 231.

In January 1958, Robeson attended the founding of the West Indies Federation (WIF) and made her first two-week trip to Port-of-Spain in Trinidad. Inaugurated on January 3, 1958, the short-lived WIF comprised a union of Caribbean colonies including Jamaica, Barbados, Trinidad and Tobago, Antigua, Dominica, St Christopher-Nevis-Anguilla, St Vincent, St Lucia, Montserrat, and Grenada, all of which intended to unify and ascend into an independent nation from Britain. Discussions about federation had been ongoing since the late nineteenth century but became more concrete from the interwar period and were shaped not only by those in the Caribbean but also inextricably informed by Black diasporic politics and the actions of West Indian intellectuals in the United States and Europe.[69]

In writings about her trip, published on her return to the United States, Robeson saw the WIF membership as "historically significant" because it was "overwhelmingly Negro in composition" with an Indian minority.[70] Foreseeing some of the future ethnic, racial, and religious divisions that would hamper the WIF Robeson hoped that "the diverse elements of this very interesting and attractive multi-racial society ... will continue to submerge their widely different interests, traditions and customs, and join together to build a healthy, happy, prosperous nation, unified in its diversity."[71] Robeson recognized that the unique WIF could help set a precedent for multi-racial political unions that could potentially be copied in areas of the non-White world.

In Robeson's writings she also remarked on the participation of women in the WIF. "There are four women in the Legislature – 2 in a total of 19 in the Senate, and 2 in total of 45 in the House of Representatives."[72] These women, Robeson argued, "seem eager and determined to participate in and contribute to the building of their new Nation" and she was confident that their voices would be heard.[73] In Trinidad, Robeson met leading Caribbean political figures, such as Grenadian journalist Theophilus Albert Marryshow, and delivered speeches to packed audiences at the Public Library in Port-of-Spain, the Communication Services and General Workers Union, a trade union for women, and the Women's League of the People's National Movement.[74] In addition, she spoke to a group of female welfare and social workers at an "all-day Rally" that "is just now crystallizing, and is called THE CARIBBEAN

---

[69] Eric D. Duke, *Building a Nation: Caribbean Federation in the Black Diaspora* (Gainesville: University Press of Florida, 2016).

[70] Eslanda Robeson, "History Is Made," April 25, 1958, 4. Box 24 EGR Papers.

[71] Robeson, "History Is Made," 4.

[72] Eslanda Robeson, "Women in a New Nation," April 28, 1958, 1. Box 24 EGR Papers.

[73] Robeson, "Women in a New Nation," 1.   [74] Ransby, *Eslanda*, 237.

WOMEN'S ORGANIZATION IN THE MAKING."[75] This group was "inter-racial, inter-Island, and represents all aspects of welfare and social work."[76] Although happy to see politically engaged women, Robeson noticed the sexism that still existed within Caribbean politics. "Perhaps the most important single result of the Federation Women's Rally, beside the new unity and consolidation achieved," Robeson commented, "was the decision of the women to protest the new Constitution now being considered for the Bahamas in which women are not granted suffrage."[77] She hoped this protest would change the constitution but regional hierarchies, personality clashes, and racial tensions led to its end in 1962, initiating the beginning of island-wide independence. Nonetheless, Robeson's travels to the Caribbean highlight her colored cosmopolitanism, her repeated emphasis on women's political involvement, and her challenge of sexism.

Later that year, Robeson ventured to independent Ghana where she attended and reported on the All-African conference for the Associated Negro Press (ANP). To her, the conference was a laudable example of Pan-Africanism, a political force that was ignored or downplayed in a racialized international public sphere. She remarked on the uniqueness of the conference, commenting that "for the first time in modern history Africans from North, East, Central, South and West Africa met in conference on African soil to discuss African Affairs."[78] At the conference, Robeson met African leaders including Patrice Lumumba, Tom Mboya, and Hastings Banda. Despite attempts to disrupt the proceedings, a number of "significant Resolutions coming out of the Conference which the Western Press played down or buried" were passed.[79] For instance, "the Conference recommended that no African State should have diplomatic relations with any country which practices discrimination."[80] Another resolution called for the formation of "an African Legion consisting of volunteers who will be ready to protect the freedom of the African peoples."[81]

Robeson agreed with the resolutions but was aware of tensions and levied a harsh feminist critique "over the absence of women at the

---

[75] Robeson, "Women in a New Nation," 2.
[76] Robeson, "Women in a New Nation," 2.
[77] Robeson, "Women in a New Nation," 4.
[78] Eslanda Robeson, "The Accra Conference," *New World Review*, February 1959, 13 Box 14 EGR Papers.
[79] Eslanda Robeson, "Summary of the Accra Conference," December 1958, 3. Box 14 EGR Papers.
[80] Robeson, "Summary of the Accra Conference," 3.
[81] Robeson, "Summary of the Accra Conference," 3.

Accra Conference."[82] In total, "there were only eight official women delegates, and only two women addressed the plenary sessions."[83] The two women were Martha Ouandie who told "the terrible story of French colonialism now rampant in Cameroons, and Shirley Graham Du Bois [who] read the clear, forceful, constructive message to the conference from her husband."[84] "A whole population cannot be properly mobilized if half of it is officially ignored," Robeson stressed.[85] Her repeated insistence on asking the gender question showed her criticism of the masculinity inherent in the "big man" politics of African independence that weakened claims about postcolonial equality.[86] At the conference she reunited with Shirley Graham Du Bois and formed friendships with other women attendees, including Nigerian activist Mallama Gambo, Egyptian feminist Saiza Nabarawi, radical Indian activist Geeta Mukherjee, and Maida Springer. Robeson's personal friendships and the political weight she put on the "woman question" reinforced each other.

US Civil Rights Abroad

Robeson interrogated the impact of civil rights campaigns abroad and the image of American democracy.[87] Writing in 1957, Robeson surmised that when Governor Faubus called out the National Guard of Arkansas to prevent nine Black pupils from entering Central High School of Little Rock, "delegates from every country to the United Nations watched and listened with amazement ... and their estimation of 'democracy' in the country 'leading the Free World' went down."[88] Although she admitted that "many of them probably decided that the United States, however undemocratic, was nevertheless too powerful to 'cross,'" this dramatically changed after Sputnik.[89] When Soviet scientists "captured the imagination and respect of the world by successfully launching the first earth satellite into outer space," she argued that this put significant pressure on a United States whose deficient democratic values could no longer be embellished by technological superiority.[90]

---

[82] Robeson, "The Accra Conference," 14.   [83] Robeson, "The Accra Conference," 14.

[84] Robeson, "The Accra Conference," 14.   [85] Robeson, "The Accra Conference," 14.

[86] Gaines, *American Africans in Ghana.*

[87] Mary L. Dudziak, *Cold War, Civil Rights: Race and the Image of American Democracy* (Princeton University Press, 2000); Borstelmann, *The Cold War and the Color Line.*

[88] Eslanda Robeson, "American Woman Number One: Daisy Lee Bates," 1957, 53. Box 14 EGR Papers.

[89] Robeson, "American Woman Number One: Daisy Lee Bates," 53.

[90] Robeson, "American Woman Number One: Daisy Lee Bates," 53.

Events at Little Rock and the launch of Sputnik marked a shift in the global perception of the United States. In an attempt to present a more appealing image of racial conditions at home, President Eisenhower promoted Black American artists such as Dizzy Gillespie and Louis Armstrong as cultural ambassadors on tours around the world. In an article Robeson wrote about the legendary musician Louis Armstrong, who had previously "deliberately evaded criticism and complaint about segregation of his audiences," leading Blacks to regard "him as some-thing of an Uncle Tom."[91] This image of Armstrong changed when he voiced disgust at the incident at Little Rock and "the continuing bomb-ings and dynamitings of Negro homes, churches, businesses; the phys-ical, economic and social persecution of the Negro people" that created "a slow fire of resentment in him."[92] With Armstrong's public state-ments, Robeson opined that, "it will be extremely difficult for the State Department to persuade Negroes to go abroad to trumpet the cause of freedom and equality." Instead, the government would have to deal more squarely with the issue of racial discrimination.[93]

At the same time that US government officials were trying to change the image of race relations for an international audience, Robeson wrote about the hypocrisy inherent in the way in which Hungarian refugees were treated compared to African Americans. In 1957, Eisenhower's administration offered support to Hungarian refugees which contrasted with, in Robeson's view, "its utter lack of concern for the victims of the invasion and bombing of Port Said, Alexandria and Cairo, and its even stranger continuing ignoring of the desperate situation of Negro citizens here in our own Deep South who are victims of dangerous and increasing White Terror."[94] Robeson went on to state that "As they continue to struggle for their constitutional rights here in their own country, Negro citizens wonder why thousands of Hungarians can come here and attain by decree, upon arrival, the rights for which Negroes have worked and fought and died, and have not yet achieved."[95] These words illustrate Robeson's persistent censure of the pretense that lay at the heart of Cold War US race relations.

[91] Eslanda Robeson, "An Entertainer Speaks His Mind: World Famous Trumpet Player Louis Armstrong on the Negro Question," *Blitz Newsmagazine*, October 1957, 2. Box 14 EGR Papers.

[92] Robeson, "An Entertainer Speaks His Mind," 2; Penny M. Von Eschen, *Satchmo Blows Up the World: Jazz Ambassadors Play the Cold War* (Cambridge, MA: Harvard University Press, 2004), 64.

[93] Robeson, "An Entertainer Speaks His Mind," 4.

[94] Eslanda Robeson, "The American Negro and the Hungarians," February 1957, 1. Box 14 EGR Papers.

[95] Robeson, "The American Negro and the Hungarians," 1.

In fact, she argued that there was much the United States could learn from Soviet Russia about how to treat minorities. What Robeson admired most about the Soviet Union was its ability to raise so-called "backward" people. "Women, Orientals, Jews, Moslems, peasants, national minority groups, traditionally despised and discriminated against in Old Russia, now live and work as equal Soviet citizens."[96] This change and the success of socialism in Robeson's view "are of profound and immediate practical interest to the Negro people and colored peoples everywhere."[97] Robeson argued that if similar strategies were implemented in the United States and elsewhere where non-White people lived, this could raise their status and remove barriers to equality. She expressed more admiration for the Soviet Union when Joseph Stalin died in March 1953. She penned a tribute, saying that, "as a woman and a Negro – I am one of those billions of people who are infinitely better off, and therefore I salute Josef Stalin, his comrades, the soviet people, and the soviet system."[98] It remains unknown to what extent either Eslanda or Paul Robeson knew of the purges that occurred during Stalin's reign. They made no mention of knowing any criminal activities and remained supportive of the Soviet Union well into the 1960s. Yet her remarks about socialism and Stalin indicate the somewhat rose-tinted lens with which Robeson viewed the Soviet Union, which was far from a haven for minorities or women. As with her calls for Afro-Asian unity, Robeson disregarded and glossed over the complexity of politics within nation-states, and oftentimes her arguments were superficial. Even if the contra-dictions in her thought were also characteristic of many other left-wing activists and intellectuals who were not fully informed of all that was occurring in the Soviet Union, Robeson was too wedded in her argu-ments to an international politics of comparison to abandon her support for the Soviet Union.

Conclusion

Eslanda Robeson's post-1945 international thought focused on women's engagement in international politics, Third World and African American freedom struggles. Through a variety of avenues – journalism, friend-ships, and international travels – and in her capacity as an

---

[96] Eslanda Robeson, "What the Soviet Union Means to the Negro People," *New World Review*, November 1951, 32. Box 13 EGR Papers.

[97] Robeson, "What the Soviet Union Means," 32.

[98] Eslanda Robeson, "On Stalin's Death," *New World Review*, March 31, 1953, 1. Box 13 EGR Papers.

"insider-outsider," Robeson was able to put into practice many of the things that she advocated. Robeson's writings were not theoretical and conceptual in a narrow sense but rooted in experience and, given that she was a public figure and journalist writing for a very distinct audience, also highly performative. She was both an intellectual and prolific writer and an activist, and this drove the unique combination of concerns in her politics, thinking, and writing. Robeson's example highlights the importance of taking seriously "ideas-in-action," rather than focusing merely on the prose of international thinkers.

The planks in her thought were a combination of varied but linked "isms": Pan-Africanism, Black internationalism, maternalism, feminism, and anti-militarism. These were not abstract ideologies for Robeson, but very much based on her identity as an African American mother, writer, traveler, anthropologist, and activist. Moreover, they contributed to the contradictions in Robeson's thought which at times presented an uncomplicated essentialized vision of women, internationalism, and colored cosmopolitanism, without detailing the challenges of multiple gendered, racialized, religious, and class divisions and hierarchies that threatened solidarity politics.[99] Yet, Robeson was not completely blind to these divisions. Her criticism, for example, of the UN's role in the Korean War demonstrates that she was not reticent to find fault with an organization embodying internationalism. Nonetheless, Robeson's politics of optimism, so to speak, was grounded in her sense of a world in a flux. Rather than becoming mired in the negative and oftentimes destructive violent politics of her time, Robeson sought to focus on a positive, hopeful vision of a world united in peace and cooperation.

---

[99] For more on solidarity politics see David Featherstone, *Solidarity: Hidden Histories and Geographies of Internationalism* (London: Zed Books, 2012).

Part II

Outsiders

Elizabeth Lippincott McQueen: Thinking
International Peace in an Air-Minded Age

Tamson Pietsch

Today Elizabeth Lippincott McQueen is best remembered as the founder of the Women's International Aeronautic Association (WIAA), an organization she established in 1929 and promoted into the 1950s. In this capacity she corresponded with J. Edgar Hoover, spoke before the California Senate, and was also pulled into the emerging world of the academic study of international relations on the West Coast of the United States. In the 1920s she had championed Anglo-American relations and British-led imperial-internationalism in Palestine. On the eve of the United States' entry to World War II she turned her attention to US influence in Latin America, defending the atomic bomb as a guarantee of protection. But in the 1930s she advanced ideas about air-mindedness and peace that drew deeply on her Christian Science background and highlight the diverse sources of international thinking in this period.

McQueen saw flying as a "wonderful medium of spreading the doctrine of goodwill around the world." "There are no boundaries in the sky," she wrote in 1936:

The barriers of mountains and seas, of times and distance, are conquered by the modern miracle of aeronautics. Whatever brings nations into a better understanding of each other is an avenue to peace. That is why airways to peace is my life work.[1]

Such comments echoed pre-war ideas about commerce and communication as a force for internationalism. In common with other thinkers of the time, they framed air travel as a technology that would reduce the "time and space which separate[d] various countries of the world, thereby establishing new interest, new trade, new friendships between nations."[2] But McQueen's thinking about international aviation went beyond these claims.

[1] Elizabeth McQueen, "Winged Ladies," 1933, Box 6/Folder: Speed Magazine 1933–1934/The Aero-Gram, USC Library of Aeronautical History, Women's International Association of Aeronautics records, Collection no. 0055, Special Collections, USC Libraries, University of Southern California (hereafter, USC 55).

[2] Elizabeth McQueen, "Peace by Air Is Their Plea," 1933, Box 6/Folder: Speed Magazine 1933–1934/The Air-Pilot April, USC 55.

She believed WIAA members could *think* the world toward peaceable international relations: "Thoughts and words," she wrote in the organization's newsletter in 1933, "are a powerful vibratory force moulding the world's affairs, so why not put our minds in the air for Peace."[3] For McQueen, the private thoughts of individuals could play a role in the fate of nations. With these ideas, McQueen translated her longstanding Christian Science beliefs and her liberal-imperialist commitments into a new language of internationalism that had wide cultural resonance.

In the period between the wars aviation was a major theme for those concerned with international relations. Some championed it as a force for peace that would bring people closer together.[4] Others, conscious of its devastating military potential, laid out plans for the regulation and organization of the new technology through international organizations such as the International Commission for Aerial Navigation (ICAN) and the League of Nations' Air Transportation Cooperation Committee, or urged preparedness for the danger it posed.[5] In this period too, aviation gained a mass popular following. In the United States, it infused every aspect of American popular culture. From Hollywood films to household consumer goods, airplanes and those who flew them became a part of the everyday lives of millions of people. In the process aeronautics became a powerful site for the popularization of ideas about internationalism. It made it possible for Americans of all kinds to imagine the world.[6] As they looked at the ubiquitous images of air routes crossing the globe, they learnt to see the United States in a global setting.

If "world-mindedness," like "air-mindedness," was a concept with wide resonance in the 1920s and 1930s, historians of international thought have tended to examine the first rather than the second parts

---

[3] McQueen, "Winged Ladies."

[4] E. Warner, "International Air Transport," *Foreign Affairs* 4.2 (1926): 278–93; Elvira K. Fradkin, *The Air Menace & the Answer* (New York: Macmillan, 1934); E. Kingston-McCloughry, *Winged Warfare* (London: Cape, 1937); Philip S. Mumford, *Humanity, Air Power & War: An Essay upon International Relations* (London: Jarrolds, 1936).

[5] Dale De Remer and Donald W. McLean, *Global Navigation for Pilots*, 2nd edition (Aviation Supplies & Academics, Inc., 1998), 370; Alan P. Dobson, *A History of International Civil Aviation: From Its Origins through Transformative Evolution* (New York: Routledge, 2017); P. Sand, G. de Sousa Freitas, and G. Pratt, "An Historical Survey of International Air Law before the Second World War," *McGill Law Journal* 7.1 (1944): 24–42. In 1919 the International Air Transport Association was also established to foster cooperation between various commercial airlines and the International Commission for Aerial Navigation (ICAN) was created as a permanent body to oversee the development of air law. A few years later the League of Nations set up an Air Transportation Cooperation Committee.

[6] Jenifer Van Vleck, *Empire of the Air* (Cambridge, MA: Harvard University Press, 2013), 9, 3.

of those concepts. They have focused on the visions for world order mapped out by historical thinkers and the international organization of aviation, but less on what contemporaries meant when they spoke about "mindedness".[7] Elizabeth Lippincott McQueen and the WIAA provide one way for historians of international thought to get at this question. Her advocacy for the international benefits of aeronautical thinking, her belief in the importance of women in making aviation "thinkable," and her notion of the intimate scale on which international thinking operated, borrowed from ideas informing two currents of interwar American culture that rarely find a place in histories of international thought: the rise of Christian Science and interwar enthusiasm for the new technology of aviation.

Christian Science and Liberal Empire in the Middle East

McQueen was an inveterate autobiographer. In accounts told again and again over the course of her life she dated her conversion "to aeronautics as an instrument for World Peace" to an experience in Palestine soon after the end of World War I:[8]

At Aden on the Red Sea, I saw seven airplanes take the place of two regiments of soldiers and in that hell hole of heat there dawned upon me the conviction that "Peace by Air" was in reality my motto for service to humanity.[9]

In some of her accounts McQueen adopted an explicitly spiritual language, describing "[a] vision, mental and spiritual" that came to her of "millions of women with the hands upraised acclaiming: 'Save my son from war, save my son from war, save my son from war!'" From that moment on, as she later put it, "the sky became the dome of my church and nature's throb the rhythm of my soul."[10] With this new motivation – so her

---

[7] On visions of world order see Or Rosenboim, *The Emergence of Globalism: Visions of World Order in Britain and the United States, 1939–1950* (Princeton University Press, 2017). On aviation and internationalism see: Waqar Zaidi, "'Aviation Will Either Destroy or Save Our Civilization': Proposals for the International Control of Aviation, 1920–1945," *Journal of Contemporary History* 46.1 (2011): 150–78; Waqar Zaidi, "Liberal Internationalist Approaches to Science and Technology in Interwar Britain and the U.S.," in Daniel Laqua (ed.), *Internationalism Reconfigured: Transnational Ideas and Movements between the World Wars* (New York: I. B. Tauris, 2011); Brett Holman, "World Police for World Peace: British Internationalism and the Threat of a Knock-Out Blow from the Air, 1919–1945," *War in History* 17.3 (2010): 313–32; David MacKenzie, *ICAO: A History of the International Civil Aviation Organization* (University of Toronto Press, 2010); Van Vleck, *Empire of the Air.*

[8] Michael Palmer, "Elizabeth Lippincott McQueen Papers," 2012, http://blogs.libraries .claremont.edu/sc/2012/08/elizabeth-lippincott-mcqueen-p.html.

[9] "McQueen Articles Undated," n.d., Box 2/Folder 7, USC 55.

[10] "McQueen Articles Undated."

accounts continue – she returned to the United States and "began to make an intensive study of all branches of aeronautics and to contact, whenever possible, flyers and air-minded people [and] ... to lecture to clubs and organizations on the subject of aviation." And from these involvements her "idea of forming an international alliance of good will through the different women flyers of the world and air-conscious women came into being."[11]

McQueen did go to Palestine in 1919–20 as a member of the US branch of the London-based Anglo-American Society on what she later described as a relief mission. At the time she believed God had sent her to Jerusalem and the *Christian Science Journal* for 1920 lists her as a Christian Science practitioner in the city.[12] Her later turn to what she called "the doctrine of aviation" and her ideas about its influence on international relations were deeply infused with ideas carried over from these earlier religious commitments.[13]

In her work as a Christian Scientist, McQueen was motivated by what she described as her desire to "be an example of virtue, to help humanity by [spiritual] healing."[14] Developed by Mary Baker Eddy in the 1860s and 1870s in New England, healing was central to the Christian Science world view.[15] Its adherents believed that reality was purely spiritual and that the material world was an illusion. They understood disease and sickness as an error in human thinking rather than a physical condition and held that ill-health could be treated by prayer. As a Christian Science practitioner, Elizabeth McQueen had been licensed by the Church to treat patients using its methods and by 1910 she was practicing in New Rochelle (just north of Manhattan).[16] For McQueen and her fellow Christian Scientists, *thinking* and *mind power* could quite literally remove the experience of suffering and restore the ultimate reality of perfect health.[17] It was the job of trained practitioners like McQueen to encourage people toward the transformative power of what those in the Church termed "right thinking," or thinking that originated in and reflected the mind of God. This was an

---

[11] "McQueen Articles Undated."

[12] *The Christian Science Journal* 38.4 (1920), xxviii; Elizabeth McQueen, "McQueen to Grant," April 10, 1920, Box 5/Folder 1, USC 55.

[13] McQueen, quoted by B. Schultz, "Elizabeth Ulysses Grant McQueen: 'Wings around the World for Peace, Prosperity, and World Friendship,'" *American Historical Society Journal* 58.2 (2013), 131.

[14] "McQueen Articles Undated."

[15] Catherine Albanese, *A Republic of Mind and Spirit: A Cultural History of American Metaphysical Religion* (New Haven, CT: Yale University Press, 2007); B. Satter, *Each Mind a Kingdom: American Women, Sexual Purity, and the New Thought Movement, 1875–1920* (Berkeley: University of California Press, 1999).

[16] *The Christian Science Journal* 28.1 (1910), xcv.

[17] P. Ross, "Security-Conscious," *Christian Science Sentinel*, January 16, 1943, 194, https://sentinel.christianscience.com/shared/view/2bsjn8txie0.

approach she would later transpose into the realms of international relations and aviation.

It was during her time working in New Rochelle, that Elizabeth McQueen met William Denison McCrackan, with whom she would develop a version of Anglo-American liberal-imperialist millenarianism. McCrackan was a cosmopolitan author and prominent journalist who had converted to Christian Science in 1900 and become very senior within the Church.[18] But sometime after the outbreak of the war he had broken with its Directors in a conflict that was part of the extended struggle for control that played out in the wake of Mary Eddy's death in 1910.[19] McQueen sided with McCrackan and in July 1919 they both took refuge at the White Mountains Christian Science resort in Tamworth, New Hampshire, where they conceived a plan to travel to Jerusalem.

Led by Field Marshall Viscount Allenby, in the last months of 1917 the British Empire's Egyptian Expeditionary Force (EEF) had conquered Southern Palestine, taking Jerusalem from the Ottoman Empire on December 9, 1917. McQueen and McCrackan were among those who understood this British presence in Jerusalem as a fulfillment of the biblical prophecy that foreshadowed the coming of the Christian millennium. McCrackan cast the English people as one of "the so-called 'lost' ten tribes of Israel," and understood the joint action of the United States and Britain as key to the "battle plan for the millennial day."[20] In doing so he was championing a version of the "Anglo-Israelism" that gained considerable traction in the half century before 1914 and in the years after the war in Britain, the United States, and other parts of the Anglo world. Notable adherents included Mary Baker Eddy, Admiral John Fisher (First Sea Lord of the British Navy), and William Massey (one-time Prime Minister of New Zealand).[21] Its tenets were an amalgam of Anglo-American racial superiority, religious millenarianism, and liberal-imperial ideology that understood the British peoples as inheriting the "birthright of Jacob," which McCrackan, among others, understood as a mandate for Anglo-American imperial and international rule. He and McQueen felt called by God to go Jerusalem, because they saw the conquest of the city as the

---

[18] Stephen Gottschalk, *Rolling Away the Stone: Mary Baker Eddy's Challenge to Materialism* (Bloomington: Indiana University Press, 2006), 57.

[19] In McQueen's words, "the lid flew off of the Mother Church in Boston": "McQueen Articles Undated."

[20] William D. McCrackan, "The Troopship of Empire," n.d., Box 1/Folder 1, USC 55. McCrackan's account of his time in Jerusalem mentioned McQueen repeatedly, though it pointedly excluded the other members of their party.

[21] For an example of British-Israelist thinking in the late nineteenth century see William Poole, *Anglo-Israel, or the British Nation the Lost Tribes of Israel* (Toronto, 1889).

beginning of a new historic era of peaceful international relations.[22] As McQueen wrote in a 1919 poem titled, "The Call of Palestine":

> The back bone of history lies bare and stripped.
> With ark and sceptre by Spirit equipped.
> The New House of Israel ushers in the divine.
> Healing the world with its thousand year's shine. ...
> They come, the tribes, the Ten and the Two;
> God's Plan, the Millenial Kingdom's come true.[23]

McQueen's letters from this time are full of praise of British rule and the Anglo-American alliance.[24] By forming a US branch of the London-based Anglo-American Society, and utilizing the connections of their fellow White Mountains resident, Talbot Mundy (who had previously led the American Committee for Armenian and Syrian Relief) they had managed to gain permission to enter a city still under the British military rule of Governor Sir Ronald Storrs.[25] Arriving in Jerusalem at the start of September 1919 they quickly became members of the Joint Advisory Committee for the Relief of Jerusalem, working closely with Allenby and Storrs, although the American Consul remained much more distant.[26] McQueen's activities were directed at the Anglo-American troops she and McCrackan saw as warriors in an "unseen destiny" and they started an English-language newspaper called *The Jerusalem News* to serve them.[27] She wrote of the ingratitude of the "native [Arab] mind," but also exhibited the anti-Semitism that would later characterize American Anglo-Israelism, particularly toward "Zionists" whom she thought were "stirring up trouble" with the Arabs.[28] These views on the natural right of Anglo-American rule ultimately led McQueen and McCrackan to break with Talbot Mundy and the rest of the party, who were more sympathetic to local Arab claims to independence.[29]

---

[22] See Mary Baker Eddy, "United States to Great Britain," *Boston Herald*, May 15, 1898, https://web.archive.org/web/20110513084035/http://www.readbookonline.net/readOnLine/49020.

[23] "The Call of Palestine," June 30, 1919, Box 1/Folder 1, USC 55.

[24] Elizabeth McQueen, "McQueen to the Editor of the London Times," September 10, 1919, Box 1/Folder 1, USC 55.

[25] Brian Taves, *Talbot Mundy, Philosopher of Adventure: A Critical Biography* (Jefferson, NC: McFarland & Company, 2006), 61, 63; "McQueen Articles Undated."

[26] Elizabeth McQueen, "McQueen to Grant," October 22, 1919, Box 1/Folder 1, USC 55.

[27] The idea was supposedly McQueen's and under the pseudonym of "M.E. Starr" she wrote a regular column for the daily one-page double-sided paper, while McCrackan assumed the role of Editor. They also set up a laundry, which provided employment to forty of the city's destitute women, many of them widows. Schultz, "Elizabeth McQueen"; Taves, *Talbot Mundy*, 61–62.

[28] McQueen, "McQueen to the Editor of the London Times"; McQueen, "McQueen to Grant," April 10, 1920.

[29] Taves, *Talbot Mundy*, 67–68, 72–74.

It was during McCrackan's and McQueen's trip home from Jerusalem to the United States in 1920 that McQueen apparently saw airplanes flying overhead in Aden and her "conversion" experience supposedly occurred. The archival record, however, suggests that this version of events is rather too neat. McQueen's time in Palestine in connection with the war no doubt gave her what she called "a vision of the universe," but it was not one that was, initially at least, connected to aviation.[30] Following her returned to the United States she continued her work as a Christian Science practitioner until 1922. To the extent that she delivered lectures in the 1920s her cause was not aviation, but Anglo-American liberal empire. British imperial rule and Anglo-American cooperation, McQueen argued, would be the "keystone of the arch of world peace."[31]

She pursued these commitments again in 1922 when she and McCrackan undertook a tour around the world in "the cause of Anglo-American friendship."[32] This was a somewhat grandiose way of framing their membership in the American Express-run luxury "Around the World Cruise" that sailed on the Cunard Line's newly built SS Laconia. The voyage once again brought McQueen into contact with many senior American and foreign diplomats, including Allenby, Governor Wood (of the Philippines), Governor Stubbs of Hong Kong, and Governor Harcourt Butler of Rangoon among others.[33] Soon after the Laconia's return to the United States in 1923, McCrackan died suddenly in Los Angeles. He left his $30,000 estate (equaling about $353,000 in 2015 values) not to his wife, who received a paltry $100, but instead to McQueen "to enable her better to carry on her work, which," McCrackan's will read, "is of vital importance to the world."[34] Exactly what McQueen did with the $30,000 is not clear, but in 1926–27 she made another trip around the world, this time on the SS Ryndam as part of the nine-month "Floating University" cruise that carried 500 American college students on a nine-month cruise in what was billed as an experiment in "world-education."

It was on this 1927 trip that McQueen first traveled in an airplane, flying from Berlin to Copenhagen in early April.[35] The year 1927 was also that of Charles Lindbergh's Atlantic crossing, and McQueen – who had returned to the United States from the Floating University cruise only a few months

[30] "McQueen Articles Undated."
[31] Elizabeth McQueen, "Letter to Editor of Egyptian Gazette," October 13, 1919, Box 1/Folder 1, USC 55.
[32] "Letter of Recommendation from Allenby for McQueen," August 12, 1922, Box 5/Folder 1: McQueen letters 1917–29, USC 55.
[33] Elizabeth McQueen, "Letter to Field Marshal Allenby," March 5, 1923, Box 1/Folder 5: Correspondence 1950–1954, USC 55.
[34] R. Edvinsson, "Historical Currency Converter (Test Version 1.0)," 2016, www.historicalstatistics.org/Currencyconverter.html.
[35] "Highlights of Pioneer University Cruise," n.d., Box 2/Folder 12, USC 55.

before the flight – cannot have failed to follow the national enthusiasm it provoked. Lindbergh was celebrated on radio and film and in the newspapers and in the months following the flight he visited forty-eight states on a national aerial tour funded by the air-minded Guggenheims.[36] Rather than the planes in Aden, it seems more likely that it was the combination of Lindbergh's crossing and her own experience of flight that led McQueen toward aviation thinking, as on her return to the United States in 1927 she joined the Orlando chapter of the US National Aeronautics Association, enrolled in flying lessons and completed a Ground Course of Aviation with Lieutenant Walter Hinton at Washington, DC.[37] When she and her husband moved to Beverly Hills in 1928, McQueen began to frame her commitment to "Peace by Air."

5.1 Elizabeth McQueen (with Dick the parrot).
Courtesy of University of Southern California, on behalf of the USC Libraries Special Collections

[36] Joseph J. Corn, *The Winged Gospel: America's Romance with Aviation* (Baltimore, MD: John Hopkins University Press, 1983).
[37] "Aviation Activities of Mrs Ulysses Grant McQueen," n.d., Box 2/Folder 3, USC 55.

The Women's International Association of Aeronautics

After McQueen's relocation to the West Coast, her activities were underpinned by a distinctive set of ideas about the international power of women's air-mindedness. World War I had been a huge stimulus to the development of aviation in the United States, but after the Armistice military spending dropped dramatically. Popular interest remained high, but large numbers of people refused to fly, associating it (not unreasonably) with danger and death. In this context women aviators temporarily became an asset to the nascent aeronautical industry. According to the historian Joseph Corn, women played a crucial role in the interwar development of aviation in the United States because, at a moment when the industry was struggling for commercial viability, they "made flying 'thinkable' by making it seem safe as well as easy."[38] Changing the way the American public thought about aviation was central to the success of the young aviation industry. If women could fly airplanes, so ran the hierarchical gendered logic that relegated women to the "natural" role of nurturing and care-giving and accorded men domain over the public and the technical, then aviation must be safe.

There were, however, serious obstacles to women's participation in aeronautics in the 1920s. Only a handful of women had managed to gain licenses before 1914 and according to McQueen, by 1928 there were only eighteen licensed women in the United States.[39] The world of aeronautical engineering was very much a man's one and women pilots faced outright discrimination at every turn. Such concerns motivated McQueen – together with the aviatrixes Marvel Crossen and Bobbie Trout – in 1928 to begin lobbying the National Air Races committee to host a Women's Air Derby and a five-day route from Santa Monica to Cleveland was mapped out. The aviation industry immediately saw the publicity value of the race and several major companies financed individual flyers. But the National Air Races committee nonetheless attempted to impose restrictive conditions on the women including limiting the distance and requiring the pilots to carry a navigator. Later the women would encounter sabotage and mismanagement.[40] But, mobilized by McQueen, both Louise Thaden and Amelia Earhart refused to participate unless the competition ran "with the same rules as the men have

---

[38] Corn, *The Winged Gospel*, 88.
[39] Only eight before 1914. Elizabeth McQueen, "California: Women in Aviation," n.d., Box 2/Folder 6, USC 55. In Britain in 1926 the number was only nine. Liz Millward, *Women in British Imperial Airspace, 1922–37* (Montreal: McGill-Queens University Press, 2007).
[40] "Report of Cross Country Derby" (*Cleveland Press*, August 26, 1929).

heretofore followed." Otherwise, wrote Thaden, "we will be the laughing stock of the aeronautical world – you know – women can't fly, can't navigate, – have to do this, and that, in order to do anything."[41] Dubbed the "Powder Puff Derby," in the end twenty pilots signed up for the August 1929 race, among them the most famous international aviatrixes of the period.[42]

On the back of the international attention the Derby was attracting, McQueen used the opportunity to establish the Women's International Association of Aeronautics.[43] Its objectives, outlined in the constitution, were threefold:

1. To associate all women throughout the world interested in aeronautics.
2. To encourage and stimulate interest in the various forms of air traffic, – carrying of mail, passenger transportation, international races and the making of world records.
3. To promote a universal spirit of friendship and service as being conducive to international peace.[44]

These aims soon assumed more grandiose expression: the organization, stated a pamphlet almost certainly written by McQueen and issued later in 1929, sought "to lift the eyes of the older generation to see the flight of the future generation" and to "Conquer Time. Overcome Space, By Air."[45] The WIAA was McQueen's vehicle for fostering public sympathy toward aviation. She was its driving force and as long as she lived, she defined its principles and philosophy.

Women pilots rallied to the organization in significant numbers, as did prominent educators and entertainers. Anne Morrow Lindbergh, the pilot wife of Charles, became the first honorary member. Lady Mary Heath (the British aviator who the year before had gained international prominence by becoming the first pilot, male or female, to fly from Cape

---

[41] Louise Thaden, "Louise Thaden to McQueen," May 18, 1929, Box 8/Women's Air Derby 1929, USC 55.

[42] They included Amelia Earhart, Louise Thaden, Thea Rasche, Ruth Nichols, Mrs Keith Miller, Ruth Elder, Blanche Noyes, Marvel Crosson, Opal Kuns, Bobbie Trout, Edith Foltz, Claire Fahy, Florence Barnes, Mary Von Nack, Gladys O'Donnell, Vera Dawn Walker, Neva Paris, and Margaret Perry. "Mrs Ulysses Grant McQueen [Biography]."

[43] Elizabeth McQueen, "McQueen to Lady Heath," May 8, 1929, Box 8/Women's Air Derby 1929, USC 55.

[44] "Constitute and By-Laws – in the Tea Room of the New York Store in PLACE," n.d., Box 3/Folder 2 – WIAA Board 1930s, USC 55; WIAA, "Minutes," May 23, 1929, Box 3/Folder 2 – WIAA Board 1930s, USC 55.

[45] WIAA, "WIAA Events Pamphlet Women's Aeronautic Association of California 1929," 1929, Box 3/Folder 4, USC 55.

Town to London) was elected the inaugural President. McQueen herself (already called the "founder") was selected as First Vice President, with noted-pilots Ruth Nicols and Amelia Earhart as fellow Vice Presidents. Lady Grace Hay Drummond-Hay (a wealthy British journalist, who although not a pilot herself, owned many planes and traveled by air prolifically) was the second President, followed by Dr. Mary Sinclair Crawford (USC Professor of French and university administrator), Mary Pickford (Canadian American actress), Olive Ann Beech (cofounder of Beech Aircraft Co.), and Matilde Moisant (second licensed woman pilot in the United States). The "File of Foreign Pilot Members" in McQueen's papers, reads as a who's who of international women aviatrixes, with seventy members from over twenty countries.[46] The majority were Anglo-Americans of the kind McQueen's earlier liberal imperialism celebrated. With the exception of Princess Der Ling (a European-educated former First Lady-in-Waiting to the late Qing dynasty's Empress Dowager Cixi, who in 1907 married the American Thaddeus C. White and moved to California) and Bedriye Tahir Gökmen (the first Turkish woman pilot), all were white. Bessie Colman, the first African American woman to hold a pilot license, was never on the WIAA lists, and there were no members from the Soviet Union. The constitution also specified a role for non-pilots: McQueen believed that "just talking about aviation, traveling by air, visiting airports, and using the airmail was sufficient to educate the general public on the merits and safety of the airplane."[47] Across the course of the 1930s many more "air-minded women" joined WIAA branches established not only across the United States and in England, Australia, New Zealand, East Africa, and South Africa, but also in France, Italy, Turkey, Hungary, Denmark, Belgium, Canada, Germany, Peru, and Brazil.[48] Arguably, they all were learning to see a world increasingly occupied by American commerce and culture.

Under McQueen's leadership, the WIAA pursued a series of activities that both emphasized women's right to the skies and borrowed from an older tradition of voluntarism and female authority embedded in sociability. Throughout the 1920s the (US based) National Aeronautics Association (NAA) refused to keep official women's records. McQueen instead lobbied the Fédération Aéronatique Internationale (of France) and in the spring of 1930 they agreed to recognize the achievements of women flyers. McQueen also encouraged the pilot members of the

---

[46] Elizabeth McQueen, "Address Book," n.d., Box 1/Folder 1, USC 55.
[47] Schultz, "Elizabeth McQueen"; "Mrs Ulysses Grant McQueen [Biography]."
[48] Schultz, "Elizabeth McQueen."

WIAA to undertake what she called "good will tours."[49] McQueen herself operated an extremely active social schedule and an extensive personal correspondence. As an office-holder of numerous associations including the California Women of the Golden West, Pan American League, and Southern California Aviation Council as well as the WIAA, she was continually attending luncheons and dinners and hosting visitors. She wrote for several flying magazines, frequently delivered lectures and radio talks on aviation and did her very best to remain ever present in the columns of the newspapers. Throughout the 1930s the WIAA organized a variety of other activities that drew upon patterns of women's sociability, including poem, song, and literary competitions as well as an "Aeronautical Art Exhibit." These contests were extremely popular. Over 360 entries were received for the 1936 poetry contest from many parts of the world, and the 1937 exhibition at the Los Angeles Museum filled five galleries with "air-minded art."[50] In a similar vein, members of the junior divisions of the WIAA – children under 7 years old were called "tailwinds," and those 7–20 years old were called "zoomers" – were encouraged to join the model plane making craze which had enormous take-up across the country. For McQueen, reading about women's aeronautic activities in local newspapers, seeing them fly planes, and meeting other air-minded women were experiences that could transform the thinking of individuals across the country.

Underpinning McQueen's WIAA activism was an unconventional understanding of the forces that shaped international relations. Although she recognized and exploited the window of opportunity for women's participation in aviation, her sense of their contribution to international affairs was a much broader one. Referencing Eleanor Roosevelt's 1933 book, *It's up to the Women* in one of her columns for *Speed* magazine, McQueen agreed that women were "a tremendous power in the destiny of the world."[51] But whereas Roosevelt placed emphasis upon practical action in the straitened economic contexts of the Great Depression, McQueen's philosophy held that it was the way women *thought* as well as the way they acted, that had an influence far beyond the home. Although she sometimes mobilized a gender essentialism that saw women as fundamentally "lovers of peace," more often she emphasized the role women had to play as mental agents who could transform the destiny of nations. In McQueen's view, by being air-*minded*, women

---

[49] "WIAA Board 1930s," n.d., Box 3/Folder 2, USC 55.
[50] "First Aviation Art Exhibition Opening Here Tonight," *LA Times*, February 5, 1937, Box 9, USC 55.
[51] McQueen, "Winged Ladies."

could help dispel fear of flying and bring about "good-will at home and friendly relations abroad."[52]

In recent work Waqar Zaidi and Or Rosenboim have highlighted the liberal internationalist belief that technologies of international connectedness demanded political thinking on a new global scale. While Rosenboim maps the thinkers who in the mid-twentieth century saw "the global" as a new "political space" in which political organization might take place, Zaidi shows how in the interwar period British, French, and American thinkers held that international control of both civil and military aviation was a necessity if the peace of the world was to be assured.[53] Up to a point McQueen's ideas about aviation are consistent with these arguments: she established the WIAA as a new international organization following her realization of the strategic and devastating military potential of flight.[54] But closer attention to McQueen's arguments suggests that at the foundation of her thinking was a belief that technologies of international connectedness operated on a much more intimate scale. If McQueen described flying as "instrument" of peace, it was an "instrument" that transformed the individual's very experience of self. "PEACE BY AIR is a hobby every woman should ride," was how McQueen put it in 1931 in a passage that evidences the continuing influence of Mary Baker Eddy's teaching about freedom from the bodily worries of material life:

[I]t will take away the earth worries and selfish details of living. It will put the white light of vision into the soul of real thinking, above the fog of ignorance. To get "off the ground" is to rise mentally as well as physically, giving a sensation of inspiration.[55]

One way to understand McQueen's commitment to the power of aeronautic-thinking is to see her translating her earlier work as a Christian Science practitioner into the "gospel" associated with the new technology of aviation. Her air-minded message was not dissimilar to that which she delivered in her rooms in New Rochelle. The world was how you thought it: "[t]he pessimist should look up and see the clear horizons ... for then he would soon see the blue sky of prosperity."[56] In this light, WIAA activities that centered on sociability or cultural production

---

[52] McQueen, "Peace by Air Is Their Plea"; Elizabeth McQueen, "Reprint from Speed 'Peace by Air,'" 1931, Box 2/Folder 5: McQueen speeches articles 1931, USC 55.
[53] Rosenboim, *The Emergence of Globalism*, 4–5; Zaidi, "'Aviation Will Either...,'" 152–55.
[54] It is possible that McQueen's involvement in Anglo-American networks in Palestine and in the early 1920s exposed her to such ideas before they had gained significant traction in the United States: Zaidi, "Liberal Internationalist Approaches to Science," 73–74.
[55] McQueen, "Reprint 'Peace by Air.'"   [56] McQueen, "Reprint 'Peace by Air.'"

were not just activities to domesticate the new technology of flight, but also ways to build and encourage a specific form of thinking. Penning aviation poetry or singing aeronautic songs enabled women to fashion air-minded subjectivities that changed how they thought and felt.

If for McQueen thinking was transformative for the self, actually flying was even more so. She described "the peace of looking up and out on the unsurpassed picture of a vast, diversified scenery, as it unfolds itself to view."[57] In the air, she suggested, the boundaries and limitations of earthly life and earthly bodies melted away. Much like the perfect spiritual reality of Christian Science, in the sky everything dissolved into the great "unlimited blue."[58] For McQueen, being in the air offered a kind of salvation that dissolved terrestrial worries and transfigured those who flew. "Pilgrim of the earth," she wrote in 1931, "either sad or joyous – if you could take to your wings and pierce the blue of the sky you would find yourself an unlimited soul."[59] Transforming the pure idealism of Christian Science, McQueen's notion of aviation thinking brought international relations into the intimacies of the mind and the depths of the soul.

Southern California and International Relations

McQueen developed much of her aviation thinking in the distinctive context of Southern California – a region in which aviation and spiritual "New Thought" were both major cultural phenomena. During the decade between 1920 and 1930 the population of Los Angeles more than doubled. Migrants were attracted by the climate and plentiful housing and by abundant employment opportunities. Carey McWilliams attributes the popularity of different faith- and mind-healing practices in the region at least in part to this population explosion. For many years the institutions of medical education and most of the hospitals were in the northern part of the state and as a consequence what he calls the "unorthodox medical sciences" established an early foothold in the south.[60] In 1922 there were already fourteen Christian Science churches in Los Angeles and over 270 practitioners offering spiritual healing, with

[57] McQueen, "Reprint 'Peace by Air.'"

[58] Elizabeth McQueen, "Why I Founded the Women's International Association of Aeronautics," c. 1940, Box 1/Folder 2, USC 55.

[59] Elizabeth McQueen, "Beverly Hills," February 8, 1931, Box 2/Folder 2 – Radio talks speeches, USC 55.

[60] Carey McWilliams, *Southern California: An Island on the Land* (1946; repr., Salt Lake City: Gibbs Smith, 1973), 258.

many more in the surrounding suburbs.[61] And Christian Science was only one of the many mystical and spiritual communities that grew up in the sunny climes of Southern California.[62]

McQueen herself seems to have had a personal energy and charisma that many found magnetic. Women associated with the WIAA were fiercely devoted to her. Lady Drummond-Hay described them as her "enthusiastic admirers and disciples."[63] Another admirer cast McQueen as a selfless worker with a "spiritual vision," who spent "lavishly of her own slender means" in service of her pioneering cause.[64] The Millers who owned the Mission Inn Hotel in Riverside, California, were among these followers. The Inn itself was largely the work of Frank Augustus Miller and his only child, Allis, and her husband DeWitt Hutchings, were keen air-enthusiasts. Not only was Allis a member of the WIAA, but she served for many years as its Honorary Secretary. They were McQueen devotees and in the early 1930s Allis, DeWitt, and Frank sought to provide a spiritual home for the adherents of the doctrine of aviation by building an "International Shrine of Aviators" at Mission Inn. They commissioned a Spanish Baroque styled chapel named for St. Francis of Assisi who, due to his affinity for winged creatures, was dubbed the "Patron Saint of Flyers." At the entrance, above St. Francis of Assisi, they placed McQueen's personal motto, "Peace by Air" and inside the chapel stood various cases containing aviation objects marked with her other slogans: "International Friendship" and "Wings around the World."[65] Just outside the entrance stood the "Famous Flyers' Wall" to which pilots were invited to affix a copper name plaque in the shape of a pair of wings. Many famous aviators made their way to the chapel, and the names on the wall included Charles Lindbergh, Ruth Law, Amelia Earhart, and Sir Charles Kingsford Smith among many others. Like so much associated with the gospel of aviation (and indeed with McQueen), the shrine was a mixture of astute publicity and genuine feeling. Its connection to McQueen's philosophy is unmistakable. McQueen herself actually lived at the Inn between 1942 and 1947 and it became something of a center for her brand of international spiritual aviation thinking.

McQueen's spiritual framing of aviation might seem peripheral now to the currents of international thought and its rationalist formulation as a

---

[61] *The Christian Science Journal* 40.5 (1922).
[62] McWilliams, *Southern California*, 249–72.
[63] Hay Drummond-Hay, "Lady Hay Drummond-Hay to McQueen," June 13, 1935, Box 5/Folder 2, USC 55.
[64] "Mrs Ulysses Grant McQueen [Biography]."
[65] Allis Hutchings, "The Internatioal Shrine for Aviation," 1937, Box 6/Folder: Speed Magazine 1933–1934, USC 55.

discipline. However it reflected a much wider popular enthusiasm for flight in the interwar period; what Joseph Corn called "a kind of secular religion" in which the airplane was invested with messianic expectations.[66] Americans perceived the "conquest of the skies as a profoundly spiritual activity, somehow linked with the divine and the supernatural."[67] Lindbergh's solo crossing of the Atlantic especially appeared as "a confrontation of man and nature [that] … recalled the country's wilderness beginning" and he was frequently portrayed in messianic terms.[68] This secular religion of flight was closely connected to a popular internationalism. In the context of the social problems caused by industrialization and the political corruption associated with railways, together with the economic hardship of the Great Depression and the United States' refusal to join the League of Nations, for a time the gospel of aviation, like the Christian gospel, seemed to many Americans to hold "out a glorious promise … of a great new day in human affairs."[69]

McQueen's combination of liberal-imperialist international thinking and spiritual aviation found a home in Southern California's distinctive version of International Relations. According to Suzanne Borghei, there the nascent discipline had a particular relationship to technologies of connectivity, migration, and travel, and was distinguished by both a development imperative advanced by a network of businessmen and civic leaders, and a concern with fostering internationalist public sentiment.[70] Moreover, at the grassroots level it was capacious, drawing in a wide array of people from lay and academic constituencies.[71] In the early 1930s McQueen was among those pulled into its fold. In 1933 the UCLA International Relations department invited her to attend its World Affairs Dinner. She spoke and hosted luncheons at more than one of the Institute of World Affairs conferences run by the University of Southern California (USC) at Mission Inn in the mid-1930s, and in 1936 she became the West Coast representative for the Pan American League, itself founded by WIAA member and West Coast activist, Dora Stearns.[72] Together with John F. B. Carruthers (former head of the Bible Department at Lafayette College) and supported by Rufus B. Von KleinSmid (who as President of the University of Southern California helped establish one of the first schools of International Relations in the

---

[66] Corn, *The Winged Gospel*, viii, 39.   [67] Corn, *The Winged Gospel*, 25.
[68] Corn, *The Winged Gospel*, 25.   [69] Corn, *The Winged Gospel*, 27, 34–35.
[70] Suzanne Borghei, "Internationalism at the Grassroots: Los Angeles and Its City Schools, 1916–1953" (PhD thesis, University of Southern California, 1995), 9–11, 23–27.
[71] Borghei, "Internationalism at the Grassroots," 27–28.
[72] "Scrapbook": October World Affairs Dinner, 1933; Institute of World Affairs, 1935; Institute of World Affairs, 1936, Box 9, USC 55.

world) she also built the International Aero Educational Research Organization (AERO) Library, which was located at USC.[73] The University of Washington's Charles E. Martin, who was Director of the World Affairs Institute, repeatedly invited her to Institute events that were held at Mission Inn, where Carruthers acted as chaplain.[74] McQueen was thus embedded in a tightly-linked network that met at the Breakfast Club of Los Angeles, which in the early 1930s attracted major celebrities and speakers from the world of politics and culture. Its manager, Harold B. Link, was a fierce supporter of aviation and prevailed upon visitors to support McQueen's USC Library.[75]

The subject of her talks on these occasions was generally "Peace by Air." In the 1930s McQueen's version of international peace was one that individuals could help bring about through the power of thought. And although the WIAA was explicitly non-sectarian, the peace McQueen wanted her members to *think* the world toward was very clearly articulated in terms that echoed those of Christian Science. It was "God's Peace."[76] "God gives us life, joy and peace," she wrote in one of her many accounts of the founding of the WIAA, but "[i]t is up to us what we make of ourselves in reflecting God."[77] This version of "Peace by Air" promised both peace between nations and internal peace within the self.

But much like the peace the British secured in Jerusalem (and like that of so many other liberal-internationalist projects) McQueen's "Peace by Air" was one ultimately backed by force.[78] In 1933 she organized the "Women's Aerial Police." Only the year before, André Tardieu, the French Minister of War, had proposed the establishment of an International Police Force of the Air to ensure the observance of international aeronautical regulations. McQueen's version, however, was more municipal.[79] Members of the Women's Aerial Police would offer assistance to pilots "lost or in distress." They might be called upon in emergencies and to supply "information as to air laws, air maps, air routes and airports." Pistol target practice was recommended for them and pilots were advised to contact "the Chief of Police" of their local city who would "no doubt ...

[73] "Air Library to be founded at USC," *Commercial News*, January 27, 1933, Box 10, USC 55.

[74] Extract from *Riverside Daily Press*, December 17, 1935, published in "Aerogram," April 1, 1936, Box 3/Folder 2, USC 55.

[75] Elizabeth McQueen, "Happy Contacts in Washington," 1933, Box 1/Folder 2, USC 55.

[76] WIAA, "Speed/(Aerogram) [Magazine]," 1937, Box 6, USC 55.

[77] McQueen, "Why I Founded the Women's International Association of Aeronautics."

[78] Roger Beaumont, *Right Backed by Might: The International Air Force Concept* (Westport, CT: Praeger, 2001).

[79] Zaidi, "'Aviation Will Either...,'" 155; Holman, "World Police for World Peace."

give [them] a police badge." In this version of collective security, the world did not need to be protected from aviation, but rather aviatrixes joined together to protect communities and pilots alike. Cooperation between women flyers would, in McQueen's words, "make a chain of air guardians around the world."[80]

And the initials of McQueen's air force were to be S.S. for "Secret Service."[81] The aesthetic that McQueen promoted in various publicity shots of herself, clad in leather and posing with pistol, certainly echoed that of fascist Italy and Germany, but there is no evidence that McQueen expressed sympathy with the rising politics of the European right. Neither is there evidence that she held anti-interventionist views or was sympathetic with the anti-war America First Committee, in the manner of Charles Lindbergh.[82] By 1935 Lady Drummond-Hay was warning McQueen that fear of war in the air was "rampant everywhere in Europe" and that everything was geared toward the military with few active women flyers.[83] These international tensions spilled over into the WIAA when its most prominent German member, Thea Rasche, visited McQueen in California in 1937. Rasche had been to the United States several times in the 1920s and had taken part in the 1929 "Powder Puff Derby." Rumors had circulated the year before in the American and international press that she had been executed by the Nazis for being a Soviet spy and Rasche spent much of her time in the United States in 1937 proving otherwise, whilst also championing the cause of peace. After the war Rasche admitted she had joined the Nazi party in 1933 and also the National Socialist Flyers Corps, but she also claimed her books had been forbidden by the Nazis because she "glorified the Anglo-American sporting spirit and fair play."[84] As the clouds of another war began to close in on Europe at the end of the decade, the WIAA and its members struggled to maintain both their activities and their internationalist aviation rhetoric. "I am afraid [the WIAA] is not so International at the moment, as far as Europe is concerned," was how Lady Drummond-Hay put it in 1940.[85]

---

[80] Elizabeth McQueen, "Winged Ladies," October 31, 1933 [Radio transcript], Box 2/Folder 2, USC 55.

[81] "Women's Aerial Police/'Goodwill Air Tour,'" n.d., Box 2/Folder 6, USC 55.

[82] Lynne Olson, *Those Angry Days: Roosevelt, Lindbergh, and America's Fight Over World War II, 1939–1941* (New York: Random House, 2013).

[83] Drummond-Hay, "Lady Hay Drummond-Hay to McQueen," June 13, 1935.

[84] "Germans Clear Flying Fraulein," *Los Angeles Times*, May 24, 1947, Box 5/Folder 2, USC 55.

[85] Hay Drummond-Hay, "Lady Hay Drummond-Hay to McQueen," May 27, 1940, Box 5/Folder 2, USC 55.

In these changing geopolitical conditions, McQueen turned her attention to a new strategic international alliance that made her once again a pseudo-diplomatic agent of the state. Sponsored by Pan American Airlines, in 1940 she undertook a ten-month "Good Will Tour" throughout Mexico, Central and South America. Throughout this trip she gave talks on radio, was written about in the newspapers, and met with officials at high levels, including United States Ambassadors, national Presidents and their wives, and leaders of the Pan American Union. At the close of this trip she submitted a Confidential Report to the Federal Bureau of Investigation, reporting on the presence of Germans in the various republics and recommending building airports to help further US interests.[86] In doing so she may have thought she was serving the cause of international air-mindedness by advancing Roosevelt's "Good Neighbor" policy. But, carried by Pan American Airlines, she was also expanding the commercial reach of American capital and consolidating an emerging geopolitical order that would only become more important as the Cold War emerged. Although her writings from the 1940s continued to place emphasis on the power of "spiritual forces" to "save the World," they increasingly underlined her commitment to American military power.[87] The "atomic bomb in the hands of Uncle Sam will guarantee sufficient protection to the people of our country," she told her members.[88] Aviation, in McQueen's emphasis, was now couched as a "defense against invasion."[89] If in 1919 it had been the Anglo-American peoples and the British Empire that would usher in a new millennium of peace, in 1949 the United States alone could keep the world safe. She encouraged her members to report subversive communist activities to the police and to the Federal Bureau of Investigation.[90] After McQueen's death in 1958, her followers attempted to keep alive her memory, bringing into print some of her unpublished writings, but the fire had gone out of the organization and without its leader, it soon dissolved.

Conclusion

Was McQueen an international thinker? Some intellectual historians might not think so, seeing her as insufficiently "serious" and more of

[86] Elizabeth McQueen, "Confidential Report," 1941, Box 2/Folder 5: McQueen speeches articles, USC 55.
[87] Elizabeth McQueen, "From McQueen to Miss Mary Pickford, President WIAA," November 4, 1948, Box 1/Folder 2, USC 55.
[88] Elizabeth McQueen, "Why Communism in America!," October 16, 1950, Box 2/Folder 2 – Radio talks speeches, USC 55.
[89] WIAA, "WIAA Inc. Literary Contest," 1949, Box 9, USC 55.
[90] McQueen, "Why Communism in America!"

an activist than an intellectual. Yet those who were organizing the nascent discipline of International Relations on the West Coast of the United States in the 1930s saw McQueen as sufficiently legitimate to be invited to their meetings. Insisting on women's equality in the air, her notion of international peace through air-minded thinking tapped into contemporary cultural currents that were widely popular. It combined the modernist technologies of the interwar period – flying, film, and the airwaves – with well-established practices of female sociability, artistic expression, and religious subjectivity, and united an older focus on communication and trade as a force for peace with an emphasis on the transformative effects of individual experience and individual thought borrowed from Christian Science.

The aviation industry's need to "domesticate" the sky in the late 1920s opened opportunities for women but it also circumscribed the roles they were allowed to play: although they were welcomed as flying saleswomen, they were not wanted around the hangers nor as commercial flyers.[91] Once the aviation industry was secure, their place in the air was swiftly marked off as stewardesses, not as pilots.[92] McQueen came from, drew on, and reimagined for an interwar American society encountering the technologies of modernity, a Christian Science spiritual milieu in which women *did* have ways of claiming status and power. Her philosophy was attractive to so many women precisely because through it they were able to think and to lead.

McQueen's approach was both distinctive and much more mainstream than it now seems. Although she might not fit the traditional description of an intellectual, she was very interested in *thinking* as itself a mechanism of change. What reaches our thoughts, McQueen believed, shapes the world. This is a version of global thinking on an intimate and individual scale. If it now seems strange to historians of international thought, that is the very reason they should engage with it. After all, this same philosophy lay behind the *Christian Science Monitor* – a paper which gave prominence to international affairs and articles from which are frequently cited in studies on the history of internationalism. Founded in 1908 by Mary Baker Eddy, it was intended not just as a counter to criticism of her ideas published in the sensationalist yellow journalism of the turn of the century, but also as a means to *counter the fear* spread by the mass media. "Through our paper," Eddy wrote, "we shall be able to reach many homes with healing, purifying thought."[93]

---

[91] Corn, *The Winged Gospel*, 88.   [92] Corn, *The Winged Gospel*, 77–89.
[93] Mary Baker Eddy quoted in Linda K. Fuller, *The Christian Science Monitor: An Evolving Experiment in Journalism* (Santa Barbara, CA: Praeger, 2011), 50.

McQueen's thinking about aviation and internationalism was neither conventional nor conventionally expressed. It is found, not in published but neglected books, nor in unpublished doctoral theses, but in the newsletters of the WIAA, magazine articles, personal correspondence, and radio transcripts. These sources in turn point to the other, more intangible sites of her intellectual production – the social gatherings and fireside conversations in which she elaborated her philosophy and worked her personal charm. They are not usual sources for the history of international thought. But uncovering them is rewarding because it points to the complexity and diversity of international thinking in the period before university-based American International Relations was consolidated as a discipline. They force historians of international thought to examine how what counts as "serious" thought is itself a historically constituted – and gendered – category.

Elizabeth Lippincott McQueen was working at a time and in a place when the boundaries not just of the discipline of IR, but also of aeronautics, and of spirituality as well, were porous and still in formation. Indeed in 1930s Southern California they were sufficiently accommodating, to allow for her brand of Anglo-American millenarianism and spiritual aviation to sit alongside other currents of thought that have made it into the post-1945 pantheon. She should be considered in a volume on the history of women's international thinking precisely because she falls outside what the discipline has learned to recognize as its past. Attending to McQueen's life and work forces historians of international thought to consider the changing politics of knowledge that has led International Relations in the post-World War II era, not so much to forget, but to erase and exclude these more complex – and perhaps now embarrassing – family members.

6 Women of the Twenty Years' Crisis: The Women's International League for Peace and Freedom and the Problem of Collective Security

Lucian M. Ashworth

The early history of women in International Relations (IR) has been rendered invisible by the changes in IR after 1950. The complexities of interwar IR served little purpose for the new predominantly American university-based field that emerged after World War II.[1] Some names, such as Shotwell, Angell, or Cecil, survived as examples of the wrong path taken in 1919, but the overwhelming number of interwar writers dropped out of IR's consciousness. This included the group of women scholars and activists that had emerged out of the suffrage movement from before World War I, many of whom identified as feminists.

The campaign for women's right to vote stimulated interest in international affairs for two reasons. First, as newly enfranchised voters many women, such as Helena Swanwick, saw their involvement in public affairs as the next logical step.[2] Second, many also saw a direct link between the right to vote in domestic politics and the campaign for a more peaceful order globally.[3] If militaristic societies were hostile to women it followed that women's suffrage would come under threat from a more violent world. Much (but not all) of the work of interwar women international experts was channeled and supported by their membership of the influential Women's International League for Peace and Freedom (WILPF), established after World War I out of existing women's peace organizations in several countries.

---

[1] Nicholas Guilhot, "The Realist Gambit: Postwar American Political Science and the Birth of IR Theory," *International Political Sociology* 2 (2008): 281–304.

[2] See Lucian M. Ashworth, "Feminism, War and the Prospects for Peace: Helena Swanwick (1864–1939) and the Lost Feminists of Inter-War International Relations," *International Feminist Journal of Politics* 13.1 (2011): 25–43. For the link between suffrage and peace in the United States see Harriet Hyman Alonso, *Peace as a Women's Issue* (Syracuse University Press, 1993), 85.

[3] Beryl Haslam, *From Suffrage to Internationalism* (New York: Peter Lang, 1999); Jo Vellacott, *Pacifists, Patriots and the Vote* (Basingstoke: Palgrave Macmillan, 2007); Ashworth, "Feminism, War and the Prospects for Peace."

The purpose of this chapter is to explore the approaches taken to international order and collective security by a group of women writers and activists in the interwar period. Combining maternalist feminism (see below), pacifism, and an analysis of international affairs, these writer-activists form an important part of the story of interwar IR. Three of these women, Emily Greene Balch, Helena Swanwick, and Vera Brittain, held senior roles in WILPF, while a fourth, Mary Agnes Hamilton, moved in the same political circles. I argue that the organization of WILPF in the years after World War I acted as a mobilizer of a specific leftist and feminist approach to international affairs that built on both pre-war suffrage organizations (especially in the United States and British Empire) and the momentum of the 1915 international Women's Peace Conference in The Hague. The early organization of WILPF focused discussions on weaknesses in the emerging post-war order, but it also led to direct engagement with the League of Nations, which regularized cooperation with WILPF. Consequently, the nature and role of the League became a central topic for many of the women writers associated with WILPF, especially senior members with regular contacts with the League such as Balch and Swanwick.

Yet, this common focus on the League's role in peace and security led to disagreements on outcomes. Balch and Swanwick in particular remained opposed to League collective security, while other feminist writers at the time, such as Swanwick's colleague on the British delegation to the League in 1929 Mary Agnes Hamilton, remained strongly supportive of collective security. Brittain, on the other hand, moved from supporting collective security to avoiding war at any price. This split came to a head after a series of crises in the 1930s. It then continued into the late 1930s, where the arguments against collective security were often marshaled in support of appeasement of Nazi Germany, and pro-collective security positions were retooled into arguments for collective defense against fascism. This part of the story also underscores the role played by women's voices in the appeasement debates.

Underlying this is my argument that the intellectual output of these writers and activists can only be fully appreciated by understanding two points. First is the role played by institutions. Here WILPF was the conduit in which earlier suffragist and pacifist ideas were directed toward discussions of the role of the League and its place in the refashioning of a pacific world order. Second is how these ideas were framed and molded by the rapid development of events after 1931. Thus, in order to understand this particular episode in the history of women's international thought the story needs to be told within the context of both WILPF and appeasement. Consequently, the first section of the chapter will deal with WILPF and how WILPF framed the debate on international order amongst a key segment of women. The second section will explore the approach to international order inspired by WILPF, and how it confronted the question of League collective security. Since collective security is a more recent term, I will use the more contemporary phrase "pooled security." The third section outlines how appeasement and the crisis of the late 1930s influenced and channeled the ideas explored in the previous section. In the conclusion, I discuss the implications of this story for both the history of international thought and the disciplinary history of IR.

The Women's International League for Peace and Freedom

WILPF is a non-governmental organization founded in 1919 that spans the globe.[4] Perhaps its major contribution to interwar international thought was that "it nurtured a new contingent of women researchers and experts in international questions."[5] Thus, it played a major role in forming and propagating the feminist international thought of Swanwick, Balch, Brittain, and Hamilton. By 1922, WILPF presented itself as a broadly-based and international women's organization dedicated to creating a just and peaceful world order. The work of WILPF boiled down to three areas: peace education by the national affiliates; liaising with various League bodies in Geneva on issues relevant to women and peace; and involvement in humanitarian relief efforts that were seen as mitigating long-term causes of war.

WILPF was a confederal organization. There was an international office based in Geneva, and initially headed by Balch, but there were also national WILPF associations. The international branch of WILPF began life as the International Committee of Women for Permanent Peace (ICWPP), which formed after the 1915 Congress of Women in The Hague, with the American social reformer and public intellectual Jane Addams as its first president. After 1919 the international section of WILPF increasingly took on an important role through its coordination of the national societies and its cooperation with the League.

Although deliberately designed as a broad set of organizations open to a wide spectrum of peace activists and advocates of women's rights, the

---

[4] Catia Confortini, *Intelligent Compassion: Feminist Critical Methodology in the Women's International League for Peace and Freedom* (Oxford University Press, 2012).

[5] Julie Gottlieb, *Guilty Women, Foreign Policy, and Appeasement in Inter-War Britain* (Basingstoke: Palgrave Macmillan, 2015), 25.

various WILPF organizations developed an ethos and a common set of priorities in its first few years of organization and consolidation. This was put into words in the 1923 Manifesto that emerged from the Dresden Conference. Here both war and imperialism were condemned for the suffering that they brought to ordinary people, and while not ruling out cooperation with governments, WILPF laid out its main task as organizing those who were or would be victimized by war.[6] WILPF was both an organization of women who were likely to suffer in the event of a war, and an organization dedicated to bringing assistance to those who already suffered. Thus, the education and humanitarian work carried out by WILPF represented two sides of the same coin.

It was also an organization of women. Underlying it was the maternalist feminist view that women had a perspective on political and social questions that was different, but equally valid, to that of men. As the givers of life and the predominant nurturers in society women had a powerful reason to oppose war's role of taking life. As Addams told the third WILPF Conference, wars destroy what mothers create.[7] War in Addams' work was contrasted with nurturing and welfare, and this was a theme that would be repeated in the work of Swanwick, Balch, Brittain, and Hamilton. For human society to survive modern war it was necessary to replace war with welfare, and women's experience of nurturing gave them an advantage over most men in understanding both the dangers of war and the possibilities offered by its opposite.[8] This also helps explain the link between WILPF's humanitarian work and its pacifism. Since nurturing was the opposite to war, WILPF's humanitarian work in postwar Vienna and Anatolia represented a positive and direct alternative to war.

WILPF, and its prominent alumni Balch, Swanwick, and Brittain would frequently evoke the unique role and viewpoint of women to great effect in their public arguments on international matters. Indeed, there was a specific feminist ethos behind WILPF that developed out of women's role in reproduction, accentuated by the structures of a society dominated by men. At one level this was a maternalist feminist argument that claimed that women had a different view on society due to

---

[6] WIL, *Women's International League* 11.6 (October), 2.1923, p. 2.

[7] WIL, Jane Addams' opening speech July 10, 1921 to the Third International Conference of the WIL, WILPF UK Branch Archives, British Library of Political and Economic Sciences, LSE, London. Box 4/5.

[8] Linda K. Schott, *Reconstructing Women's Thoughts: The Women's International League for Peace and Freedom before World War II* (Stanford University Press, 1997), 11–27; Julia Gottlieb, "The Women's Movement Took the Wrong Turn: British Feminists, Pacifism and the Politics of Appeasement," *Women's History Review* 23.3 (2014), 442–43.

physical differences. At the same time, though, this maternalism was tempered by the view that the structures of society exacerbated and often formed a negative view of women. Moreover, as discussed in more detail below, it was shaped by a liberal and socialist feminism that saw the ultimate goal being a society where women and men would be treated equally regardless of physical differences.

There was also an underlying socialist element to WILPF. The Dresden Manifesto singled out both victims of war and of capitalism, while a report on the Zurich Congress to the British branch made it clear that the rapporteurs considered their organization to be both feminist and socialist.[9] Similarly, some members of the French and German branches were even committed to overthrowing capitalism by force.[10] Anti-imperialism was also a common occurring principle in early WILPF conferences, and the Dresden Manifesto of 1923 explicitly condemned imperialism.[11] Race was discussed within the context of imperialism, and while individual attitudes were often condescending, opposition to racist policies such as the mistreatment of colonial troops was genuine.[12] Race proved a more equivocal issue in WILPF's US affiliate, where racism was condemned at its 1920 Chicago meeting, but WILPF US' roots in the suffrage movement left it with links to racism in the South.[13]

Initially, WILPF often took up a position that was critical and antagonistic both to the 1919 Peace Treaties and to the League of Nations, despite early decisions by Jane Addams and the 1919 Zurich Congress of WILPF to cooperate with the institutions of the League.[14] As late as the 1923 UK General Election the British branch was still prioritizing the "immediate drastic" revision of the treaties.[15] Catherine Marshall took a more conciliatory position in her report to the British Section on the first session of the League (1920–21). While the League Council – dominated by the cabinets of the great powers and representing the discredited old

---

[9] WIL, Report on Zurich Congress, 1919, WILPF UK Branch Archives. Box 4/3.

[10] Josephine Elgin, "Women Pacifists in Interwar Britain," in Peter Brock and Thomas P. Socknat (eds.), *Challenge to Mars: Essays on Pacifism from 1918 to 1945* (University of Toronto Press,1999), 149–68 (153).

[11] WIL, "Manifesto," *Women's International League*, October 1923, 6(XI), 2. See also the discussion in Jan Stöckmann, "Women, Wars, and World Affairs: Recovering Feminist International Relations, 1915–39," *Review of International Studies* 44.2 (2017): 215–35.

[12] See for example, Emily Green Balch's statement on colonial troops sent to Catherine Marshall (1921?), WILPF UK Branch Archives. Box 4/5.

[13] Alonso, *Peace as a Women's Issue*, 90, 101–102.

[14] See Molly Cochran, "The 'Newer' Ideals of Jane Addams's Progressivism: A Realistic Utopia of Cosmopolitan Justice," in Molly Cochran and Cornelia Navari (eds), *Progressivism and US Foreign Policy between the World Wars* (New York: Palgrave Macmillan, 2017), 156–57.

[15] WIL, "Questions to Candidates," 1923, WILPF UK Branch Archives. Box 4/3.

order – was written off as a potential partner, she saw hope in the Assembly as it represented all governments (although Marshall did not mention that out of the various colonial governments only India was formally represented). "The important fact is," she pointed out, "that the League of Nations does as a matter of fact exist, and no other working political organisation does internationally." Therefore, if WILPF was to fulfill its mandate, then working with the League was a pragmatic necessity.[16]

Added to this was the fact that the League environment proved to be more open to women than the old pre-war diplomacy, in no small measure thanks to the lobbying by WILPF and other women's organizations.[17] The Covenant, for example, guaranteed that League positions would be open to women and men equally (Art. VII), and women's representation to the League was significant by the standards of the day. Many professional women, such as the Canadian diplomat and international civil servant Mary Craig McGeachy, cut their professional teeth in the League,[18] while in 1929 the five-person British delegation to the League included two prominent women (Swanwick and Mary Agnes Hamilton). Cooperation between WILPF and the League was managed formally through the League's Liaison Committee of Women's Organizations that regularized cooperation between the formal League structure and organizations such as WILPF. At the Disarmament Conference of 1932–33 WILPF was given official status, while in 1937 the League established a Committee of Experts on the Legal Status of Women.[19]

While WILPF cooperated with the League, this did not mean that there was agreement over one of the thorniest issues of the League's international policy: pooled security. Some of the major figures in WILPF remained implacably opposed to the idea of what Swanwick called "League Wars." Indeed, Balch and Swanwick's view that war needed to be replaced with welfare led to an ambivalent relationship with the League. While they supported its "good offices," they opposed its threat to use force. That said, WILPF offered a home for all internationalist women, and many of its members also supported League pooled

---

[16] WIL, "CEM's report on first session of the LoN," 1921, pp. 7 WILPF UK Branch Archives. Box 4/6.

[17] United Nations, "Women and Global Diplomacy: From Peace Movements to the United Nations: The League of Nations," https://libraryresources.unog.ch/womendiplomacy/leagueofnations.

[18] See the discussion of her career in Mary Agnes Hamilton, *Remembering My Good Friends* (London: Jonathan Cape, 1944), 190–91.

[19] For more on the League and women's organizations see Carol Miller, *Lobbying the League: Women's International Organizations and the League of Nations* (Oxford University Press, 1992).

security. Indeed, many of the members of WILPF in the first two decades after the Hague Conference of 1915, among them Vera Brittain, were perfectly happy to consider themselves both pacifists opposed to war and supporters of pooled security. In the colder climate of the second half of the 1930s this position became untenable, but in the 1920s there was no pressure to choose between peace and security.

In WILPF this situation was manifest in two different ways. At the level of international policy there was the tension between opposition to war and League pooled security (where the latter might require "League Wars" to oppose aggression). At the level of core values pacifism could potentially find itself at odds with justice and freedom if a future aggressor was not deterred by the machinery of the League. In order to contextualize the disputes over war and pooled security, though, it is first necessary to explore what was meant by League pooled security in order to understand the major disagreements within WILPF over the place of pacifism in the League.

6.1 Vera Brittain at University.
Courtesy of McMaster University/Vera Brittain Estate

6.2 Mary Agnes Hamilton. Public domain.

WILPF Women and the Problems of Pooled Security

Engagement with the League in the interests of peace brought senior WILPF members into direct contact with the debates about the nature of pooled security.[20] The intellectual maelstrom of the war years that had produced WILPF was also responsible for a widespread rejection of the great power dominated balance of power that was seen by many international experts as the main cause of the war. In Balch's words, this failure of the pre-war order made necessary "the creation of the machinery of peace – a League of Nations with the most effective arrangements for settling differences peaceably."[21] While Brittain and Hamilton were

---

[20] While the term collective security is better known today, this was not so in the interwar period. See B. J. C. McKercher, "The League of Nations and the Problem of Collective Security 1919–1939," in United Nations (ed.), *The League of Nations 1920–1946* (New York and Geneva: United Nations, 1996), 70.

[21] Emily Greene Balch, "The Habit of Peace," *McCall's Magazine*, February 1919.

supportive of this machinery, the problem for Balch and Swanwick was that the machinery for security that the League began to build in the 1920s still relied on the threat of war.

There were three essential elements to League pooled security. These were: an effective and workable system of arbitration between states; a properly functioning system of sanctions to make the arbitration system believable; and widespread disarmament to lessen the effectiveness and promise of aggressive war. Arbitration–sanctions–disarmament were seen as supporting each other. If, however, one of these three proved ineffective, then the viability of the other two would be called into question. The initial problem, however, was that the Covenant remained vague on how states were to deal with aggression, and advocates of pooled security in the 1920s spent much of their time trying to "close the gaps" in the Covenant by working for tighter legal rules.[22]

By the 1920s there was already a history of successful arbitration on a bilateral basis, and the machinery existed for the settlement of simple judicial disputes in the Permanent Court of International Justice.[23] It was, however, recognized that no arbitration regime would be fully workable without a system of internationally agreed sanctions that could prevent states opting out. Drawing an analogy from domestic politics, Mary Agnes Hamilton argued that all successful legal systems required the threat of coercive action, while Vera Brittain (before her rejection of pooled security) saw the choice being between national and international control of armaments.[24] Discussions of sanctions were tempered by a realization that, while necessary, there was strong opposition from the publics and governments in many states to the use of military force. Overt support for military sanctions, such as the robust advocacy of military action in support of pooled security found in the writings of independent UK MP Eleanor Rathbone, was rare among public figures.[25] Indeed, these political problems led to the disappearance of

---

[22] See Lucian M. Ashworth, *International Relations and the Labour Party: Intellectuals and Policy Making 1918–1945* (London: I. B. Tauris, 2007), 96–97.

[23] William Arnold Forster, "Commentary on the British Government's Observations to the League, on Arbitration and Security," Advisory Committee on International Questions memo no. 386, February 1928. Labour Party Archives, Labour History Archive and Study Centre, Manchester, UK.

[24] Mary Agnes Hamilton, "No Peace Apart from International Security: An Answer to Extreme Pacifists," in Storm Jameson (ed.), *Challenge to Death* (London: Constable, 1934), 271; Vera Brittain, "Peace and the Public Mind," in Jameson (ed.), *Challenge to Death*, 55. See also Hugh Dalton, *Towards the Peace of Nations: A Study in International Politics* (London: Routledge & Kegan Paul, 1928), 211; David Mitrany, *The Problem of International Sanctions* (London: Humphrey Milford & Oxford University Press, 1925), 2.

[25] Eleanor F. Rathbone, *War Can Be Averted* (London: Victor Gollancz, 1938).

sanctions from UK Labour Party literature.[26] Yet, France and many of the minor powers saw a strict sanctions regime under the League guaranteed by all the major powers as a precondition for the establishment of a disarmament regime under League auspices. Interestingly, this position was close to that held by Merze Tate, discussed elsewhere in this volume, who saw disarmament as only possible once conflict had been reduced.[27] Disarmament in this context referred to a reduction of arms to a level consistent with League membership, which still allowed states to deter aggression. Advocates and critics of pooled security alike were well aware that armaments and arms races could exacerbate tensions by breeding insecurity. Or, as Balch had put it in 1927, "military preparedness is a language as well as a physical fact. One thing that it says is, 'I am seriously considering the possibility of going to war'."[28] Disarmament agreements could help ease tensions, as well as saving money. Thus disarmament, by making aggressive war less likely, would reinforce arbitration, while arbitration needed to be guaranteed by sanctions that would, in turn, allow for states to have confidence in a common disarmament regime.

The argument for the achievement of a pooled security system based on arbitration, sanctions, and disarmament rested on the successful implementation of all three elements. It also relied on the idea that members of the League would enter into legally binding agreements that would then be adhered to by states, and that military sanctions would be different to war. It was this that Balch and Swanwick saw as the Achilles' heel of the pooled security argument.

For Balch and Swanwick, opposition to pooled security came from their pacifism and feminism. Much of the institutional organization and intellectual roots of this early feminist approach to the study of international affairs came from the experiences of the suffrage movements and their interaction with the shock of World War I.[29] For Swanwick, the act of working for peace at the international level was seen as a logical corollary to working for women's suffrage and equal rights at the national level.[30] During the pre-war agitation for women's suffrage a common argument against women's participation in politics was that women lacked the physical strength to defend their country. The equally common counter-argument to this was to state that physical force in

---

[26] James Ramsay MacDonald, *Protocol or Pact? The Alternative to War* (London: Labour Party, 1925), 5.

[27] Merze Tate, *The Disarmament Illusion* (New York: Macmillan, 1942), 346.

[28] Emily Greene Balch, "The Myth of Military Security," *The World Tomorrow*, December 1927, 497.

[29] Vellacott, *Pacifists, Patriots and the Vote.*

[30] See her influential *Women and War* (London: Union of Democratic Control, 1915).

the form of violence was an outdated idea inconsistent with the growth of a civilized society.[31] Balch and Swanwick came to their position through a feminist analysis and critique of gendered roles in society. Swanwick argued that militarism, caused by the threat of war and international violence, gave support to the barbaric view that pugnacious physical force was the basis of political participation. It undervalued women's "physical force" in the form of giving life.[32] It followed, therefore, that the decline of warfare internationally would also lead to the decline of the argument against women's active participation in politics.[33] In addition, because it was presumed that women lacked the opportunity to engage in the adventures of war, but suffered unduly during wartime, Balch argued that their interests in the elimination of war were stronger than men's.[34] Important here was a mix of a maternalist gender essentialism with the argument that society exacerbated physical differences by devaluing women.

Underlying this was a feminist position that mixed both liberal/socialist feminist concerns about the rational equality of women, and a maternalist feminist conception that saw women's particular place in society as the source of a valuable and different perspective to the problem of international order. It "is natural" wrote Balch in 1922, "that the half of mankind ... which has always had the responsibility for the Children and the suffering of the weak should be especially ready to make sacrifices on behalf of peace."[35] The giving of life lent a different perspective to women on the issue of war, as Mary Agnes Hamilton suggested by beginning her contribution to the 1934 anthology *Challenge to Death* with an account of one mother's worries about her children in the light of recent war scares.[36] For Vera Brittain, in the same collection, women might be just as susceptible to "the shining martial figure of patriotism," but their particular role in society gave them the potential to take a very different line from men, while in "masculine minds there is often a confused identification of virility with the possession and use of weapons."[37]

Thus, women's differences, both physical and social, offered a fresh perspective on the problem of war, while the eradication of war was linked to the creation of a world in which women and men would be

---

[31] Helena Swanwick, *The Future of the Women's Movement* (London: Bell, 1913), 35–36.
[32] Swanwick, *Future of the Women's Movement*, 38.   [33] Swanwick, *Women and War*, 11.
[34] Emily Greene Balch, "Women's Work for Peace," *The World Tomorrow*, November 1922, 334–36; Swanwick, *Women and War*, 336.
[35] Balch, "Women's Work for Peace," 336.
[36] Hamilton, "No Peace Apart from International Security," 261–63.
[37] Brittain, "Peace and the Public Mind," 58.

equally treated. From this, two lines of development in the search for a stable peaceful order emerged: first, the creation of a formal "machinery of peace" via organizations like the League; and second a deeper change of psychology that would lead to a greater respect for peace.[38] The splits between feminists usually revolved around the interpretation of what the role of this machinery should be, and on the question of how much they should rely on changes in psychology as the main source of a peaceful world. Underlying these arguments, and what made them a debate between feminists, was the view that the eradication of war was an essential part of the creation of a society in which men and women were equally treated. The divisions were over how best to achieve this goal.

The first point of disagreement between advocates of pooled security, such as Hamilton and (before 1936) Vera Brittain, and many stricter pacifists, such as Balch and Swanwick, was on the difference between policing and military violence (an issue that still dogs humanitarian intervention today). While pooled security's supporters hoped that military sanctions would not prove necessary in any test of the League system, pooled security did rely ultimately on the use or threat of the use of force against an intransigent aggressor. Supporters of pooled security drew a distinction between the use of force in the service of a state's interest and the use of force under pooled security. Since in the latter case the military would be used in order to preserve a common global order (and to prevent violence) this amounted to a policing role, similar in character to the tasks performed by the police in domestic politics.[39] Both Swanwick and Balch contested this association of domestic policing and military sanctions, and Balch was particularly resistant to the idea, mooted by many pooled security supporters, including Hamilton, of an international League air force to act in a policing role.[40] "I understand by police force," Balch told the Women's International League Congress in Grenoble, "something absolutely unlike fire, explosives and gas, rained from the air."[41]

---

[38] Balch, "The Habit of Peace." The popularity of psychology at the time owed much to Virginia and Leonard Woolf, who had introduced the English-speaking world to the works of Freud.

[39] Norman Angell, *Peace Theories and the Balkan War* (London: Horace Marshall, 1912), 16–17, 21, 47–49.

[40] Hamilton, "No Peace Apart from International Security"; Philip Noel-Baker, "The International Air Police Force," in Jameson (ed.), *Challenge to Death*. This idea of a global air force in the service of peace appears in H. G. Wells' 1930s science fiction. On the hope that aviation could be used to further peace see Tamson Pietsch's chapter in this volume.

[41] Emily Greene Balch, "The Relation of Civil Aviation to Disarmament," Speech to the WIL Congress at Grenoble, April 24, 1932. Emily Greene Balch papers, Wellesley College, Massachusetts, Series III reel 22.

The problem, as Swanwick pointed out, was that armed forces involved in a "League War" would behave little differently from an invading military.[42]

Swanwick added two further points. First, she was convinced that the states involved in a "League War" would use their involvement to advance their own selfish interests.[43] Second, the tendency of pooled security to make every dispute between states an issue affecting the whole system would mean an escalation of all conflicts into a great power matter in the same way that the alliance systems of 1914 turned every small dispute into a dangerous system-wide confrontation.[44] Thus, Swanwick and Balch were particularly critical of the pooled security advocates' use of the domestic analogy. For them the nature of war in a system without an overall authority could not compare to the use of coercive force by the police. "League Wars" amounted to a return to a society based on men's physical force.

Yet, it was not just the issue of the policing analogy that troubled Swanwick. She also regarded pooled security as fundamentally naïve in its reliance on legal documents and the words of states. From Swanwick's point of view states had been breaking legal commitments for centuries; closing the gaps in the Covenant would not change this.[45] Swanwick argued that pooled security had been most effective when dealing with the infractions of small states, but she doubted whether the League would be willing to bring military sanctions against a great power.[46] The Covenant, rather than being a piece of unfinished business in need of further legal tightening, represented a compromise on how far states were willing to go to enforce global order.[47] Indeed, the legalistic approach was actually a threat to League credibility, she argued. By threatening sanctions, but being unable to follow through on that threat, the League system would be undermined, and the other good offices and work of the League would be tainted by the failure to impose legal rules.[48]

Disagreement within feminist ranks on this view of policing and legal guarantees in pooled security came from Mary Agnes Hamilton. While Hamilton did not address the problem of the analogy outlined by

---

[42] Helena Swanwick *New Wars for Old* (London: Women's International League, 1934), 23–24; Helena Swanwick, *Collective Insecurity* (London: Jonathan Cape, 1937), 230–31.
[43] Swanwick, *Collective Insecurity*, 89–90.
[44] Helena Swanwick and William Arnold-Forster, *Sanctions of the League of Nations Covenant* (London: London Council for Prevention of War, 1928), 22.
[45] Swanwick, *Collective Insecurity*, 19–20.   [46] Swanwick, *New Wars for Old*, 6–7.
[47] Swanwick, *New Wars for Old*, 16.
[48] Helena Swanwick, *I Have Been Young* (London: Victor Gollancz, 1935), 268.

Balch and Swanwick, she did tackle the question of the role of coercive force in all forms of society, and its relationship to military sanctions. For Hamilton, coercion was at the root of all systems for maintaining security. Even the law and the police in domestic politics rested ultimately on the threat of force. What distinguished domestic policing from international war, she argued, was that domestic policing rested on the consent and cooperation of the wider society, while war did not.[49] For Hamilton, the solution to international security was the ultimate development of a global system of security based upon the consent of both states and their peoples. This could only be accomplished if states gave up their sovereign rights to act alone and agreed to a system of pooled security. Once this order is established, consent of the community can grow.[50] In 1934, Hamilton was supported in this position by Vera Brittain. However, given Brittain's later opposition to rearmament and war in 1939 we can assume that she saw the machinery of pooled security as primarily a protection against war, rather than, essentially, a threat to wage war.[51] Balch and Swanwick's alternative to pooled security was bound up with the twin track approach to peace pursued by WILPF. That peace required the development of both formal machinery and a change of attitude all could agree. Indeed, Hamilton's argument above assumed that the development of the formal machinery of the League would lead to just such a change of attitude leading to the giving of consent for the idea of international coercion by the League. Balch and Swanwick, though, switched the emphasis, seeing psychological changes as leading. For Balch, the presence of women in political life was itself a big step toward new perspectives in society. "It is only as war in its modern guise reveals itself as a menace to the race," she argued in 1922, "that it begins to occur to people's minds that women's opposition to war may be a precious asset of humanity."[52] Swanwick suggested that the best contribution that the League could make to peace was to begin the slow change of people's attitudes through the use of "its good offices for conciliation and bargaining and compromise; its incomparable Civil Service; its adroitness at saving face."[53] At the base of this was Swanwick's view that the only sure-fire way to eliminate war from

---

[49] Hamilton, "No Peace Apart from International Security," 268–69, 271.
[50] Hamilton, "No Peace Apart from International Security," 269–71.
[51] Brittain, "Peace and the Public Mind," 49; Richard Overy, *The Morbid Age: Britain and the Crisis of Civilzation, 1919–1939* (Harmondsworth: Penguin, 2010), 246–47.
[52] Balch, "Women's Work for Peace," 334.   [53] Swanwick, *New Wars for Old*, 21.

human society was the destruction of that enemy of women and women's participation in politics: the physical force mentality.[54] Thus, it was developments in human psychology, aided by good offices and conciliation, that would be the only effective means of dealing with the problem of war.

It is here that we see a clear split in the maternalist feminist approach to international affairs. While all opposed violence (as physical force) as antithetical to women's position in society, they differed over whether the coercion associated with the pooled security machinery of the League could be regarded as a form of violence. For Swanwick and Balch pooled security would just be war by another name, and therefore violence. Hamilton's view of the machinery was that it was necessary coercion, rather than violence. The alternative to an armed league subject to common consent, for Hamilton, was leaving the arms in the hands of states, which would be a far worse option.[55] For Brittain, improvements in the League machinery, despite its imperfections, was the only defense against anarchy.[56] Thus, while maternalist feminism led all four to oppose violence, they differed over whether or not pooled security entailed violence.

The immediate aftermath of these debates was not a happy one for the position offered up by Balch and Swanwick. While Swanwick's prediction that the inability to impose pooled security on great powers would undermine the League's credibility came true, her hopes that a more psychological approach to the problem would succeed were dashed. Convinced that Nazi aggression was merely a response to Allied bad faith, Swanwick found herself supporting appeasement.[57] Balch, by contrast, eventually moved in the other direction, endorsing economic sanctions and becoming increasingly hostile to American neutrality, despite her strong pacifist convictions.[58] Events proved friendlier to Hamilton's position, but interestingly Brittain's reaction to the appeasement crisis was to move away from pooled security toward an uncompromising pacifist position. The three years before war challenged and unsettled the intellectual lines that had been drawn up in the previous years.

---

[54] Helena Swanwick, *The Roots of Peace* (London: Jonathan Cape 1938), 78–82.
[55] Hamilton, "No Peace Apart from International Security," 272–73.
[56] Brittain, "Peace and the Public Mind," 49.   [57] *Roots of Peace*, 65–75.
[58] Harriet Hyman Alonso, "Nobel Peace Laureates, Jane Addams and Emily Greene Balch: Two Women of the Women's International League for Peace and Freedom," *Journal of Women's History* 7.2 (1995): 6–26 (18–19).

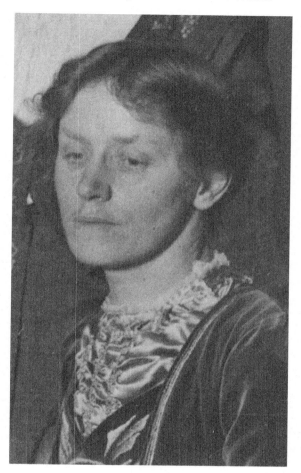

6.3 Helena Swanwick in 1909.
Courtesy of the LSE Women's Library

"I Do Not Want Peace at Any Price"

In the immediate 1936–39 period it was the former advocates of pooled security that carried the day.[59] Their support for collective action transferred easily to arguments in favor of re-armament and democratic collective defense against fascism. Meanwhile Swanwick's long-term

---

[59] The quote in the section heading above is from Maude Royden in 1939, quoted in Gottlieb, "Women's Movement Took the Wrong Turn," 17.

psychological strategy increasingly seemed out of place in the run-up to war. As Leonard Woolf put it in his review of Swanwick's *Collective Insecurity:* "Mrs Swanwick simply stands on dry land and advises a man who cannot swim and is drowning in deep water to hurry home as quickly as possible and take swimming lessons."[60]

To the extent that neither Balch nor Swanwick had a direct answer to the problem of a great power aggressor, Woolf's criticism was valid. Despite the failure of the League powers to use the pooled security machinery of the League of Nations, the advocates of pooled security could fall back on the idea of collective defense amongst the key anti-fascist powers. Indeed, this was the point of Eleanor Rathbone's 1938 book.[61] While it had been quite possible to simultaneously denounce war, the weakness of legal guarantees under pooled security, and injustice throughout the 1920s, the last years of peace often forced pacifists to confront a short-term choice between peace and anti-fascism. This was put into sharper focus by the Nazi government's brutal behavior toward the German Section of WILPF.[62]

The problem lay in how to respond to fascist aggression, especially as many recognized that fascism was now "the greatest threat to the status of women."[63] For Swanwick, this meant falling back on the argument that German aggression was merely the result of German grievances that could be relieved via appeasement.[64] Swanwick's increasing refusal to abandon peace for anti-fascism eventually led her to adopt the role of public apologist for Nazi actions.[65] Here Swanwick's own German heritage, and experience of the anti-German mania during World War I, reinforced her strong pacifism. This led her to see in the attacks on Hitler the same dynamics at play that she had seen in the earlier demonization of the Kaiser.[66]

Hamilton, by contrast, easily made the jump from pooled security to collective defense. For her the years of appeasement from 1936 to early 1939 were troubling times where her dislike of fascism trumped her pacifism. By contrast, Hamilton met the British declaration of war in September 1939 with relief.[67] For Brittain, having made the transition to peace at any price, the experience was the opposite. Refusing to take sides in 1936 over the Spanish Civil War – she argued that whatever the

---

[60] Leonard Woolf, Review of *Collective Insecurity*, *New Statesman*, September 18, 1937, 410.

[61] Rathbone, *War Can Be Averted.*

[62] Catherine Foster, *Women for All Seasons: The Story of the Women's International League for Peace and Freedom* (Athens GA: University of Georgia Press, 1989), 21.

[63] Gottlieb, "Women's Movement Took the Wrong Turn," 9.

[64] Swanwick, *Roots of Peace*, 65–67.   [65] See Gottlieb, *Guilty Women*, 97–98.

[66] Swanwick, *Roots of Peace*, 68.   [67] Hamilton, *Remembering My Good Friends*, 303–305.

issues were, war was always wrong – she was (like Swanwick) bitterly upset over Britain's declaration of war three years later.[68]

There was, however, another way out, and that was to recognize that the late 1930s represented an unusual time that forced people to put longer-term goals aside in order to deal with an emergency. The emergency for WILPF members was that fascist aggression had rendered the otherwise compatible issues of peace and justice temporarily incompatible. The choice was now between anti-fascism and peace. While Swanwick did not take this route, it was a position taken by her erstwhile intellectual ally Emily Greene Balch. While still believing that war was "the worst of public evils," she accepted that nothing could be done "till the barrier of the power of the Hitler regime is swept aside and the door opened so the forces of reason and good can function in Germany."[69] Balch joined other WILPF members, especially many in the UK section such as Maude Royden and Kathleen Courtney, who had made the leap to anti-fascism as war loomed.[70] Despite these individual journeys, both the UK and US branches remained committed to an agenda of peace throughout the crisis years, the only concession being the freedom to allow members to follow their own consciences.[71]

While these aspects of immediate relevance were important in their time, concentration on them alone hides longer-term theoretical issues that are kinder to Balch and Swanwick. Certainly, their criticisms of the policing analogy and of the overly legalistic nature of support for pooled security were relevant points that pre-dated similar criticisms from later critical, postcolonial, classical realist, and English school scholars. At another level, their concentration on longer-term psychological changes were taken up after World War II by scholars such as Karl Deutsch, and vindicated by the practical examples of the pacific union created in Western Europe. Thus, it might be fair to say that while the position taken by Swanwick and Balch had little to offer policy makers in the immediate run-up to war, they had great relevance in the era of post-war reconstruction.[72]

---

[68] Overy, *Morbid Age*, 328, 359.

[69] Quoted in Schott, *Reconstructing Women's Thoughts*, 117.

[70] For further discussion of anti-fascism and women's international thought see Field's chapter on Elizabeth Wiskemann in this volume.

[71] Schott, *Reconstructing Women's Thoughts*, 115ff.; Eglin, "Women Pacifists in Interwar Britain," 163–64 n11; Gottlieb, "Women's Movement Took the Wrong Turn."

[72] For a more detailed exploration of this issue in relation to Swanwick's thought see Ashworth, "Feminism, War and the Prospects for Peace."

Conclusion

In 1948, Merze Tate wrote an assessment of disarmament in US foreign policy that both drew on her own 1942 book on the history of disarmament and on the recent history of the role of disarmament in earlier pooled security. In the context of a world heading toward the Cold War she was critical of the high hopes for arbitration, sanctions, and disarmament displayed in the interwar period. To a certain extent she took on the criticisms of pooled security outlined by Swanwick and Balch, arguing that sovereign states were highly unlikely to submit to controls on their behavior, and advocating changes to behavior (statesmanship) that bore some resemblance to the latters' advocacy of the need for psychological changes for peace.[73] Yet, while Tate was critical of pooled security, her argument came close to elements of the collective defense position advocated by pooled security supporters in the crisis of the late 1930s. Tate backed "co-armament" to maintain peace as an alternative to disarmament,[74] and suggested that (like air power before it) an internationalization of the new atom bomb might provide the basis of an international police force (although in national hands "the bomb" would have the opposite effect).[75] Tate's work on the eve of the Cold War reveals how the Second World War and its aftermath had altered perceptions of international affairs making the pooled security debate of the interwar period moot. That said, Tate's discussion built on concepts developed in the debates over pooled security, and was clearly anchored in the terminology and interpretations of the 1930s. Indeed, her mention of the need for new machinery alongside changes in statesmanship mirrored the concerns of the interwar debates. Additionally, the basis of Tate's assessment is the need to develop collective defense. What had been a temporary measure in troubled times for pooled security advocates was now being presented as the basis for a new post-war world were sovereign states were reconciled with collective action through "co-armament" and "statesmanship" designed to lower the likelihood of war.[76]

Tate was not alone in the form of her argument, and indeed she was praised for her insightfulness by contemporaries such as Morgenthau.[77] The skepticism of the opponents of pooled security were preserved in the new Cold War thinking of British and American IR, but the collective

---

[73] Merze Tate, *The United States and Armaments* (Cambridge, MA: Harvard University Press, 1948), 5–6, 19–20, 23.

[74] Tate, *United States and Armaments*, 11.   [75] Tate, *United States and Armaments*, 13.

[76] Tate, *United States and Armaments*, 23.

[77] Hans J. Morgenthau, Review of Merze Tate's *The Disarmament Illusion* in *Russian Review* 2 (1943): 104–105.

defense policies of the pooled security advocates were equally praised as good foreign policy. This brings us to a broader question on the appraisal of past international thinkers. Do we judge them by their theoretical worth irrespective of the events of their time? If so, then probably the pacifists Swanwick and Balch come out on top over advocates of pooled security. Their criticisms of the legalistic faith that pooled security supporters had in state behavior and the Covenant would inform later postwar approaches to IR, such as Tate's. If we evaluate and interpret the approach of a group of thinkers by how their ideas interacted with contingent policy issues of their time, then the pacifists come off less well in the 1930s, and it is the advocates of pooled security, who shifted over to anti-fascism, that carry the day.

Writers like Swanwick understood the broader trends of international affairs (especially the problem of sovereign states' relationship to legal agreements, and the importance of psychological change to the development of a more stable and peaceful world), but they failed to engage with the specifics of a contingent global crisis after 1936. This boils down to the difference between assessing past thought in terms of its value as ahistorical IR theory, and evaluating how past thought successfully informed immediate policy. IR as a field tends to base its evaluation of past thinkers on the former, rather than the latter (witness how the appeaser E. H. Carr is lionized for his theoretical power). Yet, both assessments of past thinkers are valid. Indeed, given the extent to which women interwar writers on international affairs – especially those that had one foot in the activist world of WILPF – concentrated more on issues relevant to current policy, ignoring their role as public intellectuals discussing immediate problems has exacerbated their erasure from disciplinary history.

Yet, there is more to the erasure of the WILPF women than IR's proclivity to concentrate on theory over policy relevance. This is seen most clearly in the role that Swanwick played in the debates on appeasement. In the latter half of the 1930s Swanwick was a prominent and active supporter of the appeasement policy of the British government. Indeed, by 1939, her commitment to appeasement led to her ideological isolation from many of her colleagues.[78] Despite the prominence of women like Swanwick amongst the advocates of appeasement, the role of women has hardly featured in the history of appeasement, as Gottlieb has made clear.[79] The evocation of the appeasement trope within both IR and popular discourse has focused on the guilty men, but little has been

---

[78] Haslam, *From Suffrage to Internationalism*, p. xxiv.   [79] Gottlieb, *Guilty Women*, 3.

made of how important women were in promoting appeasement policy. Even in the roll-call of the "guilty," it seems, there has been a marginalization of women.

Another feature of the international thought of the interwar WILPF women was their overt reference to their gender as a central part of their claim to be heard on international issues. Given that gender (and masculine superiority) had played a role in an earlier generation of conservative writers on international affairs,[80] the evocation of gender by Swanwick, Balch, Brittain, and Hamilton was a strategic tool that turned an earlier misogynistic tradition on its head, and which in turn justified their inclusion in wider discussions of peace through their representation of women's perspectives. The League's recognition of WILPF's special position was one such example, but it was equally found in the place that these women had within organizations such as The Union for Democratic Control (which published Swanwick's *Women and War*), the British Labour Party (that engaged both Hamilton and Swanwick), and Storm Jameson's relatively gender-balanced collection *Challenge to Death* (which included pieces by Brittain and Hamilton). This evocation of gender as a justification for inclusion in debates on foreign affairs is not present in Merze Tate's work from the 1940s, signaling a change in how gender was perceived in the emerging university-based field of IR.

Perhaps the main contribution of a historical narrative that makes early IR feminism and WILPF's activism visible is not the recreation of their ideas, but in the questioning of the historical narrative that we have been taught in IR since our first introductory undergraduate course. The simplistic myth of the realist–idealist debate assumes a uniformity of non-realist thinkers, and presents realism as the victor of the contest over the intellectual soul of Western policy making. In fact, a deeper analysis of this story reveals the absence of a well-formed and distinct realist position at this time, but a sharp conflict over pooled security that embroiled an internationally-minded feminism as a substantial player. The way that the conflict actually played out contradicts the realist claim that power politics offered the solution to the twenty years' crisis. Rather, the advocates of pooled security (including Hamilton) are the ones who supported (and finally got) confrontation with fascism. Feminists like Swanwick and Balch offered a robust criticism of pooled security that mirrors later realist criticisms, but their position leads not to confrontation with fascism, but to an uneasy support for the policies

---

[80] See the summary in Lucian M. Ashworth, *A History of International Thought* (London: Routledge, 2014), 103–107. See, for example, Brooks Adams, *The Law of Civilization and Decay* (New York: Vintage, 1943 [1896]).

of appeasement. Even here, feminist thought is not united, and Mary Agnes Hamilton shows that it was possible for feminists to take a strong pooled security line.

Equally damaging, the realist–idealist myth also succeeds in writing both feminism and activist women out of the early history of IR, and even reduces the activism of organizations like WILPF to something that exists outside IR. Not only are feminists rendered invisible, but the role for women and feminism in international affairs opened up by the League and WILPF is ignored. The net result of this is that feminism can be presented by non-feminist IR as a recent arrival from "outside" that should only be taken seriously once it can properly learn the "accepted language" and "subject matter" of IR. As a perceived post-1985 "add-on," feminism is rendered marginal. This marginalizing narrative does not survive a closer reading of the policy debates in the interwar period. What emerges instead is the relevance of WILPF as a community of activists and writers that fostered a distinctly feminist approach to international issues, even if their policy prescriptions were often shared by non-feminists who had come to the same conclusions by different routes. Here feminism is shown to be central to the early questions about the nature of the international sphere in the English-speaking world. It is the university-based IR after 1950 that is the newer arrival.

7   Theorizing (with) Amy Ashwood Garvey

Robbie Shilliam

Amy Ashwood Garvey moved hundreds of thousands of people with her ideas and influence. She was an original co-conspirator, with her husband Marcus Garvey, in one of the largest and most remarkable social movements of the twentieth century: the Universal Negro Improvement Association and African Communities League (UNIA). She traveled the globe, creating and sustaining networks of activists, thinkers, and politicians which reached through West Africa, the Caribbean, North America, and Europe. Her relentless initiatives spanned the worlds of entertainment, commerce, politics, social care, domestic economy, and publishing. She fraternized with the high and the low, the famous and the infamous.

An expansive Pan-Africanism framed Amy Ashwood's contribution to Black liberation. Moreover, that a women's contribution could and should be made to the intellectual landscape of Black liberation was one of her core beliefs. At just seventeen years of age, Amy Ashwood publicly debated in Kingston, Jamaica, on the question: "is the intellect of woman as highly developed as that of man's?"[1] In her late forties, toward the end of World War II, she sought to publish an international women's magazine "to bring together the women, especially those of the darker races, so that they may work for the betterment of all."[2] And in 1953, during the early years of the Cold War, Amy Ashwood gave a speech in Trinidad entitled "Women as Leaders of World Thought." The speech challenged the women of the West Indies to raise their political consciousness so that they might "join the great women of the world in writing [their] own history across the pages of world history."[3]

---

[1] Tony Martin, *Amy Ashwood Garvey: Pan-Africanist, Feminist, and Mrs. Marcus Garvey No. 1 or a Tale of Two Amies* (Dover, MA: Majority Press, 2007), 24.
[2] Cited in Hakim Adi, "Amy Ashwood Garvey and the Nigerian Progress Union," in Judith A. Byfield, LaRay Denzer, and Anthea Morrison (eds.), *Gendering the African Diaspora: Women, Culture, and Historical Change in the Caribbean and Nigerian Hinterland* (Bloomington: Indiana University Press, 2010), 212.
[3] Cited in Rhoda Reddock, "Feminism, Nationalism, and the Early Women's Movement in the English-Speaking Caribbean (with Special Reference to Jamaica and Trinidad and Tobago)," in Selwyn Cudjoe (ed.), *Caribbean Women Writers: Essays from the First International Conference* (Wellesley, MA: Calaloux Publications, 1990), 77.

Amy Ashwood considered herself to be one of those thought-leaders. Throughout her life she regularly updated her biography of Marcus and the UNIA. During her many travels she collated (often through "native informants") information on the position of women in West African societies.[4] With this comparative data she planned to publish books with titles such as *Liberia, Land of Promise* as well as a multi-volume series entitled *Mother Africa*, which acknowledged women – especially those of poor rural areas – as "true repositories" of African histories.[5]

But Amy Ashwood's grand publishing designs never materialized. Perhaps the closest she reached to publication success was the preview of her Liberia book written by her friend Sylvia Pankhurst, the famous suffragette, socialist, and Ethiopianist.[6] Otherwise, the book manuscripts are presumed lost; at best, the archives possess only sets of un-edited notes. Few – if any – of her powerful speeches were recorded in detail. What remains in print of her philosophy and opinions are mostly titles, outlines, as well as personal and autobiographical notes. Compound this archaeological paucity with the fact that in life and in death her political and intellectual contributions were refracted through a polyamorous lifestyle, obsession with an ex-husband, at times inventiveness with the truth, indebtedness, and the unsustainability of a host of projects; her funeral in 1969 was attended by just twelve people.[7]

What does it mean to produce international thought? Who is a theorist, and in what location and register does their thought become recognizable as such? These questions are entertained regularly enough in International Relations (IR), at least by its feminist and postcolonial theorists.[8] We should, by now, be acquainted with a series of methodological segregations and excisions by which international thought is rendered as a provincial canon of mostly elite white, European, (dead), men.[9] Indeed, to frame the boundaries of what is recognizably international thought is too often to make vicarious elite white European men out of non-elite non-white non-European non-men. The distorting nature of such an enterprise should be clear enough.

---

[4] Martin, *Amy Ashwood Garvey*, 225.   [5] Martin, *Amy Ashwood Garvey*, 227.
[6] Martin, *Amy Ashwood Garvey*, 241.   [7] Martin, *Amy Ashwood Garvey*, 314.
[8] For example Christine Sylvester, "Editor's Interview," *Journal of Narrative Politics* 2.2 (2016): 91–97; Arlene Beth Tickner and David L Blaney, *Claiming the International* (Abingdon: Routledge, 2013).
[9] For example Robert Vitalis, *White World Order, Black Power Politics: The Birth of American International Relations* (Ithaca, NY: Cornell University Press, 2015); Errol A. Henderson, "The Revolution Will Not Be Theorised: Du Bois, Locke, and the Howard School's Challenge to White Supremacist IR Theory," *Millennium* 45.3 (2017): 492–510.

Amy Ashwood presents a further challenge. How might we reconstruct international thought from only fragments of archives, most of which are not written in a theoretical register recognizable to academics? One might argue that not all political actors should or need be treated as theorists. Still, it is impossible not to discern the contours of Amy Ashwood's intellect upon twentieth-century global politics, especially through her Pan-Africanist circuits. Is it satisfying, then, for this intellect to be lost in the crack between politics and theory, movements and texts? Such challenges are considered by the editors of this volume as they caution against straightforward recoveries of forgotten women, especially when such recoveries reproduce the exclusions and hierarchies congenital to canons of IR theory.

Brittney Cooper argues that the theories of women such as Amy Ashwood need to be retrieved from unexpected places such as autobiographies, medical records, etc.[10] This consideration brings to the fore the salience of "living knowledge traditions."[11] I have mobilized this phrase to argue that theory does not appear only or even mainly in the form of a recognizable text and its author. "Theory" gives too much to written composition; and while theorists might balk at the prospective collapse of their professional wall against, say, ethnography, theorizing is more consequential than writing theory, and living knowledge traditions exceed text. In the context of this chapter, and given Cooper's instruction, I seek these living traditions in the praxis of "race women" – those who in the early twentieth century publicly stood for the uplift of Black peoples.[12]

Theorizing with Amy Ashwood is a journey not only in sketching the contours of an unpublished contribution to international thought. It is also a journey through lives that could never quite be categorized through academic canons due to the fine-grain of relations that wove them into lattices of being and action. Therefore, by theorizing (with) Amy Ashwood, I seek to present her contribution to international thought as a sophisticated critical praxis of Black liberation on a global scale. Specifically, I situate the living knowledge traditions through which she

---

[10] Brittney Cooper, *Beyond Respectability: The Intellectual Thought of Race Women* (Urbana: University of Illinois Press, 2017), 12.

[11] Robbie Shilliam, "Discovering Knowledge Traditions through Co-Creation: Learning from and with Communities," *QMUL Public Engagement* (blog), 2016, www.qmul.ac.uk/publicengagement/blog/2016/items/discovering-knowledge-traditions-through-co-creation-learning-from-and-with-communities.html.

[12] Cooper, *Beyond Respectability*; Imaobong D. Umoren, *Race Women Internationalists: Activist-Intellectuals and Global Freedom Struggles* (Oakland: University of California Press, 2018).

reflected and acted as part of the contested respectability politics that surrounded Black patriarchy. I argue that the distinctive nature of her praxis can be identified in her fractal rather than categorical disposition toward Pan-Africanism. That is, instead of cleaving to a pre-given unitary blackness, Amy Ashwood critically worked through a set of what we would nowadays call oppressive "intersections" of race, class, sex, gender, and nation.

I proceed in two parts. The first part of the chapter lays out the challenge of Black patriarchy at the *fin de siècle* and the ways in which "race women" negotiated its paradoxical entanglement of dependency and liberation through respectability politics. This part gleans Amy Ashwood's life as praxis, and thus as theory-inducing. The second part shows how her pursuit of Black liberation was framed by a critique of respectability politics that gave a fractal disposition to her Pan-Africanism. A fractal disposition does not undertake struggle as something that aspires to create an existential break in affairs; rather, struggle is pursued in recursive terms. A fractal disposition of this kind would be typified by an ever expansive critique of power within power, and an ever expansive pursuit of liberation within liberation.[13] I finish by folding Amy Ashwood's own intellectual trajectory into such a fractal critique of Black liberation and respectability politics.

In making this argument I have marshaled evidence from a number of secondary sources, and mainly from the empirical, conceptual, and methodological contributions of Black women intellectuals. Tony Martin has written probably the most authoritative biography of Amy Ashwood,[14] and I have used his work as my key archive. One of the foremost scholars on Garveyism, Martin's effort is the result of decades of care and careful investigation, archival work and interviews. It is both erudite and judicious, and the narrative undoubtedly gives space for Amy Ashwood to grow as a person and as a political figure. Yet ultimately, as the subtitle of his book suggests (*Pan-Africanist, Feminist and Mrs Marcus Garvey No. 1 or, a Tale of Two Amies*), Martin's Amy Ashwood is a foil to Marcus' grand project. Contra to this framing I have liberally but reasonably imputed a logic into Amy Ashwood's praxis that at the very least cannot be subsumed under her – or anyone else's – obsession with Marcus.

---

[13] I am influenced here by my engagements with Māori cosmology and self-determination struggles, and with Rastafari cosmology and Pan-African struggles; see Ron Eglash, *African Fractals: Modern Computing and Indigenous Design* (New Brunswick, NJ: Rutgers University Press, 2005). For a political application see Horace Campbell, *Barack Obama and 21st Century Politics: A Revolutionary Moment in the USA* (London: Pluto Press, 2010).

[14] I was unable to source the one other major biography of Amy Ashwood published by Lionel Yard in 1990.

Amy Ashwood's Praxis

The challenges that I have outlined in the introduction are entirely familiar to scholars who seek to recover the ideas and practices of women from their elision by the "great race man" narrative of Black liberation.[15] Of key importance in this recovery is a sensitivity toward being inside and outside a politicized community at the same time. For instance, Carole Boyce Davies uses the work of Audre Lorde to situate Caribbean women such as Amy Ashwood outside of the standard narration of Black radical and Pan-African intellectual traditions while at the same time having substantively worked very much inside of these traditions.[16]

In *fin de siècle* North America, this inside-outside problematique manifested in the work of "race women" who discharged their public duty of uplifting the people through the execution of their domestic responsibilities of child-rearing and husband-nurturing. Above all, the public activities of race women were not expected to detrimentally impact upon these responsibilities.[17] Yet while certainly patriarchal, Black expectations necessarily differed from those experienced by white middle-class women whose domesticity also implied a duty to breed the white race.[18] Ula Taylor usefully describes this difference in terms of the "community feminism" of race women such as Amy Jacques Garvey (Marcus' second wife).[19] The politics of community-focused feminism implied the nurturing of a "race" that, under white supremacy, should never have been nurtured. Hence, the inside-outside problematique contoured Black patriarchy in white supremacist societies by politicizing the presence and work of Black women in ways excessive to white patriarchy.[20]

Black women intellectuals variously used this oppressive/liberatory space of race-gender slippage to pursue distinct projects. This was not an unprecedented undertaking. The garnering of women's power by

---

[15] Cooper, *Beyond Respectability*, 23–24.

[16] Carole Boyce Davies, "Sisters Outside: Tracing the Caribbean/Black Radical Intellectual Tradition," *Small Axe* 13.1 (2009): 217–29.

[17] Ula Y. Taylor, "Intellectual Pan-African Feminists: Amy Ashwood-Garvey and Amy Jacques-Garvey," in Charles M Payne and Adam Green (eds.), *Time Longer than Rope: A Century of African American Activism, 1850–1950* (New York University Press, 2003), 180; Cooper, *Beyond Respectability*, 13.

[18] Cooper, *Beyond Respectability*, 13.

[19] Ula Taylor, *The Veiled Garvey: The Life and Times of Amy Jacques Garvey* (Chapel Hill: University of North Carolina Press, 2002).

[20] E.g., Rhoda Reddock, "The First Mrs Garvey: Pan-Africanism and Feminism in the Early 20th Century British Colonial Caribbean," *Feminist Africa* 19 (2014): 58–77 (59–60).

circuitous means already had a long history in the Black church.[21] Nonetheless, the UNIA was somewhat exceptional in that it channeled such power through a secular, public-facing, mass organization. Still, the association was from the very start organized through a gendered division of labor. Women's spaces within the UNIA often reproduced middle-class norms of female respectability, including traditional issue areas such as charitable work, and chasteness represented by the formal canonization of the Virgin Mary as a Black woman.[22] Moreover, maternal, inward-facing roles were reserved for the leadership of women as in the Black Cross Nurse auxiliaries; masculinist, outward-facing roles were reserved for the leadership of men, as in the paramilitary African Legions. Hence, the "dual-sex" principle of organization proposed an equality in difference, but one that was still hierarchically ordered in terms of governance and leadership.[23]

And yet Black patriarchy in white supremacist societies unintentionally produced openings that white patriarchy did not. By publicly attributing feminine qualities to Black women, the UNIA challenged their bestialization just as it challenged the feminization of Black men. More, still: on occasion, the UNIA even projected an image of Black women equivalent to that of men. For instance, a female paramilitary unit existed – the Universal African Motor Corps – which complemented the African Legions.[24] Such an innovation introduced Black women into the public space as neither sub-female beasts nor as diminutive-(white)-females in training. In this respect, we could say, in contemporary academic parlance, that the UNIA's Black patriarchy "queered" white supremacism.

Above all, despite (or because of) its internal hierarchies, the dual-sex structure of the UNIA provided public leadership roles to Black women unparalleled to those positions offered to white women in white associations.[25] Indeed, as Honor Ford-Smith points out, UNIA women capitalized upon these openings in ways that further destabilized race-gender

---

[21] E.g., Jualynne E. Dodson, "Church Women's Legacy of Power: The Case of the U.S. African Methodist Episcopal Church," in William Ackah, Jualynne E. Dodson, and R. Drew Smith (eds.), *Religion, Culture and Spirituality in Africa and the African Diaspora* (London: Routledge, 2017), 17–32.

[22] Barbara Bair, "True Women, Real Men: Gender, Ideology and Social Roles in the Garvey Movement," in Dorothy O. Helly and Susan M. Reverby (eds.), *Gendered Domains: Rethinking Public and Private in Women's History* (Ithaca, NY: Cornell University Press, 1992), 159–60; Honor Ford-Smith, "Women and the Garvey Movement in Jamaica," in Rupert Lewis and Patrick E Bryan (eds.), *Garvey, His Work and Impact* (Trenton, NJ: Africa World Press, 1991), 75.

[23] Bair, "True Women, Real Men," 155–57.

[24] Bair, "True Women, Real Men," 156; Tony Martin, "Women in the Garvey Movement," in Lewis and Bruan (eds.), *Garvey, His Work and Impact*, 70.

[25] Reddock, "The First Mrs Garvey," 65.

hierarchies by making a public image for themselves as intellectuals, activists, and policy makers.[26] For example, Lyllian Galloway ran the UNIA's printing press; while Henrietta Vinton Davis, a key Baltimorean associate of Frederick Douglass, became the UNIA's first official International Organizer.[27]

Amy Ashwood was, of course, an original and vital force in the self-making of UNIA women. Whether or not her claim to be co-founder of the association was overblown, she and her family were central in material and ideological ways to its beginnings. Amy Ashwood held associate and/or general secretary positions in the early years of the UNIA, and by 1919 she had become the director of the Black Star Line – Marcus' famous shipping venture.[28] Such was Amy Ashwood's prominence in the UNIA that secret agents for the US government described her as "a kind of managing boss."[29] It is also clear from the documentary record that Amy Ashwood played a central role in the scoping out of the UNIA's constitution. Here lay perhaps her greatest influence in institutionalizing the dual-sex structure through the requirement for each local division to elect a male and female president and vice president.[30]

In all these respects Amy Ashwood helped to politicize the public standing of Black women in both inward and outwardly facing ways, with all their accompanying paradoxes. She herself walked the walk in the arena of international politics. Her presence at key moments in the twentieth-century contestation by Black and African peoples over post-colonial (and postracial) futures must be understood as the outcome of her earlier politicization by – and politicizing of – the UNIA. A couple of examples will situate the argument within the flow of global history.

The year 1945 saw Amy Ashwood in attendance at the epochal Pan-African Congress in Manchester, which marked the beginning of the post-war intellectual milieu of (Anglo) African decolonization. There, she addressed the predominantly male audience (comprising a number of future independence leaders) on the subject of the Black woman, "shunted," as she put it, by commentators of the race "into the background to be a child-bearer."[31] Amy Ashwood was in large part responsible for the inclusion, in the final resolution of the Congress, of five clauses that referenced women's concerns: equal pay for equal work,

---

[26] Ford-Smith, "Women and the Garvey Movement in Jamaica," 77–78.
[27] Martin, "Women in the Garvey Movement," 68–69.
[28] Martin, *Amy Ashwood Garvey*, 23, 41.   [29] Reddock, "The First Mrs Garvey," 64.
[30] Taylor, "Intellectual Pan-African Feminists," 183.
[31] Cited in Marika Sherwood and Hakim Adi, "Amy Ashwood Garvey," in *Pan-African History: Political Figures from Africa and the Diaspora since 1787* (London: Routledge, 2003), 73.

removals on bars to women's employment related for instance to their married status, legal provision for the registration of fathers, and the end of the "schoolgirl" system in domestic service.[32] This system, it should be noted, effectively placed young girls as unpaid wards of female employers; Amy Ashwood characterized the practice as "quasi-slavery under a thin camouflage of philanthropic solicitude."[33]

At the Manchester congress, Amy Ashwood also moderated sessions on Britain's "colour problem."[34] This concern remained with her during the post-war years, despite her periodic absences from the country. By the 1950s, the ostensibly "international" issues of colonialism and self-determination came to inflect (and still do) domestic politics in the form of "race relations." As Kennetta Perry puts it, the racist murder in 1959 of a young Antiguan man called Kelso Cochrane "recalibrated the parameters of public debate."[35] Against the predominating conceit that race relations simply referred to the assimilation of non-white Commonwealth subjects, Black organizers charged the state with failure to protect the rights of its citizens. In this development, Amy Ashwood took on a central organizing position through her Association for the Advancement of Coloured People and through her selection by the Mayor of Kensington (the London district in which Cochrane had been murdered) to represent Black residents on the issues.[36]

I have argued so far that, in pursuit of Black liberation in white supremacist societies, a negotiating/working through/besides/underneath Black patriarchy was crucial to the formation of Black women's agency. I have also argued that the UNIA acted as an incubator for this agency, and that Amy Ashwood was both architect and exemplar of this agency and its (global) public effect. Yet I have also argued that the UNIA – as with most spaces of Black patriarchy – was fundamentally paradoxical for Black women to navigate insofar as race liberation entangled with patriarchal dependency. So, as they took to local, national, imperial, and global public stages, how did the likes of Amy Ashwood theorize Black liberation in, through, and against such dependency?

Above all, the theorizing of race women must be gleaned in the very act of cultivating the spaces for theorizing and debating Black liberation. Imagine, for one moment, the difficulty in theorizing as a Black

---

[32] Reddock, "The First Mrs Garvey," 70.

[33] Cited in Marc Matera, *Black London: The Imperial Metropolis and Decolonization in the Twentieth Century* (Oakland: University of California Press, 2015), 108.

[34] Kennetta Hammond Perry, *London Is the Place for Me: Black Britons, Citizenship, and the Politics of Race* (New York: Oxford University Press, 2015), 51.

[35] Perry, *London Is the Place for Me*, 128.

[36] Perry, *London Is the Place for Me*, 130; Sherwood and Adi, "Amy Ashwood Garvey," 74.

intellectual in white intellectual locales wherein the meeting of Black minds is itself greeted with suspicion if not derision. Hence, for Black intellectuals in white supremacist societies, the cultivation of the space for theorizing has always been at the same time the theorization of power and resistance. This is the praxis of Black intellectual organization, one that is rarely documented or explicated in political theory texts. But furthermore, race women had to approach this underappreciated challenge fractally: the confrontation with power itself (race) was imbued with power confrontations (gender), and acts of resistance (against white supremacism) were confronted with acts of resistance (against Black patriarchy)[37].

The necessarily fractal disposition of race women's praxis is worthy of consideration when it came to the organizing of Black liberation. Consider, for instance, one of Amy Ashwood's many commercial enterprises: the Florence Mills Social Club, situated in London's West End. Mills was an African American cabaret star who fatally contracted tuberculosis in London, and was known both as a proponent of Black rights and as the "queen of happiness." The naming by Amy Ashwood of her 1930s London club was no accident, but rather signaled a popular, diasporic Blackness – i.e., a Pan-Africanism – safely ensconced within a politically inflected entertainment space. Known for its good Caribbean and African food, the Club became a premier location for "race intellectuals from all parts of the world ... to gather" as the *Sunday Express* put it at the time.[38]

In fact, C. L. R. James, famous Trinidadian Marxist, claimed that it was in Florence Mills that the International African Friends of Abyssinia (IAFA) was gestated. In 1935, the Friends sought to catalyze public opinion over fascist Italy's belligerent and colonial designs on sovereign Ethiopia (both members of the League of Nations). The networks developed by the IAFA would eventually deliver the seminal 1945 Pan-African Congress in Manchester. The formation of the IAFA thus demonstrates how the sensate elements of food, music, and dance at Florence Mills produced a Pan-African camaraderie that could not have begun in the British Library. Contrary to androcentric and individualized accounts of theory production, theorizing might also be, by necessity, a

---

[37] For thoughts on this as they pertain to the idea of the "kitchen table" see Jessica Marie Johnson, "Fury and Joy: Feminism at the Kitchen Table," *Women reVamped*, November 14, 2014, http://womenrevamped.org/2014/11/14/fury-and-joy-feminism-at-the-kitchen-table/.

[38] Cited in Martin, *Amy Ashwood Garvey*, 140.

situated, communal pursuit, and in this regard Amy Ashwood was a luminary.[39]

To understand her acuity in this respect we need to acknowledge just how gifted a conversationalist Amy Ashwood was. For C. L. R. James, Amy Ashwood was amongst four of the most "brilliant" conversationalists he had ever met, alongside the likes of Leon Trotsky.[40] Indeed, Amy Ashwood's conversational skills were fundamental to the cultivation of social networks that enabled her to raise funds and commitments for projects in almost every locale she frequented – whether that be in West Africa, Europe, the Caribbean, or North America. Incidentally, despite her own itinerant lifestyle, the relationships that she developed were remarkably "sticky" and long-lasting.

These skills, though, did not only catalyze the thoughts and actions of elites and notables; remarkably, Amy Ashwood could turn them toward popular oratory. It is important to remember that, alongside other race women, Amy Ashwood was on a par with Marcus in persuading crowds in Harlem and elsewhere to commit financially and otherwise to the UNIA. Her success was in part to do with a mastery of rhetoric. But beyond that, she took a hermeneutical orientation toward her publics and the spaces within which they would meet and talk. That is, Amy Ashwood was concerned to discuss and agitate in ways that crossed the thresholds of various situated understandings of blackness. To understand the diasporic challenges of orienting thus, a brief excursus is required regarding the demographic and social contours of Harlem, the premier site of UNIA organizing in the late 1910s and early 1920s.

Harlem was home to a significant migration of Black peoples not only from the South of the United States but also from the Anglo-Caribbean. At this point in time, manual and unskilled labor circuits in the Caribbean and South America were vibrant and well-established.[41] Many migrants had already passed through other entrepots of Caribbean immigration, especially Panama, including Marcus, Amy Ashwood's father, and Amy Ashwood herself prior to her first arrival in the United States. In Panamanian labor sites such as Colon, US interests had introduced Jim Crow segregation into the social and working regimes, thereby

---

[39] Another example might be Amy Ashwood's friendship with Claudia Jones that might have guided Jones towards deciding on the Notting Hill carnival as a response to racist murders. For these thoughts I am indebted to Colin Prescod. See also Marika Sherwood, Donald Hinds, and Colin Prescod, *Claudia Jones: A Life in Exile* (London: Lawrence & Wishart, 1999).

[40] Martin, *Amy Ashwood Garvey*, 144.

[41] Lara Putnam, "Provincializing Harlem: The 'Negro Metropolis' as Northern Frontier of a Connected Caribbean," *Modernism/Modernity* 20.3 (2013): 469–84.

politicizing many sojourners to US-style racism before they even arrived in New York City.[42] Concomitantly, the "internal" migration to northern US cities was itself a reaction to – and further encouraged – a resurgence of Jim Crow legislation and practices.[43]

The meeting of different migrants – "internal" and "external" – could not but be intractably political. Neither could it occur without tensions. Caribbean peoples sometimes faced prejudice from African Americans.[44] More acute than such prejudice, perhaps, were the class tensions within the Caribbean populations. In New York, white-collar workers were regularly color-barred from taking positions they were used to filling, while manual labor paid far better than in the islands. In this respect, the colonial class and respectability hierarchies of the Caribbean (often color-coded) were somewhat turned upside down in Harlem, just as Caribbean positionalities were challenged by African American positionalities, the latter of which were also marked by migration journeys. Therefore, any hermeneutics of race uplift utilized in Harlem had to be attuned not only to a dizzying diversity of familial trajectories and lived experiences but also to the fractal nature of Black struggle.

Ula Taylor has incisively explored the way in which the "street strollers" of Harlem theorized in sophisticated ways by negotiating such a contentious landscape as they socialized with groups in various public locales.[45] As Amy Ashwood moved from corner to corner she would have to quickly and pragmatically interpret the crowd composition, as well as the dynamic and tenor of the conversation. Furthermore, she would have to calculate her interventions in a way that seamlessly wove in the local conventions and traditions to her (multivalent) Caribbean voice so that she could cross thresholds of blackness. For this purpose, Amy Ashwood would sometimes use poetry to take advantage of what Taylor characterizes as a particular "hear-me-talking-to-you mode of discourse."[46] Tellingly, she was fond of using Paul Laurence Dunbar, the first African

---

[42] Walter LaFeber, *The Panama Canal: The Crisis in Historical Perspective* (New York: Oxford University Press, 1978), 62–65.

[43] John C. Walter, "Black Immigrants and Political Radicalism in the Harlem Renaissance," *The Western Journal of Black Studies* 1.2 (1977): 131–41 (132).

[44] Robert Philipson, "The Harlem Renaissance as Postcolonial Phenomenon," *African American Review* 40.1 (2006): 145–60 (146).

[45] Ula Taylor, "Street Strollers: Grounding the Theory of Black Women Intellectuals," *Afro-Americans in New York Life and History* 30.2 (2006): 153–71; see also the notion of "street-scholar" presented by Keisha Blain in *Set the World on Fire: Black Nationalist Women and the Global Struggle for Freedom* (Philadelphia: University of Pennsylvania Press, 2018).

[46] Ula Taylor, "Women in the Documents: Thoughts on Uncovering the Personal, Political, and Professional," *Journal of Women's History* 20.1 (2008): 187–96 (191).

American poet to gain national (and international) prestige, and who was unafraid to use a Black dialect in his work.[47] Amy Ashwood often recited from Dunbar's "We Wear the Mask," a poem that engaged themes resonant with W. E. B. Dubois' "veil" or "double consciousness."

Let me now summarize the argument of this part of the chapter. To appreciate Amy Ashwood's mode of theorizing, Black patriarchy must be apprehended not as a carbon copy of white supremacist patriarchy but as a paradoxical enabler of Black women's critique. The cultivation of the space for such critique through/despite/besides/underneath Black patriarchy, was at the same time the theorization of power and resistance, a theorization that proceeded through communal, colloquial, and practical registers and activities. The kind of praxis emerging from this theorization had to respond to the social and political constellations over diasporic blackness that were fractal in terms of the recursive nature of their struggles over class, gender, geography, and nationality.

While Amy Ashwood was perfectly capable of sketching out grand abstract designs, her praxis was cultivated by working through these fractals, experienced in multiple locales and across multiple classes of peoples. However, the strongest directions were undoubtedly cast through Amy Ashwood's interlinked pursuit of women's respectability and liberation, in which we might glean the fractal contours of her Pan-Africanism.

A Fractal Pan-Africanism

The respectability politics of Black patriarchy primarily sought to protect Black women's bodies against their bestialization by the sexual economies of white supremacism.[48] Such respectability, as announced by Marcus Garvey, presented Black women as the defenders of chasteness and of the household's moral sphere. Marcus himself frowned upon both illegitimate children and female-headed households.[49] One of the clauses in the UNIA's 1914 aims and objectives even promised to "rescue the fallen women of the island from the pit of infamy and vice."[50]

In her teenage years, Amy Ashwood seems to have strongly ascribed to such a respectable female model.[51] She first met Marcus at a Church Hall literary debate wherein she had proposed the motion that

---

[47] Taylor, "Street Strollers'; Martin, *Amy Ashwood Garvey*, 124.
[48] Cooper, *Beyond Respectability*, 15.
[49] Ford-Smith, "Women and the Garvey Movement in Jamaica," 76.
[50] Martin, "Women in the Garvey Movement," 71.
[51] Taylor, "Intellectual Pan-African Feminists," 183.

"morality does not increase with civilization."[52] Less a radical Pan-Africanist organization, the early UNIA appeared more like a literary and debating society, the archetypal organization for women's respectability politics.[53] One year into the organization's life, and Amy Ashwood was lecturing Jamaican women on the importance of providing a positive influence in the household so that Jamaican men might do "good and noble things."[54]

Still, Amy Ashwood's very association with Marcus strained the respectability politics that were expected of her. For example, who was dependent upon whom? Her own mother considered Marcus to be a lower-class suitor who suffered from "flights of fancy" that were none-theless bankrolled by Amy Ashwood's father.[55] More importantly, as Rhoda Reddock puts it, in Amy Ashwood's relationship with Marcus, "personal and racial liberation mingled."[56] Above all, the Black liberation offered to Amy Ashwood via her working for the UNIA was somewhat confounded by her required deference to Marcus. She was famously feminist in her retrospective on this qualified independence:

> Marcus Garvey stood before me and said in a very earnest voice, 'Amy Ashwood, I appoint you secretary of the Universal Negro Improvement Association'. I replied with an equal earnestness, 'and Marcus Garvey, I appoint you president'.[57]

Their split, as Amy Ashwood put it later, enabled her to "work in a more intimate fashion in order to help the Afro-American women to find themselves and rise in life."[58]

The tensions between respectability politics and Black liberation were, in good part, responsible for the couple's extremely short marriage. Marcus cited adultery with multiple partners and unseemly public behavior such as drinking alcohol.[59] For her part, Amy Ashwood never accepted the divorce yet at the same time publicly belittled Marcus' bedroom skills and his increasingly shoddy physical appearance.[60] The first musical comedy that she produced in New York, entitled *Hey, Hey!*,

---

[52] Amy Ashwood Garvey, "The Birth of the Universal Negro Improvement Association," in Tony Martin, *The Pan-African Connection: From Slavery to Garvey and Beyond* (Dover, MA: Majority Press, 1983), 220.
[53] Martin, *Amy Ashwood Garvey*, 24.   [54] Cited in Martin, *Amy Ashwood Garvey*, 325.
[55] Sherwood and Adi, "Amy Ashwood Garvey," 69; Garvey, "The Birth of the Universal Negro Improvement Association," 223.
[56] Reddock, "The First Mrs Garvey," 64.
[57] Garvey, "The Birth of the Universal Negro Improvement Association," 226.
[58] Cited in Martin, *Amy Ashwood Garvey*, 74.
[59] Ford-Smith, "Women and the Garvey Movement in Jamaica," 77.
[60] Martin, *Amy Ashwood Garvey*, 36.

parodied Marcus' Pan-Africanism through a subversion of his own respectability politics: two men, thrown out of their homes by their wives, seek new wives on the African continent, only to find their continental spouses to be their old wives who had followed them in order to expose their infelicitous conduct.[61]

In Amy Ashwood's (sometimes vitriolic) public admonitions and artistic output can be identified a striking critique of Black patriarchy's respectability politics and its constraining of the liberation promised to Black women. At the least, Amy Ashwood's very public – and self-publicized – falling out with Marcus raised the issue as to when Black patriarchy's protective ethos undercut Black women's self-liberation from white supremacy, including its gender conformity codes. The systematic way in which she pursued this critique in relation to Pan-Africanism is suggested, for instance, by her abiding interest in polygamy on the continent. While Amy Ashwood was cautious to embrace such practices, she nonetheless argued that they should be understood in their own historical and cosmological contexts rather than through the white supremacist morality of the Western church.[62]

Above all, Amy Ashwood's was a very personalized critique of respectability politics, especially considering the fact that debates in the UNIA over respectability often implicated her own conduct. I want to suggest that this intimacy super-charged her confrontation with and working through the diverse relationalities via which Black liberation had to be recursively pursued in Harlem (and elsewhere). Indeed, in Amy Ashwood's fractal disposition can be identified what we would now call the oppressive "intersections" of race, color, sex, class, and nationality, which rendered blackness and informed her street-strolling praxis.

In this respect, it is useful to dwell upon Amy Ashwood's careful engagement with "miscegeny" in distinction to Marcus' promotion of race purity. In marking this difference, I do not wish to reduce the politics of the Black Moses to a caricature. Marcus was no eugenicist of the Fabian or fascist ilk: he was concerned primarily with the iniquitous and violent power relations that had historically structured miscegeny in the Caribbean. It should be noted that color hierarchies were perhaps far more finely etched into the majority-Black Caribbean from whence Marcus came than in the minority-Black North American continent where he politically "arrived" and in which "one [Black] drop [of blood]" rules of race identification usually held sway. Still, Marcus viewed

[61] Martin, *Amy Ashwood Garvey*, 100.   [62] Martin, *Amy Ashwood Garvey*, 90.

"race mixing" as a political dead-end for Pan-Africanism and dismissed it as such.

Alternatively, Amy Ashwood seemed to find the psychological and social mechanisms and consequences of "mixing" worthy of careful study and intervention rather than a priori moral dismissal. The complicities of race, color, sex, class, and nation would no doubt have been apprehended by Amy Ashwood before her move to Harlem but were most certainly appreciated even more there, especially considering her own public battles. Her artistic output that followed *Hey, Hey!* placed such issues to the fore. *Brown Sugar*, for instance, followed the travails of a father who wished his brown-skinned daughter to marry an Indian prince instead of a lowly mechanic whom she loved. During a European sojourn in the 1920s, Amy Ashwood wrote a novel, *The Jungle of Civilization* which, as she put it, provided a "psychology of mixed marriages."[63] In Britain, during and after World War II, she turned her attention to the children of Black American servicemen, which at the time constituted one of the main "race problems" in the heart of empire.[64]

As suggested by the plot of *Brown Sugar*, Amy Ashwood's concerns for "mixing" also extended to interest in the politics of Black and non-white-but-non-Black relations. For instance, Amy Ashwood's second Caribbean tour in 1953 saw her reach out to Black and non-Black women groups.[65] Her address, "Women as Leaders of World Thought," was in fact given at the Indo-Trinidadian Himalaya Club.[66] During the same time period, she began to model her Afro People's Centre in West London as a residency for women which might help engender a "multiracial society" that included Black, Indian, and white women. As part of this project, and as a partial confrontation with respectability politics, she partnered with sex-workers with an ambition to improve their lives.[67]

Integral to her growing disposition toward the fractal nature of Pan-Africanism and its recursive implication of economic, sexual, national, and racial elements ran Amy Ashwood's own personal re-commitment to her African roots. Her mother was a Haitian "mulatto"; her grandmother on her father's side went by the name Grannie Dabas. Family legend held that Dabas, meaning of "strong or iron will," had been born on the continent – in a place called Juaben – and was kidnapped across the

[63] Martin, *Amy Ashwood Garvey*, 106, 89.
[64] St. Clair Drake, "The 'Colour Problem" in Britain: A Study in Social Definitions," *The Sociological Review* 3.2 (1955): 197–217.
[65] Martin, *Amy Ashwood Garvey*, 70.   [66] Reddock, "The First Mrs Garvey," 71.
[67] Martin, *Amy Ashwood Garvey*, 257–59.

Atlantic. In her later years, Amy Ashwood met the Asantehene of Ashanti who eventually confirmed Grannie Dabas' story. She subsequently took on the Ashanti name Yaa Boahimaa (also her grandmother's name).[68] These autobiographical notes suggest that Amy Ashwood's Black consciousness was congenitally cultivated along with her consciousness of continental roots.[69] Put another way, the journey toward her own Ashanti heritage was at the same time a reclaiming by Amy Ashwood of her own independent Pan-African credentials. Not all roads to the continent – or Blackness – passed through Marcus' paternalistic persona and standing.

In this sense, Amy Ashwood's fractal disposition sought out routes of Pan-Africanism rather than a root of Blackness. Consider, for instance, the way in which she took issue with Marcus' presentation of the Pan-African mantra: "Africa for the Africans, at home and abroad." The idea of a singular African kingdom, Amy Ashwood proposed, was a "geographical blunder," with "too many tribes each differing from the other in customs that it is quite impossible to form them into a simple people."[70] While her critique was certainly driven by acrimony over divorce proceedings, Amy Ashwood nonetheless had staked out an early position in one of the most defining Pan-Africanist debates of the twentieth century: what to do with the continent's colonial borders. And while her position might seem to defend such borders, it is clear from her own evolving ethnographic investigations and personal investments in a series of West African locales that Amy Ashwood was thinking primarily in terms of meaningful self-determination at the level of peoples and communities rather than "race" per se.

Amy Ashwood further argued, in a thinly veiled criticism of Marcus' organizational penchant for pomp and title, that continental Africans wanted "no Afro-Americans or West Indians as rulers over them," nor did they fancy "kings or dukes or earls created over here sent there to them."[71] This critique was perhaps even more salient to Pan-African diplomacy than the issue of colonial borders. As Edward Blyden, a nineteenth-century Pan-Africanist forerunner to Marcus, had made clear with regards to Liberia's colonization, Black peoples in North America were constantly being taught that their proximity to white society (even through slavery) had prepared them to rule over continental primitives.[72]

---

[68] Martin, *Amy Ashwood Garvey*, 16–18, 216–20.
[69] Garvey, "The Birth of the Universal Negro Improvement Association," 223–24.
[70] Adi, "Amy Ashwood Garvey and the Nigerian Progress Union," 203.
[71] Martin, *Amy Ashwood Garvey*, 88.
[72] Edward Wilmot Blyden, *The Aims and Methods of a Liberal Education for Africans* (Cambridge: John Wilson and Son, 1882).

In my estimation, then, Amy Ashwood's street-strolling praxis, her critique of Black respectability, and her personal retrieval of Ashanti heritage all intertwined in her movement toward independence from Marcus. This movement opened up – in many ways necessitated – a fractal disposition toward Pan-Africanism and an ever-expansive engagement with the recursive struggles that rendered Blackness. In some national or social contexts, Blackness might be articulated through class rather than race per se; in some political contexts the Diaspora might have to qualify its singular claims to Blackness; in some contexts, anti-Blackness might take on a pro-"brown" veneer, and in other contexts, Black women's freedoms might be usefully pursued in solidarity with non-white women of, for example, Asian heritage; in some contexts, the discrimination experienced by children of "miscegenation" revealed itself to be a central issue for Pan-Africanism; in some contexts, respectability oppressed rather than protected Black women and in this case the Pan-Africanist might even have to positively support sex-workers of many hues. Each case had lessons to bear for each other case.

None of this is to diminish the fundamental and irreplaceable importance of Marcus as a well-spring of twentieth-century Pan-Africanism which cascaded over the continent. Still, as Marika Sherwood argues, "if ever there was a life of *lived* Pan-Africanism, it was that of Amy Ashwood Garvey";[73] or, as Tony Martin perceptively suggests: she was far more a Pan-Africanist than a Black nationalist.[74] Above all, unlike Marcus, Amy Ashwood pursued Black liberation through a fractal disposition toward Pan-Africanism that had been cultivated as part of a critique of Black patriarchy and the politics of respectability.

However, elements within a fractal disposition are never disappeared or completed; they continue to be activated, albeit in different constellations where different political stakes are at play. And sure enough, despite her own living critique of it, Amy Ashwood never disavowed the tenets of respectability as they pertained to and structured the public – and global – presence of Black women. These tenets are especially pronounced by her consistent focus upon women's social work and domestic labor.

The UNIA began as a traditional Caribbean social welfare organization and Amy Ashwood considered social work to be the most appropriate pursuit for the association's race women.[75] Amy Ashwood herself started the Ladies Division, which subsequently developed into the Black

---

[73] Sherwood and Adi, "Amy Ashwood Garvey," 69, my emphasis.
[74] Martin, *Amy Ashwood Garvey*, 319.
[75] Martin, "Women in the Garvey Movement," 68; Ford-Smith, "Women and the Garvey Movement in Jamaica," 77.

Cross Nurses arm.[76] She never rescinded such a seemingly middle-class commitment to respectable women's work. Her Afro-Woman's center in London was also organized along the lines of a voluntary welfare society;[77] and her African tour, begun in 1946, addressed the conditions facing the continent's women in a register that was comfortably "respectable," focusing especially on female education.[78]

Concomitantly, Amy Ashwood considered domestic work to be a potential vehicle for poor Black women's mobility, despite its complicities with the white patriarchal division of labor. For instance, during much of World War II, Amy Ashwood worked in Jamaica to help found and promote the J.A.G. Smith political party. While the party had a mandate to support the poor, Amy Ashwood also envisaged it advancing the interests of women through a program of "domestic science training."[79] It is reasonable to presume that Amy Ashwood gleaned a positive potential in such training as by 1944/1945 she was connecting women's liberation through these means to Black and African self-determination. In fact, in the last years of the war, Amy Ashwood took on the immigration system of the United States, arguing that the scheme to recruit male Caribbean labor for farms and war industries was discriminatory toward the region's women. To rectify the situation, Amy Ashwood agitated for a domestic labor scheme.[80]

Thus, when it came to considering the proper kind of work that both middle-class and working-class Black women should undertake for Black liberation, Amy Ashwood was doggedly accepting of the divisions of labor aspired to by respectability politics. She remained so even as the constellations of Black liberation shifted and as new generations of women pursued the cause in new circumstances with different political stakes at play. Crucially, in these new constellations, Amy Ashwood's acceptance of respectability politics was rendered oppressive, as demonstrated in an interview for the *Harlem News* in October 1968, one year before her passing.

During this, her final sojourn in the United States, Amy Ashwood capitalized upon the resurgence of Black power ideology, including a revived interest in her husband. Seeking to return herself to the center of Black liberation struggle, Amy Ashwood read some of Marcus' speeches for a charitable recording, and even undertook a lecture tour of

---

[76] Reddock, "The First Mrs Garvey," 62.   [77] Martin, *Amy Ashwood Garvey*, 256.
[78] Martin, *Amy Ashwood Garvey*, 222.   [79] Martin, *Amy Ashwood Garvey*, 167.
[80] Fitzroy Andre Baptiste, "Amy Ashwood Garvey and Afro-West Indian Labor in the United States Emergency Farm and War Industries' Programs of World War II, 1943–1945," *Ìrìnkèrindò: A Journal of African Migration*, 2003, www.africamigration .com/archive_02f_baptiste.htm.

California under the auspices of the Black Panthers.[81] Her interview for the *Harlem News* was entitled "The Black Woman" and, in part, presented a defense of Black patriarchy. Amy Ashwood bemoaned the Black matriarchy that she claimed developed during slavery insofar as it had robbed Black males of their masculinity thus disarming them in terms of their duty to defend Black women. The newly assertive Black Power man, Amy Ashwood claimed, was "the kind of man the black woman would gladly love, honour and respect."[82] Under this arrangement, the Black woman would be able to retain her modesty and virtue and, through them, inspire the Black nation.

Black matriarchy was an extremely contestable and arguably damaging idea at the time. Just a few years earlier, sociologist Daniel Moynihan had written a report on *The Negro Family* while appointed to the US Department of Labor to guide policy making for President Lyndon Johnson's War on Poverty. In the report, Moynihan contrasted the pathologies of Black family life – including the eclipsing of male presence by female agency – to the normality of patriarchal-nuclear white family life.[83] By this logic, the "Black matriarchy" thesis explained away the historically sedimented inequalities of white supremacism simply as cultural pathologies of the victims.

Amy Ashwood's commentary is even more uncomfortable in historical retrospect given the inauguration of the Black Women's Liberation Committee just a couple of months after her interview. The Committee was subsequently to promote "intersectional" analyses that challenged social movements to account for women's liberation as they pursued Black liberation. This, of course, was a position once pioneered by Amy Ashwood and others in the UNIA as they engaged with Black patriarchy through a fractal disposition. Intellectuals in the Committee took direct issue with the way in which the Black matriarchy thesis damaged the pursuit of Black liberation which, they claimed, required a confrontation with the capitalist system rather than a resurgent cultural patriarchy.[84] This put the Committee fundamentally at odds with Amy Ashwood's defense of respectability politics.

Still, I hesitate to consider Amy Ashwood's intellectual legacy obsolete. Recall that a fractal disposition must relate every struggle to the

---

[81] Sherwood and Adi, "Amy Ashwood Garvey," 75.

[82] Cited in Martin, *Amy Ashwood Garvey*, 301.

[83] United States Department of Labor, Office of Policy Planning and Research, *The Negro Family: The Case for National Action*, 1965.

[84] Frances Beal, "Double Jeopardy: To Be Black and Female," in The Third World Women's Alliance (ed.), *Black Women's Manifesto* (New York: World Women's Alliance, 1970), 19–34.

larger struggles that that struggle is part of, and the struggles within that struggle. Nothing is left behind, or finished. The movement of struggle is, rather, creatively recursive, and thus infinitely expansive. I want to also connect this argument to my position stated in the introduction to this chapter that the defense of Theory can attenuate theorizing, and that living knowledge traditions always exceed text. Putting these two considerations together, I am loath to simply jettison "respectability" from Black liberation struggle. Is liberation possible without respectability? For instance, there is a conversation to be had about the way in which some Black youth currently utilize "respect" as a more politically consequential term than "rights" (to the chagrin of some older activists). Put another way, is there a way to recast it as something other than solely an aspiration toward middle-class patriarchy?

I must admit, my concerns primarily arise out of my own relatively provincial and amateurish "street-strolling" in Pan-African movements – Rastafari especially. There are many Black women whom I have known and learned from who doggedly pursue Pan-African liberation in practical, mundane, globe-trodding terms, yet who are as devastatingly radical in action as they are conservative in disposition. The editors of this volume caution over a conflation of women intellectuals with "progressive" feminism. Perhaps respect remains a communal good to be radically wielded by those who face drastically constrained choices for their and their (various) family's wellbeing at the same time as they pursue liberation "work on the self."

Conclusion

This chapter has struggled with the challenges of theorizing (with) Black women who have contributed to Black liberation through a fractal Pan-Africanism. Before closing, though, I want to dispel one assumption that might be made from the pitch of this chapter. There is a tendency to engage with Black thought as not really theory, but rather, "lived experience," the "street," "anecdote," "feeling." Such exoticism abounds and leaves the white androcentrism of social and political thought intact. Yes, Black thought is all this ... *and* it is written and read and enacted in logical analytical constructions by Black intellectuals.[85] It is not a case of either/or. The simple fact of the matter is that we possess hardly any of Amy Ashwood's writings; it is not that she categorically did not write – logically, analytically. That a record exists through which the contours of her international thought can be

---

[85] William Henry, *What the Deejay Said: A Critique from the Street!* (London: Nu-Beyond, 2006).

reasonably reassembled (albeit not without controversy) is testimony to the praxis of race women who left their mark not only on the dry, white pages that narrate world politics. I submit this chapter as a small accretion to Black women's liberation understood as a living knowledge tradition, a tradition that is excessive to the texts written about and for it.

Those of us who wish to curate a more capacious and less Eurocentric/ androcentric archive of international thought have much to learn from and with Amy Ashwood. Her Pan-Africanism not only tutors us in the specific abiding tensions between liberation and respectability, but at the same time impresses upon us a non-categorical Blackness that is globally mobile and socially motile. To theorize global order with Amy Ashwood is also – and necessarily – a lesson in praxis. It is to travel widely in body and soul; to converse in conditions not always of your own choosing; to rebel against what you used to free yourself with; yet to stick doggedly to a commitment toward the liberation of humanity; to be infuriatingly audacious in doing so; to fail – at least by certain standards; above all, to cultivate time and again the spaces that make such commitments a possibility, and to accept the challenge of those who might cultivate your work seemingly against you.

In this respect, I have learned from theorizing with Amy Ashwood that, instead of curating the archive of international thought in an exclusionary and hierarchical fashion, we might do better working with a fractal disposition. This would compel us to consider how we might retrieve the praxis of the race women whom even Amy Ashwood's star eclipsed. I am thinking, for instance, of another UNIA race woman, Satira Earle, Lady President of the St Andrews division in Jamaica.[86] A working-class woman, and union organizer, Ms. Earle on one occasion challenged the middle-class leadership of the UNIA thus: "wake up men, if you are afraid to carry on, I will organize a committee of women and launch out against capitalists in this island and leave you drowsy men behind!"[87] The fractal disposition renders a straight line as a set of infinitely recursive relations. Similarly, we might think of working with living knowledge traditions instead of only discrete individuals as we try to recall and retrieve the fullness of women's international thought.[88].

[86] Honor Ford-Smith, "Unruly Virtues of the Spectacular: Performing Engendered Nationalisms in the UNIA in Jamaica," *Interventions* 6.1 (2004): 18–44.

[87] Ford-Smith, "Women and the Garvey Movement in Jamaica," 79.

[88] My thanks to Empress Ijahnya Christian for a critical eye. Empress Ijahnya has since transitioned to the ancestors. She was a stalwart defender of Rastafari and a tireless advocate for womens' voices in the movement. I dedicate this chapter to the Empress. Thanks also to Colin Prescod for confirming my approach to Amy Ashwood Garvey. Colin is a longstanding member of the Institute of Race Relations. Upon arrival to London in the late 1950s, the first person whom he met in London apart from his mother was Amy Ashwood.

8 "The Dark Skin[ned] People of the Eastern World": Mittie Maude Lena Gordon's Vision of Afro-Asian Solidarity

Keisha N. Blain

On September 20, 1942, FBI officials arrested Mittie Maude Lena Gordon, the founder and president of the Peace Movement of Ethiopia (PME) in Chicago. A working-poor black nationalist leader with limited formal education, Gordon rose to prominence as a "street-scholar" in the city, speaking for the interests of the black masses during a global economic crisis.[1] "Grounded in specific lived realities," historian Ula Y. Taylor argues, "'street scholars' are … in the forefront of giving voice to the complicated issues of the day."[2] Similar to other street-scholars of the period, including black nationalist Amy Ashwood Garvey and civil rights leader Ella Baker, Gordon relied on public spaces, including parks and crowded street corners, as critical platforms from which to disseminate her political ideas during the late 1920s and early 1930s. Her efforts yielded significant results. By December 1932, Gordon had established the PME, the largest black nationalist organization founded by a woman in the United States.[3] A year after the PME was established, she initiated a nationwide emigration campaign and mailed a petition to President Franklin D. Roosevelt with an estimated 400,000 signatures of African Americans willing to leave the country. By the mid-1930s, Gordon had amassed a national following and the PME had attracted an estimated 300,000 supporters, particularly members of the black working-poor, in various parts of Chicago and in several cities across the United States.

---

[1] Ula Y. Taylor, "Street Strollers: Grounding the Theory of Black Women Intellectuals," *Afro-Americans in New York Life and History* 30.2 (2006): 153–71. Taylor's conceptualization of "street-scholar" mirrors Antonio Gramsci's concept of an "organic intellectual." See Antonio Gramsci, "The Formation of the Intellectuals," in Quintin Hoare and Geoffrey Nowell-Smith (eds.), *Selections from the Prison Notebooks of Antonio Gramsci* (London: Lawrence & Wishart, 1971), 134–47.

[2] Taylor, "Street Strollers," 154.

[3] Keisha N. Blain, *Set the World on Fire: Black Nationalist Women and the Global Struggle for Freedom* (Philadelphia: University of Pennsylvania Press, 2018).

179

From 1932 until her arrest ten years later, Gordon worked tirelessly to galvanize thousands of black activists in the city and in more than a dozen states across the nation – including Indiana, New Jersey, Pennsylvania, Alabama, and Mississippi – largely around the issues of black emigration and internationalism.

Through her writings and speeches during this period, she agitated for Afro-Asian solidarity, calling on black men and women to collaborate with Japanese people as a viable strategy to combat racism and global white supremacy. In Gordon's political vision, the potential collaboration between African Americans and Japanese people would not only bolster each group's political standing on a global scale, but it would also help to end white colonial rule in Africa, Asia, the Caribbean, and other parts of the globe. She looked to Japan's military accomplishments as evidence that the nation would be well equipped to challenge white rule in the United States and abroad. Gordon's position on Japan, especially in the years leading up to World War II, represented a minority opinion and a perspective that ran counter to the ideas of mainstream black leaders. Moreover, her ideas, which gained increased currency among working-class black activists, complicated the public image of African American patriotism that many civil rights leaders during this period sought to reaffirm. Not surprisingly, Gordon's endorsement of Afro-Asian solidarity and her public support for Japan – especially in the aftermath of Pearl Harbor – sealed her fate in 1942. Along with twelve black activists in Chicago, she was charged with the crime of sedition for her pro-Japanese stance and later sentenced to two years in prison.

Although Gordon's pro-Japanese sentiments drew the ire of federal officials, they underscored the significance of internationalism in black political discourse during the twentieth century. Building upon a long tradition and history dating back to the era of the American Revolution, Gordon's call for Afro-Asian solidarity reflected her endorsement of black internationalism – best described as a commitment to "universal emancipation" unlimited by "national, imperial, continental, [racial] or oceanic boundaries."[4] A central aspect of the black intellectual tradition, internationalism has shaped the political ideas and praxis of black men and women in the United States and across the diaspora for centuries. Indeed, black people in the United States have always been concerned

---

[4] Michael O. West, William G. Martin, and Fanon Che Wilkins (eds.), *From Toussaint to Tupac: The Black International since the Age of Revolution* (Chapel Hill: University of North Carolina Press, 2009), p. xi. In this chapter, I use the term "black internationalism" based on the definition West, Martin, and Wilkins offer in *From Toussaint to Tupac*. In this formulation, "black internationalism" is not confined to the nation-state but describes the transnational flow of ideas and movement of peoples.

with international politics, linking the struggle for black rights in the United States to the struggles for freedom in Asia, Africa, the Caribbean and elsewhere. By calling on people of African descent to ally with Japanese people – despite the danger of maintaining such a perspective during a period of intense government repression – Gordon was drawing upon the black intellectual tradition, one that has always been deeply internationalist.[5]

Much has been written about how towering male figures such as W. E. B. Du Bois, Marcus Garvey, and Booker T. Washington have articulated global visions of freedom and advocated Afro-Asian solidarity in an effort to secure civil and human rights.[6] In recent years, scholars have also worked to center the ideas of elite and middle-class black women such as Shirley Graham Du Bois, Eslanda Robeson, Merze Tate, and Louise Thompson Patterson.[7] But how might our understanding of black intellectual history deepen if we centered black working-class and impoverished women and black women with limited – or no – formal education? How might our understanding of twentieth-century black internationalism deepen if we carefully considered their ideas, their visions of the world in which they lived, and their proposed solutions for addressing societal problems? This chapter grapples with these questions and in so doing expands the scholarly discourse on who counts as an intellectual.

[5] Rod Bush, *The End of White World Supremacy: Black Internationalism and the Problem of the Color Line* (Philadelphia, PA: Temple University Press, 2009); Keisha N. Blain, Christopher Cameron, and Ashley D. Farmer (eds.), *New Perspectives on the Black Intellectual Tradition* (Evanston, IL: Northwestern University Press, 2018).

[6] Reginald Kearney, *African American Views of the Japanese: Solidarity or Sedition?* (Albany: State University of New York Press, 1998); Fred Ho and Bill V. Mullen (eds.), *Afro Asia: Revolutionary Political and Cultural Connections between African Americans and Asian Americans* (Durham, NC: Duke University Press, 2008); Yuichiro Onishi, *Transpacific Antiracism: Afro-Asian Solidarity in 20th Century Black America, Japan, and Okinawa* (New York University Press, 2013); Robeson Taj Frazier, *The East Is Black: Cold War China in the Black Radical Imagination* (Durham, NC: Duke University Press, 2014); Gerald Horne, *Facing the Rising Sun: African Americans, Japan, and the Rise of Afro-Asian Solidarity* (New York University Press, 2018).

[7] See Gerald Horne, *Race Woman: The Lives of Shirley Graham Du Bois* (New York University Press, 2000); Barbara Ransby, *Eslanda: The Large and Unconventional Life of Mrs. Paul Robeson* (New Haven, CT: Yale University Press, 2013); Erik S. McDuffie, *Sojourning for Freedom: Black Women, American Communism, and the Making of Black Left Feminism* (Durham, NC: Duke University Press, 2011); Dayo F. Gore, *Radicalism at the Crossroads: African American Women Activists in the Cold War* (New York University Press, 2011); Barbara Savage, "Professor Merze Tate: Diplomatic Historian, Cosmopolitan Woman," in Mia Bay, Farah Jasmin Griffin, Martha S. Jones, and Barbara D. Savage (eds.), *Toward an Intellectual History of Black Women* (Chapel Hill: University of North Carolina Press, 2015), 252–72; Robert Vitalis, *White World Order, Black Power Politics: The Birth of American International Relations* (Ithaca, NY: Cornell University Press, 2015); Keith Gilyard, *Louise Thompson Patterson: A Life of Struggle for Justice* (Durham, NC: Duke University Press, 2017).

Significantly, it broadens our understanding of black women's internationalist thought and highlights the unconventional sites from which these women's ideas were formulated and disseminated in the 1930s and 1940s.

Drawing insights from her speeches and personal writings, this chapter highlights how Gordon articulated black internationalism and attempted to forge networks and pursue political collaborations with other people of color worldwide. It demonstrates how this "street-scholar" with limited formal education drew upon, challenged, and even shaped black internationalist discourses. During the 1930s and 1940s, Gordon's PME provided a crucial platform for the activist-intellectual to popularize her internationalist ideas among mostly working-poor black people. Unlike many educated middle-class and elite black activist-intellectuals of the period, Gordon did not produce books and articles for mainstream publications. As a working-poor black woman during the Great Depression, she relied heavily on unconventional mediums – especially letters and self-published pamphlets – to disseminate her internationalist ideas among other working-poor black activists across the United States.

PME leaders used weekly meetings to read aloud letters from Gordon and share copies of organizational pamphlets. These letters and pamphlets, which circulated widely among thousands of black activists, provide glimpses into Gordon's internationalist ideas. Recognizing that the condition of black men and women in the United States was "but a local phase of a world problem," Gordon deployed internationalist rhetoric to underscore the shared strategies of resistance, the political exchanges, and historical connections between people of African descent and persons of Asian descent.[8] For Gordon, Japan represented a model of racial progress and potential ally in the struggle for black liberation.[9] Through her writings and speeches, she attempted to sway black public opinion and actively pursued contact and collaborations with Japanese activists and diplomats to challenge the global system of white supremacy and impact global developments.

The Deep Roots of Afro-Asia

The historical experiences of peoples of Asian and African descent have been deeply intertwined for centuries. "From the earliest days of the

---

[8] Robin D. G. Kelley, "'But a Local Phase of a World Problem': Black History's Global Vision, 1883–1950," *Journal of American History* 86.3 (1999): 1045–77.

[9] Ernest Allen Jr., "When Japan Was Champion of the 'Darker Races': Satokata Takahashi and the Flowering of Black Messianic Nationalism," *Black Scholar* 24 (1994): 23–46.

United States," Fred Ho and Bill Mullen explain, "Africans and Asians in the Americas have been linked in a shared tradition of resistance to class and racial exploitation and oppression."[10] Indeed, both groups have experienced racial oppression and as a result have collaborated to resist racism and discrimination. Following the abolition of slavery during the mid-nineteenth century, thousands of Chinese and Indian laborers were sent to work on sugar plantations in the Caribbean, including Trinidad, Cuba, and British Guiana (now Guyana). The manner in which Asians were brought to the Caribbean mirrored the kinds of experiences that Africans endured during the transatlantic slave trade. Under the trans-Pacific "coolie trade," as it became known, Asian laborers were often transported to the Caribbean in the same ships that had once carried Africans and, in many cases, were captured and coerced into a life of planation labor.[11]

Although Asian indentured servants were generally given contracts ranging from five to eight years, they had no guarantees that they would be able to return to their native lands. With no means of enforcing these contracts, many Asian indentured servants found themselves in a perpetual state of servitude with minimal financial compensation – if any. The lack of economic and political power under a system of white domination and control mirrored the experiences of Africans under chattel slavery. These overlapping histories provided impetus for Afro-Asian solidarity as a revolutionary collective effort to challenge racial oppression throughout the diaspora. In nineteenth-century Cuba, for example, people of African descent joined forces with people of Asian descent to challenge the Spanish empire.[12]

In similar fashion, several black leaders in the United States during the twentieth century pursued collaborations with Asian activists in a unified effort to contest the global color line. Recognizing the shared historical experiences of peoples of Asian and African descent, W. E. B. Du Bois, the Jamaican black nationalist Marcus Garvey, and others emphasized the significance of Afro-Asian solidarity as a viable strategy for combating racial oppression. A number of earlier historical developments strengthened this point of view, including the Russo-Japanese War (1904–5), which sparked a rise in pro-Japanese sentiments among black men and women across the United States. The war began in February

---

[10] Ho and Mullen, *Afro Asia*, 3.

[11] Walton Look Lai, *The Chinese in the West Indies 1806–1995: A Documentary History* (Kingston: The University of the West Indies Press, 1998); Ho and Mullen, *Afro Asia*, 3.

[12] Ho and Mullen, *Afro Asia*, 45; Also see Kathleen M. Lopez, *Chinese Cubans: A Transnational History* (Chapel Hill: University of North Carolina Press, 2013).

1904 over tensions between Russia and Japan concerning territorial claims in Manchuria and Korea, and officially ended with the Treaty of Portsmouth on September 5, 1905. For many black leaders, Japan's successful defeat of the Russian military was no small accomplishment. It served as a powerful "example of people who demonstrated the fallacy of white assertions that people of color were innately incompetent or inferior."[13] In the aftermath of World War I, many African Americans viewed Japan as a model of racial progress and found much appeal in Japan's opposition to Western imperialism, embodied in their "Asia for the Asians" slogan. For many African American activists and intellectuals, especially those who embraced a black nationalist position, the Japanese slogan resonated with their own anti-imperialist call for "Africa for the Africans." Japan's defiance of European colonial powers left a favorable impression on black Americans during this period as did Japan's imperialist aspirations. The 1931 Japanese invasion of Manchuria, though a source of contention, reinforced these pro-Japanese sentiments among black activists and intellectuals.[14] According to historian Gerald Horne, "black leaders ... looked to Japan as a living and breathing refutation of the very basis of white supremacy, that is, that one had to be of a 'pure European descent' in order to construct an advanced society."[15]

This was certainly the case for Madam C. J. Walker, a pioneer in the black beauty culture industry who presided over a global beauty empire. Born Sarah Breedlove in 1867 in Delta, Louisiana, Walker rose to fame during the early twentieth century after making a fortune marketing beauty and hair products. Walker's widespread influence, however, extended far beyond the world of cosmetology. Like Du Bois and Garvey, the self-made millionaire envisioned collaborations with Japanese people as a strategy for ending racism, colonialism, and imperialism. On January 2, 1919, Walker established the International League of Darker Peoples (ILDP), a short-lived but significant black internationalist organization in the United States. In a meeting held at Walker's home on the banks of the Hudson River, she joined forces with several other well-known black activists, including Marcus Garvey, labor organizer A. Philip Randolph, and Harlem clergyman Adam Clayton Powell Sr., to launch the ILDP in an effort to advance the interests of people of color in the United States and across the globe. Against the backdrop of World

---

[13] Kearney, *African American Views of the Japanese*, p. xxv.

[14] Kearney, *African American Views of the Japanese*, 72.

[15] Gerald Horne, *Race War: White Supremacy and the Japanese Attack on the British Empire* (New York University Press, 2004), 43.

War I, the ILDP provided a platform for Walker and her associates to advocate for the rights and dignity of marginalized groups across the world and tap into a surging anti-imperial and anti-colonial fervor.

Walker and others in the ILDP promoted Afro-Asian solidarity, calling for black men and women to collaborate with people of Asian descent in the global struggle for political rights and freedom. Building on a long history of political alliances between people of African and Asian descent, the ILDP provided a space for both groups to collaborate in the immediate aftermath of World War I. In January 1919, only five days after founding the ILDP, Walker coordinated a historic meeting between the ILDP and Japanese editor S. Kurowia, publisher of the Tokyo newspaper *Yorozu Choho*. Kurowia was also one of the Japanese representatives who had been selected to participate in the 1919 Paris Peace Conference. Planned for January 18, 1919, the Paris Peace Conference brought together more than thirty nations for the purpose of establishing peace terms following the end of World War I. Hoping to capitalize on this significant event, Walker coordinated a meeting with Kurowia to request Japan's assistance in advocating for racial equality at the Paris Conference.[16] Although the issue of racial prejudice was ultimately sidelined at the Paris Peace Conference, Walker's actions laid the groundwork for a new generation of black women activists and intellectuals in the decades to follow. Viewing Japan as a model and potential ally, black women were among the most vocal proponents for Afro-Asian solidarity.

Afro-Asian Solidarity during the 1930s

The political demands that were raised by activists during the early twentieth century continued to inform black political thought and praxis in the decades to follow. The 1930s, in particular, gave rise to the proliferation of black internationalist political organizations, which provided platforms from which African Americans could build alliances with Asian activists in the global struggle against white supremacy. These organizations included the Pacific Movement of the Eastern World (PMEW), the Development of Our Own (TDOO), and the PME. Building on the pro-Japanese sentiments that circulated in black communities in the aftermath of the Russo-Japanese War, the leaders of these organizations viewed Japan as a model and potential military ally in the struggle against global white supremacy.[17] Japan's withdrawal from the League of Nations after the 1931 invasion of Manchuria strengthened this point

---

[16] Onishi, *Transpacific Antiracism*, 33.
[17] See Allen Jr., "When Japan Was Champion of the 'Darker Races.'"

of view. After facing mounting international criticism, leaders of Japan parted ways with the League in 1933 as a direct refutation of Western control. Japan's withdrawal from the League in 1933, combined with the earlier victories in the Russo-Japanese War, amplified the place of Japan in the black political imagination. By the early 1930s, Japan had become a "symbol of pride for the darker races."[18]

Significantly, Japan helped to amplify this point of view by sending the message, at least publicly, that they welcomed African Americans' visions of solidarity. In 1919, Japan's delegation to the Paris Peace Conference submitted an amendment to the League of Nations, the international peacekeeping organization established at the end of World War I, in support of racial equality.[19] In reality, Japan's racial equality proposal was driven by nationalistic aspirations – a quest for power – rather than a genuine desire to advance racial equality for *all*.[20] While the Japanese delegation was calling for racial equality at the Paris Peace Conference, the Japanese government was working actively to block Korean efforts for self-determination.[21]

Yet many black activists would still view the proposal as a bold stance for equality, and as a symbol that Japan was on their side in the global struggle for freedom. In the 1920s and 1930s, various Japanese politicians, activists, and writers, including retired army general Kojiro Sato and ultranationalist political theorist Uchida Ryohei, contributed to the rhetoric that Japan was in full support of African Americans.[22] Japan's support for Ethiopia, following Italy's invasion of the country in 1935, also amplified black activist-intellectuals' efforts to advance Afro-Asian solidarity. Japanese journalists, such as Shoji Yunosuke, a special correspondent for the *Osaka Mainichi* newspaper, played a significant role in bolstering Japanese support for Ethiopia in the 1930s.[23] These public messages of support resonated with many black activists who maintained the belief that Japanese people reciprocated their visions of Afro-Asian solidarity.

During this period, black activists in the Midwest found a space in which to advance Afro-Asian solidarity in the PME. Founded by Gordon

---

[18] Kenneth Barnes, "Inspiration from the East: Black Arkansans Look to Japan," *Arkansas Historical Quarterly* 69.3 (2010): 201–19 (204).

[19] Allen, "When Japan was Champion of the 'Darker Races,'" 29.

[20] Naoko Shimazu, *Japan, Race and Equality: The Racial Equality Proposal of 1919* (London: Routledge, 1998).

[21] Onishi, *Transpacific Antiracism*, 27.

[22] Allen, "When Japan was Champion of the 'Darker Races,'" 29.

[23] David J. Stocker and Jonathan A. Grant, *Girding for Battle: The Arms Trade in a Global Perspective, 1815–1940* (Westport, CT: Praeger, 2003), 152, n.58.

in Chicago in December 1932, the organization drew a massive following of black activists in the city and across the United States. Gordon's early childhood years were critical in shaping her interest in black internationalist politics. Born Mittie Maude Lena Nelson on August 2, 1889 in the small rural Webster Parish of Louisiana, Gordon spent her early childhood in Louisiana, but it was not long before her family moved to Hope, Arkansas in an effort to find better job and educational opportunities. The education system in Webster Parish thwarted her parents' plans to provide a decent education for Gordon and her nine siblings. According to Gordon, "[S]chool facilities for colored children were so bad in Webster Parish, that the third-grade was as high as one could go, because pressure was so strong against educating [N]egroes."[24] Local resistance against black education coupled with vast disparities in the quality between white and black schools confirmed her parents' decision to move out of Webster Parish in 1900. To their dismay, however, the educational opportunities for African Americans in Arkansas were no different from what they had left behind. To address the disparity of education, Gordon's father, the son of a former slave who had been denied access to formal education, decided to homeschool his children with the limited education that he had received.

Although Gordon had access to limited formal education, the education she did receive from her father was critical in shaping her internationalist ideas. Through her father's teachings, Gordon was exposed to the writings of Bishop Henry McNeal Turner. A preacher in the African Methodist Episcopal (AME) church, Turner began advocating emigration when his political prospects abruptly ended after Reconstruction. Convinced that extinction was the only likely outcome for African Americans who chose not to emigrate, Turner appealed to African Americans to leave the country during the late nineteenth century. An avowed Pan-Africanist, Turner maintained a strong affinity for Africa, which he described as the "thermometer that will determine the status of the Negro the world over."[25] Importantly, Turner maintained an internationalist vision, recognizing that the challenges facing black people in the United States were inextricably linked to the experiences of people of color across the globe.[26] Gordon would embrace these ideas later in life, emphasizing the shared struggles of people of color in the United States

---

[24] Mittie Maude Lena Gordon to Earnest Sevier Cox, October 27, 1939, Box 5, Folder 2, Earnest Sevier Cox Papers, 1821–1973, Rare Book, Manuscript, and Special Collections Library, Duke University, Durham, North Carolina.

[25] Quoted in Tunde Adeleke, *UnAfrican Americans: Nineteenth Century Black Nationalists and the Civilizing Mission* (Lexington: University Press of Kentucky, 2015), 96.

[26] Adeleke, *UnAfrican Americans*, 95.

and abroad. Her call for the "confraternity among all dark races," which became a mantra for the organization she established years later, underscored this internationalist vision.[27]

Gordon's relocation to Chicago during the early twentieth century marked a key turning point in her life. Like many other black southerners who collectively resisted Jim Crow and white supremacy during the World War I era, Gordon moved to Chicago during the early years of the Great Migration. There Gordon and other working-class "New Negro" migrants joined a thriving black consumer culture and intellectual community in the city.[28] Her ideas about Japan and Afro-Asian solidarity became crystalized in this period, coinciding with her involvement in the Universal Negro Improvement Association (UNIA). Established in Jamaica in 1914 by Marcus Garvey, with the assistance of Amy Ashwood, the UNIA was the largest and most influential black nationalist organization of the twentieth century.[29] While Garvey certainly endorsed Pan-Africanist politics – by emphasizing the belief that African peoples, on the continent and in the diaspora, share a common past and destiny – he maintained a commitment to black internationalism in the broadest sense of the term.[30] He articulated a global vision of liberation that sought to address not only the concerns of people of African descent but the plight of *all* people of color worldwide.

One of the crucial aspects of Garvey's internationalism was his vision of Afro-Asian solidarity. Through the pages of the *Negro World*, the UNIA's official newspaper, Garvey expressed pro-Japanese sentiments and encouraged political collaborations with Japan. In 1918, the charismatic black nationalist leader publicly endorsed Afro-Asian solidarity, insisting that the "next war will be between the Negroes and the whites." "With Japan to fight with us," Garvey went on to argue, "we can win such a war."[31] In 1919, Garvey praised Japan's assertiveness and went on to appeal to his supporters to anticipate the "great day ... of the war of races,

---

[27]   Keisha N. Blain, "'Confraternity among All Dark Races': Mittie Maude Lena Gordon and the Practice of Black (Inter)nationalism in Chicago, 1932–1942," *Palimpsest: A Journal on Women, Gender, and the Black International* 5.2 (2016): 151–81.

[28]   Davarian L. Baldwin, *Chicago's New Negroes: Modernity, the Great Migration and Black Urban Life* (Chapel Hill: University of North Carolina Press, 2007).

[29]   Tony Martin, *Race First: The Ideological and Organizational Struggles of Marcus Garvey and the Universal Negro Improvement Association* (Dover: The Majority Press, 1986); Adam Ewing, *The Age of Garvey: How a Jamaican Activist Created a Mass Movement and Changed Global Black Politics* (Princeton University Press, 2017).

[30]   Hakim Adi and Marika Sherwood, *Pan-African History: Political Figures from Africa and the Diaspora since 1787* (New York: Routledge, 2003).

[31]   Quoted in Allen, "When Japan was Champion of the 'Darker Races,'" 29.

when Asia will lead out to defeat Europe."[32] Black journalist T. Thomas Fortune expressed similar sentiments in the *Negro World*, praising Japan after a visit to the country. Drawing a contrast between "glorious Japan" and the United States, Fortune noted that he was "very much at home" in the former.[33]

Other black writers grappled with the significance of Japan during this period. In an editorial for the *Negro World*, Harlem radical Hubert Harrison described Japan as "the most powerful" of the "darker nations" and went on to suggest that Japan was "only relevant insofar as it served as 'an index' to advance the ends of black liberation."[34] In another *Negro World* article entitled "The Line-Up of the Color Line," Harrison endorsed Afro-Asian solidarity and articulated his commitment to black internationalism. "We need to join hands across the sea," Harrison argued. "We need to know what they are doing in India; we need to know what they are doing in China; we need to know what they are doing in Africa; and we need to let them know what we are doing over here."[35]

Harrison's statements, like Garvey's, illuminate how the UNIA and its periodical provided crucial avenues for strengthening ties between black activists and Asian activists during the 1920s and early 1930s. Indeed, the UNIA brought Gordon and other like-minded black activists into contact with several Asian activists, including Ashima Takis who delivered a speech at a UNIA meeting at which Gordon was present. Born in the Philippines in 1900, Takis, whose real name was Policarpio Manansala, had adopted a Japanese persona in an effort to secure approval among Japanese sympathizers in the African American community.[36] In the early 1930s, he had joined forces with a group of black and Asian activists in St. Louis, Missouri to establish the Pacific Movement of the Eastern World (PMEW), a pro-Japanese organization that supported the unification of people of color globally.[37] Representing their commitment to transracial unity, Takis and other PMEW leaders designed a banner with the colors black, brown, and yellow – symbolizing the organization's appeal to people of color across the globe.[38] By the

---

[32] Quoted in Robert A. Hill, *Marcus Garvey and the Universal Negro Improvement Association Papers*, Vol. II (Berkeley: University of California Press, 1983), 42.2.

[33] T. Thomas Fortune, "Some Dream Hours in Glorious Japan," *Negro World*, 14 June 1924, 4.

[34] Hubert Harrison and Jeffrey B. Perry, *A Hubert Harrison Reader* (Middletown, CT: Wesleyan University Press, 2001), 230.

[35] Harrison and Perry, *A Hubert Harrison Reader*, 128.

[36] Marc Gallicchio, *The African American Encounter with Japan and China* (Chapel Hill: University of North Carolina Press, 2000), 97.

[37] Gallicchio, *The African American Encounter with Japan and China*, 97.

[38] Barnes, "Inspiration from the East," 207.

mid-1930s, chapters of the organization could be found in several states including Arkansas, Pennsylvania, Maryland, and Missouri. The organization drew a following of mostly working-class black activists who came to embrace the vision of Japan as a "Champion of the Darker Races." For example, Burt Cornish, an elevator operator in St. Louis, joined the organization in the early 1930s and later recalled having an interest in Takis' plans to facilitate black emigration to Japan. With Takis' promise that impoverished African Americans would find better job opportunities in Japan and equal opportunities in other sectors of society, several thousand African Americans in Missouri became actively involved in the PMEW.[39] The emphasis on potential job opportunities for black Americans no doubt appealed to those who were struggling to make ends meet. This was certainly the case for Mittie Maude Lena Gordon who managed to keep a small restaurant running for a few years before it folded around 1934. Against the backdrop of the global depression, Gordon relied on government relief for some semblance of financial stability. "Many times I [went] without food yet traveled to carry out the work," she wrote. "And I have never received one penny salary."[40] Despite the limited financial resources, Gordon worked diligently to organize black activists and actively sought out new political alliances during the late 1920s and early 1930s.

Sometime in 1931, she held a meeting with Takis in Chicago, immediately following his talk on Japan at a local UNIA meeting. Reminiscent of his earlier statements to UNIA members, Takis laid out his vision for the PMEW and suggested that the Japanese people would lend their support for black emigration efforts. Gordon found the proposition appealing but admitted that she was most intrigued by Takis' support for black political self-determination and emigration. "I had already decided to go ahead with the [PMEW]," she later remarked, "after I found there was no hope of our going to Africa through the U.N.I.A."[41] The two activists collaborated in the months that followed, circulating an emigration petition in Chicago and later in Indiana, until their relationship began to unravel. While records from the Federal Bureau of Investigation (FBI) indicate that the source of the conflict was financial, Gordon attributed the conflict to ideological differences.[42] Recounting the course of events

---

[39]   Ernest Allen, Jr., "Waiting for Tojo: The Pro-Japan Vigil of Black Missourians, 1932–1943," *Gateway Heritage* 16 (1995): 38–55.

[40]   Gordon to Cox, June 26, 1936, Box 4, Folder 2, Cox Papers.

[41]   *United States of America v. Mittie Maud Lena Gordon*, Reply Brief for Appellants, Box 34, Cox Papers.

[42]   Robert A. Hill, *The FBI's RACON: Racial Conditions in the United States during World War II* (Boston: Northeastern University Press, 1995), 524.

years later, Gordon insisted that she parted ways with Takis when he proposed emigration to Manchuria instead of West Africa. Unlike PMEW member Burt Cornish and other local black activists in St. Louis, who welcomed the opportunity to relocate to Japan, Gordon rejected the proposal. She was unwilling to support African American emigration to Japan's newly conquered territory. This is especially significant, revealing some of the ideological tensions among black internationalists during this period. Although Gordon maintained an interest in Afro-Asian solidarity, and certainly understood its utility in the global struggle against white supremacy, she was also unwilling to abandon her Pan-Africanist vision of uniting people of African descent in "Liberia or some other place or places in Africa."[43] Gordon reasoned that Africa was the only logical destination for people of African descent.

Despite parting ways with Ashima Takis and the PMEW in the early 1930s, Gordon maintained pro-Japanese sentiments, believing that the struggle for black liberation could not be divorced from the struggle to end racial oppression worldwide. Mirroring the views of Marcus Garvey, W. E. B. Du Bois, Hubert Harrison, and others, Gordon embraced the view that the struggle against white supremacy in the United States was intertwined with the larger struggle against white imperialism worldwide. Drawing a direct link between the manifestations of white supremacy in the United States and Asia, Gordon argued that the "destruction of the white man in Asia is the destruction of the white man in the United States."[44] In one instance, Gordon emphasized the connection between the challenges facing African descended people and the plight of Indians. "The India situation is somewhat connected," she argued, "and the complete freedom of India will bring complete freedom to the American black people, because the same men are holding them in slavery."[45] Her statements mirrored those of other working-class black women activist-intellectuals during this period. Detroit-based activist Pearl Sherrod, for example, emphasized the necessity of Afro-Asian solidary during the 1930s.[46] In a June 1934 article, published in the *Detroit Tribune*

---

[43] Peace Movement of Ethiopia, *Constitution of the Peace Movement of Ethiopia: One God, One Country, One People; also, a Brief History, Memorial to President, Funeral Oration and Burial Ceremonies, Battle Hymn of the Peace Movement* (United States: s.n., 1941?), 15 [hereafter Peace Movement of Ethiopia Constitution].

[44] Gordon to Theodore Bilbo, January 27, 1942, Exhibit 132 in Report by Special Agent John Colin Robinson, FBI Investigative File no. 100-124410.

[45] Gordon to Tommie Thomas, August 28, 1942, Exhibit 125, FBI File no. 100-124410.

[46] On Pearl Sherrod, see Keisha N. Blain, "'[F]or the Rights of Dark People in Every Part of the World': Pearl Sherrod, Black Internationalist Feminism, and Afro-Asian Politics in the 1930s," *Souls: A Critical Journal of Black Politics, Culture and Society* 17.1 (2015): 90–112.

Independent newspaper, Sherrod argued that black people could only increase their political power by forging alliances with Japan: "[O]ur minds have been diseased, and we have tried 'Mr. White's' medicine and failed; tried 'Mr. Black's' medicine and failed. *Now we must try 'Mr. Brown's medicine.*" "No doubt he will cure us of the mental disease which was caused from a lack of organization," Sherrod continued, "then we can develop ourselves."[47] Sherrod's statements, similar to Gordon's, underscore how a commitment to black internationalism shaped black working-class women's political vision during this period. Significantly, their statements exemplify how black working-class intellectuals drew an explicit link between racism in the United States and colonial subjugation in Asia and other parts of the globe.[48]

In Gordon's political vision, white colonial rule could only be dismantled if people of color united to challenge it. Through Afro-Asian solidarity, based on shared histories, similar struggles, and mutual political interests, Gordon hoped to improve the lives of black people in the United States and abroad. As a result, she attempted to forge new alliances with Asian activists from her base in Chicago during the 1930s. In May 1934, she sent a letter to Kenji Nakauchi, then Japanese Consul General in Chicago, introducing her organization and requesting his support. "We are seeking the assistance and cooperation of your people in this our darkest hour," she wrote. "We have suffered untold misery in America over three hundred years and now our condition is far worse than ever," she continued. Gordon requested a "private interview" and assured Nakauchi that she would be willing to "meet on [his] own terms."[49] Similar to other black radical activists during this period, Gordon maintained the view that Japan would come to the aid of people of African descent in the fight against US racism. To that end, she attempted to forge a collaboration with Sadao Araki, a Japanese military general. In the letter to Araki, Gordon requested a truce between the PME and "the dark skin[ned] people of the East[ern] world [sic]" in the

---

[47] Mrs. P. T. Takahashi, "Development of Our Own," *Detroit Tribune Independent*, June 16, 1934.

[48] On African Americans' political engagement with India, see Gerald Horne, *The End of Empires: African Americans and India* (Philadelphia, PA: Temple University Press, 2008); Nico Slate, *Colored Cosmopolitanism: The Shared Struggle for Freedom in the United States and India* (Cambridge, MA: Harvard University Press, 2012).

[49] Gordon to Sadao Araki, n.d., Exhibit 160a in Report by Special Agents Francis A. Regan, Aubrey Elliott, Jr., Andrew J. Rafferty, and Richard W. Axtell, FBI Investigative File no. 100-124410. FBI file on the Ethiopian Pacific Movement, 100-56894-129.

event of a war between Japan and the United States.[50] "The war is between the white man and the Japanese," Gordon insisted, "and we are not included."[51]

Gordon's comments, while emblematic of her interest in forging transnational alliances, also reveal the "uneven, inconclusive, and sometimes contradictory" nature of "black manifestations of imperial discourses."[52] Indeed, Gordon failed to acknowledge Japan's own imperialist aspirations – especially its aggressive efforts to control China – and she overlooked Japan's exclusionary policies and mistreatment of Koreans. She failed to recognize that Japan was primarily concerned with "the attainment of a 'white' imperial power status."[53] Instead, she remained preoccupied with a vision of Japan as "champion of the darker races" and advocated this message through her writings and speeches. Ultimately, the activist-intellectual was far more concerned about bringing an end to *white* imperialism than to imperialism in general. Although she viewed Japanese people as important allies in the fight against racial oppression and colonialism, Gordon overlooked Japan's own military aggression toward other people of color. She viewed Japan's aggression in China and their imperialist aspirations as somehow less severe than white imperialism – so much so that she told one PME leader in Arkansas to use "the same method that the Japanese used on the Chinese" when he solicited her advice on how to organize indifferent local black residents.[54] Her position on Japan was similar to the views of many other black intellectuals of the period, including W. E. B. Du Bois who excused Japanese imperialism.[55] "The thing that must impress us as colored people," he explained in a 1936 article, "is that the chances for economic reform [in China] under Japanese imperialism are infinitely

[50] Gordon to Sadao Araki, n.d., Exhibit 160a in Report by Special Agents Francis A. Regan, Aubrey Elliott, Jr., Andrew J. Rafferty, and Richard W. Axtell, FBI Investigative File no. 100-124410.

[51] Gordon to Sadao Araki, n.d., Exhibit 160a in Report by Special Agents Francis A. Regan, Aubrey Elliott, Jr., Andrew J. Rafferty, and Richard W. Axtell, FBI Investigative File no. 100-124410.

[52] Stephanie Batiste, *Darkening Mirrors: Imperial Representation in Depression-Era African American Performance* (Durham, NC: Duke University Press, 2011), 258.

[53] Yuichiro Onishi, "The New Negro of the Pacific: How African Americans Forged Cross-Racial Solidarity with Japan, 1917–1922," *The Journal of African American History* 92.2 (2007): 191–213 (202).

[54] Letter to Tommie Thomas, July 9, 1941, Exhibit 189 Report by Special Agents Francis A. Regan, Aubrey Elliott, Jr., and Richard W. Axtell, FBI Investigative File no. 100-124410, National Archives, Washington, DC.

[55] See Onishi, *Transpacific Antiracism.*

greater than any chances which colored people would have under the most advanced white leaders of Western reform, except in Russia."[56]

Although Gordon's admiration of Japan was consistent with Du Bois' vision, the two activist-intellectuals diverged on the matters of war and militarism. The outbreak of World War II marked a turning point in Gordon's political activism. In the aftermath of Germany's attack on Poland in September 1939, and the immediate military response from British and French Allies, it became apparent to Gordon that a global crisis was at hand – one that would forever change the world in which she lived. Naturally, she became increasingly concerned about the future of millions of people of color in Africa, Asia, and the Caribbean whose lives would be greatly impacted by the global war. As Western Allies began to mobilize for war, Gordon also feared for the lives of black men who were being recruited to fight for freedom and democracy in Europe when they were being denied the same privileges in the United States and in the colonial territories. "Our hearts are broken, our eyes are filled with tears to think that our brothers and sons, weak from hunger and ragged are being recruited to go back to Europe to another war" she wrote in 1939. "We hope that this nation will stay out of this war," she continued, "or at least keep the black man out of it. It is not our war; we have nothing to do with it."[57]

PME weekly meetings, held in various cities across the United States, provided a significant platform for Gordon to disseminate these ideas among working-class and impoverished black activists. These meetings not only brought members of the community together, but they also provided private spaces in which activists could discuss key developments taking place across the globe. This was especially significant because the organization did not have an official periodical like other black organizations such as the National Association for the Advancement of Colored People (NAACP) and National Urban League (NUL). In a 1939 letter to a political ally, Gordon expressed disappointment that the PME lacked the resources to launch a "small newspaper to circulate among the people at least twice a month."[58] In the absence of a newspaper, however, Gordon held mass meetings and relied primarily on letters and pamphlets to express her views on various issues. In this way, the black nationalist "street-scholar" used letters and pamphlets as easily accessible mediums to reach the black masses. PME leaders read aloud from these letters and pamphlets, which Gordon diligently sent out

---

[56] W. E. B. Du Bois, "No Chance," *Pittsburgh Courier,* February 29, 1936, A2.
[57] Gordon to Bilbo, October 15, 1939, Box 1090, Bilbo Papers.
[58] Gordon to Cox, October 15, 1939, Box 5, Folder 4, Cox Papers.

to local chapters on a monthly basis. These letters often contained references to international developments, an indication that Gordon wanted to ensure that her followers would not lose sight of global freedom struggles of the period.

One of the key topics Gordon addressed during this period was African American involvement in World War II. "America has too many enemies within to go abroad and fight," she argued.[59] "It seems to me," she later explained, "that before we go abroad to clean other people's houses, we should first clean our own."[60] Like many other black radical activists, Gordon maintained serious misgivings about supporting US interests in a war against Japan and other nations. Without mincing words, she insisted, "It is the white man's war and we hope that our government will not force us to take part in another white man's war."[61] With disenfranchisement, racial violence, and Jim Crow segregation at home, many African Americans were ambivalent about supporting American military aspirations even if they did not necessarily desire an alliance with Japan or relish the idea of an Axis victory. While mainstream civil rights activists, including leaders of the NAACP and NUL demanded an improvement in racial conditions at home, Gordon called for stronger ties with Japan in order to secure black political self-determination and universal emancipation. "What credit do we get for being so loyal and patriotic to the U.S. government?" she asked rhetorically.[62] Given the history of enslavement and the mistreatment of black Americans, Gordon saw no benefit in supporting US interests in the war. To the contrary, she envisioned collaborations with Japan as the logical response. Moreover, she was convinced that the Japanese people would obtain victory in the war and come to the aid of African Americans.

Her perspective on World War II differed vastly from many of her contemporaries, including Du Bois who called on African Americans to join the war effort to improve their political standing in the United States.[63] Although she was critical of war, Gordon viewed World War II as a pivotal opportunity for black people to confront global white supremacy. Writing to a group of supporters in 1942, Gordon urged them to "be of good cheer for those who are suffering now will not have to suffer much longer. Everything is working in our favor all over the world." "In the very near future," she optimistically predicted, "the black

---

[59] Gordon to Cox, November 5, 1939, Box 5, Folder 4, Cox Papers.

[60] Gordon to Cox, July 31, 1940, Box 5, Folder 5, Cox Papers.

[61] Gordon to Cox, December 31, 1940, Box 5, Folder 5, Cox Papers.

[62] Gordon to Cox, March 10, 1942, Box 6, Folder 1, Cox Papers.

[63] See Gerald Horne, *Black and Red: W. E. B. Du Bois and the Afro-American Response to the Cold War, 1944–1963* (Albany: State University of New York Press, 1986).

man will be free."[64] Gordon's statements, which PME leaders in Mississippi shared in local meetings, reflected her anti-colonial position. One year before Kwame Nkrumah, future prime minister of Ghana, black nationalist leader Amy Ashwood Garvey, Trinidadian journalist George Padmore and other activists gathered at the Fifth Pan-African Congress (1945) to confront European colonization, Gordon lent her support, using her letters as a forum for advocating African liberation. Writing to one ally, she expressed frustration over European imperialism in Africa: "Speaking of Italy and Germany controlling of Africa has left me bewildered. It is the desire of the Nationalist in America as well as Africa that our country be free of all whites."[65] While Gordon maintained an anti-colonial position, she held fast to the belief that an alliance with Japan, despite its imperialist proclivities, would bolster the political standing of people of African descent in the United States and across the world.

Conclusion

The significance of a political alliance with Japan appeared all the more pressing as many feared that the war would bolster white imperialist aspirations. The Japanese attack on Pearl Harbor on December 7, 1941, and the other Japanese military "victories" that followed, signaled to many black radical activists that an alliance with Japan was necessary since Japan appeared to have the upper hand.[66] According to one FBI informant who discreetly attended one of Gordon's meetings in Chicago in 1941, the black nationalist leader had not only dissuaded her supporters from serving in the US army but offered a positive outlook on Pearl Harbor, arguing that "on December 7th, 1941, one billion black people struck for freedom."[67] Although Gordon later denied making this statement, her earlier letters to Japanese activists, combined with her public endorsement of Afro-Asian solidarity, suggest that she embraced this point of view. Indeed, many of her letters and pamphlets emphasizing her pro-Japanese sentiments ended up in the hands of federal officials who viewed Gordon as a threat to national security. Her unprecedented

---

[64] Gordon to T. H. Bernard, July 29, 1942; Exhibit 110 in Report by Special Agents Francis A. Regan, Aubrey Elliot, Jr., and Richard W. Axtell, FBI Investigative File no. 100-124410.

[65] Letter to Earnest Sevier Cox, March 2, 1942, Exhibit 142 in Report by Special Agents Francis A. Regan, Aubrey Elliott, Jr., and Richard W. Axtell, FBI Investigative File no. 100-124410, National Archives, Washington, DC.

[66] See Gallicchio, *The African American Encounter with Japan and China*.

[67] Quoted in Hill, *FBI's RACON*, 526.

influence among the black masses, and her uncanny ability to galvanize working-poor black activists during the 1930s and 1940s provided impetus for the FBI's crackdown of her movement. Despite an appeal in the months that followed, the court upheld Gordon's guilt and sentenced her to two years in prison. Although she attempted to resume her efforts in 1945, she was forced to temper her internationalist activities.

Mittie Maude Lena Gordon's story offers a window into black women's internationalist thought during the 1930s and 1940s. Amidst the social and political upheavals of the Great Depression and World War II, Gordon was part of a cohort of black activist-intellectuals who envisioned collaborations with Japanese people as a strategy for challenging racism and global white supremacy. This "street-scholar" captured the imagination of the black masses in Chicago and beyond, and utilized unconventional mediums, including pamphlets and personal letters, to spread her ideas. Through her writings and speeches, which reached thousands of mostly working-class and impoverished black people, Gordon articulated a global vision of freedom in her attempt to secure civil and human rights. Centering her ideas about Japan and her efforts to collaborate with Asian activists broadens our understanding of the diverse ways working-poor black women in the United States shaped internationalist thought and praxis in the twentieth century.

Elizabeth Wiskemann, Scholar-Journalist, and the Study of International Relations

Geoffrey Field

On July 6, 1971 British newspapers reported the suicide of Elizabeth Wiskemann; she had taken a lethal dose of pills washed down by alcohol. Letters to *The Times* soon appeared praising her as an "outstanding scholar, a sensitive and loyal friend and a brave woman who risked her life for her country."[1] Her books and articles were once fixtures on the reading lists of students of international affairs and Eastern Europe, as well as undergraduates studying twentieth-century European history in the 1960s, but today Wiskemann's name mostly draws blank looks from those whose intellectual formation came later. As scholars revise the disciplinary history of IR, expanding its boundaries and recovering the contributions of women pioneers, her story illuminates both the challenges faced by women in British academia before the mid-1960s and the late and slow institutional emergence of both IR and contemporary history as distinctive fields of study.

An historian by training, Wiskemann's interest in international affairs, like many of the women international thinkers examined in this book, began with post-World War I liberal internationalism and matured in the fight against Nazism and government service in World War II. Very few formal academic IR programs existed before the 1950s and those who wrote about international relations were usually journalists, historians, economists, diplomats, or legal scholars. Wiskemann was 59 years old when she got her first real university job in 1958, a Chair in International Relations at Edinburgh. Before that she was a highly respected commentator on contemporary Europe; indeed, she always liked to think of herself as a scholar-journalist, although in doing so she risked being depreciated as merely or primarily a journalist. The author of ten books, including several of lasting significance, scores of essays, translations and innumerable reviews (over 300 for the *TLS* alone, in those days unsigned), she was both prolific and remarkable for her breadth

---

[1] *The Times*, July 9, 1971, 14.

of expertise. With equal mastery she wrote about Germany, Switzerland, Italy, and Eastern Europe, focusing especially on Europe's minority and nationalist disputes and contested borderlands. Few scholars had an equal knowledge of documentary sources and she combined that with constant travel, immersion in the cultures she studied, and personal acquaintance with many of the politicians and officials about whom she wrote.

Wiskemann's omission from disciplinary histories of IR is in some respects unsurprising. She was empiricist in her approach, uncomfortable with IR's integration into the social sciences, and toward the end of her career identified more as a contemporary historian. But her publications deserve to be "recovered" and re-inserted into the history of IR both for their sheer quality and for her rigorous application of historical methods to analyzing international affairs. They also illuminate a period when IR was in its infancy, a conjunction of several disciplines and plural approaches before the grooming of professionally trained IR scholars. Her career also illustrates the enormous challenges faced by women in professional life, especially if they lacked private means. By most measures Wiskemann enjoyed a great deal of success and she was supported along the way by both male and female networks. But in none of the realms in which she operated – journalism, government service, and academia – did she enjoy the same opportunities as men and she encountered barriers, slights, sometimes outright obstruction because of her sex. "She represented for me the prototype of the emancipated English woman," wrote German TV correspondent Franca Magnani.[2] However, like many of her generation, Wiskemann did not describe herself as a feminist and she was ambivalent about aspects of 1960s feminism. She was always something of an outsider, doubly so in academia as a journalist and a woman. As scholars now recover the missing women of IR, her story provides yet another reminder that they were always there, hidden in plain sight.

Cambridge to Berlin: The Making of a Journalist

Elizabeth Wiskemann was born in 1899 in the upper-middle-class London suburb of Sidcup, the youngest of three children. Her father, a German from Hesse-Kassel, ran a business trading in chemicals at the London Wool Exchange; her mother, to whom she felt closer, came from

---

[2] Franca Magnani, *Eine italienische Familie* (Cologne: Kiepenheuer & Witsch, 1990), 283.

a prominent and wealthy Ipswich family. She attended Notting Hill High School and in 1918 won a scholarship to Cambridge to read History at Newnham College. Women could sit examinations in many subjects but before 1948 were awarded diplomas rather than formal degrees. Wiskemann got a First in the History Tripos, but two things overshadowed her success: her mother's sudden death in the influenza epidemic just before she left for college and her father's financial troubles which ended in bankruptcy in 1922. She hoped for an academic career and embarked upon a doctorate in diplomatic history under the supervision of H. W. V. Temperley. This proved a disaster. Temperley provided little help or guidance and she believed him seriously resentful of an independent woman. Very few research grants were open to women and to pay her way she began teaching first at a private girls' school and then tutoring Newnham undergraduates. Several years passed, and when she submitted her thesis in late 1928 it was awarded an MLitt not a PhD – a serious setback to her career aspirations. The reverse, Mark Cornwall suggests, fueled "a lifelong subconscious quest to prove that her qualities as an historian matched those of any professional male academic."[3]

Hitherto Wiskemann's intellectual interests had focused on France and Italy rather than Central or Eastern Europe, but in 1930, bitterly disappointed over the downgrading of her thesis, she took a step that was crucial in shaping her future. Feeling the need to get away from Cambridge, she decided to move to Berlin for several months. "I wanted," she told a friend, "a big city out of England where I could improve a language, get a little history written, and be able to earn some money."[4] Unlike many of her friends, she could not rely on family support or a private income, but Berlin was cheap and she managed to cobble together a living teaching English and doing translations. Always adept at networking, she quickly gained a wide circle of acquaintances, including academics, government officials, artists and writers, several of them well-known, like Arthur Koestler, George Grosz, and in Munich Thomas Mann and his family. Most importantly, she was soon riveted by the deepening political crisis of Weimar democracy and the rise of Nazism, and developed ties to the stellar band of British foreign correspondents in Berlin – including Norman Ebbutt of *The Times*, Darsie Gillie, then working for the *Morning Post*, and especially F. A. Voigt of the *Manchester Guardian*. They became her mentors, encouraging her to write and to

---

[3] Mark Cornwall, "Elizabeth Wiskemann and the Sudeten Question: A Woman at the 'Essential Hinge' of Europe," *Central Europe* 1.1 (2003): 55–75 (57).

[4] E. Wiskemann to Julian Trevelyan, April 5, 1930. Trevelyan Papers, Trinity College, Cambridge.

carve out a career in journalism. A Cambridge friend, Kingsley Martin, had recently become editor of *The New Statesman* and her first article – analyzing the Presidential election campaign between Hindenburg and Hitler – appeared there in April 1932. She continued tutoring undergraduates at Cambridge but spent university vacations in Central Europe.

Within two years Wiskemann had become the *Statesman's* lead correspondent in the German capital, albeit on a freelance basis, as well as writing occasional articles for *The Contemporary Review*, *The Nineteenth Century*, *The Scotsman*, and *The Manchester Guardian*. Her journalistic talents were quickly recognized: acutely intelligent, she was able to capture in concise, pungent prose both the atmosphere of the time and the salient developments in a fast-changing political scene. She also got interviews with leading figures like Chancellors Brüning, Papen, and Schleicher and after Hitler became Chancellor provided readers with detailed analyses of both factional conflicts within the Nazi movement and the spiraling lawlessness and violence against Jews and socialists. In March 1934 she was in Vienna reporting on Chancellor Dollfuss' use of army units and the fascist Heimwehr to smash the Socialist party. The following year she witnessed the plebiscite in the Saar province, which had been under League of Nations control for fifteen years, but now returned to Germany after a relentless Nazi campaign of intimidation. Back in England she worked hard to gain access to politicians and government officials, trying to convince them of the danger posed by Hitler, but often finding her alarm downplayed as inflated.

The danger for foreign journalists had grown and many of Wiskemann's closest colleagues in Berlin had either been expelled or had left Germany because they felt threatened. Sources had to be interviewed in secret; reporters acquired such habits as not talking on the phone, checking rooms for bugs, choosing meeting places with care, and being ever-vigilant for spies and police. In July 1936, traveling to Danzig (an autonomous city-state under the League of Nations) to report on the wave of terror that the pro-Nazi city government had unleashed against opposition deputies and newspapers, she felt understandably nervous visiting Sean Lester, the League's increasingly powerless High Commissioner, who showed her a cupboard full of weapons left behind by Nazi thugs after a recent brawl: "I went in and out of his house a good deal and I suppose Gestapo agents were watching; this could not be helped and had to be faced."[5] In fact, she had been under surveillance for

---

[5] E. Wiskemann, *The Europe I Saw* (London: Collins, 1968), 54.

six months. Returning to Berlin she was arrested and briefly interrogated by the Gestapo on grounds that her articles "abused the German Reich and National Socialism in the most outrageous fashion."[6] She was then released and ordered to leave the Reich. In the summer of the Berlin Olympics the authorities wanted her out of the country. In Britain her arrest was front page news and questions were put to Foreign Secretary Anthony Eden in the Commons.

Wiskemann's journalism relied heavily upon travel and first-hand observation. Expelled from Germany, she now turned increasingly to the so-called successor states (Austria, Czechoslovakia, Hungary, Romania, Yugoslavia) that had replaced the Habsburg Empire, examining Nazi economic penetration and the regime's manipulation of ethnic minority conflicts. But, above all, what determined the direction of her research was an invitation from A. J. Toynbee, director of Chatham House (Royal Institute for International Affairs), to write a book about the increasingly antagonistic relationship between the Czech state and its large, hostile ethnic German minority. From 1935, having made impressive election gains, the Sudeten German Party, led by Konrad Henlein, became increasingly aligned with Nazi ideology and escalated its demands for national autonomy, threatening the very existence of Czechoslovakia. In May 1937 Wiskemann moved to Prague and for the next six months worked at a feverish pace, interviewing major political figures, both Czechs and Germans, and traveling throughout the German-populated areas. Returning to London, she wrote what became a 300-page book in four months, finishing it in March 1938, two months ahead of schedule.[7]

The result was a remarkable book that surveyed the long, troubled history of Germans and Slavs in Bohemia, then examined the intensification of national conflict since World War I and the myriad ways in which this played out in economic, cultural, and political relations. Even today Wiskemann's research remains indispensable, since the ethnic German enclaves that she described in such detail disappeared with the mass expulsions of 1945–46. She was by no measure a neutral observer, having previously met and admired President Thomas Masaryk, his son Jan, and successor Edvard Beneš. She viewed Prague as an oasis of freedom compared to neighboring states and also believed that Nazi

---

[6] Bayerische Politische Polizei, Fa 119/2 S225, February 1936. Institut für Zeitgeschichte, Munich.

[7] E. Wiskemann, *Czechs & Germans* (London: Oxford University Press and The Royal Institute of International Affairs, 1938).

anti-Slav and anti-Semitic Pan-Germanism traced its origin to the fiercely contested borderlands of Bohemia, Moravia, and Austrian Silesia. But Wiskemann was also critical of Czech chauvinism and excesses and did not disguise that, goaded by economic depression and Nazi-fueled separatism, the Prague government had become increasingly authoritarian, violating basic rights and resorting to increasingly repressive police methods. Deeply frustrated, she saw Masaryk's state, which she still admired, splitting apart from these nationalist divisions. Successive efforts to ease the tensions and negotiate a political compromise collapsed because of long-festering internal grievances and mistrust and from external pressures exerted from Berlin. She understood why and how this was happening but could find no feasible political solution that might resolve the German–Slav rift.

However, her pessimism and sympathy for the Czechs was unwelcome in some parts of Whitehall where pro-appeasers were more sympathetic to Henlein. When Toynbee sent chapters of her draft manuscript to the Foreign Office for comment, Sir Robert Hadow, a staunch advocate of appeasement, attacked them as anti-German and called for changes. He suggested postponing publication since the Czechs "might use it for all they are worth in an endeavor to refute Henlein's claims and 'stir up opinion in England'." Toynbee consulted a second Foreign Office official who judged the chapters as "interesting, objective and unobjectionable," but he did insist upon some revisions and "toning down" of those parts of the book dealing with the period since 1935.[8] Hadow viewed the situation in geo-strategic terms: to preserve peace Hitler's aims should be accommodated. E. H. Carr arrived at the same conclusion in his famous polemic about utopian and realist thinkers, *The Twenty Years' Crisis*. Indeed, when in November 1938 Chatham House considered sponsoring an additional study of the German minority in Denmark, Carr, an influential board member, wrote Toynbee that "it should not be entrusted to Elizabeth Wiskemann with her marked and well-known anti-German slant"; he added: "The temptation to follow the current intellectual fashion and turn Chatham House into a highbrow anti-fascist propaganda bureau is obvious: the undesirability of yielding to it not less obvious."[9] As for Wiskemann, she was skeptical of geopolitical theorizing; historical analysis and close observation convinced her that Hitler's expansionism would be inflamed, not satisfied by concessions over the

---

[8] RIIA 16/23, "Czechs and Germans," 1938, Chatham House Archives, London.
[9] RIIA 4/Carr, Personal Correspondence Files, Chatham House Archives, London.

Sudetenland. As she wrote in a review of Carr's book: "there may be a German problem which cannot be solved by the application of generalized formulae."[10]

Czechs and Germans appeared in June 1938 just as the crisis seemed to slide toward war. It immediately received dozens of reviews, almost without exception glowingly positive: "distinguished throughout by a tone of judicial impartiality," "indispensable to every student of international affairs," "should explode many of the superficial theories that still linger in certain sections of the British press."[11] Lord Runciman, sent to Prague by Neville Chamberlain on an ill-fated mission to resolve the Czech–German problem, was photographed in the train reading it. In consequence Wiskemann's reputation as an expert on Nazi Germany and Eastern Europe soared. She was soon inundated with speaking invitations and offers of book contracts; she also embarked on a three-month lecture tour of cities in the United States and Canada. A second book soon followed: *Undeclared War*, largely a condensation of articles she wrote in the last year of peace.[12]

By the outbreak of war in September 1939 Wiskemann had achieved considerable individual prominence as a foreign correspondent and an expert on Central and Eastern Europe. But, as Julie Gottlieb has shown, she should also be viewed as a member of a whole cohort of political women who actively campaigned against Nazism and Chamberlain's appeasement policy in Britain.[13] Most were originally influenced by the liberal internationalism of men like Toynbee, Gilbert Murray, and Alfred Zimmern, but found their hopes for collective security through the League of Nations increasingly untenable. For many, Spain's civil war or the Czechoslovak crisis was the turning-point, but Wiskemann had experienced Nazism close-up years earlier. At Cambridge, influenced by Keynes' *Economic Consequences of the Peace*, she was an enthusiastic supporter of the League of Nations Union. The League, she always believed, had offered the best hope for international cooperation and its failure to a large degree was the fault of the major powers in not committing to it. By 1936 she was convinced that no accommodation was

[10] E. Wiskemann, "Forgetting Reality: A Scourge for Utopia," *The Observer*, January 28, 1940.

[11] J. C. Johnstone, *The Daily Telegraph*, July 5, 1938; *The Times*, June 3, 1938; R. W. Seton Watson, *The Spectator*, July 1, 1938.

[12] E. Wiskemann, *Undeclared War* (London: Constable, 1939).

[13] Julie V. Gottlieb, *'Guilty Women': Foreign Policy and Appeasement in Inter-War Britain* (Basingstoke: Palgrave Macmillan, 2015).

possible with the Nazi regime. "Soon," she warned, "we may have to decide whether a German peace ... is better or worse than war."[14] On her lecture tour in the United States she met Clarence Streit and was drawn to his idea for a federal union of democracies to withstand the Nazi and fascist threat, telling an American friend it was "just what I've been fumbling for these last two or three months."[15] But it's doubtful she viewed such a scheme as more than a pipe dream.

Wiskemann's early career is also illustrative of a number of women who became pioneers in the field of international relations. Born roughly 1898–1912 they graduated from university at a time when the Foreign Service and academia were largely closed to them and pursued their interests in foreign affairs through journalism, broadcasting, and pressure-group activism or the League's bureaucracies. When a *Times* roundup listed the best studies in international affairs from 1938, three of the top four mentioned were written by women, all non-academics – Wiskemann, Shiela Grant Duff, and Elizabeth Monroe.[16] Chatham House was another important formative context in many of their careers, offering a stimulating intellectual environment as well as providing research projects and opportunities to publish. Finally, a third (and often neglected) shared experience was government service in World War II, especially in intelligence or propaganda. A few examples will suffice: Ann ("Nancy") Lambton, Britain's foremost Persian scholar, was press attaché to the British embassy in Tehran where she was deeply involved in propaganda and SOE (Special Operations Executive) activities. Doreen Warriner, celebrated for her courage in rescuing Jews from pre-war Vienna, served in the Ministry of Economic Warfare and in Foreign Office intelligence. Elisabeth Barker, whose career included important positions in the BBC and Reuters, became the Political Warfare Executive (PWE) director of intelligence for Southeast Europe. And Elizabeth Monroe, a leading figure in Middle East studies, spent the war at the Ministry of Information where she was director of the Middle East Division. As was true of Wiskemann, wartime experiences were crucial in determining the future direction of their scholarship and in forging networks of personal ties in the post-war era.

[14] E. Wiskemann, "Hitler's Rhineland Election," *New Statesman and Nation*, April 4, 1936, 519.
[15] E. Wiskemann to Hamilton Fish Armstrong, December 20, 1938, Hamilton Fish Armstrong Papers, Princeton University.
[16] "Books and Exhibitions of the Year," *The Times*, January 2, 1939, 42.

9.1 Elizabeth Wiskemann during World War II.
Courtesy of Julian Brigstocke

Secret Agent and Starting Over in Post-War Europe

In September 1939 Wiskemann joined the Foreign Research and Press Service, really an offshoot of Chatham House in Oxford, which A. J. Toynbee envisioned as a body that would advise the government on foreign policy planning. But she grew bored and within a few months found a more interesting and active role, working as an agent in Switzerland for what became PWE. Large numbers of refugees from Nazi Germany and Fascist Italy had settled there and, as a neutral country with extensive trading connections, there was a constant and largely unchecked flow of officials, businessmen, and agents back and forth across its borders. Hitler's lightning victories in the West in 1940 further enhanced Switzerland's significance; now encircled by Axis-held territory and with other intelligence centers overrun, it became especially important as a "listening post." Wiskemann spent almost the entire war there, ostensibly as an assistant press attaché, but in fact recruiting agents and gathering a wide range of intelligence about enemy states and occupied Europe.[17]

The skills she had honed as a journalist served Wiskemann well as a secret agent, as did a huge range of personal contacts across Central and Eastern Europe and among the exile communities. Numerous Whitehall agencies used her information, either as straight intelligence or for propaganda purposes. "Not only," PWE noted, "is she ideally placed to reach the most influential persons connected with Vichy France in Switzerland, not only has she developed suitable channels to get material into occupied France, but we know that whenever she has received material she has been able to dispatch it to Eastern and Central Europe as well."[18] She supplied London with information about economic conditions in Axis Europe, popular morale, forced labor, the Nazi euthanasia program, mass killings of Jews in Romania, and the deportation of Hungarian Jews to Auschwitz. Effectiveness did not, however, make her popular in the British Legation in Berne, where she faced resistance and non-cooperation from diplomatic colleagues and members of rival covert units. Indeed, she often worked more amicably with Allen Dulles, the OSS station chief in Berne, than she did with her own compatriots. Different sections of British intelligence were embroiled in internecine struggles throughout the war. But the vagueness of Wiskemann's instructions from London, her lack of full diplomatic status until 1941, and the fact that she was a woman undoubtedly also increased the tension: "I was," she wrote, "for the first time perhaps since Temperley up against resentment of the independent female."[19]

Already in 1942 PWE's Italian directorate praised her reports as among the most valuable information they were receiving from secret sources. With the overthrow of Mussolini in July 1943 and German occupation of the peninsula, her contacts among the large new influx of Italian exiles to Switzerland proved even more valuable. She was soon providing London with much of its best intelligence on the partisan struggle in the north which she viewed as a "second *Risorgimento*," this time embracing the whole population, including peasants, workers, and women. Like many intellectuals she supported the *Giustizia e Libertà* group and the Action party (*Partito d'Azione*) as the best hope for liberals

---

[17] Neville Wylie, *Britain, Switzerland, and the Second World War* (Oxford University Press, 2003).

[18] H. Paniquian to P. Scarlett, October 22, 1942, FO898/256, The National Archives, Kew.

[19] Wiskemann, *The Europe I Saw*, 141.

and the far left to achieve both urgently needed social reform and the protection of individual rights. "The whole story of the Italian Resistance," she recalled, "was one of the most moving I have ever lived close to."[20] The fragmentation of the anti-fascist "resistance" coalition in 1946–47 was deeply disillusioning and she never again experienced the same idealism about politics. "There was," she wrote, "something very sad watching these brilliant people subside into political insignificance and isolation, and to realize that their party had been only an idealistic dream in wartime."[21]

When peace came there was talk of Wiskemann continuing to work for British intelligence or joining the British program for German "re-education," although she had little desire to live in occupied Germany. Instead she chose to move to Rome and focus on Italy. Her main aim was to write a book about the Axis between Hitler and Mussolini. Documentation for the German side had become available in a huge cache of captured files at the Foreign Office in London, while the Nuremberg trials provided an additional mass of evidence. Official documents for Italian foreign policy were unavailable, but in Switzerland she had mixed with diplomats, politicians, and intellectuals, many of whom went on to distinguished careers in post-war Italy, and she soon gained access to former high officials from the fascist era. To pay her way she arranged to report on Italian politics for *The Economist*, *Spectator*, and *The Observer*. Arriving in Rome in October 1945, she spent much of the next two years there, covering in astute, well-researched articles the birth of the Italian Republic: the mistakes of Allied occupiers, the poverty and land hunger of the *Mezzogiorno*, and the rapid demise of the Action party which proved incapable of attracting mass support. It was an exciting time to be a journalist in Italy and the circles she moved in included writers like Silone, Moravia, and Carlo Levi, industrialists like Adriano Olivetti, Benedetto Croce's daughter Elena, and the radical banker Raffaele Matteoli, a central figure in post-war Italy's economic reconstruction.

She also accomplished a prodigious amount of work, completing two books and many articles and reviews in the space of three years. *Italy* was a brief overview, part of a popular series to examine European nations as they emerged from the war.[22] The second book, *The Rome-Berlin Axis*, was the first detailed analysis of the Hitler–Mussolini relationship and remained for many years the standard account in English. Through the two leaders' letters and eye-witness testimonies, it reconstructed the strains and changes in the Axis alliance over time, from their early rivalry

---

[20] Wiskemann, *The Europe I Saw*, 185.   [21] Wiskemann, *The Europe I Saw*, 218.
[22] E. Wiskemann, *Italy* (Oxford University Press, 1947).

over Austria and Southeast Europe to the *Duce*'s total subservience and abject reliance on Hitler's power and decisions. Wiskemann's contrast between the two – Mussolini, volatile and opportunistic; Hitler, fanatical, resolute, unswerving in his goals – may have been too stark; certainly, recent scholars have found more consistency and continuity in Mussolini's foreign policy.[23] Also, her effort to link the two dictators as perverse bowdlerizers of Nietzsche's doctrines and her depiction of Nazi ideology as a "revolution of nihilism" echoed views current in the late 1940s.[24] But in the details of their personal chemistry the book remains fresh and insightful even today.

The Rome-Berlin Axis confirmed Wiskemann's status as a leading authority on fascism and Nazism. Reviews were overwhelmingly positive. "*Czechs and Germans,*" wrote G. P. Gooch "established Miss Wiskemann as one of our leading authorities on international affairs, and her latest volume is even more remarkable."[25] In Martin Wight's opinion it ranked with "the half dozen definitive secondary works on the diplomatic history of Hitler's age," and Hugh Trevor-Roper was equally appreciative: "that rare thing, a definitive work of contemporary history."[26] But scholarly books paid little, and Wiskemann lacked the security of an academic job. Financially, her situation was precarious in the early 1950s. Aside from journalistic assignments, to make ends meet she did almost weekly book reviewing for the *TLS*, *The Spectator*, and other journals, translations for publishers, and she even took in "paying guests" and ran a bed-and-breakfast. When Toynbee began editing volumes of Chatham House's *Survey of International Affairs* covering the war years, Wiskemann wrote long sections on the Italian resistance movements, Czechoslovakia, Hungary, Romania, Bulgaria, and Yugoslavia. But, apart from a visit to Hungary in 1948, she no longer traveled to Eastern Europe and found the tightening grip of Stalinism tragic. In Prague the mysterious death/murder of her old friend Jan Masaryk and the consolidation of a hardline communist regime was an especially bitter blow (in the purges that followed, her name surfaced in connection with Allen Dulles in the Slansky show trial) and she petitioned for the release of incarcerated intellectuals like the Hungarians Paul Ignotus and Istvan Bibo.

[23] Alan Cassels, *Mussolini's Early Diplomacy* (Princeton University Press, 1970); MacGregor Knox, *Mussolini Unleashed 1939–1941* (Cambridge University Press, 1982).

[24] E. Wiskemann, *The Rome-Berlin Axis* (Oxford University Press, 1949).

[25] G. P. Gooch, *The Contemporary Review*, July 1, 1949, 313.

[26] M. Wight, *International Affairs*, July 1949, 370; H. Trevor Roper, "Unholy Alliance," *The Observer*, May 1, 1949, 7.

It was not until 1950 that Wiskemann returned to Germany where, like many observers, she was deeply disturbed by the prevalence of former Nazis and a failure to engage with the past. Most of her friends there were "engaged democrats" who insisted that Germans could only rebuild their collective identity by confronting their collective guilt; they had spent the occupation years advocating grass roots democracy where citizens actively participated in political life and self-rule.[27] By the early 1950s many felt marginalized or alienated in Adenauer's new Germany. An amnesty law had allowed tens of thousands of former Nazis to escape justice altogether; government pressure secured early release for numerous others, while Article 131 of the Basic Law reinstated and restored the pensions of hundreds of thousands of civil servants, judges, and career soldiers, including Gestapo members. Arguably, Wiskemann was too critical and underestimated the difficulties Adenauer faced as he tried to fashion a new national identity, which required integrating former Nazis and vast numbers of German refugees from the East (16 percent of West Germany's population). That said, indisputably, in the early Bonn years concern for the victims of Nazism took a backseat to building solidarity among West Germans regardless of past crimes.[28]

Again in 1953 it was an offer from Chatham House that determined Wiskemann's next major project: a book, financed by the Rockefeller Foundation, about Germany's eastern borderlands from which some 12 million ethnic Germans had been expelled after 1945. The idea came from Hugh Seton-Watson, a leading scholar of Russia and Eastern Europe and an influential member of the Chatham House board. In 1952 Stalin had put forward a proposal for a reunited, neutral, and demilitarized Germany which both Adenauer and the West rejected. If a final peace with Germany and the issue of reunification were ever taken up, Seton-Watson argued, the social situation in these frontier lands would be central to all discussions: "It is simply fantastic that so little is known of this subject in this country & [the] U.S. There is hardly a problem in world affairs today of greater basic importance." There was Board resistance to the idea with some members preferring an edited book of essays, but Seton-Watson pushed for Wiskemann as the sole author and got his way. The research was in some respects a sequel to her pre-war study of German–Slav conflicts in Eastern Europe. If her work were to play a role in ongoing policy discussions, speed was essential and

---

[27] Sean A. Forner, *German Intellectuals and the Challenge of Democratic Renewal: Culture and Politics after 1945* (Cambridge University Press, 2014).
[28] Norbert Frei, *Adenauer's Germany and the Nazi Past* (New York: Columbia University Press, 2002).

Wiskemann agreed to finish the manuscript in 1954, ready for publication the following spring.[29] However, when the communist regimes of Poland and Czechoslovakia refused to grant her visas for travel, the project had to be reshaped, focusing less on the situation in the borderlands and more on West Germany's integration of expellees.

Germany's Eastern Neighbours: Problems Relating to the Oder-Neisse Line and the Czech Frontier Region was the first major study in English of the post-war expulsion of ethnic Germans.[30] Few topics were more controversial or more likely to arouse extreme views. Wiskemann endeavored to be detached and impartial, to weigh both the suffering of German expellees and the inevitable thirst for revenge from populations that had endured the horrors of forced labor, concentration camps, and mass murder. But she sympathized more with the victims of Nazism. "If one considers the recent record of German minorities in eastern Europe," she wrote, angering German reviewers, "it is difficult to wish them back there."[31] The economic sections of the book that described West Germany's successful absorption of expellees and their contribution to the German *Wirtschaftswunder* were positive and uncontroversial. But her depiction of the negative influence of refugee *Landsmannschaften* upon West German politics was unequivocal. She had been deeply alarmed at the extreme chauvinism and Nazi-sounding rhetoric of their meetings, viewing it as evidence of overt revanchist goals. Post-1989, with the collapse of communist regimes and the opening of Eastern European archives, scholarship has become more sympathetic to German expellees.[32] But Wiskemann's optic was the 1930s and Munich, and the horrors of Nazism were closer. Arguably, she never fully appreciated the abstract, cultural power of *Heimat* as a focus of imaginary longing rather than as a demand for return. While Adenauer's government still officially insisted on the borders of 1937, she asserted that, after almost a decade had passed, it was time to recognize the population transfers as irreversible and to accept the Oder-Neisse frontier as not simply *de facto* but *de jure*.

It was a brave book and one that she found more difficult than anything she had written before. British and American reviewers applauded her achievement in glowing terms. Prague offered no public

---

[29] RIIA 17/73 "Germany's Eastern Neighbours 1953–58," Chatham House Archives, London.

[30] E. Wiskemann, *Germany's Eastern Neighbours* (Oxford University Press, 1956).

[31] Wiskemann, *Germany's Eastern Neighbours*, 294.

[32] Ian Connor, *Refugees and Expellees in Post-War Germany* (Manchester University Press, 2007); Andrew Demshuk, *The Lost German East: Forced Migration and the Politics of Memory 1945–1970* (New York: Cambridge University Press, 2012).

response, while pro-Polish writers were everywhere delighted with its vindication of their territorial claims. However, Wiskemann was completely unprepared for the apoplectic response to her book in West Germany where it was reviled as a diabolically unfair, an "apologia of inhumanity." Attacks orchestrated by the refugee lobby and officials at the Bonn government's Federal Ministry of Refugees became increasing nasty and personal, vilifying her motives and integrity, calling her a dilettante, a Czech mouthpiece, even a onetime lover of Beneš's adviser, Hubert Ripka.[33]

Seeing her personal reputation at stake, to say nothing of her livelihood as a journalist, Wiskemann turned to Chatham House for support. It had commissioned the book and her friends Alan Bullock and Hugh Seton-Watson had accepted the manuscript with scarcely any revisions. She would have liked some public riposte – a statement that could then be communicated to the British press and would be picked up by continental papers. Alan Bullock said he would bring the request before the Board: "We have, as you know," he admitted, "been persistently ignoring attacks from Germany on the book," but he was also "personally most strongly opposed to publishing formal denials or retorts of any kind." Monty Woodhouse, the Director, was less sympathetic to Wiskemann than his predecessor Toynbee and the Research Committee, while agreeing that the imputations against her were "entirely deplorable," decided "as a matter of principle it would be undignified for the Institute to take any public position in reply to such an attack."[34] There is no evidence of Foreign Office involvement in the dispute, although Richard Crossman had predicted that the book might be construed as unhelpful in that quarter.[35] British policy in the mid-1950s was engaged in a delicate dance, trying to move toward détente with the communist bloc, which required tacit acceptance of the Oder-Neisse line, while doing everything possible to avoid openly offending West Germany. Feeling snubbed, Wiskemann got her friend Hugh Gaitskell, leader of the Labour Party, to intercede with the German Embassy. The *Manchester Guardian* also rallied to her defense: "That leader of yours," she wrote editor Alastair Hetherington, "did exactly what was needed, and the

[33] Hilmar Toppe (Osteuropa Institute, Munich), "Elizabeth Wiskemann und Deutschlands Nachbar Polen," *Wirtschaft und Wissenschaft*. *Sonderdruck des Stiftenverbandes für die deutsche Wissenschaft*, 1957.
[34] RIIA 17/73 "Germany's Eastern Neighbours 1953–58."
[35] R. Crossman, "The Oder-Neisse Line," *New Statesman and Nation*, August 4, 1956, 125.

wicked Nazi professor [Hilmar Toppe] has been made to feel a tiny bit foolish, I gather."[36]

Teaching at Edinburgh and Sussex

Wiskemann had last taught Cambridge undergraduates in 1936 and she had no expectation of landing an academic post at age 59. But in March 1958 she wrote Alastair Hetherington: "I've been asked up to Edinburgh to discuss a professorship – can't think I'll get it, but if I did I should try to call on you in Manchester one day."[37] The Edinburgh position for which she successfully interviewed was the Montague Burton Chair of International Relations, a professorship established in 1948 to foster the study of international relations and peace, based on the ideals of the United Nations.

At the time there were still very few academic programs, teaching positions, or endowed chairs in international affairs. They included the Wilson Chair of International Politics at Aberystwyth (1919); the Montague Burton Chairs at Oxford and LSE (1930; 1936); and the Stevenson Chair of International History at LSE (1926). Additional programs developed slowly and at Oxford, while strapped for funds in the early years, St Antony's College (1950) began to emerge as a center for contemporary history and international studies. In Britain, in contrast to the United States, International Relations barely existed as a theorized discipline with its own claims for a distinctive mode of thinking about international issues. Approaches to the subject were pluralistic, less connected to the social sciences than in later years, and its relationship to the fledgling field of "contemporary history" was ambiguous. Those teaching it were mostly trained as classicists, political scientists, philosophers, or (increasingly) historians.[38] Wiskemann had earlier taught diplomatic history, but her major publications were recognized as significant contributions to IR and, except for *The Rome-Berlin Axis*, each had an underlying objective to influence policy. This was also true of her current research project when she went to Edinburgh: a study of the Italian–Yugoslav territorial dispute over Trieste, funded by the Carnegie Foundation.

---

[36] E. Wiskemann to A. Hetherington, February 25, 1958, Editors' Correspondence Files, C2/W9/Wiskemann, Manchester Guardian Archives, Manchester.

[37] E. Wiskemann to A. Hetherington, March 25, 1958, Manchester Guardian Archives, Manchester.

[38] Ian Hall, *Dilemmas of Decline: British Intellectuals and World Politics 1945–1975* (Berkeley and Los Angeles: University of California Press, 2012), 7–9.

As the first woman to occupy a Chair in any discipline at Edinburgh, it would be gratifying to see Wiskemann's appointment as a major break-through for gender equality. But the truth is a little more complex, for the Burton endowment's terms made the position more difficult to fill than one might expect. The pay was far from generous and the job was only part-time, requiring an incumbent to reside each spring term for three years in Edinburgh and to give a series of lectures. This made it difficult to attract distinguished scholars with full-time positions elsewhere – their universities were unlikely to agree. The previous occupant had been C. A. Macartney, a renowned scholar of Central Europe, who was a fellow of All Souls, Oxford, where he had no formal teaching or adminis-trative responsibilities. Also, Edinburgh did not have a separate depart-ment or degree course in IR and so the Burton lectures (not fully integrated into the existing degree syllabus) had trouble attracting stu-dents. Already in 1957 there was some discussion about revising the endowment's terms and converting the Chair into an annual lecture series given by several distinguished scholars. W. N. Medlicott, Steven-son Professor of International History at LSE, was consulted about the situation and he made a strong case that Edinburgh should seek add-itional funding, make the post full-time, and establish a new degree-awarding department. These suggestions did not get very far (the Burton endowment was unwilling to increase its contribution substantially, while –presumably fearing competition – "neither the Faculty of Law nor the Department of History considered that such a step would be in accordance with their educational policy for the next decades"). Medli-cott then put forward three candidates for the existing post with Wiske-mann as first choice and, he suggested, the one most likely to accept the position since she could live in London part of the year and still travel regularly to the Continent as a journalist.[39]

By the end of Macartney's tenure the Burton lectures seem to have become rather moribund. Wiskemann worked hard to resuscitate them, developing a following among students and staff in other disciplines, taking pains to publicize lectures and choosing topics that, in her view, students ought to be discussing irrespective of her own areas of research. Her offerings for spring 1959 seem to have been lost from the files but in spring 1960 she gave two courses: "Retreat from Empire to Common-wealth and Community" and "International Negotiations in the Modern World." The following year she lectured on "Aspects of the German Question" and, being particularly interested in the rapid pace of

---

[39] EUA-A-83: Correspondence Relating to Wiskemann's Tenure of the Montague Burton Chair in International Relations, 1958–61, Edinburgh University Archives.

independence movements in Ghana, Nigeria, and the Congo, decided to tackle a completely new area: "The United Nations and Africa." Further, to raise the public profile of the Chair, she began a regular series of Thursday evening seminars and invited eminent outside experts to open the sessions. In 1960 they included: Peter Calvocoressi (Assistant prosecutor at Nuremberg and editor of five volumes of Chatham House's *Survey of International Affairs*); Hester Marsden Smedley (a journalist in Europe and Africa); historian Margaret Lambert (Editor of the captured German Foreign Office Documents); W. Horsfall Carter (former head of the Foreign Office's West European section); and John Goormaghtigh (Director of the Carnegie Endowment's European Centre). Her invitees the following year were equally distinguished, including Elisabeth Barker on the Balkans and historian Golo Mann, son of Thomas Mann, on Germany.[40]

Wiskemann was clearly successful at Edinburgh and she enjoyed the recognition that came with a professorship. But in July 1960, to the dismay of the university administration, she gave notice that she would not stand for re-election for a further three years. The reason was her deteriorating eyesight. She first had trouble with her left eye in 1955, but further complications led to a cataract operation at the end of 1959 which seems to have been botched. As she explained to Professor A. H. Campbell of the Law Faculty: "Three specialists have now told me that [my left eye] should not have been operated and that I shall just have to make the best of present discomforts perhaps for 10 or 15 years." Especially in the dark winter months of January and February this made moving around Edinburgh hazardous. To her novelist friend, Richard Hughes, she explained: "Through the tomfoolery of a quite eminent eye-surgeon I've lost the use of my left eye, the detachment of the retina being quite unnecessary. I hope it hasn't happened to you."[41]

She probably believed that her teaching career was over, but another opportunity soon arose closer to London at the new university of Sussex. Sussex was an exciting place, eager to experiment with innovatory curricula that promoted interdisciplinary work and committed to teaching by seminars and tutorials rather than large lectures. Asa Briggs had been recruited as Professor of History and Dean of Social Studies and he hired Martin Wight, then beginning to emerge as an important figure in British IR, as the first Dean of its School of European Studies. Wiskemann and

---

[40] EUA-A-83, Edinburgh University Archives.
[41] E. Wiskemann to A. H. Campbell, July 28, 1961, EUA-A-83, Edinburgh University Archives. Elizabeth Wiskemann to Richard Hughes, December 10, 1961, Richard Hughes Papers, Lilly Library, Indiana University.

Wight had worked together on the *Survey of International Affairs* at Chatham House and had also reviewed each other's books in glowing terms. Wiskemann was hired as a Tutor in Modern European History and stayed three years. Very little information has surfaced about her time there, but she clearly enjoyed tutoring undergraduates and liked the structure of cross-disciplinary area studies. At times she was mystified by the Sixties' generation of students and felt something of an anachronism. To her friend Leonard Woolf, who lived nearby, she wrote: "Two young creatures, *first* years at Sussex, are much excited about 'Bloomsbury'. Would it amuse you to talk to them? They would think it FABULOUS or whatever their word is by now."[42] She could commute to Sussex from her London home and had easy access to Fleet Street and the BBC. Despite a high-pitched voice she had become a proficient broadcaster; in the mid-1960s she organized several radio series on recent history and made appearances on BBC TV. She also wrote regularly for the *Listener* magazine, and from its inception in 1951 contributed articles and reviews to the popular magazine *History Today*, believing strongly that scholars had a duty to address as wide a public as possible.

Contemporary Historian

The distinction between international history and IR was extremely vague in British universities at least until the early 1960s and, arguably, well beyond that. Scholars in both areas focused largely upon statecraft and interpreting the perceptions, beliefs, and actions of the leading foreign policy makers. The approach in many cases was straightforwardly historical and cultural, coupled with skepticism about social science concepts. Wiskemann's work, empirical in character, was not untypical of 1950s scholarship. She was happier emphasizing the specificities of each situation than theory-building, underscoring, for example, differences between Nazism and Italian Fascism rather than positing a generic model of fascism, much in vogue in the 1960s. She admired, for example, Martin Wight's range and erudition, but was never tempted to intervene in theoretical debates about power, mass politics, or the international system. A regular contributor to *International Affairs*, she did not engage with debates in the journal about IR as a discipline. Indeed, as IR drew closer to the social sciences, Wiskemann increasingly described herself as scholar of modern and contemporary history.

---

[42] E. Wiskemann to L. Woolf, November 21, 1964, Woolf Papers, The Keep, University of Sussex.

Contemporary history, one should remember, had almost no institutional presence in British universities in the 1950s, although things began to change by the late 1960s. Few university courses extended far into the twentieth century – at Oxford the Modern History syllabus went to 1878 in 1946 and had reached 1939 in 1966. Conservative colleagues sniffed that historians writing about their own lifetimes was really journalism with footnotes and those rash enough to venture into these waters often made a point of separating their "journalistic" and "scholarly" sides. The "objective" study of the past, many insisted, required large collections of official documents, archives, and the passage of several generations to transform "current events" into "history." Most nations imposed 50- or 70-year delays on the opening of government documents. In the 1940s the most recent British ones available were from 1885 and for much of the 1950s it was 1902; only after a sustained campaign was a 30-year rule adopted in 1967.

Both world wars were a catalyst, but it was especially after 1945 that pressure intensified for expanding the traditional periodization of history. At the heart of this project was a recognition that it was imperative for historians (along with other humanists and social scientists) to put analytical history to work to understand and explain the extraordinary ruptures and turmoil of their lifetime: two world wars, communist revolutions and fascism, concentration camps and genocide, and the collapse of liberalism in so many places. Historians, wrote Eva Reichmann, had "a moral duty" to understand and explain "the collapse of the bastions of reason ... of common human decency."[43] Nowhere was this urgency felt more than in West Germany where it was crucial to discredit the historical falsehoods of the Third Reich and to document reliably the Weimar and Nazi years. There, from the beginning, contemporary history was central to the construction of public memory, a stable democratic polity, and new civic morality. The Institut für Zeitgeschichte (IfZ) coincided with the founding of the Federal Republic of Germany, and its journal, the *Vierteljahreshefte für Zeitgeschichte* began publication in 1953. Wiskemann, who had been deeply critical of conservative German scholarship and the flood of sanitizing memoirs in the early 1950s, became a fervent admirer of IfZ publications and attended its conferences. Her reviews helped publicize the work of historians like Karl Dietrich Bracher, Wolfgang Sauer, and Martin Broszat whose research,

---

[43] E. Reichmann, "The Study of Contemporary History as a Political and Moral Duty," in Max Beloff (ed.), *On the Track of Tyranny* (London: Valentine and Mitchell, 1960), 191.

she wrote, was "far and away the most illuminating … about Hitlerism that there has been in the last thirty years or so."[44]

It is not surprising that in Britain, a country less directly affected by the crises and ruptures of the recent past than continental Europe, the push for "contemporary history" came especially from scholars specializing in Central Europe and international affairs. Several new universities (like Sussex) led the way, while in Oxford, where curricula change lagged, Alan Bullock, A. J. P. Taylor, James Joll, and F. W. Deakin had formed a Recent History Group in 1950 to stimulate research. The Institute of Contemporary History grew out of London's Wiener Library, specifically devoted to the study of the Nazi era, and researchers of the recent past were mostly scholars whose lives were profoundly shaped by their war experiences. However, compared to West Germany, debate about the status, periodization, and methodology of contemporary history was "rather pallid" and defensive, intent on establishing its respectability and Rankean professionalism – insisting that for historians to leave the terrain to political scientists or non-professionals would be an abdication of responsibility, while also warning that the new field must not "degenerate into quasi-historical journalism."[45] Perhaps the perceived fragile status of this sub-discipline contributed to the enormous furor that erupted over A. J. P. Taylor's *The Origins of the Second World War.*[46] The controversy is too well known to require elaboration here, but in a Shavian, provocative way Taylor sought to upend the growing scholarly consensus over the foreign policy of the 1930s. His selective use of evidence, his desire to shock, arguing, for example, that Hitler was "no more wicked and unscrupulous than many other contemporary statesmen," was widely condemned as perverse and potentially dangerous. Dozens of historians leapt into the fray, including Wiskemann, who excoriated the book as a "travesty of the facts" and "a virtuoso's display of impish inconsistency in the name of rationality." She also worried that Taylor's claim that the war resulted from an unintended sequence of events, rather like a road accident, would sustain German revisionist politics.[47]

---

[44] H. Krausnick, H. Buchheim, M. Broszart, and H. Jacobsen (eds.), *Anatomy of the S.S. State* (London: Collins, 1968), ix (Introduction by Wiskemann).

[45] J. Caplan, "Contemporary Europe: Reflections from Britain and Germany," *History Workshop Journal* 63 (2007): 230–38; Reichmann, "The Study of Contemporary History," 191; also, A. Bullock, "Is It Possible to Write Contemporary History?" in Beloff (ed.), *On the Track of Tyranny.*

[46] A. J. P. Taylor, *The Origins of the Second World War* (London: Hamish Hamilton, 1961).

[47] Wiskemann letter to *Times Literary Supplement*, June 2, 1961, 341. Also, Wiskemann, "Hitler's Reputation," *History Today*, June 1961, 429.

Until her death five years after leaving Sussex Wiskemann's schedule was exhausting. There were articles, media appearances, lectures, innumerable reviews, and she wrote four books of "contemporary history." Three were brief syntheses designed for students; the fourth was a memoir focusing on her experiences in the 1930s and 1940s. *Fascism in Italy*, drawing upon years of detailed reading, was aimed at undergraduates, while *Italy since 1945* (published posthumously) contained many astute observations on Italian politics; it was not her best work, but even finishing it was a victory.[48] Plagued by failing eyesight and now in her late sixties, she could not produce the kind of deeply researched major book that many prominent scholars publish as a capstone to their careers.

Her most popular book, *Europe of the Dictators, 1919–1945* was part of the Fontana History of Europe series edited by J. H. Plumb.[49] Full of lightly worn erudition, and sharply drawn vignettes of policy makers she had met and events she had witnessed first-hand, it was written more from a continental perspective than most British accounts and devoted closer attention to how events looked from an East European vantage point. In many ways, without mentioning him, it was also a rejoinder to Taylor's *Origins*. In the preface Wiskemann declared that she made "no claim to detachment about the history of Europe" in this period and the result, as Robert Pois put it, was "a work of compelling power, tinctured with strong emotion" and "much more than the mixture of studied objectivity and platitudes one often associates with histories of this era."[50] Her views had changed very little. She still believed that the League of Nations could have done much to modify and improve the Versailles peace settlement had the major powers been willing to defend it. For all his tactical flexibility, she argued, Hitler never varied his territorial and racial goals, which were evident in *Mein Kampf* and documents like the November 1937 Hossbach Memorandum (largely dismissed as a policy blueprint by Taylor). Nor had her criticism of Neville Chamberlain and appeasement softened. G. P. Gooch called it "a little masterpiece" and it sold over 80,000 copies.[51]

Wiskemann's memoir –*The Europe I Saw*, a poignant title for someone going blind – dealt mainly with her role in the fight against Nazism which she saw as the great cause of her life. Always a very private person, she said little about her private life or feelings – self-revelation was not her

---

[48] E. Wiskemann, *Fascism in Italy: Its Development and Influence* (London: Macmillan, 1969); E. Wiskemann, *Italy since 1945* (London: Macmillan, 1971).
[49] E. Wiskemann, *Europe of the Dictators 1919–1945* (London: HarperCollins, 1966).
[50] R. Pois, *The Historian* 30.1 (1967), 100.
[51] G. P. Gooch, *The Contemporary Review*, July 1966.

style. Reviewers praised her as one of the best-informed and, in judgment, most balanced observers of the international scene, but those who knew her best were disappointed and wanted more. There were marks of academic recognition in these years: C. L. Mowat asked her to write the section on "Germany, Italy and Eastern Europe 1898–1945" for the *New Cambridge Modern History* and she was delighted by the award of an honorary DLitt from Oxford, especially when the ceremony's public orator described her as a Cassandra who lived to record the war she had foretold. Wiskemann continued to travel, though less than before, and returned to Czechoslovakia briefly in late 1968 where Soviet invasion forces had recently destroyed the democratic aspirations of the Prague spring. But her eyesight got worse. Early in 1969 she wrote a friend: "I'm very bad at growing old and can't face the prospect of death with much satisfaction. But it is the problem of my sight which plagues me most. I am to go to an eye-surgeon tomorrow and I'm sure he will want to operate." And a year later: "My sight is bad, everything looking fearfully smudgy, but with a very good reading lamp etc., I manage somehow, though winter is awful to get through. I lose my nerve if I look ahead, so I just try not to."[52] "I don't think any of us realized," an old friend wrote, "just what it meant to the scholar and historian that slowly and inexorably her eyes dimmed, her vision failed."[53] When her good eye began to deteriorate, she grew terrified that another operation might fail, leaving her totally blind. In late April 1971 she made a brief lecture trip to Israel and seemed cheerful enough in her correspondence. Two months later she was dead, characteristically making her own decision about when her life should end. Typically, she attended to details, leaving instructions for the charlady whom she knew would find her.

[52] E. Wiskemann to H. Bergholz, February 6, 1969 and March 25, 1970, Wiskemann Papers, Newnham College Archives.
[53] *The Times*, July 9, 1971, 14. The author was probably Lord Arran who worked with her in wartime Switzerland.

Part III

Thinking in or around the Academy

10 From F. Melian Stawell to E. Greene Balch: International and *Internationalist* Thinking at the Gender Margins, 1919–1947

Glenda Sluga

If it were not for F. Melian Stawell's book *The Growth of International Thought* few intellectual historians, let alone IR scholars, might bother with the classicist, or reflect on the gender-masking "F." Ironically, in the mid-1920s, Florence Melian Stawell (1869–1936) had set out to write a different book: a popular account of the League of Nations published with the Home University Library series, which could be of use to the League of Nations Education Committee.[1] Her intention was to educate a broad readership in the novel international organization. But instead she unexpectedly turned to writing a *longue durée* history of international thought due to the intervention of Oxford Regius Professor Gilbert Murray, her classicist mentor and Australian compatriot. Having been asked by the publisher to appraise Stawell's proposal for a book on the League, Murray claimed the project for himself. He then suggested the publisher advise Stawell to tackle something historical instead. Within a year – by the end of 1926 – Stawell had written *The Growth of International Thought*. As Murray procrastinated over the League book (which, ultimately, he never wrote), the publishers delayed releasing Stawell's until she insisted that to postpone further would risk her study requiring updating.[2]

New work in intellectual history is making it increasingly difficult for historians who ignore women as agents of ideas to blame "the lack of women's historical thinking."[3] Stawell's unpredictable career as a public intellectual is one small example of the insidious ways in which personal and institutional practices could stymie and impact the fate of women's

---

[1] F. M. Stawell, *The Growth of International Thought* (London: Home University Library, 1929).

[2] Letters between Murray, Williams, and Norgate (London), and Stawell, in G. Murray (1926–1928) Papers, Oxford, MS 407, f.58, f.60, f.102.

[3] Patricia Owens, "Women and the History of International Thought," *International Studies Quarterly* 62 (2018): 467–81

actually existing intellectual work. To be sure, the recent resuscitation of Stawell – nearly a century after the publication of *The Growth of International Thought* – suggests a significant shift in this pattern. Now, Stawell's contribution to the canon of international thought is being extolled as "pioneering."[4] This recognition has been accompanied by the accumulation of biographical detail: that Stawell's middle-name "Melian" was her classicist father's idea; that she studied at Melbourne University and then at Newnham College, Cambridge; ill-health undermined her career; she worked on classical editions; her collaborators were well-known British classicists-*cum*-internationalists such as Goldsworthy Lowes Dickinson and Gilbert Murray, as well as the educator F. S. Marvin and, like these men, Stawell was involved with the British League of Nations Union.[5] For all we are learning about women such as Stawell, their inclusion does not always lead to the integration of their actual ideas and arguments into larger narratives of the growth of international thought since Stawell's own time. Instead, it is the title of Stawell's work, her invention of the term "international thought" that seems to be capturing all the attention in the process of constructing "international thought" as a distinctive field of intellectual history.[6]

In hindsight, Gilbert Murray may have inadvertently done Stawell a favor by adopting her writing project on the League, and leading her to

---

[4] In a recent essay on the relative virtues of contextualism in the history of international thought, Ian Hall gives Stawell genealogical pride of place – even though Murray usurping her book plan may not be the kind of "context" that Hall has in mind: see I. Hall, "The History of International Thought and International Relations Theory: From Context to Interpretation," *International Relations* 31.3 (2017): 241–60.

[5] Details on Stawell's work outside of academia are difficult to find in the archives of any of the institutions to which she belonged, including the League of Nations Union; within the academy she directed Historical Studies at Girton, wrote on classics texts, and was regarded more generally as a useful narrator of ideas for a broader public (including Goethe); see Karen L. Levenback, "Florence Melian Stawell and Virginia Woolf: Home-Front Experience, The Price of Freedom, and Patriotism," in Julie Vandivere and Megan Hicks (eds.), *Virginia Woolf and her Female Contemporaries* (Liverpool University Press, 2016); Rosie Wyles and Edith Hall (eds.), *Women Classical Scholars: Unsealing the Fountain from the Renaissance to Jacqueline de Romilly* (Oxford University Press, 2016).

[6] See David Armitage, *The Foundations of Modern International Thought* (Cambridge University Press, 2013); and Glenda Sluga, "Turning International: Foundations of Modern International Thought and New Paradigms for Intellectual History," *History of European Ideas* 41.1 (2015): 103–15. Compare with, for example, Edward Keene, *International Political Thought: A Historical Introduction* (Cambridge: Polity Press, 2005), which covers the same terrain as Stawell, from the ancient to the modern world, which is much more detailed, but has no mention of Stawell or these earlier texts. It mentions international society, but not internationalism. The period of the interwar, and the League movement is incorporated in a discussion of liberal civilizationalism. See also, Emma Rothschild, "Arcs of Ideas: International History and Intellectual History," in Gunilla Budde, Sebastian Conrad, and Oliver Janz (eds.), *Transnationale Geschichte: Themen, Tendenzen und Theorien* (Göttingen: Vandenhoeck & Ruprecht, 2006), 217–26.

write the book which, after her death, he "applauded" as a "small treatise."[7] *The Growth of International Thought*, I will argue, turns our attention not only to the question *who* counts as an international thinker, but also *what* counts as international thought. Here, I want to argue that it is worth taking the ideas of F. Melian Stawell seriously because including them in the repertoire of international thought helps us refine our answers to both "who" and "what."

10.1 F. Melian Stawell.
Courtesy of Newnham College, Cambridge

By the time Stawell wrote *The Growth of International Thought*, international relations was firming up as an appropriate subject of scholarly analysis. In the British context, these developments were the work of academics, many of them men (by virtue of institutional bias) and classicists such as Arnold Toynbee, who had prime positions during the war advising the Foreign Office on the terms of the post-World

---

[7] [G. Murray], "Miss Melian Stawell. Greek scholarship and philosophy" (obituary), *The Times* (London), June 11 1936, 18.

War I peace, from the contours of territorial settlements, to the significance of international government.[8] By the mid-1920s, Stawell's fellow
classicist Alfred Zimmern had taken up (and lost) the world's first Chair
in International Relations in Aberystwyth, while Gilbert Murray
established himself as a leading figure in the League of Nations movement. In this institutional context, Stawell was one more classicist operating in the web of Oxbridge internationalist networks, melding scholarly
endeavors and political activism.[9]

The Growth of International Thought emanates from these interwar
intersections between international politics and a mainstream internationalism reflected through the prism of the League of Nations
system.[10] Taking Stawell seriously now – that is, reading beyond the title
of *The Growth of International Thought* – leads us to a history of international thought that fits only awkwardly with conventional historical
narratives of the emergence of international politics and IR as a discipline. The marginalization of Stawell's work coincided with the marginalization of *internationalist* international thought more generally, even when
it informed the praxis and publications of Stawell's male peers. This is
despite the fact that over the same period that IR took root as a discipline,
League of Nations-focused internationalism inspired academics of all
kinds to address international ideas in the public domain, and women
to engage international politics.

This chapter delves between the covers of *The Growth of International
Thought* in order to parse this early twentieth-century internationalist
international thought, and what it tells us about Stawell's intellectual
work, even her status as an "intellectual." It then pursues the question
"what difference did gender make to the historical neglect of *internationalist* international thought?" by situating Stawell's ideas in relation to the

---

[8] Glenda Sluga, *Nation, Psychology and International Politics* (Basingstoke: Palgrave Macmillan, 2008).

[9] During the war, classicists had made up the majority of expert advisers to the Foreign Office in anticipation of the peace: see Sluga, *Nation, Psychology and International Politics*, ch. 2; Julia Stapleton, "The Classicist as Liberal Intellectual: Gilbert Murray and Alfred Zimmern," in C. Stray (ed.), *Gilbert Murray Reassessed: Hellenism, Theatre and International Politics* (Oxford University Press, 2007), 261–91; Casper Sylvest, "Interwar Internationalism, the British Labour Party, and the Historiography of International Relations," *International Studies Quarterly* 48.2 (2004): 409–32; Sylvest describes "internationalism" as contradicting "the dominant, realist view in International Relations (IR), which stresses the difficulty (or impossibility) of transforming the basic conditions of international politics."

[10] For more on this period see Glenda Sluga, *Internationalism in the Age of Nationalism* (Philadelphia: University of Pennsylvania Press, 2013), ch. 2; Daniel Laqua (ed.), *Internationalism Reconfigured: Transnational Ideas and Movements between the World Wars* (New York: I. B. Tauris, 2011).

internationalist international thinking of another woman, Emily Greene Balch.

By the mid-twentieth century, Balch had taken internationalist international ideas in radical new directions. As a recipient of a Nobel Peace prize, it can hardly be argued that she was marginalized. But the prize was awarded for her activism, rather than her status as an intellectual. While feminist historians have long appreciated the significance of Balch's internationalist ideas, she has only begun to have a place in accounts of international thought, thanks in part to the work of Catia Confortini. In this volume Confortini examines the contribution of Balch to international thought at the peak of her public career. Here I add the focus of the later Balch on sovereignty as an international idea and highlight the qualitative difference in her conceptualization of the place of the state in international thought, particularly in contrast to Stawell's more limited appraisal of the scope of internationalism. By reading Stawell and Balch together, my intention is to return to these mutually reinforcing questions: What ideas matter for intellectual historians of IR and international thought? How can we explain the over-determined historical erasure of women, such as Balch and Stawell, in the canon of intellectual history and the history of ideas? And how should we contextualize and evaluate women in international thought, within and beyond feminist histories of the international past?

The Growth of International Thought

In *The Growth of International Thought* F. M. Stawell's search for an international past is led by a foundational premise:

that a sane nationalism, when it understands itself, points the way to internationalism as its completion. The principle that builds the single State cannot end with the single State. This has been felt, sometimes clearly, more often dimly, by all the best thinkers of Europe.[11]

With the benefit of hindsight, the "principle" that political life evolves through stages of ever-expanding forms of political association (sometimes identified as "stadism") now seems quaintly misguided. In the nineteenth and twentieth centuries it was a familiar basis for the internationalist thinking that captured progressive liberal imaginations.[12] There are explicit clues to the influence of this *internationalist* thought

---

[11] Stawell, *Growth of International Thought*, 7.

[12] For more on the history of internationalist thought, see Sluga, *Internationalism in the Age of Nationalism*, chs. 1 and 2; and the essays in Glenda Sluga and Patricia Clavin (eds.), *Internationalisms: A Twentieth-Century History* (Cambridge University Press, 2017).

on *The Growth of International Thought*, in Stawell's references to her readership as "the student of internationalism" and "thoughtful students of internationalism."[13] This same internationalist perspective is the context in which Stawell insists that "[a]ll the great movements of thought in Europe have been international, even before the days of printing and cheap transit."[14] Wending its way through *The Growth of International Thought* is the assertion that "from Paganism to Christianity" "European" thinkers, regardless of country, nation, or religion, by definition, aspired to the creation of associations beyond their immediate community.[15]

In Stawell's mapping of these internationalist strands of international thought, she lingers in the familiar landscapes of the ancient world, with Socrates, Plato, Euripides, and Aristotle; she ventures through the medieval and Renaissance periods, pausing with Dante, Marsiglio di Padua, Pierre Dubois, Duc de Sully, Machiavelli, and Grotius among others before arriving at the eighteenth century to contemplate William Penn, Rousseau, Burke, and Kant. As Stawell builds up this itinerary of European thinkers in *The Growth of International Thought*, she applies a test: What have they added to the growth of international thinking? By this she means the specifically internationalist thinking premised on the progressive evolution of ever-enlarging political communities to the ends of peace.

From her chosen perspective, Stawell determines the Greeks were problematic because they were not pacifists. However, the Stoic Amphictyons "will always deserve a place in any review of Internationalism because theirs was the first Council in Europe ... to attempt a definite limitation of cruelties in war."[16] Jews added religion, a sensitivity to foreign cultures, as well as a concern for the future, which the Greeks did not have: "Hebrew thought" opened a "vista of internationalism" by embracing "the vision of the world at peace."[17] From the Romans Stawell draws the example of the law of nations applied universally; in the medieval world she locates the relevance of Charlemagne's universal empire. When she looks at the fourteenth century, she finds Dante contributing a universalist outlook in the form of a common goal or destiny for mankind. His limitation, however, in the internationalist schema of things, is that he shared with the medieval era a failure to

---

[13] Stawell, *Growth of International Thought*, 35.
[14] Stawell, *Growth of International Thought*, 204.
[15] Stawell, *Growth of International Thought*, 204.
[16] Stawell, *Growth of International Thought*, 23.
[17] Stawell, *Growth of International Thought*, 28.

"take sufficient account of the actual divisions between the nationalities, still less do they attempt to frame any scheme which, fitting those facts, would give room for the ideal to grow."[18] Stawell launches the same criticism at Machiavelli, who did "most harm to internationalism" by lauding humanity's worst instincts; Thomas More's *Utopia* was too exceptionalist in favor of the English to be of interest to internationalists, as she imagines them.

Quakers fit Stawell's bill better, as long-time advocates of the confederation of states.[19] For the same reasons, Stawell considers Rousseau and Kant important. By comparison, Grotius was too hung up on precedent, on "what had been"; Rousseau, Stawell explains, added "what might be." On her readings, Rousseau's theory of the General Will recognized the legitimacy of both national and international communities and acknowledged the need for instruments of coercion if national or international law was to be obeyed. Stawell makes clear that one of her benchmarks for these evaluations is the contemporary League of Nations. She notes, for example, that while Rousseau imagined a confederation that would intervene in the affairs of states to prevent rebellion, by comparison the actual League can intervene only through consent, not coercion, in issues such as slavery, trafficking, and opium.[20] However, she also considers the internationalism of the actual League to be broader than earlier iterations of confederation, even Rousseau's, which only included Europe, albeit with some space for Russia and Turkey.

While the geography of Stawell's thinking is fixed, throughout *The Growth of International Thought* Stawell acknowledges the problematic fungibility of international ideas. They can be utilized on behalf of either world government or world dominion; they can build on a more *or less* "sane nationalism." Alexander the Great's inclination to create an ever-larger empire exhibited a conquering spirit rather than interest in winning the confidence of the world. Pierre Dubois, a medieval Normandy lawyer and counsellor to Philippe le Bel, preferred a confederation among the powers of Catholic Europe that, as in "the procedure

---

[18] Stawell, *Growth of International Thought*, 53.
[19] On the enduring internationalism of Quakers, see, for example, Daniel Maul, "American Quakers, the Emergence of International Humanitarianism and the Foundation of the American Friends Service Committee 1890–1920," in Johannes Paulmann (ed.), *Dilemmas of Humanitarianism in the Twentieth Century* (Oxford University Press, 2016), 63–87.
[20] Stawell, *Growth of International Thought*, 163.

advocated by modern internationalists" would use arbitration; but he too, she concedes, was motivated by an exclusivist religious imperialism.[21]

Stawell had more faith in the French Duc de Sully's early seventeenth-century grand design for a "Universal Christian Commonwealth of Europe," because it balanced international and national ambitions. Europe would be transformed into a universal commonwealth by respecting not only its Christian roots, but also "the natural dispositions and peculiar characteristics of peoples and races and thus guard against the folly of trying to unite in any one State ... men whose differences of temperament or diversity of language, law and tradition are so great as to be incompatible."[22] Even so, she admitted Sully's ideas could be used negatively to perpetuate a status quo, especially given his emphasis on military power rather than consensus. Similarly, Napoleon, who otherwise liberated nations, propounded a problematic version of internationalism because he was after world dominion. "[T]houghtful students of internationalism," Stawell suggests, should consider resuscitating the Holy Alliance, an otherwise much-maligned notion of the European alliance of all *Christian* powers – Protestant and Catholic – proposed by the Russian Tsar in 1815.[23]

Stawell insisted that international thinking was the foundation of *European* identification, and present through all periods and major movements of European politics and culture: "the darkness of the Dark Ages, the Renaissance, the Reformation, the growth of science, the Industrial Revolution, the rise of Democracy, the formation of a Labour party, the Emancipation of Women, the advocacy of Socialism and Communism."[24] On the evidence of her own ideas, international thinking was entangled in both the light and dark of early twentieth-century European thought – not excluding its racism, nationalism, and imperialism. Stawell herself is aware that the European focus of her history belies the book's international ambitions, although she argues there simply is not enough space to venture further afield in her intellectual survey.[25] She does find some space for the United States, as an actually-existing example of diversity working through federal systems. On the rare occasion, Stawell gestures to the cross-fertilization of European and

[21] Stawell, *Growth of International Thought*, 64.

[22] Stawell, *Growth of International Thought*, 110.

[23] On the Holy Alliance, see C. Crawley, "International Relations, 1815–30," in C. Crawley (ed.), *The New Cambridge Modern History*, vol. 9: *War and Peace in an Age of Upheaval , 1793–1830* (Cambridge University Press, 1965), 668–90.

[24] Stawell, *Growth of International Thought*, 228.

[25] Stawell, *Growth of International Thought*, 7.

non-European, even non-Christian intellectual traditions. Thus, "[w]hile Christian Europe was inciting itself in the Crusades to destroy the Mussulmans root and branch," she reminds us, "it was Mussulman thought which was bringing back to Europe by way of Cordova the invaluable legacy of Aristotle."[26]

The Growth of International Thought reflects general nineteenth-century intellectual trends that connected internationalism to the historical inevitability of the nation-state, the ontological realism of patriotism, and the "right and duty of every full citizen to share in the making of the State and its laws."[27] The ideal form of the nation-state – still relatively new in this historical schema – is a structural component of Stawell's internationalism, as much as "sane nationalism." We find Stawell describing how Kant brought to the history of international thought the idea that a functional federalism required each constituent state to be free. She also incorporates into her survey the 1830s – which, she offers, was more about nationalism than internationalism – because that decade's best-known nationalist thinker, Giuseppe Mazzini, conceived of nations as *associazione*. In democracies, her explication of Mazzini runs, experience of association trains individuals to have consideration for *national* others. As importantly, by extension, national associations provide training for internationalism.

There is less discussion of nationalism and patriotism in *The Growth of International Thought* than in Stawell's other published essays. In an earlier 1915 pamphlet on *Patriotism and Humanity*, for example, written against the background of a Europe at war in the name of patriotism, Stawell insists on the national object of patriotism, that is "the true nation, not to be confounded with the artificial empires held together merely by force. Such empires sin, themselves, against nationality." She urges the readers of *The International Journal of Ethics* to "keep patriotism, and yet go beyond it." Critical of "an unthinking nationalism," Stawell suggests training "national feeling that it leaves room for internationalism."[28] A decade later, the function of *The Growth of International Thought* is in part to assist this process, as an educational resource that proves and promotes the evolution of international thinking through the dissemination of the long history of international thought for a broad audience.

---

[26] Stawell, *Growth of International Thought*, 52.
[27] Stawell, *Growth of International Thought*, 52. On the relative novelty of patriotism, see G. Sluga, "Passions, Patriotism and Nationalism, and Germaine de Stael," *Nations and Nationalism* 15.2 (2009): 299–318.
[28] F. M. Stawell, "Patriotism and Humanity," *International Journal of Ethics* 25.3 (1915): 292–306.

Stawell's mid-1920s intellectual *milieu* kept mutual company with League of Nations internationalism, English nationalism, and British imperialism. For the most part, Stawell's own nationalism and internationalism are inextricable from her understanding of the English roots of British imperialism. Indeed, British internationalists had by this time developed a rich repertoire of arguments about why Britain was different from the defeated "artificial" Ottoman and Habsburg empires, thanks to its English core. To begin with, one argument ran, the British empire exuded a "gift for colonialization" that allowed it to govern the "backward races" in a manner that gave colonized subjects the opportunity to realize their potential.[29]

In a period when the League of Nations bureaucracy paid lip-service to the idea that empire needed regulation in the interests of the colonized, Stawell insists that "our international system would be unhealthy if it could not make room" for the British Empire, when it meant "training the backward races" (a common concept at the time that she repeats without contest), "in the true missionary spirit without humbug or domineering."[30] The spirit of the League mandate system, she maintains, is of value only if those races are not "only taught to be hewers of wood and drawers of water for the dominant race ... until the generous heart is ready to sicken at the talk of 'the white man's burden', as nothing but so much tyrannical cant."[31]

An expatriate from a self-identified white British settler colony that practiced a "White Australia" immigration policy, Stawell also emplots the relationship between internationalism and British imperialism on a world map of trade determined by the conventional (at the time) presumptions of racial biology. On this argument, since the tropics – a place where "unfortunately" "the black, the brown and the yellow" thrive but not the white – are the only places to grow key resources such as rice and rubber, the "world" could not consent to leave those places alone.[32] For the "student of internationalism" who accepts her racialist geography, colonialism is inevitable. The only question is, under what conditions is this trade to proceed?

Now the white men are firmly convinced of their own superiority, and whatever may be the ultimate truth on this matter there can be little doubt that they are the

---

[29] Glenda Sluga, "Bodies, Souls and Sovereignty: The Austro-Hungarian Empire and the Legitimacy of Nations," *Ethnicities* 1 (2001): 207–32; Stawell, *Growth of International Thought*, 171.

[30] Stawell, *Growth of International Thought*, 184.

[31] On the mandate system see Susan Pedersen's excellent recent study, *The Guardians: The League of Nations and the Crisis of Empire* (Oxford University Press, 2015).

[32] Stawell, *Growth of International Thought*, 173.

more efficient; nor yet that intermarriage between themselves and the darker breeds fails to produce a good stock. Thus, over and over again, one race is put in the power of another with which it cannot amalgamate, yet which demands its loyalty. These are commonplaces, but they are repeated to recall the difficulties and intricacies of the problem.[33]

Into this racialized imperial landscape Stawell introduces Edmund Burke as a thinker whose agency, rather than ideas, are exemplary of the *English* character of British imperialism that establishes that empire's fundamental decency. She has in mind Burke's public criticism of the East India Company's bad imperialism in the late eighteenth century. Burke, Stawell argues, showed the value of England that would "in centuries to come," be recognized for having paved the way for world-federation, "by showing that it was possible for 'sovereignties' to unite in common action and common defence" with men of the same race.[34] When she considers Kant in this same context, as "alive to the problem of the races," "he implies that any attempt by the 'commercial govern-ments' of Europe to control Eastern or barbaric lands was bound to end in a 'litany of horrors'."[35] Stawell's own view is that those lands are likely to be Russia and Japan, not Britain.

Borrowing from the pseudo-science of eugenics, and its corpus of imperi-ally convenient convictions about the relation between the biology and psychology of "the darker breeds," Stawell awkwardly resolves on the need for scientific objectivity and impartiality. Here she is thinking of a different kind of science – not the science that established biological racism, but of international government exemplified in the potential of the League itself: "The distribution of the world's natural resources, limited as they are and must be, the relation of backward races to those abreast of modern sci-ence ... need the forum of the world for their settlement."[36]

These potentially paradoxical positions on geopolitics, race, and trade, present Stawell with familiar conundrums in the interwar landscape of international thought.[37] Indeed, her arguments have much in common with those of her better-known internationalist peers such as Gilbert Murray.[38] In general, British internationalists – male and

---

[33] Stawell, *Growth of International Thought*, 174.
[34] Stawell, *Growth of International Thought*, 184.
[35] Stawell, *Growth of International Thought*, 205.
[36] Stawell, *Growth of International Thought*, 175.
[37] R. Vitalis, *White World Order, Black Power Politics: The Birth of American International Relations* (Ithaca, NY: Cornell University Press, 2015).
[38] S. Pedersen, "Metaphors of the Schoolroom: Women Working the Mandates System of the League of Nations," *History Workshop Journal* 66 (2008): 188–207; Sluga, *Internationalism in the Age of Nationalism*.

female – envisioned the League as an extension of the British Empire, or even as modeled on the British Empire – even though, unlike national-ism, empires did not have a prescribed place in the stadist world view of the evolving enlargement of political association because they were not identified with democratic progress. Stawell even concedes that the history of the nineteenth century offers up examples of bad imperialism aplenty, which, she believes, advocates "of a sane internationalism" have a duty to publicize: from negro slavery to reprisals at the time of the Indian Mutiny, the forcing by the British of opium on the Chinese, the forms of extortion used by companies under the protection of empire to extract rubber and cocoa in the colonies, and atrocities inflicted by white armies during the Chinese Boxer rebellion. However, the English example persists as an international model for managing what she terms "the problem of the coloured races." Stawell is confident that in a world where, on her view, the facts of race differences are reflected in different levels of civilizational achievement, empire could be an agent for good. "Native misgovernment," she offers, "may often reach a point at which it is far better to interfere. And without some civilized government it is hardly conceivable that certain savage races could ever advance at all. Instead they would become the victims of irresponsible traders."[39]

Taking Stawell seriously is to see her as a proponent of an increasingly mainstream early twentieth-century repertoire of international thinking that rendered the international the complement, and fulfillment, of the national – insofar as national patriotism is a facet of human nature, *and* the national level of association is an expression of freedom. In a geneal-ogy of international thought, Stawell also stands for a history of ideas written to educational ends, for the "general reader," by an intellectual defined through this public role. Even before the League of Nations was established, in early 1919, Stawell announced in a letter to the new journal *History* – written on behalf of "a Committee of the League of Nations Union" – that the League was "on the lips of everyone and in the hearts of many," but it could only become real if it had a social base educated in knowledge of the unfamiliar, through "the wise and large-hearted teaching of History," including a European history, and not only the history of England, "which is only part of something much greater."[40] Her point was that building the League's social base required knowledge of elsewhere. At the same time, her advocacy invoked a "we" that was simultaneously internationalist and "English," and that included

---

[39] Stawell, *Growth of International Thought*, 186.
[40] F. Melian Stawell, "History and the League of Nations," *History*, New Series, 3.12 (1919): 224.

herself – an Australian British citizen, who happened to build her career in England, a woman who could vote in her homeland but not in the motherland. Taking Stawell seriously means recognizing the depth of her imperial and gender positioning, not least as a colonial at the female margins of the center of Oxbridge history.

When we put Stawell back in her internationalist context, she is less a pioneer, and more a public intellectual with a well-prescribed social and political agenda. We cannot claim that *The Growth of International Thought* invented a genre, although it coined a term. It was certainly not the first history of international thought as internationalist thought. That path had already been trodden by Christian Lange's *Histoire de l'internationalisme* (1919).[41] In writing his history of internationalism, Lange assembled examples of international thinking since the "Greeks" too and worked his way forward. Lange's aim was to illustrate that early twentieth-century internationalism was the antithesis of eighteenth-century cosmopolitanism, because it acknowledged the social and cultural indelibility of nations.[42] Lange was critical of the destructive power of the modern sovereign state, while insisting that "nationality" was a spiritual phenomenon that could not be eradicated. The gloomier (and in some ways more Kantian) rationale for his version of internationalism was that in order for nations to survive they had to become more international, or they would wipe each other out. Stawell's study did not strike the same dark chords as Lange, although she cited his work in her bibliography commending it as an "invaluable book for the student."[43]

Then there was the precedent set by Stawell's own earlier *longue durée* history of Western thought from Hellenism through Hebraism, Christianity, ancient Rome, the medieval world of Charlemagne and

---

[41] C. Lange, *L'Histoire de l'internationalisme* (1919), vol. 1: the first volume covered the period from antiquity to 1648 ; a second volume was published posthumously.

[42] Lange argued that, unlike the moralism endemic to pacifism, internationalism had its basis in solid economic, historical and sociological and biological facts. In 1915 and later Lange was active in the work of the Central Organization for a Lasting Peace, the OOP, an organization founded by the Dutch, and which counted among its members Emily Greene Balch.

[43] Lange, *L'Histoire*, 247. Lange won the Nobel Peace prize in 1921 and was a prominent name in internationalist circles. He won the prize primarily for his work on behalf of the Inter-Parliamentary Union (IPU), an international inter-governmental institution set up in the late nineteenth century, with branches in the UK, and widely regarded as having provided an institutional precedent for the creation of a League of Nations. The IPU's aims were to encourage governments to solve international disputes by peaceful means and arbitration and annual conferences were held to help governments refine the process of international arbitration; its structure consisted of a Council headed by a President, which would later be reflected in the structure of the League.

"Mohammedism," to the Renaissance, Enlightenment, and Romanticism. In 1923, Stawell published a co-authored study entitled *The Making of the Western Mind*.[44] Most of the forty-three chapters are by her hand, although three – on science, maths, and the modern era (including the League) – were written by her erstwhile collaborator F. S. Marvin, a (male) teacher and education bureaucrat. *The Growth of International Thought* feels like the abridged and re-tasked version of *The Making of the Western Mind*. It is not difficult to imagine that, given the change of topic forced onto her by Murray and her publisher, Stawell may have found it easiest to return to that familiar *longue durée* framing for her more focused international history.

So, we have in *The Growth of International Thought* a text determined in part by Gilbert Murray's sense of entitlement, Stawell's possible pragmatism, her accrued expertise as a popular historian of ideas, and her classicist training. Then there was her engagement (like that of Murray and other high-profile British classicists and historians) with a liberal internationalist version of international thought identified with the League of Nations. The motifs of her internationalism accumulate in her account of the later nineteenth and twentieth centuries: the invention of the Red Cross and the Hague peace congresses as critical contributions to internationalist thinking; the growing acceptance of international law and international conventions against certain practices in warfare, including a humanitarian purpose; the belated international recognition given in 1919, at the moment of the League's founding, to the principle of nationality. She notes too the effects of big business working across borders, and the virtue of scale for efficiencies of production. From her international perspective, these are all elements of the modern world that work toward or assist the realism of internationalism.

It is impossible to read Stawell's survey of international thought without hearing the ideological strains of a 1920s conception of internationalism or seeing a millennium of thought reflected through the mirror of the League of Nations, as she does. Stawell's history and analysis are so embedded in the 1920s, it tells us as much about the state of international thought in that period as the centuries before. Its key tones speak to a historically specific moment in thinking about the possibilities of internationalism relative to the conceptual, moral, and emotional primacy of nations and races. All the characteristic tropes of progressive internationalist thought are there: nationalism as a necessary complement to internationalism, rendering the international consensual rather

---

[44] F. M. Stawell and F. S. Marvin, *The Making of the Western Mind: A Short Survey of European Culture* (London: Methuen, 1923).

than coercive; empire as an economic correlative of internationalism and nationalism; patriotism twinned with humanity.[45] The book's timing accounts for the confidence with which Stawell wielded the term internationalism and made it her framing idea.

Stawell's "Greeks to the League" account of international thought brings the intellectual weight of "the western mind" to bear on the growth of international thought. It traces the presence and absence of an internationalism that combines stadism, federalism, pacifism, humanitarianism, an ambivalent imperialism, and sublimated race-based eugenics.[46] If we accept the centrality of internationalism to the origins of international thought, and with that the discipline of IR, then Stawell fits right in. The history of women and international thought with Stawell added reinforces the transnational relevance of Robert Vitalis' recent conclusions regarding the importance of race and nation-thinking in the American origin story of IR, but with a British internationalist twist.[47]

Women and Internationalist International Thought

Writing *The Growth of International Thought* back into the history of international ideas is one thing, claiming Stawell a place in a canon of international thinkers is another. Both activities return us to fundamental questions of historical method: Where should we look for the international past? What kind of publications, writing, and thinking count as intellectual history, let alone as contributions to the conceptual grounding of IR? If women have lacked access to institutional status and publication (even when men have not borrowed their ideas), what should be the qualification for including them in the canon of international thought, as chroniclers of the past, as public intellectuals and activists deploying international ideas? Should we consider F. M. Stawell an historian of international thought, or an even an intellectual? For all the recent interest in her conceptualization of "international thought," she is representative of a class of women who have been relatively ignored as thinkers because they do not fit a gender, institutional and publication

---

[45] Sluga, *Internationalism in the Age of Nationalism*, ch. 2.

[46] Hall, "History of International Thought," 243 notes that Stawell's history is a "Greeks to the League" account, a whiggish history that prefigures a trend – although that trend in Hall's own accounting, quite conventionally, never encounters another woman writing on international thought, until Jennifer Pitts and Or Rosenboim. See also Keene's *International Political Thought*.

[47] Vitalis, *White World Order*.

profile, just as the history of internationalist thinking has long been discarded by IR scholars as either Marxist, or irrelevant.[48]

In Stawell, we have the frame of a British imperial view taken by a woman from the colonies who did her own thinking in the networks of classicist internationalists, at the cusp of a new era in the teaching and research of international politics. In the circumstances I have preferred to portray her as a "public intellectual" – although again not unlike many of her male classicist internationalist peers. Stawell's milieu was not only Oxbridge classics, but the rise of the WILPF, and broad expansion of League of Nations movements across the British world.[49] Indeed, she stands for a larger trend in this period, in the developing stages of IR as a discipline, when politically active internationalist women (not only British) otherwise kept out of the Academy, took to the summer school forum, publishing and pamphleteering as a means of teaching a new generation.[50] These women were often located in feminist internationalist organizations and networks, and less often in the spaces of unwelcoming universities. They were motivated by an overlapping commitment to internationalism (including the League of Nations Union), nation, and empire.[51] Other chapters in this volume discuss the work of women partly educated through networks, some of whom, such as Merze Tate, made it into universities, but remained marginalized in institutional memory.[52] That few of these women have been integrated into the history of international thought, even as F. M. Stawell herself is being given a place there, at least superficially, confirms a deeper gender problematic. Just as international history has found no place for internationalist thought, intellectual history has been antipathetic to women.[53]

---

48 See my discussion in *Internationalism in the Age of Nationalism* afterword, and Sluga and Clavin, "Rethinking the History of Internationalisms."

49 See Helen McCarthy, *The British People and the League of Nations: Democracy, Citizenship and Internationalism c. 1918–45* (Manchester University Press, 2011), and Aden Knaap, "'Apart Altogether from Idealistic Sentiments': Domesticating the League of Nations in Australia, 1920–39," Honours thesis (University of Sydney, 2014).

50 Glenda Sluga, "Gender," in Patrick Finney (ed.), Palgrave Advances in International History (Basingstoke: Palgrave Macmillan), 300–19.

51 Helen McCarthy argues that women were overrepresented in the foundational branches of the LNU.

52 For a discussion of Lucy Philip Mair, who graduated from Classics at Newnham in 1923, see Owens, "Women and the History of International Thought."

53 Glenda Sluga, "Women, Feminisms and Twentieth-Century Internationalisms," in Sluga and Clavin (eds.), *Internationalisms*. The fact that international thought is often linked with feminine influence – not unlike the status of international organizations in the context of the identification of "governance feminism" today – is more simply the intersection of these trends.

Stawell was not unaware of her difficult position as a woman. There are few documentary traces of Stawell's association with the contemporary feminist internationalist or League bodies that were as influential in this period in the political networks she inhabited – which is not evidence that she was not involved, but rather reflects her particular circumstances, a low institutional profile, and chronic illness. However, an earlier 1907 text on "Women and Democracy," suggests that the question of the place of women in the growth of international thought was on Stawell's mind.[54] Stawell claimed the right of women to the vote was an argument not for "the ridiculous fancy that everyone has equal abilities, but the conviction that every one's self-development, whatever their abilities may be, is in itself to be taken as of equal importance." The franchise was necessary "to develop the characters of women"; when "each sex" could think "for itself," "the full differentiation of the sexes" would also be realized.[55] Stawell's point in both the gender and race cases was that there existed an obligation to educate women (and the non-white races) to distinctive ends, including an acknowledgment of *unequal* difference.[56]

Adding women to the intellectual history of international thought is not only problematic because of the long history of women's difficult place in the institutions that gave time and space to cultivate an intellectual life, and be recognized for it, but because some women such as Stawell were unlikely to make an argument for equality on the same bases as men on behalf of themselves. Stawell's support for the collective rather than individual role of intellectuals is, however, a basis for defending a more generous version of intellectual history, and of international thought, in which popular publications and public education are legitimate locations of ideas that matter. To that same end, here I want to briefly turn to the internationalist thought of American economist Emily Greene Balch.

When it came to making an impact, Balch, six years Stawell's junior, and operating out of the United States (which had abstained from the League of Nations), was no wallflower. In World War I and after, Balch was an energetic high-profile figure in an extended network of feminist internationalists, known not only for her pacifism (and being fired from Wellesley because of it), but also her writing on immigrants, international economics, international cooperation, and colonialism. Stawell,

[54] F. M. Stawell, "Women and Democracy," *International Journal of Ethics* 17.3 (1907): 329–36.
[55] Stawell, "Women and Democracy," 330, 333, 335.
[56] Stawell, "Patriotism and Humanity," 293, 298.

by contrast, remained in the rarefied domain of the university college, increasingly constrained in her intellectual and political projects by illness.

In her careful survey of Balch's extensive interventions in international thought, Catia Confortini has identified similar themes to those that concerned Stawell: race, empire, and trade.[57] But in contrast to Stawell, Balch was a much more careful critic of racism, the "unholy alliance" of cannon and capital, and the state. For example, Balch engaged the US occupation of Haiti as a question of race-based imperial occupation. Internationalism on Balch's view was a means of weeding out the exclusivism and discrimination produced by national, imperial, and racial manifestations of political power and community. In the circumstances, Balch's most important contributions to international thought are her originality and refinement in conceiving international forms of sovereignty that recognize the state and move beyond it. This is particularly the case in her role as a public intellectual in the 1930s and 1940s, when Stawell was no longer on the scene. Through the interwar years and into the 1940s, Balch turns her hand to the ideas of one of the intellectuals in Stawell's study, Hugo Grotius – the Dutch jurist who focused on the law of the sea.

For Stawell, Grotius' version of the law of the seas had a contemporary resonance, particularly when he asked: "whether any one power could claim a jurisdiction over any part of the high seas as complete as it could claim on land"?[58] Before and during World War I, as the idea of the League of Nations took form, the law of the seas was a component of international thinking, and Grotius' question still informed international legal debate. At the 1915 Hague Peace Conference run by internationalist women, including Balch, their resolutions call "for open seas and free trade routes ... and for the establishment of a permanent international conference which shall deal with practical proposals for future international cooperation and shall appoint a permanent council of conciliation for the settlement of differences arising from social and economic causes."[59] The principle of international waterways made its way into Woodrow Wilson's "Fourteen Points," and became a staple of twentieth-century international thinking.[60] In 1926, however, Stawell notes that although the high seas are now "free" in times of peace, their status during war

---

[57] See the chapter in this volume by Catia Confortini.

[58] Stawell, *Growth of International Thought*, 128.

[59] Mary Chamberlain, "The Women at the Hague," *The Survey* 5 (1915): 219–22. Available at: http://journals.sagepub.com/doi/full/10.1177/0047117817723061.

[60] The Point stated: "absolute freedom of navigation upon the seas, outside territorial waters, alike in peace and in war, except as the seas may be closed in whole or in part

remains legally uncertain. Balch takes up the debate circulating around the law of the seas and over the next two decades extrapolates a conception of international sovereignty as it pertains to not only the sea, but also to airspace and the polar regions. Along the way, Balch stretches the parameters of internationalism by putting her mind to rethinking sovereignty as international.[61]

In the mid-1940s, a period that Balch describes as "plastic" because of its openness to international thought, Balch stretches the parameters and possibilities of internationalism by re-imagining territorial boundaries and political citizenship. Her ideas assume practical form: how to appoint an International Maritime Authority "with wide powers covering all the waterways of the world which have an international character, including the oceans, narrow seas such as the Mediterranean, straits, canals such as Suez, Kiel, and Panama, and so far as may seem indicated, international rivers such as the Rhine and Danube, although very possibly the latter might be best left to a purely European authority."[62]

Whereas in the 1920s Stawell pictures the world's resources at the behest of imperial commercial interest, Balch's formula for thinking sovereignty subjects resources to international sovereignty. Balch sums up her international re-conception of the status of the sea in 1947, after the United Nations has been born out of the ashes of the League:

The world of waters, the international waterways of the globe, are as yet unpreempted. Until yesterday Britannia ruled the waves, and her place has not yet been taken in this regard. Why should not the United Nations now create a supreme authority over both the "ocean seas" and the channels and canals, artificial and natural, which are of peculiar importance and create peculiar political problems? To suggest but one instance, the internationalization of the Dardanelles under properly equipped world authority would take the poison out of one of the "hottest" spots on the political map.[63]

Balch works her international thinking through her influence in various League of Nations NGOs.[64] She writes up her international ideas in

by international action for the enforcement of international covenants." See Sluga, *The Nation, Psychology, and International Politics.*

[61] Glenda Sluga, "The International History of International Sovereignty," in Matthias Middell and Steffi Marung (eds.), *Spatializations and the Global Condition* (Leipzig University Press, 2019).

[62] Emily G. Balch, "UN and the Waters of the World," *Survey Graphic* 36 (1947): 529–30, 555–57 (555).

[63] Emily G. Balch, *Toward Human Unity or beyond Nationalism: Nobel Lecture, Delivered at Oslo, 7 April 1948* (Stockholm: Kungl. Boktryckeriet P. A. Norstedt & Söner, 1949).

[64] Balch's proposal was referred to the WILPF's International Executive Committee, which voted to send a petition to the UN requesting the appointment of a committee

wartime opinion pieces, in the *New York Times* and magazines such as *Survey Graphic*, and the reports of international organizations. Does this mean Balch has no place in an intellectual history? Is she a thinker, and Stawell a chronicler? Or perhaps, it is more important to ask what allows one woman to imagine a post-imperial world of international spaces and laws, when both write in the context of the same international past, and negotiate the same international and imperial institutions, nation and race ideas? Answers to those questions, I would argue, require taking both women seriously, and recognizing that the question of context extends beyond the landscape of ideas, or even an individual's geopolitical positioning as a British or American subject. It includes the historical domains of activism and exclusion, and the shifting political tenor of "international" in the interwar period and the 1940s.

In Stawell and Balch, we have two women who added considerably to the canon of the intellectual history of international thought, often by more public and educational means. While a new trend in intellectual history proposes the utility of the category "mid-level" thinker for capturing and salvaging the ideas of individuals who by virtue of their gender, race, or class were unlikely to earn prominence as "thinkers," but who still were influential by other means, neither Balch nor Stawell are in need of this kind of recategorization in order to earn a place in the history of international thought.[65] Both were actively and consistently internationalist in their international thinking and disseminated their ideas through less conventional methods than is the norm for "intellectual history." Neither were any more "mid-level" than E. H. Carr, or other more obvious internationalists such as Norman Angell or Alfred Zimmern. If anything, Stawell's efforts place her in the same space of intellectual thinking as her masculine peers, the other classicists who so ardently engaged the internationalism and international politics of the first half of the twentieth century. In this same milieu, Balch stands out as an original activist thinker. The onus is on historians. Adding both

---

to study the subject, "both its substance and the practical methods of realizing it." Each national section of the WILPF was asked to secure signatures for the petition from a "small number ... of persons of known competence, official or unofficial." In this way, the idea was said to be "presented to various leading persons in eleven different countries"; Balch, "UN and the Waters of the World," 555.

[65] Glenda Sluga and Tim Rowse, "Forum: Global Liberalisms – Introduction," *Modern Intellectual History* 12.3 (2015): 523–28; Sluga, "Turning International"; Mia Bay, Farah J. Griffin, Martha S. Jones, and Barbara D. Savage (eds.), *Toward an Intellectual History of Black Women* (Chapel Hill: University of North Carolina Press, 2015); Chris Bayly, "The Ends of Liberalism and the Political Thought of Nehru's India," *Modern Intellectual History* 12.3 (2015): 605–26.

women to the history of international thought requires not only fitting them into the existing canon, but expanding the canon to fit a spectrum of ideas and public engagement that extends back and forward through yet undiscovered strands of international thinking – not only the limits of Stawell's "pioneering" approach, but also the liminality of Balch's imagined international sovereignty.

11 Race, Gender, Empire, and War in the International Thought of Emily Greene Balch

Catia C. Confortini

The discipline of International Relations (IR) is slowly addressing the centrality of race in the field's origins, theories, and practices, including how IR's canon developed hand-in-hand with racist justifications of war and imperialism and excluded those arguing against both.[1] In this context, I wish to recover the pacifist and anti-imperialist thought of the white woman scholar Emily Greene Balch.[2] Known and appreciated by feminist historians, Balch is overlooked in IR.[3] Apart from *Our Slavic Fellow Citizens*, her book on Slavic immigration, she never collected her thoughts on race "prejudice," imperialism, and war in one manuscript.[4] Nor did she acquire a degree higher than her BA from Bryn Mawr College in 1889. However, she worked as professor of economics and

---

[1] For example, Alex Anievas, Nivi Manchanda, and Robbie Shilliam (eds.), *Race and Racism in International Relations: Confronting the Global Color Line* (New York: Routledge, 2015); Robert Vitalis, *White World Order, Black Power Politics: The Birth of American International Relations* (Ithaca, NY: Cornell University Press, 2015); Siba N'Zatioula Grovogui, *Sovereigns, Quasi-Sovereigns, and Africans: Race and Self-Determination in International Law* (Minneapolis, MN: University of Minnesota Press, 1996).

[2] I would like to thank Sara Ludovissy, of the Wellesley College Archives for her assistance in locating material on Emily Greene Balch, Cecelia Lynch for her careful reading of different versions of this chapter, and this book's editors and anonymous reviewers for their helpful comments and suggestions.

[3] For example, Linda K. Schott, *Reconstructing Women's Thoughts: The Women's International League for Peace and Freedom before World War II* (Stanford University Press, 1997); Melinda Plastas, *A Band of Noble Women: Racial Politics in the Women's Peace Movement* (Syracuse University Press, 2011); Kristen E. Gwinn, *Emily Greene Balch: The Long Road to Internationalism* (Urbana: University of Illinois Press, 2010). And in economics, sociology, and the social sciences in general. See Andrew Johnston, "The Disappearance of Emily G. Balch, Social Scientist," *The Journal of the Gilded Age and Progressive Era* 13.2 (2014): 166–99; Robert W. Dimand, "Emily Greene Balch, Political Economist," *The American Journal of Economics and Sociology* 70.2 (2011): 464–79.

[4] Her writings mainly appeared as transcribed speeches in social work, pacifist, labor, or women's magazines like *Charities and The Commons* (later *The Survey*), *The New World* (later *The World Tomorrow*), *The Intercollegiate Socialist* (later *Socialist Review*), and *The New Republic*; and in reports for Women's International League for Peace and Freedom (WILPF) – the organization that she helped found. Many of the thinkers of what Robert Vitalis has termed "the Howard school" also published in some of the same outlets.

sociology at Wellesley College from 1896 to 1919, chairing the department from 1913. As Glenda Sluga argues in this volume, genre, degrees, personality, or academic-institutional status are rationalizations for women's exclusion from IR's disciplinary history, which insufficiently takes account of gendered structures of power in the field and beyond. Yet Balch, unlike her white male counterparts in the emerging field of IR, was in fact "a key interwar era critic" of US racially-justified imperialism.[5]

Balch's thought was not free of contradictions and tensions, and her struggles were evident in speeches and in the policies that she supported. As Cecelia Lynch argues, one cannot dismiss such contradictions and tensions as inevitable given the times.[6] But one need not romanticize Balch or ignore the troubled history of white feminism as regards questions of race to acknowledge and analyze the significance of Balch's international thought.

In this chapter, I bring to bear feminist historians' insights on the thought of Emily Greene Balch on the disciplinary history of IR and make the following claims. First, Balch's work stands out among her contemporary analysts of international relations not only because of her critique of the interrelated problems of racism, nationalism, imperialism, and war, but also because she grounded this analysis in a commitment to the "ontological unity" of a humanity "with common interests and a common destiny."[7] Her form of cosmopolitanism diverges from the nationalist fervor that, as Glenda Sluga's work extensively documents, permeated the internationalism of the time.[8] In Balch's vision of international relations, states – and the "unholy alliance of state and capital" – are but an obstacle to the realization of this unity, rather than an ontological given.

Second, for Balch, the foundation of a just and peaceful world system had to rest on this cosmopolitan ethos in order to provide a moral compass that would guide interpersonal as well as international relations. There was no distinction for Balch – as there was, instead, for self-proclaimed realists – between state and personal morality, or – as for both realists and liberals/idealists – between Western and non-Western

---

[5] Melinda Plastas, "A Different Burden: Race and the Social Thought of Emily Greene Balch," *Peace & Change* 33.4 (2008): 469–506 (470); Vitalis, *White World Order*, 12.

[6] Cecelia M. Lynch, *Wrestling with God: Ethical Precarity in Christianity and International Relations* (New York: Cambridge University Press, 2020).

[7] Emily Greene Balch, "The Trouble the Remedy," 1940, Swarthmore College Peace Collection, Microfilms, Records of Emily Greene Balch, Reel 3.

[8] See for example Glenda Sluga, *Internationalism in the Age of Nationalism* (Philadelphia: University of Pennsylvania Press, 2013).

"others."[9] Neither were imperialism and war solely motivated by "defensive and aggressive forms of racial nationalism,"[10] or by purely economic motives. Rather they were the result of a fundamental failure of the moral imagination to realize humanity's ontological unity: they rested on an economic system based on profits rather than human well-being; on a cultural system built around notions of racial and sexual inferiority; and on an international system of power-as-dominance-hungry states. Finally, Balch's writings about women and international politics presage the 1980s adage that "feminism is the radical notion that women are people,"[11] rather than attributing to women natural qualities essentially different from men's. For Balch, humanity's ontological unity included – and indeed necessitated – women, and it was a matter of justice to elevate women's roles in international politics, although they were not exempted from the responsibility to act according to the cosmopolitan ethos that Balch advocated.

Perhaps it is not surprising then that Balch came of age as an intellectual-activist in spaces carved out for women. Her all-girls high school, the settlement house for women that she co-founded, the three US women's colleges where she studied or taught (Bryn Mawr, Radcliffe, and Wellesley), and WILPF, the organization to which she devoted most of her adult life, provided the freedom, networks, and political communities where her and other women's international feminist thought could develop, flourish, and be challenged. The years Balch spent at Wellesley, in particular, are an important prelude to her interwar and post-war thought. Since Alice Freeman became Wellesley's first president after the death of founder Henry Durant in 1881, the college had become a full-fledged and unapologetically liberal arts institution for women, progressively shedding the religious rigidity of the beginnings and consolidating both social reform aims and feminist academic leadership.[12] By the beginning of the twentieth century, Wellesley with other institutions had become instrumental in the development of a strong and successful feminist movement – although one that did little-to-nothing about race and class biases and often had essentialist understandings of political and social bonds.[13] It was at Wellesley that Balch's first thoughts

---

[9] See Cecelia M. Lynch, "The Moral Aporia of Race in International Relations," *International Relations* 33.2 (2019): 267–285.

[10] Plastas, *Band of Noble Women*, 85.

[11] Marie Shear, "Review of Cheris Kramarae and Paula Treichler's *A Feminist Dictionary*," *New Directions for Women* (May/June 1986).

[12] Patricia Ann Palmieri, *In Adamless Eden: The Community of Women Faculty at Wellesley* (New Haven, CT: Yale University Press, 1997).

[13] Estelle Freedman, "Separatism as Strategy: Female Institution Building and American Feminism, 1870–1930," *Feminist Studies* 5.3 (1979): 512–29.

on race and imperialism took shape, placing her work in sharp contrast with the increasing popularity and influence of scientific theories of race and immigration restrictions.

In this chapter, I offer a snapshot of an intellectual, whose complex thought has been forgotten, ignored, or overly simplified. Feminist peace scholars revere her but too easily dismiss her contradictions, while others criticize her as hopelessly racist.[14] The following section foregrounds Balch's magnum opus, *Our Slavic Fellow Citizens*, as an important prelude to her later engagement with questions of empire, gender, and war. I then turn to her interwar writings, devoting a section to a co-authored report on the US occupation of Haiti. I end with some concluding remarks summarizing the particularities of Balch's international thought, so that we can understand its varieties and contradictions at a significant time in international relations as well as the history of the academic field of IR.

Socialism, Race, and Nationalism in *Our Slavic Fellow Citizens*

Balch arrived at Wellesley after working for a couple of years at Denison House, the first settlement house for immigrant women in Boston, which she co-founded with other women's colleges graduates. Denison House, like Jane Addams' Hull House in Chicago, provided welfare and health services, employment, vocational and academic classes, and it became a center of labor organizing, linking the settlement and labor movements in Boston. Balch's labor activism and her concern particularly with the conditions and rights of immigrant workers, as well as her idea of the settlement house – where workers and immigrants resided together[15] – as a model of international community, started at Denison House and continued at Wellesley.

Her networks of female colleagues and friends at the college strengthened her connections with feminism and socialism: Ellen Hayes "kept the beacon of feminism alive" through her columns in the college newspaper, *The Courant*.[16] She also published at the time in *The Intercollegiate Socialist*, the newsletter of a homonymous coalition of US colleges, which stood consistently against racism and imperialism.[17] With Vida

---

[14] For example, Nancy Folbre, *Who Pays for the Kids? Gender and the Structures of Constraint* (London: Routledge, 1994), 185–86.

[15] Balch chose to live in her family home, a decision she seemed to regret in her late years. Gwinn, *Emily Greene Balch*, 32.

[16] Palmieri, *In Adamless Eden*, 39.

[17] Craig N. Murphy, "Relocating the Point of IR in Understanding Industrial-Age Global Problems," in Synne L. Dyvik, Jan Selby, and Rorden Wilkinson (eds.), *What's the Point of International Relations* (New York: Routledge, 2017), 71–82 (75).

Scudder, Balch brought John Hobson to Wellesley in 1902, and in 1909 they organized a conference in Boston on "Socialism as a World Movement."[18] Balch's first courses included one on the "Evolution and Present Conditions of Wage-Labor" which, according to a retrospective self-study of the Wellesley Department of Economics and Sociology, "preceded by eight years the appearance of the first text book on the subject."[19] In 1907 she also taught a course on immigration, by her own account the first of its kind in undergraduate institutions.[20]

Between 1904 and 1906, Balch took a two-year sabbatical to immerse herself in ethnographic research, going to Austria-Hungary to understand the reasons for migration as well as the effects of migration on the communities of origin. Across the United States she lived in the houses of immigrants as well as settlement houses. This fieldwork and the resulting book, *Our Slavic Fellow Citizens*, published in 1910, was her first sustained engagement with imperial formations.

It is impossible to overestimate the degree to which this book challenged the intellectual trends of the time regarding race, immigration, and nationalism. At a time of increased immigration from Southern and Eastern Europe, race, as Matthew Guterl has shown, "was marked by language, nationality, religion, and social status, as well as by color."[21] The "science" of eugenics – classifying these "new" immigrants as inferior to Anglo-Saxon stock and a threat to America's racial purity – provided the intellectual justification for increasing immigration restrictions. According to the 1911 US Congress' Dillingham Commission's Report, Slavs, in particular, "possessed a fanaticism in religion, carelessness as to the business virtues of punctuality and often honesty, [and were prone to] periods of besotted drunkenness [and] unexpected cruelty."[22] Racially-justified immigration restrictions went hand-in-hand with nationalist and imperialist fervor. The construction of an American empire (in Hawaii, the Philippines, Cuba, and Haiti) was justified with gender-coded appeals to the superiority of Anglo-Saxon

---

[18] Mercedes M. Randall, *Improper Bostonian: Emily Greene Balch* (New York: Twayne Publishers, 1964), 108.

[19] "The Teaching of Economics at Wellesley," 3L Collection, Wellesley College Archives, Library and Technology Services. Economics Department: General, Box 1.

[20] Balch, cited in Mercedes M. Randall (ed.), *Beyond Nationalism: The Social Thought of Emily Greene Balch* (New York: Twayne Publishers, 1972), 50.

[21] Matthew Pratt Guterl, *The Color of Race in America: 1900–1940* (Cambridge, MA: Harvard University Press, 2001), 5–6.

[22] John M. Lund, "Boundaries of Restriction: The Dillingham Commission," *History Review* 6 (December 1994). Available at: www.uvm.edu/~hag/histreview/vol6/lund .html. A perhaps unsurprising example of the contradictions in Balch's thought, she wrote a tepidly positive review of the commission's findings, summarized in Jeremiah W. Jenks and W. Jett Lauck, *The Immigration Problem* (New York: Funk and Wagnalls Company, 1912).

civilization and the "manly virtues of the 'race'."[23] Even the internationalism of these decades "revolved around the conceptual, moral, and emotional primacy of nations,"[24] complementing, rather than contrasting, both nationalism and empire.[25]

By contrast, together with a few others, such as anthropologists Franz Boas and sociologist William I. Thomas, Balch articulated a conception of "race as culture" that challenged the prevalent understandings of "scientific" race theories,[26] a trend that engulfed IR theorists as well, including women such as F. Melian Stawell.[27] Boas and his followers instead refuted eugenicists' claims that human moral, temperamental, and social characteristics were hereditary and related to biological traits. Rather, environmental and cultural factors determined human personality as well as social and moral characteristics. In other words, although physical types and races might exist, they claimed, physical differences did not translate into moral, social, or political ones.[28] Unlike quite a few of her teachers and friends – progressive academics, social reformers, and socialists such as Franklin Giddings, Albion Small, Victor Berger, Sidney Webb, and Robert Woods – Balch was not seduced by eugenics' illusionary promise of human advancement via natural or social engineering. Nor did she take part in the influential Immigration Restriction League of Boston.

Instead, in *Our Slavic Fellow Citizens* she dismantled eugenicists' claims to scientific authority by exposing the internal logical and empirical contradictions of eugenicist positions. Rather, she asserted "our comprehensive ignorance of the actual results of race crossings"[29] and highlighted the wildly divergent opinions of so-called experts. In 1917, she concluded her review of Madison Grant's anti-immigrant and eugenicist treatise *The Passing of the Great Race* with the following admonition: "Rash is the man who passes lightly from skull measurements to vast unprovable sociological and historical generalizations."[30] Further, Balch dismantled the racist stereotypes about Slavs' supposedly innate characteristics by highlighting the varieties of their beliefs, languages, and practices based on the extensive evidentiary material from her years of fieldwork, as well as secondary sources in multiple languages.

---

[23] Guterl, *Color of Race*, 24.   [24] Glenda Sluga, this volume.

[25] Sluga, *Internationalism*, ch. 2.

[26] Plastas, "A Different Burden"; Plastas, *Band of Noble Women*; Schott, *Reconstructing Women's Thoughts*.

[27] See Glenda Sluga's chapter in this volume.

[28] Franz Boas, "Eugenics," *The Scientific Monthly* 3.5 (1916): 471–78.

[29] Emily Greene Balch, *Our Slavic Fellow Citizens* (New York: Charities Publication Committee, 1910), 404.

[30] Emily Greene Balch, "Review of The Passing of a Great Race by Madison Grant," *The Survey* (December 1, 1917): 262.

For example, she demonstrated how the overcrowding of urban dwellings was due to low wages and high rents, rather than to the supposedly loose morals and poor hygienic habits of Slavic immigrants. She challenged feminists' views of Slavic women as both lewd and oppressed, noting their economic roles in the family, their organizations and newspapers, and reporting the mixed effects of immigration on gender relations. In contrast to both racially obsessed theories of human relations and strictly material or class arguments, Balch outlined a political economy of Slavic immigration where intersecting economic, political, and social factors drove the movement of labor across borders. They also influenced in various ways customs, traditions, languages, cultures, and political organizing of Slavic immigrants to the United States, as well as the relations between them and the communities in which they settled.

Although she conceded that the English were the primary group of first immigrants to the continent, she dismissed the notion of a uniformly Anglo-Saxon "stock" and, rather, saw Americans as "something distinctive and different," a stock created through "an amalgamation, a fusion" of many different people.[31] She also ignored, however, the violence of the conquest and the genocide of Amerindian populations in the process of this "fusion": when reading *Our Slavic Fellow Citizens* one would think that the process of land acquisition in colonial America had been through entirely voluntary transactions, and missionary conversion of Amerindians a benign enterprise. *Our Slavic Fellow Citizens* displayed as well traces of a paternalistic, while benevolent, attitude toward poor and working-class people, an example of what we may now call the "politics of respectability." For example, while Balch decried the devaluing and belittling of southern European immigrants by Americans, she did so by highlighting a distinction between upper and lower classes, claiming that "especially is there always a tendency to undervalue any nationality which is known in real life only by representatives of its lower social strata."[32] Dispersed throughout there are references to "primitive" life, or "backward" education, agriculture, and industry. If she gave a value judgment to these terms, it was not univocal: there was something romantically appealing for her in this supposed backwardness, with some "beauty and harmony" as well as "narrowness, suffering and degradation," as there were "bright features" as well as "shadows [in] our tenements and industrial life."[33] In any case, she argued, Americans should certainly not demand or impose changes on others' social mores.

---

[31] Balch, *Our Slavic Fellow Citizens*, 403.   [32] Balch, *Our Slavic Fellow Citizens*, 409.
[33] Balch, *Our Slavic Fellow Citizens*, 57. This ambivalence, as well as Balch's unequivocal position on empire, also stand in contrast with F. Melian Stawell's unquestioned use of these terms, documented by Glenda Sluga in this volume.

Whatever the book's limitations, it also exposed the hypocrisy and inconsistencies of American society by turning a reflexive lens on its own practices, superstitions, and prejudices.[34] Balch pointed out that immigrants' poor conditions "would not long be tolerated" if suffered by Americans. She indicted Americans for their "inability to share the sensations of a foreigner."[35] Immigration restrictions were "more or less arbitrary exclusion rules," that would have direct and tragic impacts on individual families, as it was "not possible to lower the portcullis without cutting into living flesh."[36] America may well tell itself the glorious story of a nation united by the common belief in lofty ideals,[37] but the immigrants' own impression was of the United States as "'the land of the almighty dollar'."[38] In this land often the "most elementary ethics of civilization" were lost,[39] and newcomers were at the same time treated as less than fellow human beings, and despised for the poor sanitary conditions and living arrangements forced on them by such treatment.

In sum, Balch's was a morally grounded critique of an economic system based on greed and the "intoxication of making money,"[40] rooted both in a socialist view of economic relations, and in a cosmopolitan ethos antithetical to nationalism. It is in *Our Slavic Fellow Citizens* that we find the embryo of Balch's later articulation of the connections between nationalism, capital accumulation, imperialism, and war. In this work, nationalism as "the active ferment of the nineteenth century" had "revealed fresh human treasures and called forth some of the rarest and finest blossoms of the spirit of mankind."[41] But it also divided people, "narrowed men's sympathies to their own little group,"[42] and gave rise to the desire to subjugate others. In the United States, nationalism translated into fear of and disdain for the immigrant and conversely, on the part of the immigrant, a concern about losing one's own national identity in the context of a hostile environment.

Balch's vision for co-habitation was one of integration and mutual influence, rather than straightforward assimilation, a living democracy where old settlers and newcomers would work together "for justice, for humane conditions of living, for beauty and for true, not merely formal,

---

[34] See Plastas, "A Different Burden."
[35] Balch, *Our Slavic Fellow Citizens*, 356 (citing a study by Elizabeth Butler).
[36] Balch, *Our Slavic Fellow Citizens*, 406.
[37] See also Emily Greene Balch, "What It Means to Be an American – 1916," in Randall, *Beyond Nationalism*.
[38] Balch, *Our Slavic Fellow Citizens*, 420 (citing informant).
[39] Balch, *Our Slavic Fellow Citizens*, 425.   [40] Balch, *Our Slavic Fellow Citizens*, 420.
[41] Balch, *Our Slavic Fellow Citizens*, 396.   [42] Balch, *Our Slavic Fellow Citizens*, 397.

liberty."[43] The living democracy she envisioned for the United States was the early articulation of a human society beyond nationalism, not far from her later idea of a "planetary civilization"[44] – expressed, for example, in her work on the internationalization of waterways documented in this volume by Glenda Sluga – and that she saw embodied in WILPF as a women's organization.

With the onset of war, Balch took a sabbatical leave in 1915 to join Jane Addams and forty other US women at the International Congress of Women in The Hague (the precursor of WILPF) which called for an arbitrated end to the war. In contrast to some of her Wellesley friends, she remained staunchly against US entry into war and against the "conscription of mind, hierarchical stratification of society ... [and] obedience as primary virtue"[45] that war and the preparation for war brought with them. It was likely her membership in the People's Council of America for Democracy and Terms of Peace, the short-lived but most radical and explicitly socialist of the wartime peace groups,[46] that cost her her job at Wellesley. The trustees of the College refused to reappoint her in 1919, and she found herself unemployed at the age of 52.

Implications of *Our Slavic Fellow Citizens* for Balch's Feminist Pacifism

As Balch's attention shifted from US domestic to international politics, her early work on immigration and race came to inform her analysis of international politics, including the problems of war and imperialism. When she joined WILPF as a full-time employee – she was Secretary General of the organization from 1919 to 1922 and dedicated the majority of her time to the organization for the rest of her life and until her death in 1961 – her analysis inspired and drew inspiration from fellow WILPFers.[47] In turn, Balch's feminism which had been shaped during

---

[43] Balch, *Our Slavic Fellow Citizens*, 425.

[44] Emily Greene, "Toward a Planetary Civilization – 1942," in Randall, *Beyond Nationalism*, 162.

[45] Emily Greene Balch, "Socialists and the Problems of War: Answers," *The Intercollegiate Socialist* 4 (April/May 1917): 9.

[46] H. H. Alonso, "Nobel Peace Laureates Jane Addams and Emily Greene Balch: Two Women of the Women's International League for Peace and Freedom," *Journal of Women's History* 7.2 (Summer 1995): 6–16.

[47] Joyce Blackwell, *No Peace Without Freedom: Race and the Women's International League for Peace and Freedom, 1915–1975* (Carbondale: Southern Illinois University Press, 2004), xix, 241; Wendy Sarvasy, "Militarized Occupations: Evolution of Women's International League for Peace and Freedom's 1920s Intersectional Conversation," *New Political Science* 37.4 (2015): 476–93.

the Wellesley years easily merged with WILPF's approach to inter-national politics.

An 1915 article on "Racial Contacts and Cohesions" in *The Survey*, one of Balch's first public writings after the start of the war, drew a clear connection between eugenics, nationalism, imperialism, and war. Balch wrote this piece at a time when American discourses on race had shifted significantly. When she published *Our Slavic Fellow Citizens*, a book that was focused on land-based empires, US ideas about race had not yet congealed around skin color.[48] In this article, by contrast, Balch joined contemporary anti-racist theorists in directly referring to racially-justified colonialism in Africa and Asia.

Balch lauded nationalism for producing great cultural treasures, but highlighted how the same phenomenon went hand-in-hand with "the pseudo-science of race ... with its effort to interpret human history in terms of the innate superiority of one racial group."[49] Insofar as nationalism created an impetus to dominate those deemed inferior, it was "a curse":

national vanity, and national greed masking under national vanity, give us the war cries of the jingo and the imperialist, and of *pan* this and *pan* that. The dogma of the white man's burden veils the colony-grabbing that lies behind it. The idea that it is a national mission to force others into the national mould, springs from contempt for those who differ from us.[50]

Colonization of "backward territories" brought "results that European states in their present stage of development hotly covet" – material, as well as less material ones.[51] They came at the cost of peace, but also at the cost of freedom for populations who had "no effective guarantee against exploitation and generally [were] in fact exploited."[52]

As Balch went against the *zeitgeist* of the time in many ways, in more subtle ones she went along with it, her assumptions coming to clash with her emancipatory aspirations. And because, as others have argued, racia-lized coding was not just accidental but constitutive of morality for theorists of the international in interwar years,[53] it is important that we recognize the limitations and contradictions in Balch's thought and practice. At the same time that she warned against "intellectual" or other

---

[48] Guterl, *Color of Race.*

[49] Emily Greene Balch, "Racial Contacts and Cohesions as Factors in the Unconstrained Fabric of a World at Peace," *The Survey* (March 6, 2015): 611.

[50] Balch, "Racial Contacts," 611.

[51] Emily Greene Balch, "International Colonial Administration – 1916," in Randall, *Beyond Nationalism*, 89.

[52] Balch, "International Colonial Administration," 89.   [53] Lynch, "The moral aporia."

kinds of "snobbery" as some of "many kinds and depths of ignorance,"[54] Balch proclaimed her belief in the existence of "various stages of development," from modern, industrialized, and centralized political systems, to mid-level areas with a mix of institutions, to the "lower extreme" in Central Africa.[55] She talked of the Zulus as "savage folks" and of the Moroccans as "semi-civilized,"[56] even as she decried the lack of access to decision-making bodies for the nations under US control.

In the early 1920s, German propaganda seemed to garner the support of Balch, Addams, and other WILPF leaders for a petition to end the use of French colonial troops in the occupied Rhineland. The protests used racial stereotypes and gendered tropes about dangerous black men and pure German women to incite animosities and ultimately serve Germany's revisionist aims.[57] These stereotypes found fertile terrain in a racialized society such as the 1920s United States, experiencing a high point of racist violence and hatred in the form of lynchings and a rising Ku Klux Klan membership. Mary Church Terrell, an African American WILPF leader, wrote to Addams and Balch exposing the connections between the campaign's racist ideology, its appeal to US audiences, and the incitement to nationalism and militarism. She also pointed to sexual violence against women during military occupations in general, including the examples of Haiti and German-occupied France, as well as the disgraceful and common rape of black women by white men.

Wendy Sarvasy compares two documents authored by Balch, one before and one after Terrell's letter.[58] In the first one, a December 1920 letter, Balch criticized the conscription of colonial troops as a tool of imperialism but limited her recommendation to training colonial troops only for policing purposes inside the colonies – a policy already in effect in the League of Nations' mandates. The second is Balch's remarks at the 1921 WILPF Vienna Congress, in support of a resolution stating that the "League make every possible effort to oppose the military use of 'native' populations."[59] The resolution may have been a

---

[54] Emily Greene Balch, "What's Hecuba to Me or I to Hecuba? – 1907," in Randall, *Beyond Nationalism*, 67.

[55] Emily Greene Balch, "Economic Imperialism with Special Reference to the United States – 1926," in Randall, *Beyond Nationalism*, 140.

[56] Balch, "International Colonial Administration," 88.

[57] Erika Kuhlman, "'Women's Ways in War': The Feminist Pacifism of the New York City Woman's Peace Party," *Frontiers: A Journal of Women's Studies* 18.1 (1997): 80–100; Sally Marks, "Black Watch on the Rhine: A Study in Propaganda, Prejudice and Prurience," *European History Quarterly* 13.3 (1983): 297–334.

[58] Sarvasy, "Militarized Occupations."

[59] Emily Greene Balch, "Military Use of Native Populations of Colonies," *Report of the Third International Congress of Women, Vienna* (Geneva: WILPF, 1921), 76.

compromise, with Balch reiterating her 1920 points, but it also reflected on the racialized politics of colonial troops' conscription, equating it to "chattel slavery." Balch also protested the blurring between army and civilian population that "conscription of entire peoples" implied.[60] Ultimately, Terrell – as well as other African American WILPFers in the 1920s – persuaded Balch and Addams that "racialized sexual politics structured militarized colonialism and imperialism abroad, and white supremacy at home."[61]

To an extent, then, Balch was embedded in the symbolic framework of what Mark Salter calls the "European geopolitical imaginary."[62] This symbolic framework, for liberal internationalists as well as for the social scientists that entered the IR canon, was part of the "discursive traditions ... that suppressed or simply erased non-European subjectivity"[63] and allowed Europeans (and later Americans) to justify colonial expansion. Making a similar argument, Melinda Plastas (citing Michelle Newman) notes that "opposition movements retain the residue of that which they oppose."[64] Such "residue" constitutes an important limitation in Balch's thought, one that became evident in her writings on the post-war administration of colonies, as well as in her work for WILPF, particularly in her strained relations with some of her African American colleagues in the US Section.

Nevertheless, when seen in its totality, Balch's body of work departs from IR's first liberal theorists who were mostly unequivocal apologists of empire, if not all in the same way.[65] She had no attachment to either empire or the state. Imperialism provoked "jealousy, suspicion and trouble in international relations,"[66] while "ethical considerations ... and the rights of native populations lay outside the sphere of the European conscience."[67]

Imperialism, the State, and Women

Imperialism was a violation of two interrelated fundamental principles of democracy, which were important for international and national life: one

---

[60] Balch, "Military Use of Native Populations," 76.
[61] Sarvasy, "Militarized Occupations," 489.
[62] Mark B. Salter, *Barbarians and Civilization in International Relations* (Sterling, VA: Pluto Press, 2002), 23.
[63] Grovogui, *Sovereigns, Quasi-Sovereigns*, x.   [64] Plastas, *Band of Noble Women*, 136–37.
[65] See here for example Jeanne Morefield, *Covenants Without Swords: Idealist Liberalism and the Spirit of Empire* (Princeton University Press, 2005).
[66] Balch, "International Colonial Administration," 89.
[67] Balch, "International Colonial Administration," 88.

was the liberal understanding of self-determination as "the refusal in principle of the subjection of one person or one set of people, against their will, to masters, one or many."[68] Coercion was the antithesis of democracy for Balch – personally, nationally, and internationally.[69] The other principle was "universality," intended as "welfare of all without exception."[70] As in *Our Slavic Fellow Citizens*, universality meant the appreciation of human differences and human interdependence coupled with the recognition of humanity's "common interests and ... destiny."[71] Together, Balch argued, these principles of democracy implied "not only rejection of such obsolete doctrines as the divine right of kings, but also the negation of racial subordination and exploitation, whether internally or in a colony, the end of sex domination – women are also people – and of class domination and exploitation."[72] In a liminal space between liberal internationalism and socialism, Balch's analysis was also distinctly feminist.

Unlike liberal internationalists or socialists, Balch had no attachment to the state. In fact, she ceased to call herself a socialist in 1916 not because she "had moved more to the right in [her] social politics," but because the war "had made [her] more sceptical [sic] of governments as such and much more afraid of trusting them with great new powers."[73] Other American Progressives shared Balch's distrust for the state. For example, Randolph Bourne's outspoken opposition to World War I was founded on a critique of the state "as a repository of force, determiner of law, arbiter of justice," whose very health rested on war.[74]

Similarly, Balch thought that, among other forms of human association, for the most part peaceful, the state was an aberration. Its uniqueness lay in its "coercive and divisive character, but above all [in] the fact that it is the group which commands armies and navies."[75] Balch's analysis was, however, distinct from Bourne's in its gender analysis: the simultaneous and interdependent fear of and constant preparation for

---

[68] Emily Greene Balch, "The Principle and Practice of Democracy – n.d.," in Randall, *Beyond Nationalism*, 214.

[69] Emily Greene Balch intervention, *Report of the Second International Congress of Women*, Zürich (Geneva: WILPF, 1919), 109.

[70] Balch, "The Principle and Practice," 214.   [71] Balch, "The Trouble the Remedy."

[72] Balch, "The Principle and Practice," 214.

[73] Emily Green Balch, "Acceptance and Transcendence of Socialism," in Mercedes M. Randall (ed.), *Beyond Nationalism: The Social Thought of Emily Greene Balch* (New York: Twayne Publishers, 1972), 50.

[74] Randolph Bourne, "Unfinished Fragments on the State," in *Untimely Papers* (New York: B. W. Huebsch, 1929), 230 and 145.

[75] Balch, "The Trouble the Remedy," 1.

war embedded in the sovereign "national state" were underpinned and perpetuated by gendered symbolic systems and rules. As the

representative of all its people [the state] is personified, idealized, romanticized. It is given a conventional figure as an [sic] semi-deified woman and is referred to as "she" even in times and places where women are shut out from political life and even openly despised.[76]

It is easy to see here the "foreshadowings"[77] of feminist engagements with the state, and critiques of the ways in which gendered representations are used to garner support for militarization, while in practice subjugating women. War and militarism were, for Balch, primary causes of women's devalued status in society, in ancient as in contemporary times. The relegation of women to the private sphere and "the correlated scorn for any sphere which is regarded as peculiarly feminine"; the "exaltation, in the hierarchies of virtues, of those most useful to the military man"; the socialization of boys, but not girls, into those virtues; and the resulting branding of women as "spiritually inferior"; all were "a natural result of the militaristic point of view."[78] "Women," Balch wrote for *The World Tomorrow* in 1922, "have the same emotions than men and with them are inflamed by nationalism, intoxicated by the glories of war, embittered by old rancors," but had also more to lose in war than men.[79] As in the case of race, differences between the sexes that determined their different propensity for war may exist, but their biological sources were both indeterminable and vastly less important than socialization into sex roles.[80]

Women's lack of political power was, therefore, not an excuse for inaction: "public opinion is power; strong and reasonable feeling is power; determination, which is the twin sister of faith or vision, is power."[81] Women had particular responsibilities toward and skills to contribute to the world community, precisely because they were excluded from it. The relevance of WILPF was that it united women of

---

[76] Balch, "The Trouble the Remedy," 2.

[77] Anne Marie Pois, "Foreshadowings: Jane Addams, Emily Greene Balch, and the Ecofeminism/Pacifist Feminism of the 1980s," *Peace & Change* 20.4 (1995): 439–65.

[78] Emily Greene Balch, "The Effect of War and Militarism on the Status of Women," *Papers and Proceedings of the Tenth Annual Meeting of the American Sociological Society* X (Washington, DC, December 1915), 46 and 43–44.

[79] Emily Greene Balch, "Women's Work for Peace," *The World Tomorrow* 5.11 (November 1922), 334.

[80] Emily Greene Balch, "The Effect of War and Militarism on the Status of Women," *Tenth Annual Meeting, American Sociological Society: Papers and Proceedings* (Washington, DC, December 28–31, 1915).

[81] Emily Greene Balch, "At the Northern Capitals," in Jane Addams, Emily G. Balch, and Alice Hamilton, *Women at The Hague* (Amherst, NY: Humanity Books, 2003), 98.

different political beliefs to work together for a world without war. It was also that it recognized "the reciprocal facts that women have political duties and that they must be politically free in order to fulfil those duties."[82] Thus achieving her "planetary civilization" depended on the full participation of women in political and economic life.

If for Balch the state was a masculinized apparatus for the pursuit of power and constraining of human freedom and fundamental goodness, then its collusion with capital was all the more troubling. Capitalism was a topsy-turvy system to generate profit rather than serving human needs. Therefore, it was incapable of dealing with the existence and functions of women, because it was unable to account for and value the work of social reproduction and care.[83]

Balch favored the internationalization of trade – in alignment with liberals of the time – but, importantly, she differed from them in seeing the contradictions between free trade and a world at peace.[84] First there was the moral danger of creating economic interdependence without a corresponding "psychological or emotional counterpart."[85] In a report she delivered at the fourth International Congress of WILPF – held significantly at Howard University in Washington, DC – she remarked: "We drink our tea from China and our coffee from Arabia or Brazil, and dress in wool from Australia ... without any sense of community of indebtedness, or any sense of personal relation to the coolie who picked the tea leaves or the Australian bushman, if that's the proper name, who took care of its sheep."[86]

The second danger, for Balch, was "the unholy alliance of cannon and capital,"[87] between business and the state. In the most "extreme case" businesses traded directly in or profited from war, and therefore had a direct interest in inciting war. More subtly and more pernicious yet were the mundane alliances between businesses and governments. It is easy again to see in her interwar analysis the legacy of her pre-war research on Slavic immigration to the United States, where she had related the economic exploitation of immigrants with racial "prejudices" and government anti-immigration measures. In cases of capital–state alliances at

[82] Balch, "Women's Work for Peace," 335.
[83] Emily Greene Balch, "The Education and Efficiency of Women," *Proceedings of the Academy of Political Science in the City of New York* 1 (October 1910). See also Emily Greene Balch, "The Economic Role of the Housewife," *Home Progress* 4.1 (September 1914).
[84] See Morefield, *Covenants*, ch. 3.
[85] Emily Greene Balch, "Economic Aspects of a New International Order," in *Report of the Fourth Congress of Women's International League for Peace and Freedom* (Washington, DC: WILPF, 1924), 73.
[86] Balch, "Economic Aspects," 73.   [87] Balch, "Economic Aspects," 77.

the international level, governments were at the service of business interests abroad and in competition with each other for the control of resources and the domination of territories. Or, vice versa, governments used trade and businesses to promote their nationalistic and imperialist bellicose agenda. It was of paramount importance, therefore, to break this alliance, and "to end economic imperialism in all its forms."[88] For Balch, personal and political values based on "interest ... in material possessions, and more especially in possessions as a way to get social prestige and power" conflicted with the fundamentals of democracy,[89] and with her cosmopolitan ethos.

11.1 Emily Greene Balch.
Courtesy of Wellesley College

[88] Balch, "Economic Aspects," 77.   [89] Balch, "Economic Aspects," 76.

Visions for the Realization of Humanity's Ontological Unity

The ontological unity of humanity could only be realized through the creation of a new international system and a new international organization. She envisioned this not to be a "super-state, but a real organic body with business to do and not merely to keep each other from going to war."[90] Her cautious support for the League of Nations rested on her belief that the League represented the first "permanent official organized representation of the mass of mankind continuously concerning itself with the common interests of humanity."[91]

The League, she wrote in a 1923 proposal for American entry into the League of Nations,

strengthens and spreads the consciousness of a world-wide community of interests, it gives practice in the difficult art of cooperation between states, it is developing trained international public servants ... men and women appointed for special competence and not as nationals of one or another country who are expected to act not as representatives of one country or with regard to the interests of one country more than another, but for all.[92]

The importance of the League of Nations, then, was not in its actual structure or powers, but in enabling the development of a cosmopolitan conscience.[93] Of course, liberal thinkers often thought of the League as a training ground for international public servants. In this passage, however, Balch was not only referring to the technocratic formation of an international cadre, but to the growth – through the development of international bureaucrats – of a more widely shared spiritual and ontological unity (not by chance she called the League, as it was in the Romance Languages, "Society").

It was, however, in her proposals for the future of the colonies that her cosmopolitan imagination cracked. While the growth of empires had been both predictable and evil, and retreat into an independent isolationism "impracticable" and "unthinkable,"[94] the option of "native independence along with commercial relations" carried a new risk: she presciently feared "the rise of native tyrannies owing their wealth and

---

[90] Emily Greene Balch, "Impromptu Memorandum as to Peace Terms," SCPC, Reel 1, Emily Greene Balch Papers, 2.
[91] Emily Greene Balch, "Peace Plan," SCPC, Series III, Box 23, Folder 16 (1923), Writings by Emily Greene Balch, 9.
[92] Balch, "Peace Plan," 9.
[93] Emily Greene Balch, "Impressions of the First Assembly of the League of Nations," *Women's International League Monthly News Sheet* 6.4 (February 1921), SCPC, Reel 4, Papers of Emily Greene Balch.
[94] Balch, "Economic Imperialism," 141.

power to the income and support derived from foreigners" seeking profits.[95] Removing one form of direct domination without removing the structural inequalities built into a system of power/profit would simply generate a more "veiled" form of domination, where "foreigners" and their local allies rather than "natives" would benefit.

As an alternative to the three options she saw above Balch offered a fourth option in the form of mutual guarantees of independence or internationally regulated agreements. In 1916 the alternative she suggested took the form of "international commissions" to regulate the economy and trade, but not the political or social affairs of the then-colonized countries. This system was not particularly imaginative, rather quite similar to the one envisaged by some of the early liberal architects of the mandates system for the League of Nations,[96] who wanted all colonies brought under international control (but ended up compromising with the "partisans of imperial annexation").[97]

Although the Mandates Commission was effectively (if not formally) composed of representatives of colonial or mandatory powers, Susan Pedersen argues that the system began a transformative shift in international governance because it "obliged [mandate powers and imperial states] to say they were governing [mandated territories] differently."[98] In other words, the system provided a public forum to voice opposition to colonialism and make abuses visible, thus slowly stripping the colonial powers of any perceived moral authority or legitimacy.

But in Balch's vision, the interim stage of international administration of former colonies could last indefinitely "in some cases."[99] After all, she implied, some people could not govern themselves. Balch imagined co-habitation with Slavs or Italians, particularly as she cultivated contacts with these different "races" in her settlement and social welfare work, as well as in her academic research. But that cosmopolitan imagination did not extend fully to black and brown people, from whom – even in her international work with WILPF – she lived relatively isolated. What Balch's proposal for the colonies reveals then is a crucial contradiction that she could not fully resolve between her aspirational cosmopolitanism and some ingrained liberal imperialist assumptions about non-Western people. A crucial opportunity for self-reflection presented itself in 1926

---

[95] Emily Greene Balch, "The White Man's Burden," *The New World* 1.2 (February 1918): 37–39.

[96] See Randall, *Improper Bostonian*; Gwinn, *Emily Greene Balch*; Schott, *Reconstructing Women's Thoughts*.

[97] Susan Pedersen, *The Guardians: The League of Nations and the Crisis of Empire* (New York: Oxford University Press, 2015), 3.

[98] Pedersen, *Guardians*, 4.   [99] Balch, "White Man's Burden."

when, as part of a delegation of six, Balch led an investigation into the situation of US-occupied Haiti.

Occupied Haiti, Balch, and the US Empire

Matthew Guterl claims that the 1920s marked a crucial moment in US race relations as "the lines of racial classification were redrawn with a heightened emphasis on race-as-color."[100] As race and skin color became one and the same in IR theory as well, Balch's original work on Slavic immigration allowed her to go beyond her contemporaries to understand racialized social constructions in the United States' relationship with its own empire.

Nowhere is this connection clearer than in Balch's reflections on the conditions of Haiti. The island had been under American occupation since 1915, and a group of Haitian members of WILPF had asked the organization to address the situation.[101] A delegation composed of Balch and five other people conducted a thorough investigation, based on several weeks of interviews and conversations across the island. *Occupied Haiti*, the report they issued – mostly written by Balch with the exception of two chapters co-authored with African American WILPFers Charlotte Atwood and Addie Hunton – was a scathing condemnation and incisive analysis of US occupation.

Melinda Plastas highlights three elements of the report, which are relevant here.[102] First, the delegation dismantled the idea of benevolent US rule. Notwithstanding the good intentions of many Americans in Haiti, "the fundamental fact of the armed occupation" was a moral evil.[103] It was not only a danger to the survival of American democracy, as well as to the people and democratic development of Haiti, but it was "in itself an unjustified use of power."[104] The determining element was that the occupation rested on force and violated the non-negotiable principle of self-determination, regardless of the alleged improvements to Haitian infrastructure or education system. On the contrary, Balch noted, for the Haitians, occupation had destroyed self-government with its attendant experience and self-confidence.[105]

---

[100] Guterl, *Color of Race*, 155.
[101] Emily Greene Balch (ed.), *Occupied Haiti: Being the report of a Committee of Six disinterested Americans representing organizations exclusively American, who, having personally studied conditions in Haiti in 1926, favor the restoration of the independence of the Negro Republic* (New York: The Writers Publishing Company, 1927), v.
[102] Plastas, *A Band of Noble Women*.   [103] Balch, *Occupied Haiti*, vii.
[104] Balch, *Occupied Haiti*, 151.   [105] Balch, "Economic Imperialism," 145.

Second, Balch denounced the way in which American racism justified and sustained the occupation and cultivated in Haitians "an 'inferiority complex' so well known among disadvantaged groups."[106] No matter how hard the occupiers tried to hide their contempt, it was clear that racism underlay all their actions and prevented genuine cooperation.[107]

Finally, in a co-authored chapter, Balch and Hunton dismantled the myth of the predatory black man, spread through cultural artifacts such as the film *Birth of a Nation*. They pointed out that before the occupation white women were safe traveling alone around the island. Conversely, they noted the lack of safety for Haitian women under military occupation, the predatory nature of militarized masculinity, the existence of and tolerance for militarized prostitution together with the criminalization of romantic inter-racial relations. Their conclusions highlighted that "the mechanism of enforcing racial segregation through the regulations of sexual relations anchored the militarized occupation."[108] Contemporary feminist IR scholars will certainly find Hunton and Balch's analysis familiar.

While the occupation had to end, Balch did not find it advisable that the United States leave the country without establishing first "a practical governmental mechanism of which [Haitians] are in control."[109] But such a mechanism needed to be determined and arrived at through agreements between representatives of the Haitian people and the US government. Balch called for "a real 'meeting of minds' of American and Haitian, a feeling-out of Haitian opinion and a real understanding, from the inside out, of how they feel and what they want." She wished for "a willingness [on the part of the United States] to have things done not in the American way, which we are always so sure is best, but in their way."[110] Her final recommendation was "for a new foreign policy based on humanitarian mutuality."[111]

Our Slavic Fellow Citizens had been in no small part a mirror to American society, exposing the hypocrisy of a rhetoric of liberty for the self that denied liberty to others. Likewise, in *Occupied Haiti* Balch's internationalism turned its lenses reflexively back onto the United States: humanitarian mutuality meant that US refusal to grant Haitians the enjoyment of the quintessential American values of freedom and liberty was tantamount to a denial of those same values for oneself. While the

---

[106] Emily Greene Balch, "Social Values in Haiti – 1926," in Randall, *Beyond Nationalism*, 145.
[107] Emily Greene Balch, "Memorandum on Haiti: Submitted by Emily Greene Balch to the Hoover Commission – 1930," in Randall, *Beyond Nationalism*, 152.
[108] Sarvasy, "Militarized Occupations," 492.   [109] Balch, "Social Values in Haiti," 147.
[110] Balch, "Memorandum on Haiti," 153.   [111] Plastas, "A Different Burden," 479.

contradictions in her thought were never fully resolved, the Haiti report highlights Balch's continuous efforts at transcending her limitations and interrogating her own assumptions.

Conclusions

Despite the Haiti report, inconsistencies and contradictions regarding race and empire surfaced time and again in Balch's thought. Her assumptions were tested on several occasions throughout her years of engagement with WILPF, particularly vis-à-vis prominent black activists in the organization, and were reflected in WILPF's own contentious race relations.

On the one hand, then, my examination of Balch's thought on nationalism, empire, gender, and war helps to correct the record and highlights the relevance of her work in a historiography dominated by men as well as to recover more fully a long tradition of feminist pacifist tradition of IR. On the other hand, Balch has been written out of IR and her own disciplines, idealized by peace scholars and activists, and criticized as irreparably racist by others. I have instead suggested a more complex reading of a multifaceted intellectual and activist.

From her early fieldwork in Austria-Hungary to the Haiti report Balch went against the grain of much of contemporary international thought. Her analysis of immigration in the United States led directly to a critique of nationalism and, with it, a condemnation of empire and war. In her life, Balch interacted with liberal internationalists, social workers, socialists, and trade unionists, in a liminal space between the academy and political activism. Her work too is situated in a liminal space between liberalism and socialism: never quite as nation-based as the former, nor as class-based as the latter. It certainly positions Balch squarely among those early feminists who analyzed international politics through gender lenses. Her intellectual trajectory offers further evidence of a gendered field in which men who navigated between the political and intellectual worlds are considered among the founders of IR, while someone like Balch (or other (peace) activists) is not.

Yet, in Balch we encounter the unusually self-conscious "ethical precarity"[112] of a thinker who, while espousing a universal ethos, could not fully shed a racially coded morality. As I have shown, Balch's belief in the ontological unity of a diverse humanity had its limits. Ultimately, she was genuinely committed to emancipatory politics at home and

---

[112] Lynch, *Wrestling with God.*

internationally; she engaged in sharp critiques of racism, empire, and gender oppression, but never did so perfectly or consistently. Balch was well aware of this ethical precarity, which motivated her to wrestle continuously with her own assumptions. Writing for the *Bryn Mawr Alumnae Bulletin* in 1933, she described her inner struggles at the onset of World War I when she refused to support the war. Aware of the political and ethical implications of intransigent pacifism ("What if Germany wins and militarizes the world?"), she admitted that her "conscience was uneasy." That uneasiness was, however, both inevitable and a continual and forceful reminder of the thin line between "inner integrity and fanatical self-will."[113]

My contribution then has been to highlight the tensions in Balch's thought and practice, not to discount these tensions and moments of contradictions as uncharacteristic or odd, and neither to discount her thought and life as hypocritical. Rather, I hold them as they are, in tension, to highlight our human imperfections and always incomplete project of human emancipation. "Self-examination" – told Balch to Wellesley College audiences in a 1916 President's Day speech – can also be "'very salt and bitter and good,' leading to stronger and clearer and better purpose."[114]

---

[113] Balch, "Working for Peace," 80.
[114] Balch, "What It Means to Be an American," in Randall, *Beyond Nationalism*, 39.

12   Beyond Illusions: Imperialism, Race, and Technology in Merze Tate's International Thought

Barbara D. Savage

When Merze Tate made her first trip to Europe, she was a 26-year-old Indianapolis high school history teacher who planned to study French history at the Sorbonne, to visit the Colonial Exposition of 1931, and to tour historical sites in Europe. Traveling alone, she found herself the only black woman aboard the Canadian Pacific line's mail steamer *Montrose* as it traveled from Montreal to Cherbourg. A train took her to Paris where, by lingering at the American Express offices, she soon met other black Americans. Through them, Tate also met Grace Walker, a black American woman who had studied at London's Academy of Dramatic Art in London that year and who told her that she was heading to the Geneva School of International Studies for a summer session. Intrigued and being both supremely confident in her own abilities and a risk taker, Tate also decided to go to Geneva where she talked herself into the summer program which was founded and directed by Alfred Zimmern, named that year as the first Montague Burton Professor of International Relations at Oxford. After a month in Geneva, she resumed touring Europe and England and ended her trip in Liverpool where she boarded the *Duchess of Richmond* for her return trip to Quebec after eight weeks away, arriving just in time to return to her teaching job.[1]

In many ways, that trip held many clues to the life and career that Tate was inventing for herself, inspired by the worlds she wanted to discover and driven by the intellect and ambition that would bring her a year later to Oxford, where she became the first black American woman to earn a graduate degree, a 1935 BLitt for a thesis on the disarmament movement. Later, in 1941 while teaching at a black women's college in North Carolina, she became the first black woman to receive the PhD in

[1] Barbara D. Savage, "Professor Merze Tate: Diplomatic Historian, Cosmopolitan Woman," in Mia Bay, Farah J. Griffin, Martha S. Jones, and Barbara D. Savage (eds.), *Toward an Intellectual History of Black Women* (Chapel Hill: University of North Carolina Press, 2015).

government from Harvard (Ralph Bunche had preceded her as the first black person in 1934). Finally, in 1942, at age 37, Tate joined the faculty at Howard, the first black woman in the history department at a time when the university's stellar cohort of professors made it a beacon of intellectual excellence. None of this would have been predicted for a black girl born on a farm in rural Michigan in 1905. An honors graduate from Western Michigan Teacher's College in 1927, she had to leave her home state because it did not hire black high school teachers; she took a job at Indianapolis' Crispus Attucks high school, newly formed to segregate black migrant children.

Tate was among that minority of African American scholars who did not focus their work on domestic racial matters. A versatile intellectual, she moved from one specialty to another, producing pioneering and definitive work not only on the disarmament movement, but later on imperialism in the Pacific and on railways as tools of corporate empires in southern Africa. Tate's long life spanned much of the twentieth century, a time when professional, scholarly ambitions for black people, and especially black women, were all but foreclosed or prohibited by economic, racial, and gender restrictions. Those facts she saw not so much as impediments, although they were, but as motivators for her to fight herself as "free" of the constraints of gender and race as possible in order to do the scholarly work she felt compelled to do. Tate has all but disappeared from the narrative of American and African American diplomatic, political, and intellectual life in the twentieth century, or for that matter, black women's history.

In this chapter, I trace Merze Tate's international thought up to the post-World War II era. Her ideas were formed through her exposure in Geneva in 1931 to scholars associated with the League of Nations, her training in three years at Oxford from 1932–35, her doctoral work in Harvard's government department in 1938–39, and her arrival in 1942 to teach at Washington's Howard University. She confronted discriminatory practices in daily and scholarly life and carried the obligations of racial and gender representation; that too shaped the contours of her thinking and her work. Tate witnessed the struggles over racism at home and imperialism abroad right alongside the evolution of weapons of mass destruction. All of these strands of her education, her life, and her times are embedded in her early intellectual formation.

Transnational Intellectual Formation

Although she had studied modern European history in the United States, Tate's initial exposure to the nascent field of international relations came during her time in Geneva at the School of International Studies. Zimmern opened the session with four lectures, one on the ideals of the school and three others on international relations. Tate also heard scholars and officials associated with the League of Nations lecture on economics, the mandate system, political philosophy, the opium crisis, and current tensions in specific nations.

Examples of African American culture and the history of racial inequality in the United States also were featured in three sessions. Walker lectured on "The American Negro in Art and Literature," framing her presentation of poems by writers Countee Cullen, Claude Mackay, Langston Hughes, and Jean Toomer with dramatic power and elocution skills. In a later session, Walker joined with the black American classical concert pianist Lorenza Jordan Cole in an evening recital where Walker highlighted the meanings of the texts of Negro spirituals before Cole played them. Both of these presentations received rapturous attention and applause, according to Tate who also seemed awed by their power. She also attended a lecture on "The Negro Problem in the U.S.A." presented by Professor Everett Stonequist, a Robert Park student who in 1937 would publish *The Marginal Man: A Study in Personality and Culture Conflict.*[2]

This deployment of African American culture and its inclusion of the unjust treatment of black people in the United States presented Tate with a concept of international relations that treated racial injustices in that instance, but which at the same time remained silent on the status and treatment of colonial peoples of color. That also would be consistent with Zimmern's elevation of African Americans into a higher cultural or civilizational status than Africans or Pacific Islanders. Although he had supported Japan's failed attempt to insert support for racial equality at the founding of the League of Nations and subscribed to notions of American-styled cultural pluralism, he also supported the mandate system for people he viewed as culturally under-developed.[3]

Tate's time in Europe and England that summer made her even more resolute to become a scholar, a longstanding quest. That fall, she won a $1,000 foreign fellowship sponsored by her sorority, Alpha Kappa Alpha, and announced that she intended to study with Zimmern at Oxford. The fellowship was a recent initiative designed to support international graduate study for their members. But going to Oxford was easier said than

---

[2] Merze Tate, "Travel Diary," 1931. Merze Tate Papers, Moorland Spingarn Collection, Howard University.

[3] Tomohito Baji, "Zionist Internationalism? Alfred Zimmern's Post-Racial Commonwealth," *Modern Intellectual History* 13.3 (2016): 623–51 (649).

done, and that Tate was able to study there at all came only after the intervention of women associated with the Society of Oxford Home Students, especially its principal Grace Hadow. Admitted only provisionally, Tate later wrangled her way into the BLitt program. During her second year, when she was writing her thesis on disarmament, Zimmern, who had suggested the topic, was away in the United States and she was left on her own with little supervision. As would become her tendency as a scholar, she read and amassed an excessive amount of material; but as a student, her expansive research overwhelmed her analytic skills and her mastery of European history. Her eventual success came the next year under close supervision from Agnes Headlam-Morley, a near contemporary of Tate's who in 1948 would become the Montague Burton Professor of International Relations. Headlam-Morley helped Tate focus not just on government and military officials but on the role of non-state groups in public disarmament campaigns, an aspect of the work that would distinguish it. With her help, Tate was able on a second attempt to satisfy her two examiners, James Brierly, professor of international law at Oxford, and C. A. W. Manning, a South African professor of international relations at the London School of Economics who was later known for his ardent defense of apartheid.

With her BLitt in hand, Tate spent the remainder of the summer of 1935 studying German at the University of Berlin, where she witnessed the anti-Semitism of the new Nazi regime and where she was required as a foreign student to attend a large public rally where Hitler spoke. When she left Germany, Tate made a special trip to Geneva so that she could witness the League of Nations' first debates on Italy's attacks on Ethiopia, a prelude to its failure to intervene. With those two experiences as her final impressions of pre-World War II Europe, Tate left for the United States where she had accepted a teaching job in North Carolina.

After five years teaching at a black women's school, Bennett College, Tate earned her PhD in government at Harvard in 1941. The thought of doing that only came to her as she read the titles of PhD topics while attending Harvard's 1938 graduation with a friend whose son was earning an undergraduate degree. Her admission in the government program was facilitated by Bernice Brown Cronkhite, Radcliffe's first graduate dean, who herself held a PhD in international law and government from Harvard. Later, Cronkhite would help Tate take her dissertation to publication with a subvention from the Rockefeller-funded Bureau of International Research. Tate first started her study at Harvard with a summer course taught by Frederick Schuman, who would become well-known for his textbook on international politics and his later work on the Soviet Union. Her dissertation advisor was Payson S. Wild,

Jr. who specialized in international law, sanctions, and treaties which suited Tate who had decided to stay with the topic of disarmament for her doctorate. Both men would eventually come under state scrutiny from their liberal political stances.

12.1 Merze Tate.
Courtesy of Western Michigan University Archives and Regional History Collections

Disillusionment With Power Politics

Tate's first book, *The Disarmament Illusion: The Movement for a Limitation of Armaments to 1907*, was published just before she arrived at Howard University in 1942 to take a temporary appointment in the history department.[4] The extensive research she had done for her BLitt had exceeded what was needed, but she seems to have re-purposed and expanded that material.[5] Her first book was virtually identical to the 499-page dissertation. Tate's book was a transnational intellectual history of debates about war as a mechanism for dispute resolution, about the conflict between state sovereignty and the need for international cooperation, and about the perpetuation of historical power imbalances.

[4] Merze Tate, *The Disarmament Illusion: The Movement for a Limitation of Armaments to 1907* (New York: Macmillan, 1942).
[5] Merze Tate, "Movement for a Limitation of Armaments to 1907," PhD Dissertation, 1941. Harvard University Archives.

Tate had an engineer's mind and an easy facility for the technological and algebraic aspects of armaments, whether ships or gunnery, but she insisted that they were mere mechanisms or tools in ideological and political debates:

The limitation of armaments is not a matter of mathematics nor of morals but of politics; states seek to give effect to their national policies through armaments as well as through monetary and immigration policies, tariffs and embargoes. Armament competition is inextricably interwoven with political tension, and international agreement on armaments is possible only when the national policies of states are not in conflict; for international disarmament standardizes the relative diplomatic power of the countries involved and prevents the use of armament competition to upset the political equilibrium.[6]

She also made clear that her book was "not peace propaganda," but a "critical historical treatment of the pre-World War efforts towards a limitation of armaments, for in the last quarter of the nineteenth century the history of the movement for arbitration and disarmament became an integral part of international relations."[7] Her emphasis was on proposals and ideas "for a general, simultaneous reduction or non-augmentation of armies and navies or military budgets," not on "the complete abolition of armament as implied in the phrase 'lay down your arms,' but in the wider significance given to it in popular language, as meaning 'limitation and reduction of armaments.'"[8]

The book was a methodical rendering of ideas from many different quarters and nations about the current and future risks of escalating competition among nations over the strength of their standing armies, their navies, their fortresses, and ever more technologically sophisticated tools of destruction. She argued that "after 1870 the size and efficiency of the military and naval establishments of a state were considered by many to be the best indication available of the aggregate power and wealth of a nation. So long as this view prevailed, the rivalry in armaments was not an accidental evil, but a fundamental necessity."[9] Tate also made explicit the links between armaments and the work to maintain or build colonial empires. "Economic imperialism encouraged this competition, for one of the chief purposes of armaments," she wrote, "especially naval armaments, is to defend colonies against seizure and to enhance diplomatic prestige."[10]

With a not too subtle sense of skepticism, Tate dissected the work of various advocates of a nascent "disarmament movement" under

---

[6] Tate, *Disarmament Illusion*, 346. [7] Tate, *Disarmament Illusion*, ix–x.
[8] Tate, *Disarmament Illusion*, ix. [9] Tate, *Disarmament Illusion*, 348.
[10] Tate, *Disarmament Illusion*, 351.

directives from Headlam Morley and Zimmern. Her research led her to examine peace congresses, churches, international jurists, interparliamentary groups, and the newly recognized "force in political life" of "public opinion," in which she included the press. Tate articulated what would now be called a social movement theory as she weighed the various levers of power and players on this issue, spending an equal amount of time on figures who embody the "official class" and those who inhabit or advance "public opinion."[11] Engaging new theories by Walter Lippmann and others, Tate concluded that there was at best only an "inchoate" movement toward limiting armaments in England, Europe, and the United States despite the flurry of meetings, writings, organizing, petitions, and resolutions on the issue over the several decades detailed in her book. Tate had much less confidence than Zimmern and others that an educated public might bring pressure to bear on these issues, or that more open diplomacy might yield different results. Her conceptualization of power remained focused on more traditional power politics: "When diplomats, kings and emperors approached the problem of limiting armaments they did so not on account of the pressure of public opinion but because they were finding their budgets increasingly more difficult to balance, and, in some instances, were piling up huge deficits in time of peace; they dreaded the terrible hazards of modern war; they feared internal revolution and economic and political convulsions in the social order – all of which might prove fatal to their position."[12]

The participation of women among those advocating on the issue of armaments and war also received Tate's attention after prodding from Headlam Morley. But she resisted the idea that women were early or especially effective advocates of disarmament and she also seemed ambivalent about any maternalistic anti-war impulse. "It is only natural that women should hate war – which breaks up their homes, robs them of their sons, husbands, and support – but," she argued, "this hatred had done little by 1898 to assist the struggle for a limitation of armaments." Even after recognizing the founding in 1895 of the International Peace League of Women, Tate still contended that "[i]t took the cataclysm of a World War to awaken women from their lethargy."[13] Her analysis was consistent with her resistance to the idea either that women were especially interested in anti-war activism or that they could be particularly effective as long as state power remained in the hands of men.

---

[11] Tate, *Disarmament Illusion*, 351–52, 358.   [12] Tate, *Disarmament Illusion*, 162–63.
[13] Tate, *Disarmament Illusion*, 158–59.

Tate's explanations of tepid debates about the dangers endemic to the increasing competition for armaments were fair, balanced, and thorough, but obviously she did not avoid expressing her own assessments of ideas and proposals. For example, on calls for arbitration of international disputes, Tate was not optimistic that governments would do anything other than "rely on the arbitrament of war." Peace would only come from "a juster conception of international relations" and some "rational international political system." Without that, she concluded, "war is to be expected; although it may be avoided on one occasion, it will inevitably occur on some other."[14] She saw as enduring structural impediments the continued refusals to limit sovereignty or to submit to an international authority with the power to execute and enforce agreements. Ultimately, she argued that agreements would only work if those who entered them were content with the political status quo, which few if any wanted to freeze in place, neither those who were satisfied with current armaments or those dissatisfied. So, neither the strong nor the weak had sufficient incentive to commit to limiting or reducing military capability, and least of all, those who had or desired empires and colonies.

After outlining the emergence of discussions about limiting armaments among a wide range of groups, Tate devoted the second half of the book to the dramatic turn of the Tsar's Rescript and the First and Second Hague Conferences. Of the first meeting, Tate concluded that it "failed in its primary mission," but the "greatest benefit of the Peace Conference was in the fact of the Conference itself; in the spectacle of all the great powers meeting in the name of peace." Tate saw value in having the topic no longer relegated to debates "merely by philosophers, jurists and Utopians, but by responsible governments." For her, this marked an important moment in the "sphere of international relations" even if the conference had concluded with only a referral for individual states to study the issue further. Tate still saw the locus of power at the nation-state level, despite her earlier treatment of non-state actors in disarmament debates.[15]

Whatever glimmer of hope she expressed, if it can be called that, was soon overtaken in the book by her description of the rush of historical events that followed: "The twentieth century opened with conflicts fought in the Far East and South Africa. Russia struggles in distant Manchuria; a combined European and American army avenged the outrage of the Boxers by sacking Peking; England fought in the Transvaal, five thousand miles from her base of supplies; the United States had

[14] Tate, *Disarmament Illusion*, 83–84.   [15] Tate, *Disarmament Illusion*, 278, 293.

just conquered and now held under military rule possessions an even greater distance from home waters." These new wars to protect or build new empires spawned a new round of naval armament competition. By the time of the Second Hague Conference in 1907, she noted that Russia had dropped all mention of discussing disarmament after its own recent military defeat. As for the United States, Tate concluded that "Roosevelt's opinion was that sufficient naval and military force should be kept up to make the higher civilizations masters of the world." At the conclusion of the second meeting, the delegates resolved to meet again within seven years, "a period," as Tate noted, "which expired when the most powerful and deadly means of destruction devised to that time were engaged in one of the most ghastly annihilations in history."[16]

Published propitiously in the midst of another world war and after the demise of the League of Nations, Tate's work generated much review attention in political science, international affairs, and historical journals, as well as in broader forums. Academic reviewers uniformly lauded the book as the definitive history on the subject, describing it as erudite, scholarly, and the result of untiring research. She was praised for looking beyond the state to other actors in the public debate about armament policies, although her own enthusiasm for that was limited. Hans Morgenthau commended Tate for her treatment of the limits of arbitration, but her materials on public opinion led him to question whether there could or should be more "democratic control of foreign policy," implying a negative in the asking. Two reviewers, Louis Martin Sears and L. Arnold Forster, wanted more explicit treatment of nationalism and imperialism as culprits in the late nineteenth-century build-up in arms. Tate's refusal to blame Germany alone for the failures at the Hague conferences drew praise. The book title's reference to "disarmament illusion," an allusion perhaps to the classic Norman Angell text *The Great Illusion*, had led some reviewers to expect that she would damn pacifist "illusions," but the book demonstrated instead Tate's conclusion that it was an "illusion" that there had been any real movement toward limiting armaments. Many of the reviewers suggested the urgent need for the rest of the story, suggesting that Tate produce a second book that expanded its coverage to the current era.[17]

---

[16] Tate, *Disarmament Illusion*, 294, 321, 330, 345.

[17] Louis M. Sears, "Review," *The Annals of the American Academy of Political and Social Science* 224.1 (1942): 201–202; W. Arnold-Forster, "Review," *International Affairs Review Supplement* 19.10 (1942): 532–33; J. Wesley Hoffmann, "Review," *The Journal of Modern History* 15. 1 (1943): 62–63; William O. Shanahan, "Military Problems," *The Review of Politics* 5.3 (1943): 387–92; Elton Atwater, "Review," *The American Journal of International Law* 36.4 (1942): 742–43; Hans J. Morgenthau, "Review," *The Russian*

The variety of reactions to Tate's work was an apt reflection of tensions and paradoxes in the academic fields which the book entered. This was true not only among traditionally recognized scholars of international relations, but also in the field of African American studies which consistently embraced an explicit anti-imperialist impulse. So, scholars from that discipline highlighted the aspects of the book most useful for establishing links between armaments, colonization, and empire. That was made clear when the three most prominent African American historians of her day reviewed the book. W. E. B. Du Bois praised the quality of Tate's research and writing, but criticized her interpretation for failing to give more attention to the economic reasons for expanding armaments. This he blamed on her training, writing that "Harvard University," also his alma mater, "ignores the epoch-making philosophy of Karl Marx."[18] Tate was probably disappointed by his criticism; she admired his scholarship and had specifically requested that he consider reviewing her book.[19] Tate's colleague Rayford Logan, whose Harvard history dissertation was on US diplomatic relations with Haiti, hoped the book would serve as a warning "to those Pacifists whose ignorance of history or whose distortion of it helped to make World War II possible and who, unless they take a more realistic attitude toward the basic causes of war, may well precipitate a third holocaust." Like Du Bois, Logan praised the quality of Tate's work as meticulous and scholarly, assuring her "a permanent place among American historians regardless of color."[20] Finally, Carter G. Woodson, the dean of black historians and founder of the field of black history, also praised Tate's analysis: "Chauvinistic doctrines, insane nationalism, and imperialistic expansion at the expense of unoffending natives in distant lands have served as enormous stimuli to the inevitable death march of these nations."[21]

Each of these reviewers brought an explicitly anti-imperialist interpretation to the question of armaments, another reminder of the early prevalence and persistence of that critique among a diverse group of black intellectuals, including Tate. Indeed, that assessment dominates African

---

Review 2.2 (1943): 104–105; Pitman B. Potter, "Review," *The American Political Science Review* 36.5 (1942): 973; Julian P. Bretz, "Review," *The Mississippi Valley Historical Review* 30.1 (1943): 89–90.

[18] W. E. B. Du Bois, "Scholarly Delusion," *Phylon* 4.2 (1943): 189–91.

[19] Tate to Du Bois, May 22, 1942; Du Bois to Tate, May 28, 1942. W. E. B. Du Bois Papers, Special Collections and University Archives, University of Massachusetts Amherst Libraries.

[20] Rayford Logan, "No Peace for the Pacificist," *Journal of Negro Education* 12.1 (1943): 92–93.

[21] C. G. Woodson, "Review," *Journal of Negro History* 28.2 (1943): 251–53.

American studies and figures in a larger black public's recognition of the kinship between racism and imperialism. Nearly two decades ago, Robin Kelley explained eloquently that black studies insists on an anti-racist global vision and is a field that always has been "relentlessly international and comparative."[22] For that reason, a recent claim that ideas held by Tate and others constitute a new "Howard school of thought" is a misnomer, although it admirably has provoked long overdue attention to the works of an important group of black scholars and intellectuals.[23] Like other myths, schools, and paradigms in the history of international relations this label has its limitations; it implies that these ideas were attributed to or restricted to a single site of influence despite their widespread acceptance among a very broad black public. What seems most important is to subject the under-studied works produced by black scholars to the sustained reading and critical analysis they deserve. If one does that, as I am attempting to do here with Tate, it quickly becomes clear that no one "school" or political label or discipline can serve as a short-hand for the range and theoretical sophistication of this large body of scholarship, or for that matter, even for Tate's works and ideas.

It is understandable that a late "discovery" of the works of Tate and others might bring a shock of recognition that the critiques they deployed were missing in action from the works that defined several academic fields, including history, international relations, and political science. That is part of a broader problem within academic politics where the work of black scholars and thinkers is less likely to be studied, taught, or used, and more often subject to blunt categorization or appropriation. Ironically, discovering plentiful evidence of African American thought on the nexus between race, empire, capitalism, and colonization merely highlights the fact that most white scholars, with rare exception, continued to deny or ignore the racialized political reality in the topics they studied and in the worlds where they lived. This then is the more compelling line of inquiry: how did Tate and others – all trained at Harvard, Chicago, Oxford – manage to reject the prevailing notions in their fields and produce stellar scholarship that defied convention while their white colleagues and classmates continued to follow received wisdom, not challenge it, and earn great academic success.

---

[22] Robin D. G. Kelley, "'But a Local Phase of a World Problem': Black History's Global Vision, 1883–1950," *Journal of American History* 86.3 (1999): 1045–77.

[23] Robert Vitalis, *White World Order, Black Power Politics: The Birth of American International Relations* (Ithaca, NY: Cornell University Press, 2015).

An Anti-Racist Geopolitics

Tate had arrived at Howard in 1942 obviously with her own ideas including a complex appraisal of political and economic conditions facing colonized people of color around the world even if she did not express it as strongly in her first book as Du Bois, Logan, and Woodson emphasized. Tate published other articles and book reviews on imperialism and colonialism and displayed the versatility of her knowledge of world affairs. A clear illustration of this is found in an article that she published in 1943, "The War Aims of World War I and World War II and Their Relation to the Darker Peoples of the World" in a special issue of the *Journal of Negro Education*. That article was based on a speech she had given at the predominantly black Morgan State College in May of that year.[24]

Tate employs language in her oratory and in the article that is not cloaked in objectivity and a voice that is as direct and powerful as one would expect from someone with her confidence and bravado. She defines the "darker peoples" in her title expansively to include people of African descent and other people of color in the Americas, Africa, and Asia. Casting them all as "peoples of color," she warned that: "They are no longer willing to accept the white man's exalted view of trusteeship; they no longer quake at the teachings of the white man's missionaries, who bring them the white man's God but a God in whom the white man does not believe; no longer are glass beads and trinkets marvelous to them; they are much more interested in the marvels of the white man's guns."[25] Paying separate attention to the injustices throughout Africa and in India and within each imperialist empire, Tate lined out abuses ranging from wage and labor exploitation, illegal land usurpations, and destructive economic and political partitions. As for the United States, she reminded readers that black Americans know "that there are elements in this country which practiced Nazism long before Adolph Hitler celebrated his first birthday and which today dominate the Federal Government and the Army and Navy." She ended by calling for a new global order with freedom guaranteed for all, and an end to vast empires.[26]

---

[24] Merze Tate, "The War Aims of World War I and World War II and Their Relation to the Darker Peoples of the World," *Journal of Negro Education* 12.3 (1943): 521–32; Merze Tate, "Speech – The War Aims of World War I and World War II and Their Relation to the Darker Peoples of the World" (*Morgan State College Bulletin*, June 1943). Tate Papers, Howard University.

[25] Tate, "War Aims," 521.   [26] Tate, "War Aims," 529, 532, 521.

Fearing a repeat of the politics that created the mandate system and a continuation of what she called "the imperialist mentality" of "master and subject," Tate argued that a return to the pre-World War II status quo would not satisfy, especially since so many soldiers of color were serving in military service. Tate could write so eloquently about the injustice of sending "colored" troops into battle at a time when they were denied their basic rights and freedoms because she knew some of those troops. One of her duties at Howard was to teach history, economic geography, and geopolitics to 300 black engineering, medical, and dental students from around the country who were brought to Howard University in the Army Specialized Training Program before being shipped out.

Of special concern to Tate and other black scholars in the post-war period was the question of whether the UN would engage effectively, or at all, with questions of racial inequality and colonialism. The UN's new "mandate" system came under special scrutiny when the Division of Social Sciences at Howard hosted a major annual conference in 1947 on UN-designated trusts and non-self-governing territories. In 1946, Tate had been finally offered a professorship in history at Howard, after four years in a temporary, untenured position. Her department chair, Logan, had assigned Tate the task of organizing the conference and editing the volume of its proceedings. The large audience attending the two-day event heard talks by Du Bois, Max Yergan, the co-founder with Paul Robeson of the Council of African Affairs, and Eleanor Roosevelt, a newly appointed trustee at Howard and member of the UN Commission on Human Rights. Tate prefaced the 127-page printed proceedings with a reminder that African Americans felt a deep "kinship with minorities and depressed peoples everywhere" and that Howard's student body included many from Africa, the Caribbean, and Central and South America.[27]

Although she handled the invitations and logistics for the conference, Tate was not accorded any formal opportunity to speak at the gathering, neither to introduce speakers nor to moderate the presentations or discussions. That role was reserved for male colleagues and administrators. Her resentment would not go unvoiced or be forgotten; she complained to her dean that "I have had to do considerable work that should have been carried by the chief," specifically citing the conference, and concluding that "this delegated work relieved the chairman, allowing him time for his varied activities, but limited me in my

---

[27] Merze Tate, "Trust and Non-Self-Governing Territories," in *Papers and Proceedings of the Tenth Annual Conference of the Division of Social Sciences, The Graduate School, Howard University, April 8th and 9th, 1947* (Washington, DC: Howard University Press, 1948).

professional research."[28] Near the same period, she was forced to chair the department twice against her wishes, also interfering with her ability to do her own work. Tate later repeatedly complained to the deans that she was unfairly treated and received less pay and privileges than her male colleagues. She reported that during her first decade there, she taught nearly twenty-five different courses "including European, English, American, Diplomatic, and Military History, International Politics, Political Science, Geography, and Geopolitics."[29]

Tate saw herself as an historian of international relations, a field she conceptualized as broadly multidisciplinary. When she gave a talk in 1947 at Miners Teachers College in Washington on the teaching of international relations in black colleges, Tate first dismissed the conceit of the invitation by declaring that "there is *no* justification for teaching International Relations in any different way in a Negro College from the way it should be taught in a white college." She argued for presenting the subject in exactly the same way, saying the "only departure that I feel is justified is the constant reminder that the American Negro is only one of many minorities in the world and that his problem is not unique but only one phase of a much larger issue."[30] With that phrasing, Tate aligned herself with Du Bois' well-known 1906 assertion that the "Negro problem in America is but a local phase of a world problem."[31] Tate's endorsement of this view once again reflected her global political orientation, her anti-essentialism on race, and her concern that strictly domestic approaches to "the Negro problem" were parochial and ineffectual.

Tate then turned the talk into a theoretical disposition on international relations and on geopolitics in particular. "Power politics," she argued, could only be understood through a multidisciplinary embrace of all of the social sciences because she found "economics, geography, political science, political philosophy, international law and geopolitics inextricably interwoven" with history:

One cannot teach 19th and 20th century imperialism, the partitioning of Africa, of Asia, of the Pacific, of the Arctic and Antarctic regions, and the scramble for world markets and spheres of economic penetration without a background of geography. An examination of 19th and 20th century laissez-faire liberalism, leads inevitably to a consideration of the last phases of capitalism and a study of scientific socialism or Marxism; while a history of 20th century Russia and the

---

[28] Tate to Dean J. St. Clair Price, October 29, 1951. Tate Archive, Howard University.
[29] Tate to Price, October 29, 1951; Tate to Price, July 17, 1945. Tate Archive, Howard University.
[30] Merze Tate, "Teaching of International Relations in Negro Colleges," *The Quarterly Review of Higher Education Among Negroes* 15 (1947): 149–53 (149).
[31] Kelley, "Local Phase," 1054.

U.S.S.R. compels one to examine Lenin's great contribution to socialism in deciphering the 'dictatorship of the proletariat' through the device of the soviet.[32]

For each discipline or field, she outlined the reasons each was integral to the teaching of international relations, whether international law, or modern philosophy.

Tate reserved her longest treatment for "geopolitics," a field that captured her imagination because of her fascination since childhood with geography and maps, subjects later central to her training and teaching in global and military history. As she understood it, geopolitics was "primarily concerned with a consideration of the political state in its geographical environment," but, she warned, "the study of neither geography nor political science alone is sufficient for the understanding of geopolitics." Here, she introduced her audience to the work of the Swedish political scientist Rudolf Kjellén; she took care to distinguish the German engagement with the concept, through the Geopolitical Institute at Munich, with the caution that "the German theory of Geopolitics leads to war."[33] But implicit in her presentation was her own conceptualization of something quite different, an anti-racist geopolitics which had been expressed in her earlier 1943 talk and article. The remainder of her talk cautioned about the new demands for bases in the air age and more starkly, the dangers of competition over nuclear weapons.

Technologies of Imperialism

These concerns were on her mind because during the war, Tate had expanded her earlier work on disarmament for the period 1907 forward, with a focus on the United States. Her second book, *The United States and Armaments*, was published in 1948 by Harvard University Press, with another subvention from the Bureau on International Research. Even in the preface, Tate's authorial voice was more assertive, expressing a greater sense of urgency after the ferocious destructiveness of World War II. She paraded facts about armaments, aircraft, carriers, atomic bombs, fleets, and technological advances in a steady drumbeat of chilling detail. She made clear that a new arms race of extraordinary proportions and dangers would be the principal outcome of the "peace" that followed World War II. Tate also envisioned that in order to secure its naval and air strategies, the United States would need to control the

---

[32] Tate, "Teaching of International Relations in Negro Colleges," 149.
[33] Tate, "Teaching of International Relations in Negro Colleges," 150.

Pacific region with strategic air bases although many of those islands were then held by other powers.[34]

Tate's concluding paragraph captured her views on the dangers of a new intertwining spiral of civilian technology development, armaments, and military infrastructure:

> Tomorrow time will be measured in the twinkle of an eye. Stratospheric projectiles and jet-propelled superbombers carrying atomic bombs at supersonic speeds will become the competitive weapon of prearmed nations against which there is no defense, except to use them first. Therefore, we argue that our security lies in keeping our research going, regardless of cost and effort, so that we can maintain the lead and stay ahead of the world in the development of atomic energy. Thus a competition in a new and awesome field threatens to supersede the old race in armaments.[35]

The conjoined nexus of scientific research, technological advance, and new weapons she described so ably in her book would come later to be known as the "military industrial complex," laid out here by Tate as a cautionary futuristic tale. Indeed, one of the hallmarks of Tate's work here and later was her fascination with the technological tools that nation-states employed to establish and maintain power, both with one another and with their twentieth-century colonial empires, subjects she would explore in great detail in her later writings on missionaries in Hawaii and railroads in Africa.

Reviewers praised Tate's second book for providing a timely and comprehensive treatment of the subject as well as for being restrained and fair, resting on years of meticulous research and newly available documents. The somber tone of the reviews reflects well the profound sense of pessimism about any prospect for limitation of arms. In some ways, the subtitle to her first book may have been more appropriate for this one since the "disarmament illusion" seemed to now be confirmed as reality. Although it did not receive as much review attention as her earlier work, this book would prove to have staying power and would be reissued with renewed interest twenty years later in 1969 when attention turned once again to arms limitation.[36]

Tate's work and her connections in Washington brought her to the attention of the UNESCO official in the State Department who invited

---

[34] Merze Tate, *The United States and Armaments* (Cambridge, MA: Harvard University Press, 1948), 273–74.

[35] Tate, *The United States and Armaments*, 273–74.

[36] E. Atwater, "Review," *Annals of the American Academy of Political and Social Science* 258 (1948): 141–42; William M. Boyd, "Diplomacy and War," *Phylon* 9.3 (1948): 279–81; C. J. Child, "Review," *International Affairs* 25.1 (1949): 114–15; W. Henry Cooke, "Review," *Pacific Historical Review* 18.1 (1949): 150–52.

her to be one of three to represent the United States at a six-week UNESCO summer seminar 1948 at Adelphi College near the UN's temporary headquarters at Lake Success. With participants from twenty-six other countries, Tate joined what was primarily a gathering of high school teachers who were each to produce useful teaching materials on the UN and its agencies, an intention for which this early intercultural exchange seminar was known.[37] But Tate, in typical fashion, went her own way and submitted a 30-page single spaced paper entitled "The International Control of Atomic Energy: A Vital Problem," not exactly pitched at the high school level nor on topic.[38] In the piece which was later produced as a UNESCO pamphlet, Tate warned of the "danger of an atomic armament race," arguing that prevailing concepts of security and sovereignty would need to be adjusted to avoid destruction and that some "affirmative action" by a new international nuclear control authority was essential. She wrote: "Statesmen must constantly be kept aware that there can be no absolute sovereignty in an atomic world. The word has lost its meaning in an era where the choice is between international cooperation or international disintegration, between world peace or world destruction, between 'the quick and the dead.'"[39]

At the end of the 1940s, Tate was a recognized expert in diplomatic history and international relations, but her intellectual interests would expand over the course of a long scholarly career that would reach into the 1980s. She would become one of the earliest holders of a Fulbright which she used to go India in 1950–51 where she was assigned to Tagore's World University, Visva-Bharati at Santiniketan near Calcutta. Although she was invited primarily to lecture on geopolitics and international relations, she also was expected by her hosts to lecture on the history of "the Negro" and of race relations in the United States. Tate used the Fulbright to lecture all over India exhaustively and in Myanmar and Sri Lanka, to make her first around-the-world tour, and to travel in Asia, including Thailand, Cambodia, Singapore, the Philippines, Hong Kong, and Japan. Finally, she arrived in Hawaii, her last stop before returning to the United States.

In 1948, two years before she left for her Fulbright, Tate had developed an expansive conceptual framework for a comparative empires project in the Pacific, to her an overlooked region where "the power lines

---

[37] Glenda Sluga, *Internationalism in the Age of Nationalism* (Philadelphia: University of Pensylvania Press, 2013), 1.

[38] Merze Tate, "The International Control of Atomic Energy: A Vital Problem," 1948. Tate Archive, Howard University.

[39] Tate, "International Control of Atomic Energy," 3, 19.

of the great powers had crossed" in a "rivalry of the sea power age" that was now "intensified in the age of air power." Visiting Hawaii for the first time in 1951 made it clear to her that her own country could serve as the exemplar for that study. She published two books in the 1960s that became, and remain, a standard treatment of the history of the annexation of Hawaii in 1898 and its conversion into a "near colonial" status from that time until statehood in 1959.[40] The Pacific islands, large and small, remained Tate's intellectual focus for three decades, yielding a large, unexamined body of work.[41]

After completing her work on the Pacific, Tate turned to Africa, about which she had written and taught for decades. It was one of the places she long had been interested in visiting. She finally made it there in two trips in the 1970s to research the history of the mineral extraction industry and the privately funded web of railroads and ports then under construction in southern and east Africa. She completed two manuscripts on Africa that never made it into print but not for lack of trying or resourcefulness.

It is a miracle that as much of her writing made it into print as it did. She pursued her own interests, often way ahead of the scholarly mainstream, and produced work that rarely fit neatly into a single discipline. Yet what is perhaps most impressive is that she never stopped researching and she continued to write long, complicated manuscripts even after she retired from teaching in 1977.

Conclusion

The production of scholarly knowledge requires access to training and credentialing. Tate rightfully credited women mentors and supporters, professional and personal, for her success at every step of her career, from her teachers in Michigan to the AKA sorority sisters to the female tutors and administrators at Oxford to the graduate dean at Radcliffe, and to her black women colleagues at Bennett, Howard, and elsewhere. But for the generous interventions of women impressed by her determination and the quality of her mind, Tate's ambitions as a scholar would never have been realized. She also adapted the training received from her professors at Oxford and Harvard to creatively explore her own scholarly interests.

---

[40] Merze Tate, *The United States and the Hawaiian Kingdom: A Political History* (New Haven, CT: Yale University Press, 1965); Merze Tate, *Hawaii: Reciprocity or Annexation* (Lansing: Michigan State University Press, 1968).
[41] Merze Tate, *Diplomacy in the Pacific: A Collection of Twenty-Seven Articles on Diplomacy in the Pacific and Influence of the Sandwich (Hawaiian) Islands Missionaries* (Washington, DC: History Department, Howard University, 1973).

Her brilliant intellect, her capacity to do academic work, her knack for pursuing serendipitous opportunities (she called these "Providential"), and her capacity for sustained hard work prevented the tragedy of unrealized ambitions. She was never shy about insisting that she belonged in places where she was the first or only black woman. Her life as a solo traveler would take her around the world twice, and the self-possession, confidence, and sense of adventure needed for that also served her well in her professional career. It has been our loss that we are now just turning to the task of placing Tate's work in the many fields to which it speaks. That it has taken so long to do that is our tragedy and not hers.

Tate's early international thought undergirded her five decades of scholarship. Her realist bent would endure, as her conceptualization of power relations had first come from her expertise on state monopolies of arsenals of new tools of war, violence, and destruction, including air power and atomic weapons. Tate's skepticism that incentives could be found to sacrifice state sovereignty to international cooperation or agreements was deepened when even the threat of total annihilation proved ineffective. She concluded that these capital-intensive technologies had become a highly valued surrogate in international relations, especially among those intent on perpetuating imperialism.

Tate's attention to the "tools of empire" and to how imperialism actually worked would remain a thru-line in her work. She would expand her definition of those tools to include missionary education and printing presses in Hawaii. For her, the arrival of New England missionaries in Hawaii in the early nineteenth century, which led to its annexation in 1898, marked a beginning of US imperialist aims beyond its borders, well before the closing of its so-called "frontier." This was both an innovative and a politically controversial analysis when her writings on the Pacific began to be published in 1960.

Her work on 1970s Africa argued that the combination of state power and international corporate capital formed a modern technological imperialism enacted through railroads, deep sea ports, mineral extraction, and transport of underpaid labor. Establishing links between technology, war, and imperialism had been central in her earliest work in the 1930s and 1940s. An analysis of that connection would be reached by other scholars only many decades later.

Tate conceptualized an anti-racist and anti-colonial geopolitics and searched for a "juster conception of international relations." Her own understanding of the world drew on her training in interwar England and the United States, but also on her own experiences of segregation and racial and gender inequality. She shared the view with other African Americans that post-World War II international initiatives, including the UN, were tainted by the refusal of those in power to embrace human rights and oppose colonialism. But she feared that peaceful methods of effecting change seemed elusive, as the state's monopoly on the most powerful tools of violence also remained firmly intact.

Her views on imperialism were a product of her experiences living in a seat of empire at Oxford in the 1930s and then in India in 1950–51. That year came so soon after Indian independence and its imposed partition that the remnants and upheavals of the oppressions enacted under the British raj were deeply embedded in the daily life she witnessed first-hand. Her observations in India and Asia would have a profound influence on her work on imperialism in Hawaii, the Pacific, and Africa. In all these ways, what Tate thought, what she theorized, and what she wrote also reflected the particular geopolitical complexities of the times and the places in which she lived as a black American woman scholar.

13   A Plan for Plenty: The International Thought of Barbara Wootton

Or Rosenboim

In the interwar years, the British economist and sociologist Barbara Wootton (1897–1988) developed a strong interest in the international aspects of economic and political order. By the 1930s and 1940s, domestic and international politics were, to her mind, closely intertwined. She proposed a distinct vision of world order based on a democratic federal system where social justice, planning, and equality could be implemented beyond state borders. During World War II, she became a leading member of the British organization Federal Union that advanced the cause of democratic federalism. For her, Federal Union was a suitable institutional setting to promote a global vision of social justice, based on her conviction that socio-economic discrepancies caused domestic and international political unrest and war.

Wootton's federalist writings, I argue, expressed an original approach to the problem of domestic and international inequality, which emphasizes its transnational, even global dimension. Thus, in parallel to the foundation of the British welfare state, she built on her knowledge and expertise in economics and sociology to fashion an innovative vision of a new welfarist international order. Designed along federalist lines, the post-war world order would guarantee welfare to individuals and communities across state borders using central economic and social planning to mitigate inequalities and improve living standards around the world.

Although today Barbara Wootton may no longer be a household name, her original and innovative writings enjoyed a lasting impact on the British welfare system as well as on the social and economic foundations of the European Union.[1] Her federalist vision drew on liberal internationalism and domestic socialism while leveling a critique at both approaches. Opposed to abstract thinking, she used notions such as "planning," "needs," and "want" to outline a concrete vision for international change. Yet she was confident of the capacity of the law to

---

[1] Alberto Castelli, *Una pace da costruire: I socialisti britannici e il federalismo* (Milan: FrancoAngeli, 2002).

redress racial and gender discrimination. Although her proposals were not realized, she anticipated present-day debates on global justice, offering interesting insights on the interplay between the global and the domestic aspects of social and economic inequality and justice.

Wootton crafted her ideas about the international realm by examining the links between fundamental principles and policy making. She endorsed a coherent set of normative values that should be applied internationally – including social and economic equality, universal living standards, participation-based democracy, and social and political rights – which she sought to embed in her policy proposals centered on the idea of planning extended beyond the boundaries of the state. Her advocacy of federalism was therefore motivated by a sophisticated and coherent political thinking. For Wootton, as well for other thinkers of her times who were closely interested in public debates and policy, including Lionel Robbins, Friedrich Hayek, and E. H. Carr, scholars had the responsibility – and duty – to reflect on the desirable links between abstract thinking and its practical applications in society. Her ideas were informed by theoretical assumptions, but she insisted on exploring their potential application in practice, thus marking the limit of pure abstract thinking in politics. By examining her thought, this chapter seeks to highlight that policy proposals constitute theorizing and are underpinned by it.[2]

Despite her influential position in British mid-century public debate, the title she chose for her autobiography was *In a World I Never Made*, possibly reflecting the challenges she faced as a woman to valorize her knowledge and expertise against gender discrimination and narrowmindedness.[3] A sense of struggle accompanied her illustrious career. After the completion of her studies in economics at Girton College, Cambridge, Wootton shifted her focus to sociology. In 1948, she was appointed Professor of Sociology at Bedford College, London, the first higher education college for women in the United Kingdom. Her apparent professional success could not conceal the difficulties she encountered in securing academic positions in institutions such as Cambridge and LSE, where she held temporary teaching and research jobs. Later, she commented that she "supposed women in my position were so accustomed to what we would now regard as outrageous insults that we

---

[2] On policy makers as subjects of intellectual history see for example Christopher Bayly, "The Ends of Liberalism and the Political Thought of Nehru's India," *Modern Intellectual History* 12.3 (2015): 605–26.

[3] Barbara Wootton, *In a World I Never Made* (London: Allen & Unwin, 1967).

took them as all in a day's work."[4] In response, she extended her activities beyond academia to the public sphere: she was a Justice of Peace, member of national policy commissions and Royal Commissions, delegate to the League of Nations World Conference, and governor of the BBC.[5] In 1958 she was the first woman to become a life peer and used her position as a deputy speaker of the House of Lords to promote her socialist vision.[6] She published pamphlets and articles for a general readership, aimed at harnessing academic scholarship for the benefit of society.

Wootton did not consider herself part of the nascent discipline of International Relations. In the 1930s and 1940s she developed her international thought in an effort to translate her conception of economics and social justice into a thorough plan for a new political world order. By the late 1940s, she turned away from international politics, and for the rest of her career her main concerns remained domestic: penal law, criminology, and welfare in Britain. She was often invited to apply her knowledge to other countries, such as Ghana and India, but her attention remained focused on the domestic problems of British society. Nonetheless, as this chapter will show, her brief engagement with the domain of international politics merits the attention of historians and International Relations scholars today.

In the remainder of the chapter, I will examine aspects of Wootton's international thought. First, I will examine her vision of a transnational democratic federation as developed in the context of Federal Union. The following section will discuss her attempts to extend the notion of social justice beyond the state and will critically assess her relative silence on the legacies of empire, the colonial world, and transnational racial inequality. The third section will consider the notion of "planning" on transnational and international scales, which later inspired the founders of the European Union. The conclusion will assess some of the contribution and limits of Wootton's international thought.

A Democratic Federation for Welfare

In 1938, Wootton joined the British organization Federal Union, and two years later became a member of the Executive Committee, President, and Chair of the Federal Union National Council, a role she held until 1944. Against the backdrop of the war, her international vision and

---

[4] Ann Oakley, *A Critical Woman: Barbara Wootton, Social Science and Public Policy in the Twentieth Century* (London: Bloomsbury Academic, 2011), 73–75.
[5] Oakley, *A Critical Woman.*   [6] Oakley, *A Critical Woman*, 1–5.

economic thought collided most clearly. She joined other London-based economists in a lively discussion on the desirable route to economic prosperity for Britain and the world as a whole: a democratic federation. At Federal Union, she strengthened her relations with William Beveridge, who in 1919 had offered her a studentship for social research at the LSE. For Beveridge and Wootton, the war was an opportunity to establish a new social order to be planned on an international rather than merely national scale. Beveridge maintained his relations with Federal Union after Wootton had left the organization and became its honorary president in 1944.[7]

The war years saw an intense public political discussion in Britain about the post-war order: What should be its founding principles? How could economic growth and social justice be guaranteed? What international political mechanism could safeguard peace? Federal Union was hardly the only hub of debate at the time, and Barbara Wootton divided her attention between several initiatives, often at the invitation of senior (male) scholars, but she did not have a scholarly or political "patron." She operated in relative freedom within the academic and political landscape of mid-century Britain and preserved her political and professional independence. For example, in 1942 Beveridge invited her to help elaborate his famous report on unemployment in Britain, and she later published many articles in the popular press defending Beveridge's welfare reforms.[8] In the same year, Wootton became a member of the committee of intellectuals set up by H. G. Wells to formulate his universal declaration of the "Rights of Man."[9] Wootton also collaborated with G. D. H. Cole's New Fabian Research Bureau (and the Federation for Progressive Societies and Individuals (FPSI) led by Wells and by her Federal Union colleague Cyril Joad). She held roles at the Trades Union Congress and Chatham House Council. In these myriad political visions, she fashioned her own public voice as a socialist, federalist, and staunch defender of liberty and democracy, concerned with the future of international order after the war.

The political climate of wartime Britain generated not only an enthusiasm for new organizations, but also a surge in publication of pamphlets and short essays. Since the early 1930s, the pamphlet became a favorite

---

[7] Richard Mayne and John Pinder, *Federal Union, the Pioneers: A History of Federal Union* (Basingstoke: Macmillan, 1990).

[8] William Beveridge, *Full Employment in a Free Society* (London: Allen & Unwin, 1944); Jose Harris, *William Beveridge: A Biography*, 2nd edition (Oxford: Clarendon Press, 1997), 434–37.

[9] H. G. Wells, *The Rights of Man: An Essay in Collective Definition* (Brighton: Poynings Press, 1943); Oakley, *A Critical Woman*, 153–54.

publication format for scholars and activists who hoped that their ideas could influence not only decision makers but also the general public. During World War II, when the British government restricted paper usage and printing, short pamphlets were preferred as a cheaper and more feasible form of publication than books, yet longer-lasting and more respectable than a newspaper article. There was no consensual view about the positive political or ideational impact of pamphlet literature, which was very diverse in scope and quality. George Orwell wrote in 1943 that "pamphleteering has revived upon an enormous scale since about 1935 and has done so without producing anything of real value."[10] Nonetheless, he affirmed that pamphlets ought to be *the* literary form of his age thanks to their accessibility and informality. Indeed, Federal Union, Chatham House, the National Peace Council, and commercial and university presses published pamphlets by respected scholars and commentators, which sold in thousands of copies.

One pamphlet from 1940 records a London conference organized by the National Peace Council on "A New International Order," in which Wootton and Norman Angell iterated their international thought.[11] She emphasized her support for a federation, at a time when the proposal of Anglo-French union was on the table.[12] The basic conditions for a federation, to her mind, was a certain degree of shared political values, yet she conceded that the bar could be set quite low: "I should like the minimum of liberty to be a very substantial one, but I should be prepared to take substantial concessions, in that I would be prepared to work a federation with agreement on political liberty in a rather narrow sense."[13] It was compromise, rather than unity, which rendered the federation possible. While political values such as liberty were key in forming the federal constitution, their economic application was no less important.

The main aim of the federation would be to overcome "that sense of nationalism" which dominated economic policies hitherto: "tariffs, currencies, prohibitions and migration really have more a political than an economic basis," she suggests. "They are one way of achieving certain economic ends and a bad one too. They are forms of economic planning conceived only in the interests of a particular state and which emphasize before the mind of every citizen the separateness of one state from another." The League of Nations is complicit in the increase of national

---

[10] George Orwell, "Pamphlet Literature," *New Statesman and Nation*, January 8, 1943, 23.

[11] National Peace Council, *A New International Order: Political and Constitutional Aspects* (London: National Peace Council, 1940).

[12] Avi Shlaim, "Prelude to Downfall: The British Offer of Union to France," *Journal of Contemporary History* 9.3 (1974): 27–63.

[13] National Peace Council, *New International Order*, 6.

animosities as it is an organization based on the outdated principle of national statehood, yet has the merit of providing professional expertise on matters of health, labor, and economic cooperation, which could serve the federal order after the war.[14]

While targeting the League of Nations for its failure to stand up to aggressive nationalism, Wootton did not address the economic and political impact of existing imperial structures. In referring to the possibility that a member of the federation would be an empire, she said that "it would be quite essential that it should place under federal control the administration of any non-self-governing dependencies." In addition, if, for example, independent India would want to join the federation, a "practical" problem of "literacy against illiteracy" may arise and prove incompatible with the federation's democratic system of representation. Yet, she soon dismissed this problem and reassured her audience that "some experience has been gained as to how you can overcome those things" and ensure that the principles of democracy were maintained. The inclusion of ex-colonies was neither a central part of her federal plan, nor a significant obstacle for its realization. Rather, it was a marginal detail in a plan centered on the developed and industrialized countries of Europe and North America.

The potential extension of the federation to the imperial sphere was not a prime concern for Wootton or her Federal Union colleagues.[15] Their plans seem to assume the decline of the British Empire, but many, including Wootton, agreed that membership in the federation required, first and foremost, a degree of political similarity in the form of democratic constitution and some shared values.[16] She did not circumscribe her ideas to the West, but considered this vision to be globally applicable: "It is, therefore, particularly a European, or at least a Western European, Federation that I have here in mind; though much of what is said may well have a more general reference, and be relevant to any and every Federation that is democratic."[17] The reality of the war – when most of Europe lived effectively under a German dictatorship – rendered more urgent the federation of Europe after the war.

Moreover, in her autobiography, Wootton concluded that the decision to advance a European federation was based on the notion that such a scheme would be the most likely to be realized after the war.[18]

---

[14] National Peace Council, *New International Order*, 8.
[15] Andrea Bosco, *The Federal Idea* (London: Lothian Foundation Press, 1992).
[16] Barbara Wootton, "Economic Problems of Federal Union," *New Commonwealth Quarterly* 5 (1939): 150–56.
[17] Barbara Wootton, *Socialism and Federation* (London: Macmillan, 1941).
[18] Wootton, *In a World I Never Made*.

Yet focusing on Europe was more than a pragmatic decision. Evidently, Wootton based her vision on a substantially Western socio-economic experience; she remained silent on the ways to overcome the significant differences in living standards between the European and American societies and those in Africa, Asia, and South America. In 1940, "Dependent territories" would remain, for her, under colonial administration: federal rather than national.

The liberated peoples of the colonies were invited to join the federation once free and democratic; there was no provision to assist these populations to attain formal independence and establish a democratic government. Her federal vision assumed that Britain would no longer cultivate a special relationship with its imperial possessions; instead, she proposed to turn to Europe as the most effective partners for constructing a welfarist post-war order. Wootton's silence on the problem of empire did not reflect a moral or political support for imperial politics. Possibly, she might have seen her own input – as a white, British, and privileged academic – as undesirable in the context of postcolonial politics. It was time for the local population to shape their polity according to their own views. Her visit to Ghana in the 1960s may be indicative of her approach to colonial liberation.[19] She expected to find postcolonial grassroots political movements, yet she was surprised to discover that local students were more interested in pursuing a professional career. The disappointment with the students' political disengagement did not prompt her to express her own views on the desirable future of the ex-colony.

If the goal of the democratic federation was not colonial emancipation, what would it be? Wootton's democratic federation relied on a post-imperial future in which Europe was tasked with rebuilding its economic and social structures after the end of World War II. The main aim would be to outline social economic plans to provide not only basic "needs" but also "plenty": concrete economic prosperity and social welfare for all. The challenge might be, for her, "to consider how we can work together a highly collectivized economic system with one of a largely capitalistic character."[20] The great divergence for her was not between North and South, but between East and West, between collectivism and capitalism. "Could you combine under one political federal system states predominately collectivist and states like ourselves?," she asked, and hoped for an affirmative answer.[21] Such coalition would be facilitated, she argued, by the closing gap between the "collectivist" and "capitalistic" states due to the planned war economy that enhances the collectivized qualities of

[19] Wootton, *In a World I Never Made*, 110–13.   [20] Wootton, *Socialism and Federation*.
[21] National Peace Council, *New International Order*.

capitalistic economies. The underlying aspiration of her vision was that democratic federation could merge liberal capitalism and socialist collectivism to promote equality and social justice on a global scale.

One of the main hubs for sustained research within Federal Union was its research institute, known as FURI.[22] As scholars and researchers joined the organization, it became a platform for theoretical and practical studies on federation. It was in this setting that Wootton's international ideas took shape through publications and discussions on world order and federation with other key economists like Friedrich Hayek, Lionel Robbins, William Beveridge, and James Meade. She and her colleagues agreed on the economic and political advantages of federalism, yet they disagreed on the role of individual entrepreneurship and centralized planning in the federation. Wootton focused on the economic aspects of a federal world order with the aim of establishing a new transnational system of social justice: it was a proto-welfarist discourse on the potential extension of the notion of social justice beyond the state, an innovative analysis of the intertwined relations of economics and politics on the global scale.

The commitment to social and economic welfare went, according to Wootton, hand in hand with a democratic political system based on freedom and "the rights of man." In 1940, when Charles Kimber published the first Federal Union policy pamphlet *How We Shall Win*, she praised his assertion that "man has certain rights and certain needs, and the business of the political machine is to fulfil the needs and safeguard the rights."[23] Her interpretation implies that "needs" like "rights" could be discovered and agreed upon by political decision makers. Although their meaning could be interpreted in various ways, it was still possible to lay down standards as the basis of state – or federal – laws.

In the *Federal Union News* issue of March 1942, she referred to the importance of F. D. Roosevelt's "freedom from want" as a fundamental step toward transnational equality in the post-war world order. While acknowledging that Federal Union could not, at that point, outline a consensual economic plan for the future, she underlined her commitment to economic security and social wellbeing as the foundation of a democratic world order. She perceived federalism as a means to achieve a democratic socialist society in which equality was not merely legal and political but also economic. Hence, as Ransome wrote in a letter to Beveridge as early as 1940, Wootton represented the interventionist

---

[22] Melville Channing-Pearce (ed.), *Federal Union: A Symposium* (London: Lothian Foundation Press, 1991 [1940]).

[23] Barbara Wootton, "Plan for Plenty," *Federal Union News*, March 29, 1940.

faction in Federal Union, who sought to create a "new economic policy" based on planning and state intervention.[24] Her initiatives were blocked by other economists like Robbins and Hayek, who saw her vision as a menace to democracy.[25]

Social Justice beyond the State

In her early writings about economics, Wootton despaired about the abstract theorizing which dominated the British discipline at the time, and prevented, to her mind, economists from offering practical, scientific, and useful economic policies. In *Lament for Economics* (1938) Wootton offered a critique of abstract thinking in economics. The problem with abstraction was that it distanced the study of economics from real-world issues. The problem was, in her words, that "economics was no use" if economists engage in "pure science" rather than in solving real-world concerns.[26] While embracing rationalism as a method of inquiry in the social sciences, she deplored the excessive weight classical economic theory gave to individual rational choice. She claimed that a more complex understanding of human nature and social interaction, based on empirical data and statistical analysis, was necessary to identify, assess, and improve social and economic interactions.[27] Instead of theory-driven research, she called for problem-driven studies. Economics should be not only useful, but also "intelligible to the common man": "there is no merit in technicality for technicality's sake," she argued.[28] She envisioned a methodological turn away from grand theory toward social policy-oriented investigations, and demanded that economists provide clear, useful, and applicable answers to ambitious problems, such as whether Britain should restore the gold standard, or raise tariffs. Her criticism was leveled not only at the economists themselves but also at the university system that prioritized certain – abstract – forms of social knowledge that were of little use to society.

Wootton suggested that the real problems of equality and social justice should guide economists to effective solutions. This methodological position led to a critical exchange with leading economists such as Lionel

---

[24] Patrick Ransome, "Letter to W. Beveridge," 1941, British Library of Social and Economic Sciences, London School of Economics, The papers of William Beveridge, London.

[25] Or Rosenboim, "Barbara Wootton, Friedrich Hayek and the Debate on Democratic Federalism in the 1940s," *The International History Review* 36.5 (2014): 894–918.

[26] Barbara Wootton, *Lament for Economics* (London: Routledge, 1938), 15.

[27] Wootton, *Lament for Economics*.   [28] Wootton, *Lament for Economics*, 22.

Robbins, who conceded that their positions were not significantly different.[29] Yet Wootton's revolt against mainstream economics came at a price: she was unable to secure an academic post in one of Britain's prestigious universities. Instead, she accepted a professorship at a women's college specializing in social work, which agreed with her conceptual view of the disciplines of economics and sociology but relegated her to the margins of academic debate at the time.

One real-world problem emerged as a particularly strong concern for Wootton: inequality. The idea that social justice and equality were integral parts of international thought was a constant in her writings. Her pamphlet *In Pursuit of Equality* opens with an important declaration: "I seem to have been pursuing the ideal of equality all my life but have been singularly unsuccessful in catching my prey."[30] Looking back on her 1941 tract on inequality in Britain, she argued that little had changed over the past three decades. While the accuracy of this judgment may be contested, it reveals her long-sighted and innovative approach to the problem of inequality back in the 1940s. Wootton brought to Federal Union her academic experience in economics and sociology, as well as in public policy making, through her activities at the War Office and Chatham House, where she was secretary to the "Study Groups on Reconstruction" which aimed to provide social, economic, and political vision for post-war Britain. The pursuit of equality was, therefore, a particular British domestic concern, but also a potential remedy for a global malaise that posed a threat to world peace. Yet what might be the best approach for thinking about inequality in the national and global dimensions? The decision was, for Wootton, essentially political.

Wootton's international thought sought to reconcile federalism, democracy, and socialism. As becomes clear from her 1941 tract on equality, what renders "democracy" the most appropriate political form for social and economic progress was the centrality of the value of "equality" in the democratic system, which could also be extended beyond the state. The public campaign led by Federal Union enhanced her interest in federalism and its impact on economics, although federation as a political form was not, of course, inherently conducive to equality and democracy. For Wootton, a federation meant "the establishment over more than one previously independent state of a supranational government with strictly limited functions."[31] The most

[29] Or Rosenboim, *The Emergence of Globalism: Visions of World Order in Britain and the United States, 1939–1950* (Princeton University Press, 2017), ch. 5.
[30] Barbara Wootton, *In Pursuit of Equality* (London: Fabian Society, 1976).
[31] Barbara Wootton, "The Keynes Plan," *Federal Union News*, June 1943.

fundamental of these functions was war prevention. She argued – with many other British internationalists – that international control of armed forces and foreign policy could guarantee world peace. However, her interest in the federal form of government extended beyond this fundamental function.

A federation could prove more appropriate than nation-states for the attainment of social justice, if it could become a fertile land for ambitious social and economic planning. The key benefit of world or regional federalism would be its vast territorial scale, which lent itself to more complex and sophisticated economic planning. Moreover, a powerful centralized government could effectively enforce its policies. In the nation-state system, economic planning was limited by the difficulty of addressing economic issues caused by forces that were beyond the reach of individual states. Moreover, the limited territorial scale of extant states set clear boundaries to the availability of human and natural resources for the development of the economy. The world's growing technological interconnectedness accelerated the flow of capital, goods, and people across national borders. Yet national economic policies were not always equipped with the appropriate tools to deal with these phenomena. This situation rendered federal large-scale planning a necessity, but there was no particular implication for the geographic boundaries of the federation.

In one of her early federalist publications, *Socialism and Federation* (1941) Wootton made a clear case for large-scale federations, arguing that a large canvas for planning was necessary to raise the standard of living for people across national boundaries.[32] Thus, she outlined the contours of a global – or at least transnational – concept of social justice. Her vision was anchored in a universal idea of the public good, which could not be confined to the political space of the state. In this sense, equality between individuals was of prime importance. Similar ideas were proposed in Wells' declaration of the rights of man, which Wootton helped draft. Yet Wootton's conception of welfare and social justice was not individualistic, but also considered the influence of societal relations and tensions.

Wootton approached equality from two perspectives: equality of opportunities and social equality. The first related to providing access to benefits of education, profession, and welfare to individuals regardless of their income or background. The second related to the formal and informal boundaries within society based on notions of class, gender, and race. For her, no democratic society could prevail if these two aspects of

---

[32] Wootton, *Socialism and Federation*.

inequality were not addressed properly by government acts. Yet at the same time, she assumed that the formation of a welfare-oriented demo-cratic order could, eventually, lead to the elimination of inequalities. She employed the idea of "planning" as a means for curtailing inequality in society and attaining prosperity and welfare for all individuals and communities.

In her federal pamphlet, Wootton considered migration as a key aspect of the federal plan. In the late 1940s, when the 1948 British Nationality Act reflected some of her considerations about the social and economic desirability and necessity of migration, she did not provide any further reflections on the subject. Later on, her optimism about the capacity of the law to redress gender and race discrimination brought her thought closer to classic liberalism. She argued that racial discrimination was a deplorable problem that had to be tackled by policy makers and by society at large, yet she believed in the capacity of the law in modern democracies to overcome these social tensions.[33] In 1975, in a public lecture on equality, she argued that racial differences could never justify different social, political, or economic treatment: "members of different races living in this country may, of course have special cultural and religious practices, to which they attach great value, and may therefore not wish for total integration into British way of life; but these give no excuse for discrimination in regard to jobs, or housing or credit facilities or educational opportunities, or in access to places of recreation or entertainment."[34] Thus, Wootton did not see any real difference between people of different races, or between men and women. By extension, her argument would imply that equality in the law could, for her, end women's subordination in the same manner in which it could hopefully end the hierarchical relations of race in the inter-national sphere.

The federal polity was therefore charged by Wootton with the onerous task of achieving what might today be called "global justice". State intervention in the economy was necessary to obtain social justice: "social equality is, itself, plainly the product of deliberate planning."[35] It was a welfarist vision based on the fulfillment of the basic needs of individuals: housing, nourishment, employment, and health services. The advantage of the federal form of government for social justice revolved around the idea of social democratic planning. Effective eco-nomic planning had two conditions: it required extensive territorial

[33] Wootton, *In Pursuit of Equality*.   [34] Wootton, *In Pursuit of Equality*, 10–11.
[35] Barbara Wootton, *Freedom under Planning* (London: Allen & Unwin, 1945), 180.

space, and a stable balance between centralized government and popular participation.

Wootton argued that federal economic planning would be more effective if the central authority had decision-making power over matters of immigration, trade, currency, credit, tariffs, employment, and production. Here some of her ideas are more original than others. In the 1940s the notion that currency, trade, and tariffs should be internationally regulated became more readily accepted.[36] Fewer economists considered the impact of immigration on international prosperity and welfare. Since she was interested in the relations between social welfare and the individual freedom to improve one's life, she thought migration should be managed by an impartial international authority, rather than by self-interested states. Lionel Robbins, her colleague at Federal Union, also espoused a vision of free movement of people in the federation, centrally regulated only for the benefit of the federation as a whole.[37] Yet while Robbins prioritized the advantage of free migration for the economy, Wootton perceived the problem from the migrants' viewpoint, enabling individuals to improve their living conditions by relocation.

The problem of migration was similar to the problem of class inequality in the domestic context. In both cases, the social and economic gaps would be closed thanks to better state-led planning. This is the precondition for the attainment of freedom on a collective scale. For her a federation would be a means to increase social wealth and prosperity universally, in both the private and the public sectors. Largely, a unified economic and social policy had more chance of success because it would eliminate excess by improving the coordination of various aspects of consumption, production, and trade.

International "Planning"

In this section, I will focus on one important aspect of Wootton's federalist vision, that brings together the key features of her international thought: planning. The idea of a plan-based international system drew on Wootton's socialism, on her problem-driven approach to economics, and on her optimism about the human capacity to realize social justice through legal and political reform. Wootton's vision of international politics was based on two fundamental precepts: first, economic planning is politically beneficial because strife and poverty lead to political

---

[36] Martin Daunton, "Britain and Globalization since 1850: The Rise of Insular Capitalism 1914–1939," *Transactions of the Royal Historical Society* 17 (2007): 1–33.

[37] Patrick Ransome (ed.), *Studies in Federal Planning* (London: Macmillan, 1943).

radicalization and war. Second, since the war budget showed that the state could finance large-scale projects, in the post-war era these funds should be diverted toward social causes to prevent future war. Her international thought assumed that government planning was possible and desirable beyond the state's boundaries.

In her discussions of planning, Wootton had not always attached to the term the same meaning. For example, in 1939, she suggested that the world federation should follow the American New Deal experience and establish a central authority for economic planning which would gradually grow "up to the Russian level."[38] However, if initially she endorsed centralized regulation and direction of the economy, six years later, in *Freedom under Planning*, she argued that planning need not entail centralized authority following the Soviet model, which, in her mind, sacrificed individual freedom for vague economic goals.[39] This means that initially she advanced an idea of a centralized federal authority responsible for setting plans for economic outputs, but also for controlling the means of production and coordinating the whole economy.

Later her vision of planning was more limited, endowing the state with the responsibility to set plans for economic growth, and to regulate the economy accordingly. "Planning" in this sense included not only social services to the poor and unemployed, but also free or subsidized nutrition and housing for all. She denied that this idea of planning meant a centralized control of the means of production. Why did Wootton change her mind? There are several possible reasons. First, observing the political and economic situation in the USSR, she might have changed her mind about the desirability of the Soviet model. A self-defined socialist, Wootton did not feel obliged to support blindly the policies of the Soviet Union; as time went by, she became increasingly critical of the news arriving from Russia. Second, the debates in Federal Union might have persuaded her that many federalists opposed the Soviet economic model as repressive and intolerant. Finally, Wootton might have been influenced by the criticism leveled at her arguments by Hayek, who was concerned over the illiberal aspects of economic planning, and sought a non-repressive form of planning, which focused on setting plans, regulating the economy, and providing subsidies and similar measures for individual welfare.[40]

---

[38] Wootton, "Economic Problems," 156. Some American thinkers, like Rexford Tugwell and Charles Merriam who were inspired by the New Deal, proposed similar ideas without taking the USSR as their model.
[39] Wootton, *Freedom under Planning*, 5–12.
[40] See Rosenboim, "Barbara Wootton, Friedrich Hayek and the Debate on Democratic Federalism."

In her subsequent three articles on "Plan for Plenty," Wootton underlined her idea of economic democracy. For her, the better off the poor states would be, the more they could contribute to the federal treasury through taxation. Thus, it was in the rich countries' interest to promote greater economic equality on a world scale. This economic equality would translate into equality of opportunities in trade, access to resources, and financial investment. Yet, she applied a domestic analogy to argue that the universal "living standard" was flexible rather than fixed, and by no means implied "mathematical" equality between individuals or between states. The British system of social services paid for by taxation provided an appropriate model of serving a universal living standard by state subsidy of basic goods and services.

Furthermore, Wootton proposed a fiscal reform to finance these social provisions, based on three principles: individual – rather than corporate – taxation, tax on inheritance up to a maximum of 60 percent, and finally fixing an "absolute upper limit" to individual income or inheritance. These ideas sought to moderate the socio-economic gaps by mobilizing wealth across society and dismantling the wealthiest classes. However, they are obviously relevant only for Western industrialized countries. Although Wootton repeated that it was in the rich states' interest to mitigate the economic and social gap between them and the poorer states, she did not propose any specific means for overcoming the political challenges that such a proposal for global taxation and global redistribution implied. Yet she did approve of the role of migration in mitigating social and economic gaps between states.

Besides fiscal measures, Wootton expressed her views on international finance and institutional reform. Although she upheld a more radical notion of economic planning than Keynes ever envisaged, she supported some of his instruments of international financial regulation, and in particular his idea of an International Clearing Union (ICU), a global banking institution which Keynes presented to the British Parliament in 1943, and at Bretton Woods in 1944.[41] The ICU was to regulate currency exchange and trade using a new international currency, "Bancor". By penalizing creditor states, Keynes hoped the ICU would encourage states to use their capital to purchase foreign goods and improve the world economy as a result.[42] These were the sort of institutions Wootton hoped could facilitate the transition to a transnational economic – and political – system. The ICU would have helped stabilize and control

---

[41] Benn Steil, *The Battle of Bretton Woods: John Maynard Keynes, Harry Dexter White, and the Making of a New World Order* (Princeton University Press, 2013).

[42] Wootton, "The Keynes Plan."

economic markets, thus contributing to a more balanced distribution of wealth and industry. Yet, by 1943, she seemingly despaired of the lack of political willingness to undertake federal and transnational reforms and proposed to use some – not well specified – political authority to impose these schemes on reluctant states.

The reaction to her views was mixed. Some federalists supported her plan, yet others accused her of paternalism and over-emphasizing irrelevant details, which could obstruct the federalist cause. Others yet preferred social policies based on economic incentives rather than subsistence provisions.[43] Wootton was keen to persuade Hayek and her fellow economists at Federal Union that the problem of social and economic equality had to be taken seriously when thinking about a democratic world federation. Yet others doubted the feasibility – and at times the desirability – of her vision. A summary paper of the committee's activities before Wootton joined stated that a federal economy should be endowed with a common currency and a strong central authority to regulate monetary and trade policies also within the member states. However, it added, such a "radical solution would probably have to be abandoned" because the existing states would not give up their economic sovereignty and independence. The economists sought a compromise, which consisted of applying the principle of free trade to the international sphere, and leaving the fiscal, monetary, and planning decisions to the national governments. They asserted that "free trade may be taken to be the fundamental basis for the international relation of the nations constituting the International Organisation."[44] Upon joining the economists' committee, Wootton underlined the close relations between economic policy and social rights on a global scale and suggested that the new economic policy for Federal Union should be based on planning to foster equality of opportunities around the world. As Robbins noted in his interim report on the committee's activities, the final solution was to avoid any decision and concentrate on envisaging a federation with substantial economic powers that could be used only in exceptional cases.[45]

Nonetheless, Wootton did not give up on her vision of planning federal social justice and penned various publications aimed at explaining her

[43] For a collection of letters replying to Wootton's argument see *Federal Union News*, July 20, 1940.
[44] "Economic Problems of International Government," n.d., British Library of Social and Economic Sciences, London School of Economics, Federal Trust, London.
[45] Lionel Robbins, "Interim Report on Economic Aspects of the Federal Constitution," in Patrick Ransome (ed.), *Towards a United States of Europe* (London: Lothian Foundation Press, 1991), 91–97.

views to the members of the organization. Her article series in Federal Union's official publication, *Federal Union News*, "Plus Plan for Plenty" and "Plan for Plenty" focused on planning as "a recognition of certain elementary needs and of the fact that, if it were not for the war and war preparation, the satisfaction of those needs would be entirely possible."[46] This definition presupposed – rather than proved – that the public authority and not private individuals had responsibility to identify and satisfy these "elementary needs." The discovery and fulfillment of "elementary needs" was indeed the main duty of the government and the public sector en route to realizing global social justice.

Conclusion

After the 1950s, Barbara Wootton largely turned away from the question of world order. She was doubtful that federalist advocacy could generate change in the international arena. Given her preference for practical and useful rather than pure abstract research, she decided to focus her efforts on reforms in British social welfare and penal systems. It may be tempting, therefore, to dismiss her contribution to international thought as marginal or inconsequential. This chapter, however, argues that Wootton was able to weave together theoretical assumptions and policy proposals to provide an original contribution to international thought in three different aspects.

First, Wootton made a long-lasting contribution to transnational federal thought, and in particular to theorizing European integration. She outlined the economic and social principles that grounded her proposal for a new federal order as a vehicle of transnational political change, providing inspiration for the economic thought of the founders of the European Union.[47] Her idea that a federation – and especially a European one – should embrace the precepts not only of liberty but also of social justice and democracy resonated with federalist thinkers beyond the British Isles. Wootton's writings underline the great weight of inequality on international relations, and the need to actively create a global institutional and political framework to generate plenty and justice across borders.

---

[46] Barbara Wootton, "Plan for Plenty," *Federal Union News*, March 1, 1940; Barbara Wootton, "Plan for Plenty," *Federal Union News*, March 15, 1940; Wootton, "Plan for Plenty," March 29, 1940; Barbara Wootton, "Plus Plan for Plenty," *Federal Union News*, July 6, 1940.

[47] Castelli, *Una pace da costruire*.

The originality of Wootton's federalism is reflected in the conceptual content of her proposals, but also in her methodological approach that merged ideas from liberal and socialist political thought. This perspective shows the important interplay of economics and politics in twentieth-century international thought, which has often been marginalized in the accepted historiography of international thought. International thought underpinned policy proposals and provided their justification. For Wootton, the benefits of European federalism could be best identified at the intersection of Economics, Sociology, and International Relations. Thus, she outlined a sophisticated international thought which set out to realize her social and economic principles in the domestic sphere, alongside more conventional international objectives such as peace and security.

In Ventotene, the Italian prison camp island where Mussolini's opponents were incarcerated, Wootton's writings generated a great deal of interest. Ernesto Rossi and Altiero Spinelli, both left-leaning liberal democrats who opposed fascism, read Wootton's books on federalism and planning and found them particularly inspiring for thinking about a new European order after the war.[48] Their own federalist tract, known as the Ventotene Manifesto, became one of the foundational documents of the European Union.[49] In this document, which called for a common social policy in Europe based on the precepts of liberal socialism and democracy, Rossi and Spinelli embodied Wootton's vision. The Italian federalist tract merged the defense of liberty with a strong commitment to social justice and equality, replicating Wootton's original combination of liberal democracy and socialism. The legacy of Wootton's ideas in Europe suggests that her ideas outlived the Federal Union moment and provided a long-lasting intellectual foundation for the evolution of the European Union as a very loose federation, and more importantly, as a sphere of large-scale social-economic planning for liberty, welfare, and democracy.

Second, Wootton's writings reflect her conviction that practice, not abstract theory, should guide international thought. She advanced a critique of pure abstract thinking in economics and politics and challenged common legalistic approaches to international relations. For her, political thinkers should not work in a bubble and imagine an ideal world of norms and principles. Instead, she advanced an alternative, problem-driven practical approach to politics, in which theory serves as a means to effect social change. Like Wiskemann and other women who were

---

[48] Castelli, *Una pace da costruire*; Bosco, *The Federal Idea*.
[49] Altiero Spinelli and Ernesto Rossi, "Il Manifesto di Ventotene / The Ventotene Manifesto," Bilingual edition (Ventotene: Ultima spiaggia, 2016 [1944]).

activist-scholars such as Eslanda Robeson, both of whom are discussed in this volume, Wootton found merit in fact-based, practical research in the social sciences, that aimed to use theory to intervene directly in "real-world" problems. This position could be explained in two ways. On the one hand, social scientists had, for Wootton, a duty to provide clear and effective policy guidance. Thus, she advanced a utilitarian approach to research that highlighted the applicability and impact of theoretical ideas. On the other hand, her professional trajectory as a woman might also have influenced her view. Her major academic position was as a professor at a women's college that aimed to provide practical formation in social care, while she failed to obtain a permanent position in more prestigious universities. In more general terms, Wootton's life experience as a woman highlighted to her eyes the importance of practical conditions over formal and theoretical structures. Wootton's privileged background – the gifted daughter of two dons educated at an elite British university – was "marred" by gender.[50] In her 1967 autobiography, she included a chapter titled "woman," where she deplores workplace sexism and practices that we would now call "mansplaining" and "hepeating." Doubtless her professional trajectory was conditioned by her gender to a more significant extent than that of her male colleagues.[51] Gender equality, for her, was based not only on social mores but also on practical economic conditions such as equal pay, maternity leave, and social benefits. While biographic details should not be over-stressed, Wootton's career is indicative of a more general trend that encourages women activist-scholars to embrace a practice-driven approach to international thought, drawing on their experience outside the more conventional spheres of academic knowledge-production.

Third, Wootton's thought has the merit of highlighting some of the limits of mid-century visions of world order. In her writings, there is little or no discussion of empire and its structures of international inequality. By prioritizing a seemingly more feasible European federal project, Wootton turned her gaze away from major international inequalities that would eventually hinder the realization of her vision of global justice. In her largely Western narrative, the colonial and non-Western world featured very little – if at all. Possibly, Wootton lacked direct experience with the colonial world. Following her practice-based methods, such lack of knowledge excluded her intervention in planning the post-imperial world. Nonetheless, acknowledging the blind-spots of her proposals

---

[50] Albert Henry Halsey, *A History of Sociology in Britain: Science, Literature and Society* (Oxford University Press, 2004), 63.
[51] Wootton, *In a World I Never Made*, 150–55.

helps recognize the diversity and complexity of women's international thinking in the twentieth century. In Wootton's case, a progressive approach to gender and race equality may conceal a conservative pragmatism that delimits the boundaries of progress to Europe and ignores Africa. The spatial and conceptual limits of her vision reveal the challenge of global thinking in the twentieth century.

The history of women's international thought is an ongoing endeavor. Often, it requires shifting the gaze away from the "canon" of international thinkers to recover neglected or minor figures who contributed to shaping the international imaginary. Such an exercise is useful to challenge the conventional narratives about the development of international thought, but also to bring back thinkers such as Barbara Wootton whose influential and original contributions to international thought were hitherto forgotten. Her international thought embodied the conviction that politics and economics should be considered as two aspects of a common problem, that of constructing a society based on social equality, economic justice, and political liberty. As this chapter has hopefully demonstrated, her sophisticated analysis of the advantages and limits of a transnational federal order still holds relevant insights for intellectual historians and international relations scholars today.

14 Collective Security for Common Men and Women: Vera Micheles Dean and US Foreign Relations

Andrew Jewett

Do popular writers have a place in the history of international thought? If "thought" means only the systematic presentation of findings and arguments for specialized (typically academic) audiences, then the answer is by definition "no." In recent years, however, many intellectual historians have embraced the study of non-canonical texts and thinkers, recognizing that consequential ideas and their purveyors can be found throughout society.[1] This move should not be allowed, as it often has, to devalue the familiar task of exploring the internal histories of canonical discourses. Still, if scholars wish to understand the development, circulation, uptake, and social impact of ideas in the round – including the processes by which today's canons came into being – they must also include the full range of knowledge workers (rank-and-file academics, public intellectuals, popularizers, journalists, teachers, and many others) and ordinary people as well. From this perspective, as the editors argue in the Introduction to this volume, exploring the history of international thought means not just examining the subset of theoretical, empirical, and methodological contributions currently deemed "seminal" but also undertaking careful, empirically grounded analyses of arguments, assumptions, and rhetorical devices wherever they appear – indeed, studying the entire matrix of beliefs, conscious or unconscious, that have shaped views of, decisions about, and actions in the international domain.

This change of perspective brings women into focus, since they have historically been marginalized in canons and universities alike. Indeed, as several of the chapters in this volume suggest, exploring the role of women in international thought can help us understand such patterns of

---

[1] This shift has been especially common among historians of American thought: e.g., Joel Isaac, James T. Kloppenberg, Michael O'Brien, and Jennifer Ratner-Rosenhagen (eds.), *The Worlds of American Intellectual History* (New York: Oxford University Press, 2016); and Raymond Haberski, Jr. and Andrew Hartman (eds.), *American Labyrinth: Intellectual History for Complicated Times* (Ithaca, NY: Cornell University Press, 2018).

exclusion, as well as the complex interactions of formal discourses with the numerous intellectual and cultural cross-currents that surround them – and often cut directly through them. Indeed, widening the interpretive lens reveals not only that non-canonical discourses feature "intellectual content" deserving of scholarly attention but also that canonical discourses themselves have been shaped by "non-intellectual" factors as well. It is not just women and other outsiders that have unconsciously echoed popular understandings, reflected their own identity positions, let their conclusions outrun their evidence, or departed in other ways from the desiccated caricature of "thought" that intellectual historians often employ.

The work of the American theorist Vera Micheles Dean offers a particularly valuable example of the interplay of formal and popular discourses because she occupied two institutional worlds in succession. At roughly the midpoint of Dean's long and illustrious career, she shifted her base from an elite non-profit organization to academia. Despite the change of venue, however, her stance on international relations remained relatively constant. From the 1930s to the 1960s, Dean espoused a cosmopolitan, social-democratic form of internationalism rooted in collective security, economic prosperity for all peoples, and an end to racism and colonialism. Whether meeting with State Department officials, interviewing Jawaharlal Nehru, speaking to a New Jersey women's club, or teaching undergraduates at leading universities, the Russian-born Dean portrayed the world as the site of an emerging global neighborliness that would ensure peace by fostering economic wellbeing and psychological security around the world. She highlighted the inseparability of political, economic, social, and cultural changes, and she recognized quite early the centrality of the "non-Western world" to the Cold War struggle. Indeed, she assumed that each of the world's peoples would ultimately make its way down the winding path to democracy, equality, and justice.[2]

But how can we assess Dean's work if we cannot easily relate her to the canon by offering judgments of the type "Carr influenced ..." or "Morgenthau responded to ..."? A new standard of historical importance is needed. Such a standard will rely on less clearly demonstrable forms of

---

[2] For brief treatments of Dean's writings, see Alan Raucher, "The First Foreign Affairs Think Tanks," *American Quarterly* 30.4 (1978): 493–513; Charles DeBenedetti, "The American Peace Movement and Asia, 1941–1961," *Pacific Historical Review* 50.2 (1981): 192–214; Inderjeet Parmar, "The Carnegie Corporation and the Mobilization of Opinion in the United States' Rise to Globalism, 1939–1945," *Minerva* 37.4 (1999): 355–78; David C. Engerman, *Modernization from the Other Shore: American Intellectuals and the Romance of Russian Development* (Cambridge, MA: Harvard University Press, 2004); and Jeremy Weiss, "Strategizing for Peace: Approaches to Global Security in Crisis and War, 1933–1953" (PhD thesis, Boston University, 2012).

impact, among a group of people far larger and more diffuse than the set of canonical authors. Surely it made a difference that Dean penned a series of readable books, articles, and pamphlets that sold in the tens, and sometimes hundreds, of thousands. *The Nature of the Non-Western World* (1957), a fifty-cent paperback, sold over 250,000 copies and found widespread use in college classes. Dean also covered subjects from Fascist Italy, Nazi Germany, and Soviet Russia to Latin America and the "new nations" of the 1950s and 1960s. She spoke to scores of audiences each year and appeared frequently on radio and television. Through much of her career, Dean played a key role in the activities of the Foreign Policy Association, founded in 1918 to educate American policy makers and citizens about international affairs at a time when even career diplomats often lacked systematic, empirical information about other countries. FPA leaders worked closely with top officials, in the United States and elsewhere, and spoke constantly to both popular and professional audiences through innumerable reports, speeches, conferences, and discussion group materials. For decades after joining the FPA in 1928, Dean provided much of that group's intellectual armature. Heading the powerful Research Department from 1936 to 1951 and then its successor, the Publications Department, for ten more years, she oversaw publications including the periodical *Foreign Policy Reports* (1925–51) and its successor, the *Foreign Policy Bulletin* (1955–61), as well as the Headline Series of books (1935–) and numerous other pamphlets and articles. Later in Dean's career, she also left her mark on academia. After teaching at various universities in the late 1940s, she organized and directed the Non-Western Civilization Program at the University of Rochester from 1954–62. Subsequently, she joined New York University's Graduate School of Public Administration and Center for International Studies, where she taught until the year before her death in 1972.[3]

[3] Biographical information here and below is from William J. Dean, *My New York: A Life in the City* (CreateSpace, 2013); William J. Dean, biographical sketch, Vera Micheles Dean Papers, Arthur and Elizabeth Schlesinger Library on the History of Women in America, Radcliffe Institute for Advanced Study, Harvard University (hereafter "Dean Papers"), box 1, folder 1; Vera Micheles Dean (hereafter "Dean"), "Russia Revisited," Dean Papers, box 1, folder 3; Nadine Micheles, "My Russia," Dean Papers, box 1, folder 4; and "Vera M. Dean (9/45)," Foreign Policy Association Records, Wisconsin Historical Society, Division of Library, Archives, and Museum Collections (hereafter "FPA Records"), box 39, folder 34. The latter folder contains additional biographical items. Sales figures come from August Heckscher, "Vera Micheles Dean: A Personal Word," *Foreign Policy Bulletin* 40 (June 15, 1961), 147; Richard Phalon, *Foreign Policy, Democracy and the Art of Association* (New York: Foreign Policy Association, 2001), 40; Victor Weybright to Dean, February 10, 1958, Dean Papers, box 5, folder 1; Crane Brinton to Dean, October 28, 1960, ibid.; "EO" to Dean, April 6, 1942, FPA Records, box 6, folder 7; "MAS" to Dean, March 1, 1940, FPA Records, box 11, folder 18.

As a shaper of American opinion in the mid-twentieth century, Dean bears comparison to contemporaries such as the Republican presidential candidate Wendell Willkie, the journalist John Gunther, and the novelist Pearl Buck. Each reformulated American liberal internationalism in cosmopolitan terms, decrying isolationism, imperialism, and conspiratorial anti-communism. Explaining "how to make friends for the U.S.," these common-sense cosmopolitans identified the world's peoples – prominently including the Russians and the "non-aligned" nations of the global South (the "Land of Bandungia," Dean called it) – as familiarly human and potentially friendly: not alien enemies but future allies under a harmonious regime of "diversity within unity." In short, these writers portrayed the world as a global neighborhood in which appreciation and mutual aid would soon replace bitterness and domination.[4]

Yet Dean, unlike Willkie, Gunther, or Buck, was a scholar first and a popular writer second. Throughout her career, Dean argued that international decision making must rest on careful, empirical analysis – above all, realistic assessments of the individual and collective interests at stake. (Indeed, Dean identified her abiding optimism about the path of global development as an outgrowth of hard-boiled realism about both human behavior and the twentieth-century world situation.) During her early days at the FPA, fresh from writing a lengthy, densely argued PhD dissertation in international law and international relations at Radcliffe, the bookish Dean struggled to find the right tone for popular audiences. She may have resisted bracketing her hard-won professional status and intellectual attainments in addressing the masses. But as Dean embarked on hundreds of speaking engagements and ramped up her writing schedule through the 1930s, she found ways of connecting with broad audiences and quickly came to appreciate the practical importance of educating the public. Financial pressures reinforced the new emphasis; when Dean was thirty-three, her husband died and she found herself the sole provider for two young children.[5] But Dean's writings, however accessible, remained deeply grounded in her own research and that of others. She gathered innumerable documents throughout the year, via libraries and the mail, and then traveled extensively during the summers, interviewing top politicians and administrators while gathering additional

---

[4] Dean, *How to Make Friends for the U.S.* (New York: Foreign Policy Association, 1952); Dean, *The Nature of the Non-Western World* (New York: New American Library, 1957); Dean, "Politics and Human Welfare," in Henry A. Wallace et al., *Christian Bases of World Order* (New York: Abingdon-Cokesbury, 1943), 163.

[5] For Dean's struggles with tone, see H. S. Latham to Raymond L. Buell, June 4, 1934, Dean Papers, box 4, folder 51; and Paul U. Kellogg to Dean, November 25, 1932, Dean Papers, box 1, folder 8.

documents unavailable from a distance. By 1960, in addition to numerous itineraries in Western Europe, her professional travel had taken her to Russia (1932), Hungary (1937), Latin America (1941), Czechoslovakia (1949), Asia (1950, 1953, and 1957), Yugoslavia (1954), the Middle East (1955), and Africa (1959). Her many leisure trips added further to her knowledge base.

Like Elizabeth Wiskemann, then, Dean based her conclusions on a massive and ever-growing base of detailed information, including not only published and unpublished documents but also interviews and personal communications with global leaders. Dean certainly found more cause for hope in global affairs than did the post-war IR realists, but that does not place her beyond the pale of "thought," as a mere sentimentalist, sloganeer, propagandist, popularizer, or reformer. After all, her assumption that the dynamics of international relations could change is no less scholarly or empirically warranted – let alone "scientific" – than the realists' assumption that such dynamics will never change. Dean and similar figures must find their place in a comprehensive history of international thought.

Totalitarianism

Amid the chaos of her age – the totalitarian regimes of the 1930s, the brutalities of World War II, the frustration of post-war peace – Dean consistently discerned slow, halting progress toward an internationalist, social-democratic future. Her account of this overall trajectory reflected Dean's belief that a series of disruptive but ultimately inevitable shifts were fast rendering other forms of international order untenable. The core dynamics were economic in origin, as people around the world sought to improve their lot materially. Dean saw a densely connected global economy emerging, knitting even the least developed areas into a single web of material interdependence. She also argued that individualized ownership of the means of production was beginning to give way to more collective, managerial forms of economic organization in nations around the world. Dean urged American citizens and policy makers to cast off their ideological allergy to shared ownership and aid democratic socialist movements abroad, which represented both a positive good in their own right and the only antidote to totalitarian forms of socialism. Dean also called on Americans to embrace two other dynamics that economic changes made necessary: a move through and beyond the stage of unfettered national sovereignty toward greater global coordination; and the emergence of a pluralistic, inclusive orientation toward social and cultural diversity – especially an end to all racial and ethnic discrimination and the imperialism it authorized. Only by actively coord-inating its affairs across national boundaries, Dean argued, could the world survive the accelerating processes of industrialization and social-ization without succumbing to either war or totalitarian domination. Meanwhile, she held that intergroup conflict, whether subnational or international, undermined both social trust and economic development. From formal imperialism down to cultural parochialism, a refusal to recognize the value of all social groups and cultures obstructed global development and organization.

Dean's analysis located control over – and thus responsibility for – world affairs squarely in the hands of the United States and its Western European allies, even as she urged these countries to fundamentally alter their approach toward other peoples. Well into the 1950s, she argued that if the West promoted social-democratic reforms and moderated its claim to political sovereignty and cultural superiority, the resulting pat-tern of international federalism would inevitably fuel economic develop-ment and political democratization around the world. Only late in her career did she ascribe a significant degree of responsibility to the leaders of decolonizing nations and other "non-Western" areas – a category that for Dean included the Soviet Union and its satellites as well as what her contemporaries called the "Third World." Prior to that, she simply took for granted that non-Western peoples would respond constructively if the West met their legitimate needs for economic and military security.

Thus, Dean counseled self-reflection and judicious action, not blame or denial, in response to the totalitarian threats of the 1930s. Like the modernization theorists after her, she identified both European fascism and Soviet communism as pathological outcomes of the industrial tran-sition. Yet she also saw major differences between them. The Italian and German dictatorships, Dean argued, spoke for the middle class, which Marxists had wrongly expected to revolt when its economic fortunes waned. Instead, the German and Italian middle classes, facing financial ruin and the threat of communism, had opted for dictatorship to preserve their property rights. Fascism thus reversed the course of progress toward democratic socialism; the middle class abandoned its freedoms to pre-vent workers from making economic progress.[6]

Dean's policy prescriptions in the 1930s reflected her belief that fascism stemmed from legitimate underlying demands but represented a major step backward, both economically and politically. Although she

---

[6] Vera Micheles Dean, "The Attack on Democracy," in Raymond Leslie Buell (ed.), *New Governments in Europe: The Trend toward Dictatorship* (New York: T. Nelson and Sons, 1934), 22–23.

opposed concessions to Hitler and called for a forceful response to his annexation threats, which she considered a bluff, she also pressed for a redistribution of economic resources toward Germany and Italy to meet their needs for social reconstruction and thereby blunt their leaders' ambitions to dominate others. When Hitler pressed ahead, Dean worked with groups such as the World Alliance for International Friendship through the Churches and the National Conference on the Cause and Cure of War, seeking a brokered peace. But when war broke out, she warned peace advocates against "skipping over" the military conflict. Instead, Dean urged the Allies to fight for the right reasons and craft a peace based on egalitarian development and global cooperation.[7]

Dean responded very differently to Soviet communism. She interpreted the Bolshevik Revolution as a significant step down the path of human development, despite the political pathologies it had birthed – and the fact that it had torn Dean from her childhood world and then her family. (Dean was born in 1903 to a multilingual, multi-religious, middle-class family in cosmopolitan St. Petersburg that fled ahead of the Revolution to Copenhagen, from which she made her way alone to the United States for schooling. She eventually took a bachelor's degree at Radcliffe and a master's in international law at Yale before receiving the PhD from Radcliffe.) Dean maintained a lifelong, largely sympathetic engagement with the land of her birth. She urged Western governments to accept the legitimacy of the Soviet regime and to understand that its policies, however lamentable, reflected the Russian people's past history and genuine economic and defense needs, not an alien political philosophy of the type fascists upheld.[8]

From her doctoral dissertation onwards, Dean consistently downplayed the Soviet regime's Marxist orientation and traced its decisions to the specific contours of Russian economic and social development. By the late 1920s, she argued, the campaign for a global anti-capitalist revolution had already given way to a preoccupation with domestic concerns. She warned optimists that the regime's commitment to state socialism was deeply entrenched, but at the same time contended that

[7] Frank Winchester Abbott, "From Versailles to Munich: The Foreign Policy Association and American Foreign Policy" (PhD thesis, Texas Tech University, 1972), 269–71; "U.S. War Entry Opposed in Plan before Roosevelt," *Christian Science Monitor*, November 11, 1939: 2; "Women Map Items in Peace Plan," *New York Times*, January 25, 1939: 9; "U.S. Policy Told to Women Outlaws Gains by Aggression," *Christian Science Monitor*, January 24, 1940: 22.

[8] Like Krystyna Marek and many other figures from politically volatile areas, Dean had a keen interest in the birth of new states and the conditions of their international recognition: e.g., Vera Micheles, "Governments de Facto with Special Reference to the Soviet Government" (PhD dissertation, Radcliffe College, 1928).

the Soviet Union's relentless focus on economic modernization at home made it a vigorous force for global peace, not a military or ideological threat. The problem, Dean explained, was simply that the various classes and parties in Russia had long bowed to authoritarian rule. Democracy would emerge only slowly there – as it had in the West.[9]

Yet it would emerge nonetheless. By the mid-1930s, Dean believed that Russian workers had come to enjoy not only economic advantages but also opportunities for political participation, under a group of leaders who genuinely pursued the workers' interests despite their misguided choice of authoritarian methods. Unlike Hitler or Mussolini, Dean wrote, the Bolsheviks showed "imagination, resourcefulness and selfless zeal." She also saw a fundamental difference in foreign policy between the fascists, whose ideological character made them a constant threat to their neighbors, and the Soviets' purely defensive approach, based solely on Russia's longstanding need for territorial integrity. In short, the Soviets sought to consolidate the economic gains of workers, not dominate or annex other countries. Dean maintained this view of the Soviet leadership's core goals through the Stalinist upheavals of the 1930s, although she increasingly criticized specific policies and deplored many features of the 1936 constitution.[10]

Security

Dean's divergent responses to European fascism and Soviet communism reflected her belief, drawn from extensive study of Western history, that economic development, if distributed across all classes – as it was in Russia, she said, but not the fascist regimes – cleared a path for democracy: the equally wide distribution of political rights. During the 1940s and early 1950s, Dean spelled out more clearly the view of human behavior underlying this causal analysis. She rejected what she considered the sentimentalism of peace advocates and portrayed the push for greater international cooperation as the result of material forces, not utopian ideals. Her position, she wrote, reflected "the actual needs of living human beings," not mere "theoretical formulas."[11]

---

[9] Dean, *Soviet Russia, 1917–1933* (New York and Boston: Foreign Policy Association and World Peace Foundation, 1933).

[10] Dean, *Soviet Russia: 1917–1935* (New York and Boston: Foreign Policy Association and World Peace Foundation, 1935), 5; Dean, "Geneva, August 26, 1936," FPA Records, box 6, folder 8.

[11] Dean, *Why Europe Went to War*, World Affairs Pamphlets no. 7 (New York: Foreign Policy Association and National Peace Conference, December 1939), 48.

Dean's realism was not that of the canonical IR theorists, however. Rather, it was a social-psychological orientation echoing key themes from the ascendant social sciences. It is not clear how explicitly Dean drew on those disciplines, since she often wrote in forums unsuited to systematic citations. But her work strongly paralleled interwar developments in cultural anthropology and social psychology. She relied especially heavily on a version of the "frustration-aggression" framework that social psychologists crafted in the late 1930s. Both individuals and nations had deep, persistent drives and impulses that would sow conflict unless acknowledged and constructively channeled. Dean, like the architects of the frustration-aggression hypothesis, did not believe that a drive to dominate others was innate to either individuals or nations. Rather, aggressive or controlling behavior was simply a pathological expression of more basic impulses that could be redirected into productive pursuits.[12]

Like many thinkers in the late 1930s and 1940s, Dean emphasized the quest for "security" as a driving force in human affairs. In the first instance, she wrote, most people cared little for "the intricacies of diplomacy," or "territorial boundaries," or "the reshuffling of colonies," or "access to raw materials." What mattered was "food, and housing, and education, and health, and the bringing up of children." Yet Dean's understanding of security was more complex and morally charged than this statement indicates. Both individuals and human groups, Dean assumed, needed security on multiple levels. For individuals, this meant not only bodily security, in the form of a baseline of material comfort, but also psychological security: freedom from the threats of war and social chaos as well as acceptance by others of one's cultural norms. Dean's understanding of security anchored her definition of a "democracy" as a

---

[12] On the postwar social sciences, see especially Ellen Herman, *The Romance of American Psychology: Political Culture in an Age of Experts* (Berkeley: University of California Press, 1995); Andrew Jewett, *Science, Democracy, and the American University: From the Civil War to the Cold War* (New York: Cambridge University Press, 2012); Peter Mandler, *Return from the Natives: How Margaret Mead Won the Second World War and Lost the Cold War* (New Haven, CT: Yale University Press, 2013); and Jamie Cohen-Cole, *The Open Mind: Cold War Politics and the Sciences of Human Nature* (University of Chicago Press, 2014). Although Dean's analysis reflected key themes from those disciplines, she often framed it in religious terms for wider audiences. Sometimes claimed by historians of Judaism (e.g., Natalie Friedman, "Vera Dean, 1903–1972," *Jewish Women's Archive* [https://jwa.org/encyclopedia/article/dean-vera-micheles]), she was by affiliation an Episcopalian who spoke frequently to liberal Protestant audiences and contributed to many conferences and volumes organized by Protestant leaders. Even there, Dean made few explicit references to Christianity. (For a rather anodyne exception, see Dean, "The United States and the U.S.S.R.," in Paul Newton Poling (ed.), *God and the Nations* (Garden City, NY: Doubleday, 1950), 60–61.) But she saw her core ideals of "human welfare" and the common good in all of the world's faiths: Dean, "Politics and Human Welfare," 162–63.

society that met the material and psychological needs of all inhabitants, without pejorative racial, ethnic, or class distinctions. Indeed, much of her optimism about global affairs stemmed from a belief that any government's legitimacy, and thus survival, depended on its capacity to address the basic needs of "common men and women."[13]

But Dean cautioned that no state, however powerful, could meet its citizens' needs through domestic policy alone. Due to the world's growing economic interdependence, each nation had to participate constructively in the international order. Through World War II and beyond, Dean worked tirelessly to turn Americans away from strong assertions of national autonomy and toward support for a robust international organization. Academia beckoned to Dean during the war; her growing visibility and reputation brought offers of a deanship at Wellesley and the presidencies of both Mills and Radcliffe. But Dean stayed at the FPA, choosing to remain as close as possible to the policy action. (She would have preferred to work directly in the Washington policy establishment, she told Radcliffe's outgoing president, but women were unwelcome there.)[14] In that capacity, Dean was asked to serve on Herbert Lehman's personal staff at the 1943 founding of the United Nations Relief and Rehabilitation Administration, and then to represent the FPA at the 1945 United Nations organizing meeting in San Francisco. Dean also contributed to the cause by lecturing in England, France, and Germany for the Office of War Information and studying conditions in defeated Germany for the State Department.[15]

Although Dean staunchly defended the United Nations through the years – indeed, she was memorialized in its chapel after her death in 1972 – she saw that organization as simply the first step toward a much more powerful world body. Dean repeatedly told American readers that they could never expect either prosperity or peace in a world "rent by war and civil strife, and overshadowed by hunger, misery, and disease." She hoped the UN would pool defense resources and outlaw the kinds of attacks launched by Hitler, seeking to eliminate conflict altogether by making inter-state aggression prohibitively costly. Indeed, Dean foresaw

[13] Dean, "Politics and Human Welfare," 162–163, 177–178.
[14] Dean to Ada Louise Comstock, July 26, 1943, Records of Radcliffe College President Ada Louise Comstock, Arthur and Elizabeth Schlesinger Library on the History of Women in America, Radcliffe Institute for Advanced Study, Harvard University, box 56, folder 514.
[15] "Vera M. Dean (9/45)"; Dean, "Proud to Live in our Times" (autobiographical fragments), Dean Papers, box 1, folder 2; "In Memoriam Vera Micheles Dean," Dean Papers, 1997 addition, box 1, folder 1; "The Women's City Club Citation of Vera M. Dean as One of New York's Distinguished Women Citizens on May 14th, 1946," FPA Records, box 39, folder 34.

"a closely-knit world federation similar to the structure of the United States" emerging out of the UN one day.[16]

Economically, Dean envisioned an integrated, global system based on the industrial production of consumer goods in all countries. Unlike the many planners who expected the West to use raw materials from other areas, she believed that each country should develop at least a light industry to satisfy its citizens' consumption needs. Overall, she contended, the regions of the world should be "roughly equalized" in economic terms. Although the West would suffer at first from such a change, it would eventually benefit from the increased markets for its heavy industry. Dean thus took for granted the West's dominance in areas such as aircraft production and shipbuilding. However, she rejected the long-standing division between industrial and non-industrial countries. Dean believed that new scientific techniques, such as synthetic replacements for natural substances, could overcome inherent inequalities of geography and resource distribution. And of course, she added, such techniques should be freely shared by all peoples.[17]

As always, however, Dean identified her proposals as realistic rather than sentimental. Rejecting what she considered the utopianism of the League of Nations, she warned that internationalists could never expect to create a beloved community grounded in self-sacrifice and love. Any imaginable world organization would rest solely on mutual benefit, with nations participating due to enlightened self-interest, not moral obligation. Indeed, Dean echoed the Christian realist Reinhold Niebuhr in casting suspicion on moral ideals themselves. Like Niebuhr, she argued that "the fallibility of man" produced a universal and ineradicable tendency among individuals and groups to rationalize their own interests by couching them in moral terms. The first step in developing a realistic stance, Dean explained, was to recognize "that all of us are guilty of thinking our cause is just, no matter how it looks to others; that no nation can claim to be a repository of all the virtues; and that one's judgment as to the other fellow's claims depends not on some eternal principle but on the more lowly question of whose ox is being gored."[18]

---

[16] "In Memoriam Vera Micheles Dean"; Dean, *After Victory: Questions and Answers on World Organization*, Headline Series no. 50 (New York: Foreign Policy Association, 1945), 8, 50–51; Dean, "The Responsibilities of Peace," *Nation* 142 (February 26, 1936), 245.

[17] Dean, "Politics and Human Welfare," 164, 167–169.

[18] Dean, *Latin America and the War* (New York: Oxford University Press, 1942), 5; Dean, "The United States and India," *Far Eastern Survey* 21.5 (April 2, 1952), 45.

The Cold War

If enlightened self-interest lacked binding moral force, however, Dean nonetheless portrayed it as humanity's only hope in the fraught years after World War II. As the fragile post-war peace degenerated into an armed standoff, Dean urged international amity and mutual aid as the only solutions to the Soviet threat. She warned that economic and social change was coming one way or another: in Europe, in Russia, and around the world. The United States faced a choice between two possible outcomes: a peaceful, democratic form of socialism or revolutionary communism. On this basis, Dean advocated cooperation with the Soviet Union, aid to the devastated economies of Europe (including Eastern Europe and the Soviet Union itself), and a strong and effective United Nations. She welcomed the rise of socialist parties in Western Europe and argued that democratic impulses in Eastern Europe could be significantly accelerated through economic and technical aid tailored to promote agricultural modernization.[19]

Dean's steadfast belief in the Soviet regime's democratizing tendencies also survived intact amid the Cold War, earning her considerable scorn. (Dean's writings on the reconstruction of Europe, the Cold War, and the decolonization process provoked anti-communist attacks from the late 1940s up to at least 1960.) In 1947, as Cold War tensions deepened and Dean finally accepted a high-profile academic position at Harvard, she published two books on US–Soviet relations that described the Soviet regime as "crude, brutal and unjust" – but no more so than many other governments. "I believe that, in spite of setbacks and mistakes," she wrote, "Russia is traveling in a direction that will eventually bring it out on the high road of spiritual and political, as well as material, progress. And, loving both peoples, I hope Americans and Russians will travel that road together." As before, Dean insisted that Russia sought peace, not world domination. Shattered economically and socially by the war, it wanted only to secure its western border, then retreat and heal.[20]

Dean's continued faith in the capacity of economic reform to drive democratization produced some of her most starry-eyed statements about the Soviet Union. Again denying that communist principles influenced the regime's actions, she now emphasized the fact that Russia had

---

[19] Dean, *Russia: Menace or Promise?* (New York: Henry Holt and Company, 1947); Dean, "Russia and Her Neighbors in Europe," *Atlantic Monthly* 177 (March 1946), 73.

[20] Dean, *Russia: Menace or Promise?* viii. For anti-communist criticism, see especially *Counterattack*, March 12, 1948 issue, FPA Records, box 11, folder 22; "Subversive Materials in Schools," Dean Papers, box 2, folder 24.

"telescoped" multiple revolutions – "the downfall of monarchy and aristocracy, the breaking up of feudal estates, the advanced stages of the Industrial Revolution" – into a short window and simply "overleaped the period of individual enterprise." Little wonder that political niceties had fallen by the wayside. In fact, Dean claimed the Stalinist dictatorship might offer the only path to democracy in the Soviet Union. Until the heterogeneous Soviet citizenry became literate and culturally unified, she wrote, strong leaders would need to guide economic growth. Dean described a range of repressive practices and institutions as steps down the democratic path. Stalin's purges, though deeply lamentable, had nevertheless fostered political stability and consensus. So, too, had a more positive development: the gradual replacement of the first generation of ideological dogmatists by practical bureaucrats. Meanwhile, the process of ideological self-criticism was giving the masses a political education and "experience in discussion of matters that directly affect their daily work and lives." Dean even saw hope in the 1936 constitution, which she had earlier criticized more substantively. She emphasized its provision of new personal freedoms, including the ownership of consumer items. Dean discerned the emergence of a small middle class in Russia, and a broader cultural shift from libertarianism and materialism toward bourgeois proprieties. In short, she presented the Soviet Union as a thoroughly democratic regime in cultural terms, if not political ones. If one bracketed "political considerations," Dean wrote, communism offered "a way of life similar to that which is urged by the most highly developed religious movements." As the United States and USSR converged on a social-democratic middle ground beyond the personal ownership of enterprise (even land reform reflected core American values, said Dean), American policy makers could hasten democratization in the Soviet Union by understanding its needs and negotiating in good faith – most importantly, by eschewing "strategic bases and other special advantages" in Europe and elsewhere.[21]

By the early 1950s, Dean increasingly turned her attention from Europe and the Soviet Union to the "non-Western world," on which citizens, scholars, and even policy makers lacked the most basic information. As the image of the Soviet Union's "telescoped" revolutions suggests, Dean's analysis had gained a strong temporal dimension during World War II. Echoing the stadial theories of earlier centuries, and foreshadowing the modernization theories of the early 1960s, she increasingly rendered the differences between countries in temporal terms by placing them on a timeline of progress that was defined by the

---

[21] Dean, *Russia: Menace or Promise?* 23, 33, 37, 44, 50–53, 70, 90.

trajectory of Western Europe and the United States. Dean often described the peoples of the world as living in many different centuries – literally, "different periods of history," reflecting their levels of political and economic progress. Some remained in the feudal, pre-industrial phase. Others occupied intermediate points between the fourteenth century and the Western present – or rather, the West's social-democratic near future.[22]

Yet Dean also departed from modernization theorists in important ways. Like area studies specialists, she emphasized the historically rooted differences – social, cultural, economic, political – that distinguished non-Western societies from one another, despite their shared location on the pre-industrial rung of the developmental ladder. Moreover, Dean also contended that the industrialized countries had not yet fully traversed the road to social and international peace and prosperity. She explained that in the United States, as in the fascist regimes, business leaders waged rear-guard battles against social democracy – an emerging phase of economic life where individuals still owned consumer goods but public or quasi-public organizations took over the means of production. Nor had the advanced countries translated nascent insights about the implications of interdependence to the global level. In Dean's view, the developed countries could only live up to their stated values – and thereby find a hearing in the less developed areas – by pushing themselves fully into the social-democratic, internationalist phase of human history.[23]

For the non-Western world, Dean advocated a comprehensive program of technical assistance centered on agricultural improvements, of the type that would later characterize the "Green Revolution" of the 1960s. Like other post-war "low modernists," Dean favored technological development in every country, though ideally organized on a smaller, more human scale than the heavy industry of the leading powers. To this end, Dean called for no-strings-attached aid to non-industrial countries, undertaken

---

[22] Dean, "Politics and Human Welfare," 163. On modernization theory, see especially Nils Gilman, *Mandarins of the Future: Modernization Theory in Cold War America* (Baltimore, MD: Johns Hopkins University Press, 2003); David C. Engerman, Nils Gilman, and Mark H. Haefele (eds.), *Staging Growth: Modernization, Development, and the Global Cold War* (Amherst: University of Massachusetts Press, 2003); and David Ekbladh, *The Great American Mission: Modernization and the Construction of an American World Order* (Princeton University Press, 2010).

[23] Helpful accounts of the area studies approach include David L. Szanton, *The Politics of Knowledge: Area Studies and the Disciplines* (Berkeley: University of California Press, 2004); Said Amir Arjomand, *Social Theory and Regional Studies in the Global Age* (Albany: State University of New York Press, 2014); Gareth Dale, *The Politics of East European Area Studies* (New York: Routledge, 2016); Zachary Lockman, *Field Notes: The Making of Middle East Studies in the United States* (Stanford University Press, 2016); and Katja Naumann et al. (eds.), *In Search of Other Worlds: Essays towards a Cross-Regional History of Area Studies* (Leipziger Universitätsverlag, 2018).

cooperatively by the United States, offering capital; Britain, offering technical advice; and the Soviet Union, offering its experience with rapid industrialization. This program would forestall dictatorship in the developing world, strengthen Europe's commitment to the United States, and assuage Soviet fears that US policy threatened their traditional spheres of influence. Meanwhile, Dean challenged the widespread assumption that socialist sentiments in the developing world reflected a Soviet conspiracy. Twentieth-century upheavals, she argued, had sources far deeper than Soviet propaganda. Basic human needs for material comfort and psychological security had set in motion massive economic and political changes that predated Lenin and even Marx himself.[24]

Dean's accumulated knowledge of non-Western countries, a valuable commodity during the early Cold War period, facilitated her entrée into academia and eventually allowed her to give up her FPA position. (Although Dean's Harvard stint was short, she also taught at Barnard (1946–47) and Smith (1952–54) before finding a more stable position – and an opportunity to direct the resources of other scholars into congenial channels – at Rochester.) As in her discussions of Soviet affairs, she consistently argued that crude Marxist sentiments and repressive practices in developing countries reflected an underlying drive to extend economic prosperity to the masses, and thus a stepping stone on the path to democracy. Dean's category of the "non-West" always included Russia and Eastern Europe – the communist "Second World" – as well as the "Third World" of Africa, Asia, and Latin America. She thus approached the study of the non-Western world as an insider, harkening back to her childhood in non-Western Russia. Dean contended that the imperative of modernization, not the ideological content of communism, shaped political regimes across the non-Western world. Other non-Western countries followed the Soviet Union because they found its situation familiar and admired its rapid industrialization, not because they hewed to Marxist orthodoxy. Most of those regimes simply wanted what the Soviets – and, for that matter, Western leaders, in Dean's view – wanted: to meet the needs of their populations, starting with the pressing economic needs of the poor.[25]

---

[24] Dean, *Russia: Menace or Promise?* For "low modernism," see Jess Gilbert, *Planning Democracy: Agrarian Intellectuals and the Intended New Deal* (New Haven, CT: Yale University Press, 2015) and Daniel Immerwahr, *Thinking Small: The United States and the Lure of Community Development* (Cambridge, MA: Harvard University Press, 2015).

[25] "Harvard Appoints 2 for New 'Area Studies,'" *Boston Globe*, May 27, 1947, 8. Besides *The Nature of the Non-Western World*, Dean's Rochester collaborations also produced two edited volumes: Warren S. Hunsberger (ed.), *New Era in the Non-Western World* (Ithaca, NY: Cornell University Press, 1957); Dean and Harry D. Harootunian (eds.), *West and*

This push for economic modernization was the truly revolutionary force in the post-war world, Dean contended. In the first instance, it did not flow from Marxism at all, but rather from the glaring contrast with the United States, "with its powerful and unceasing propaganda for electricity, washing machines, refrigerators, automobiles, Listerine, cosmetics, and the thousand and one things that less advanced peoples have come to want, may not be able in the foreseeable future to afford, but will seek in one way or another to achieve." Whatever country or region Dean analyzed, she argued that Marxist leanings were a consequence, not a cause, of the ferment. The real causes were simple: endemic poverty and a subjective sense of deprivation in comparison to Western peoples, increasingly overlaid with resentments of colonial oppression and a fierce nationalistic pride.[26]

With Hitler and Mussolini vanquished, Dean now saw the promise of rapid economic development and slow political maturation everywhere she looked. Concluding in 1941 that post-war international relations would encompass the entire globe, she traveled through Latin America and asserted that the region featured democracy's "substance," though not its "form." Latin American dictators genuinely cared about their subjects' welfare, and public opinion was "overwhelmingly pro-democratic and anti-totalitarian," foreshadowing the eventual development of Western-style liberal democracy. Later, in the 1950s, Dean vigorously defended "non-aligned" countries such as India against American anti-communists. It was hardly unexpected, she explained – let alone dangerous – that other countries, and especially newly independent former colonies, would formulate their own goals and interests rather than aping those of the West. Dean also identified the non-aligned countries as a buffer against communism. Modifying an argument she had earlier applied to the smaller European countries, Dean predicted that the non-aligned areas would mediate between the superpowers. Lacking the power to exert their will alone, they would work collectively through the UN to ensure their survival until they had modernized and removed the real source of global conflict: unequal development. Throughout the 1950s, Dean insisted that Americans could ensure peace only if they buttressed "the strength and sense of independency of smaller nations, as well as of potentially great nations, like India and China, which are weak only because of their economic backwardness."[27]

Non-West: New Perspectives (New York: Holt, Rinehart & Winston, 1963). Another prominent Asianist in the Rochester program was Harry J. Benda. For Dean's self-identification as a non-Westerner, see *Russia: Menace or Promise?* vii.

26 Dean, "Balancing Our Assets," *Saturday Review of Literature* (November 6, 1948), 34; Dean, "The United States and India," 45.

27 Dean, *Latin America and the War*, 17, 30; Dean, "The Role of Weaker Nations," *Nation* (December 16, 1950), 584.

For Dean, India offered a test case for the question of whether rapid industrialization could proceed under democratic auspices. Her confidence rested largely on Nehru, whom Dean saw as a charismatic, intelligent leader who had a principled but realistic view of world events and local conditions, tolerated political dissent, and pursued both the welfare of Indians and a genuine "world community." Dean also saw other factors in India, including a longstanding tradition of deliberative decision making, experience with British modes of administration, and the hardiness fostered by the Hindu tradition of non-violence, that would help it steer a middle path of "indigenous democracy" between capitalism and communism. (Dean highlighted the efforts of Acharya Vinoba Bhave, who traveled around communist-infiltrated Hyderabad urging landowners, with some success, to donate one-sixth of their land to the landless. To her, Bhave's movement proved that indigenous religious movements would outdo and thus repel communism if allowed to run their course.) Through the 1950s, Dean argued that the Indian experiment with political democracy, a mixed economy, and guided technological development illustrated what the West could expect from non-Western modernization.[28]

Yet the West, and above all the United States, would ultimately shape the outcome. Modernization, Dean argued, would fuel democratization only if the West thoroughly relinquished its imperial ambitions, assertions of cultural superiority, and, in the American case, fear of socialism. Throughout her career, Dean defined imperialism in economic as well as political terms: it encompassed not only formal colonization, "but also unilateral concessions for the development of raw materials like oil, and other advantages." Around the world, she insisted, democracy would be stillborn unless the United States opposed imperialism in all its forms – including its own longstanding status as "a crude nation of money-grubbers" who feathered their nests at the expense of poorer neighbors. Anti-democratic tendencies in the developing world did not reflect Soviet dogmatism, but rather Western imperial domination and racial subordination.[29]

In her wartime book on Latin America and subsequent popular writings such as *Russia: Menace or Promise?* (1947) and *Foreign Policy Without Fear* (1953), Dean urged American policy makers and citizens to get past their endemic racism toward non-Western peoples, fetishization of private ownership, and childish fearfulness about world affairs. Rather than naïvely expecting to be loved by all, she argued, Americans needed to grasp hard realities – especially the cataclysmic shift from feudalism to modernity, in areas

---

[28] Dean, "New Patterns of Democracy in India," *Yale Review* 43.2 (December 1953), 164, 170, 176; Dean, "He Left His Country a Future," *Saturday Review* (March 27, 1965), 26.

[29] Dean, *Latin America and the War*, 60–63; Dean, *Russia: Menace or Promise?* 64.

that often lacked indigenous democratic traditions. The United States needed to give funds and expertise to non-Western countries, stop insisting they toe a pro-capitalist line, and embrace indigenous forms of socialism that would correct the global maldistribution of resources and strengthen the world community as a whole. It should also replace loans, which fostered dependence, with direct aid that promoted industrialization and raised standards of living for the masses. Such aid, she specified, should come with no political strings attached and aim especially at agricultural modernization and the development of a light, consumer-oriented industrial capacity.[30]

14.1 Vera Micheles Dean (portrait by Barbara Sutro).
Courtesy of the Schlesinger Library, Radcliffe Institute, Harvard University

[30] Dean, "Clash of Two Systems," *Nation* (September 21, 1946), 317; Dean, *Latin America and the War*, 58; Dean, *Russia: Menace or Promise?*; Dean, *Foreign Policy without Fear* (New York: McGraw-Hill, 1953).

Legacies

Yet Dean's vision of global order rested on a second pillar as well: international organization for collective security, in addition to democratic socialism at the domestic level. She expected every country – old or new, powerful or weak, large or small – not only to meet the economic needs of the masses but also to cede a considerable degree of sovereignty to the United Nations, out of enlightened self-interest. Indeed, she saw the two processes of coordination and centralization as fundamentally identical. At both the national and international levels, she contended, local units – individuals in the former instance, nations in the latter – had become deeply interdependent. Under these conditions, active cooperation between the units, with an accompanying sacrifice of their absolute autonomy, represented the only path to peace, and thus the security of all. On the national level, this meant social democracy; internationally, it called for collective security, including a global defense force. Dean argued that universal human needs would inevitably produce these outcomes in the long run. The only real question was how to minimize violence and bloodshed along the way.

By the early 1960s, Dean's rosy view of the capacity of non-Western countries to recognize and follow their enlightened self-interest began to falter, and her vision for world order became more technocratic. In a 1962 pamphlet on the United Nations, Dean asserted that the UN aimed to consolidate virtually all of the world's military resources, leaving individual countries only those resources needed for police purposes. She foresaw political centralization as well: the emergence of a true world government, with individuals voting directly for UN leaders rather than national governments mediating their views. Finally, Dean now called for the UN to coordinate all economic aid to industrializing countries.[31]

Dean's growing concern reflected the behavior of the heads of newly decolonized countries, to whom she now ascribed significant agency in world affairs. She complained that non-Western leaders had often adopted a narrow-minded, self-seeking nationalism rather than embracing the world community. (Dean abandoned her longstanding prediction that weaker countries, wary of being crushed between the great powers, would push those powers toward cooperation under a strong international regime.) Many of these leaders had also used modernization as an excuse for dictatorial rule. And some non-Western countries

---

[31] Dean, *Builders of Emerging Nations* (New York: Holt, Rinehart & Winston, 1961) Dean, *Roads to Peace*, Public Affairs Pamphlet no. 334 (New York: Public Affairs Committee, 1962), 21, 12, 18.

sought foreign aid to gain a competitive advantage over others, or used such aid irresponsibly. In short, Dean no longer trusted that non-Western leaders sought the best for their people; many now seemed to be on regressive paths, like the fascists before them.[32]

Dean did not abandon her expectation of long-term progress, but she significantly altered her sense of both the timetable and the path to universal democracy. She predicted that few non-Western countries would immediately follow Nehru and Yugoslavia's Tito in pursuing "human values" alongside material development. Given that democracy required a revolutionary "readjustment in human relationships," she wrote, the best short-term case was probably "authoritarianism without totalitarianism." Dean's expectation of global progress persisted in the 1960s, but it came to rest mainly on technology's capacity to fuel rapid and widely distributed economic growth, although she added the usual caveat that the West must share its innovations so that all peoples enjoyed the "coming wonders" of science.[33]

Still, Dean believed to the end that something deep within human nature demanded the universal security that only economic growth and redistribution, acceptance of cultural differences, and the slow but steady growth of political liberties could bring. Like Barbara Wootton in Britain, Dean centered her international vision on welfare, although she typically employed the term "security" instead and eschewed all talk (if hardly the idea) of "planning." She proposed a world vastly different from what most Americans had experienced. Yet she framed her proposals in a folksy, accessible language and played up the connections to American ideals: common sense, neighborliness, inventiveness. She also employed familiar examples, as in calling colonialism "segregation on the world scene." Above all, Dean appealed to Americans' self-understanding as practical, no-nonsense realists. In her view, taking a realistic approach to world affairs meant enlisting other countries as allies on their own terms, and not expecting them to become clones of the United States before lending a hand. Likewise, in her advocacy of women's equality, Dean worked to promote the interests and the dignity of the powerless – with the ultimate goal of bringing them to the table themselves – by appealing to the self-interest of the powerful, while also working to enlighten that self-interest. To await an impossible future state of "universal

---

[32] Dean, *Roads to Peace*, 18.
[33] Dean, *Builders of Emerging Nations*, 203, 201; Dean, *The United Nations in a Developing World*, Public Affairs Pamphlet no. 319T (New York: Public Affairs Pamphlets, 1962), 417.

self-denial" before seeking cooperation was the height of idealism and sentimentalism.[34]

Buried deep in the archives, there are stories waiting to be told about Dean's interactions with the canonical realists and cold warriors that populate histories of mid-twentieth-century IR. She certainly interacted with some of them during her years at Rochester and NYU. Back in the 1930s, moreover, Dean had joined many other notable IR thinkers as a rare female participant at the seminal International Studies Conference. Characteristically, however, Dean found the Conference's strongly academic approach hopelessly impractical and distanced herself from it.[35] Yet this distance does not indicate her historical irrelevance. Even accounting for audiences' divergent responses, Dean's approach clearly resonated with many of the hundreds of thousands of educated, middle-class Americans – including present and future leaders – who read her books or articles or heard her speak in person, on the radio, or on television. These post-war cosmopolitans created a significant counter-current to the official policies of containment, rollback, and mutually assured destruction – a countercurrent that would crest, albeit in a much more radical guise, among a new generation in the 1960s. Within that milieu, Dean worked not only to define mid-twentieth-century liberal cosmopolitanism but also to connect it to the academic discourses of area studies and modernization theory, as well as the political ideals of collective security, social democracy, and US–Soviet cooperation – or, some would say, pro-Soviet apologetics. At a time of deep anxiety about the international scene, Dean helped convince many Americans to wade into its deep waters and carve out a role for themselves as something more than isolationists or counterrevolutionaries. For that, as for much else, she deserves to be remembered by historians of international thought.

---

[34] Dean, "What U.S. and India Agree On," *Christian Century* 71 (July 7, 1954), 818; Dean, "The Responsibilities of Peace," 244. See also the materials related to the 1951 Conference on Women in the Defense Decade, FPA Records, box 93, folder 1.

[35] "Meeting of the American Coordinating Committee, International Studies Conference, December 30, 1937," Dean Papers, box 1, folder 8. For Dean's dismissal of the ISC, see her letter to Sydnor H. Walker, October 1, 1937, Rockefeller Archive Center, Tarrytown, Rockefeller Foundation Archives, RG 1, 100 S, Box 106, Folder 957. (Many thanks to Katharina Rietzler for this source.)

Natasha Wheatley

Law's World

From where does international law think?

Scholars are today trying to unpick the relationship between *international law* and *place*, and calling on a range of disciplines, methods, and registers to do so. There is the intellectual-historical question of how international lawyers of generations past understood the geographic scope of its application, confined (for example) to the "civilized" states of Europe, and withheld from the "uncivilized" or "semi-civilized" wilds of Asia and Africa beyond.[1] Then there is the substantive-historical question of *(f)actual* legal relations between different polities and world regions (quite apart from how jurists theorized the boundaries of inclusion and exclusion), which in the hands of Lauren Benton and Lisa Ford has the power to turn frayed imperial fringes into international law's central laboratory.[2] Bridging these zonings, another vein of research stresses that "the rest of the world" was always lodged in those European disciplinary theorizations, either at a conceptual level (for example: the construction of European sovereignty always involved the construction of the non-European, non-sovereign other)[3] or at the level of transcultural interactions between legal thinkers, diplomats, and others that have

[1] Jennifer Pitts, *Boundaries of the International: Law and Empire* (Cambridge, MA: Harvard University Press, 2018); Andrew Fitzmaurice, "Equality of Non-European Nations in International Law," in Randall Lesaffer and Inge van Hulle (eds.), *International Law in the Long Nineteenth Century*(Leiden: Brill, 2019), 75–104; Gerrit W. Gong, *The Standard of 'Civilization' in International Society* (Oxford: Clarendon Press, 1984).

[2] Lauren Benton and Lisa Ford, *Rage for Order: The British Empire and the Origins of International Law, 1800–1850* (Cambridge, MA: Harvard University Press, 2016); see also Charles Henry Alexandrowicz, *An Introduction to the History of the Law of Nations in the East Indies (16th, 17th and 18th Centuries)* (Oxford: Clarendon Press, 1967).

[3] Antony Anghie, *Imperialism, Sovereignty and the Making of International Law* (Cambridge University Press, 2005).

been written out of the official story.[4] In yet another formulation, the question can also be explored as academic or institutional sociology: Anthea Roberts' study tracks national variation in the way that international law is taught, professionalized, and reproduced.[5]

But the question also has a formal-philosophical or epistemological dimension, and this chapter recovers a telling conjuncture in what we might call international law's epistemological history. From "where" does international legal reasoning begin, on what premises is it based, what is the field of possible arguments, the criteria for truth, the frontier where the well-lit sphere of the knowable gives way to the dim domain of the unknowable? This chapter explores knowledge-places and knowledge-corridors – the formal "places" from which international legal arguments begin, how those coordinates delimit what international law can formally know, and how both those things (the start point of reasoning and the geography of the knowable) have changed over time.

As international law grew into a professional field in the second half of the nineteenth century, that "origin point" for reasoning was occupied by the state. Within the dominant positivist, voluntarist paradigm, states were international law's only agents and actors – its only "legal persons." International law's binding force rested on their will and consent. There was no international legal life beyond them: one could only think about international law from inside the prism of sovereignty. This had significant implications for what international law could formally know. Among other things, it logically blocked legal knowledge about state creation and state extinction. If international law was *made by* states, it was dependent on them, and always came *after* them in the sequential-logical chain: states were its precondition. How could it possibly "know" about that which *preceded* the state, that which preceded its own operation and own conditions of possibility?[6] Consequently, international law had no capacity to conceptualize or regulate the emergence and disappearance of states. Georg Jellinek's classic *Allgemeine Staatslehre* (first published 1900), for example, flatly posited the "untenability of all attempts … to

---

[4] Arnulf Becker Lorca, *Mestizo International Law: A Global Intellectual History 1842–1933* (Cambridge University Press, 2014).

[5] Anthea Roberts, *Is International Law International?* (Oxford University Press, 2017).

[6] Early, naturalist/pre-positivist writers in international law (Grotius, Pufendorf, and so forth) did not have the same conceptual problem with state creation; they also spent far less time thinking about the state in an external sense. For an overview, see James Crawford, *The Creation of States in International Law*, 2nd edition (Oxford: Clarendon Press, 2006), 6–12. The problem described in this chapter is accordingly one arising in connection with modern international law.

construe the creation of states juridically."[7] Such matters were considered questions of *fact* and not *law* – they lay beyond the frontier of the legally knowable. Such "pre-legal" matters of fact were of no consequence to international law: debate focused on the question of state recognition instead. As the Austrian jurist Alfred Verdross summarized the traditional view in 1927, "law attaches only to the finished fact of the state."[8] The state always already existed within the frame of international law, and the latter unfolded inside sovereignty's eternal present: there was no way for international law to conceptualize the outer edges of a state's existence in time.

As a result, the birth and death of states arrived only belatedly as a topic for international legal inquiry. If law's structural blindness to state creation seemed a matter of largely academic interest in the nineteenth century, in the era of decolonization its political and practical resonance was impossible to ignore. The new political urgency of such subjects could not, however, easily dissolve the problems of logical-legal sequence. Take "self-determination," that keyword of decolonization. Attempts to construe it as an international right tripped over this legal-philosophical impasse. From a formal perspective, one could not have an international legal right to self-determination (or anything) if one was not yet an international legal person: there was not yet a legal personality to whom such a right could attach. As Nathaniel Berman explained, "the process of determination, the attainment of the indica of statehood, has always already occurred; if it has not, the entity in question does not exist in the eyes of the law."[9] It was a self-cancelling loop: how could one legitimize a claim to statehood when the legal vocabulary for doing so required that you already were one?

The disappearance and succession of states proved just as legally ambiguous as their birth. What happened, for example, to the juridical entrails of erstwhile imperial states, especially in relation to things like economic concessions and rights to resources? In determining to what extent a postcolonial state could start with a "clean slate," sloughing off inherited institutions and obligations that perpetuated dependency, the law of succession conditioned the meaning of independence, indexing

---

[7] "Unhaltbarkeit aller Versuche ... die Entstehung der Staaten juristisch zu konstruieren." Georg Jellinek, *Allgemeine Staatslehre*, 3rd edition (Berlin: Verlag von O. Häring, 1914), 270.

[8] In the nice German phrasing: "Erst an die fertige Tatsache des Staates knüpfe das Recht an." Alfred Verdross, *Die Verfassung der Völkerrechtsgemeinschaft* (Vienna and Berlin: Verlag von Julius Springer, 1926), 125.

[9] Nathaniel Berman, "Sovereignty in Abeyance: Self-Determination and International Law," *Wisconsin International Law Journal* 7.1 (1988): 63.

(in Matthew Craven's words) "either the profundity or superficiality of decolonization."[10] How could international law bind the "new" states before they had consented to it? The legal uncertainty around all these questions exposed the "contagion of sovereignty"[11] as an intellectual or philosophical problem as much as a geopolitical one: law lacked a language adapted to the new liquidity of the world of states. The first edition of James Crawford's now-standard work, *The Creation of States in International Law*, appeared only in 1979. The coherence of international law itself seemed to him to be at stake: if the emergence of states remained a matter of fact rather than law, if international law forswore all say in the making of its own subjects, then it could never be a complete or coherent system. In the preface, he paused to puzzle over the remarkable paucity of scholarship on this subject. "[A]part from Marek's study on identity and continuity of States (published 1954 and reissued in 1968), and various accounts of recognition of States in books on recognition generally, there is, to the writer's knowledge, no monograph dealing with the topic of statehood as such."[12]

Apart from what? Apart from a now-forgotten book by a now-forgotten Polish exile by the name of Krystyna Marek. Her Geneva dissertation-turned-monograph, *The Identity and Continuity of States in Public International Law*, was published more than twenty years before Crawford's. It was long, lucid, thorough, careful, sprawling, brilliant. The problem at the heart of the book – the legal identity of states, and the continuity and discontinuity of that identity over changes in sovereignty – was also the problem of their "very existence," Marek wrote in opening. It concerned the foundational question how international law might even know if one state had ended and another started.[13] As perhaps the first international legal monograph on "the topic of statehood as such," its obscurity is itself compelling. Crawford was not alone in identifying Marek's book as a disciplinary departure: when it first appeared, Verdross wrote a review that hailed it as "the first comprehensive monograph on that so topical problem, the international law identity and continuity of states" – and called it learned, keen-witted, and original to boot.[14] Her work may sit

---

[10]   Matthew Craven, *The Decolonization of International Law: State Succession and the Law of Treaties* (Oxford University Press, 2007), 5.

[11]   To adapt a phrase from David Armitage, *The Declaration of Independence: A Global History* (Cambridge, MA: Harvard University Press, 2007).

[12]   James Crawford, *The Creation of States in International Law* (Oxford: Clarendon Press, 1979), vii. The second revised, much-expanded edition is cited above.

[13]   Krystyna Marek, *Identity and Continuity of States in Public International Law* (Geneva: Librairie E. Droz, 1954), 1.

[14]   Alfred Verdross, "Review of *Identity and Continuity of States in Public International Law* by Krystyna Marek," *Österreichische Zeitschrift für öffentliches Recht* 1 (1955): 107–108.

astride an epochal shift in the history of legal knowledge about sovereignty, but Marek remains absent from histories of the field. We can recover her trailblazing book as a pivotal moment in the epistemological history of international law – a moment in which international law was explicitly reconceiving its boundaries of the knowable, and in so doing, remaking its world.

International Law as a Specular Structure / Sovereignty as a World Picture

What needed to change, formally speaking, for international law to be able to "see" the birth and death of states, to be able to conceive of the birth and death of states as a legal matter? One needed to alter the "place" and premise from which it reasoned. As long as international legal knowledge began with (and depended upon) states, the topic remained legally invisible and legally unthinkable – as Marek herself explained in her introduction. The traditional characterization of state birth and state death as beyond the pale of law's operation was incontrovertibly correct, she wrote, if the problem was approached from the perspective of state-based, domestic law:

> But it is clear that this problem can be investigated only from "outside" States themselves, since the norms of municipal law are valid only "within" the State and cannot serve as a legal criterion of external happenings. Moreover, the creation of municipal norms does not precede the birth of a State, but coincides with it, – just as the end of their validity coincides with the State's extinction. Hence, the time factor alone prevents the application of municipal norms to the question of the birth and death of States. For those who regard State law as the summit of the legal pyramid, the birth, extinction and transformation of States are thus metajuridical matters, not capable of legal appraisal. Any attempt to solve these problems within the framework of municipal law fully deserves Kelsen's picturesque analogy with Baron Münchhausen's efforts to drag himself out of the mud by his own hair.[15]

One could not begin with the states themselves, could not reason out of and through their own legal orders, for they had no capacity to comprehend (let alone regulate) their own non-existence. There was no continuous "I" that could consciously comprehend its own death, or "remember" a time before it was born.[16] The state could not see around

---

[15] Marek, *Identity and Continuity of States*, 2.

[16] In this way, we can see *Identity and Continuity of States* dovetailing with philosopher Miguel Tamen's wonderful work on legal personality. As he writes: "The 'I' cannot remember what *I* cannot remember, cannot go beyond its origin." "My literal autobiography of a former nonperson would be a story whose initial chapter would be about how my own story is permeated by the possibility, to which I am now quite foreign,

the corners of its own life. International law needed to take an existential turn. One had to move to a place "outside" the state – into the soup or river in which states swam, the thicker stream within which their appearance and disappearance was logged or recorded. States, in the end, could know so little about themselves, and only international law could remedy that lack of self-knowledge.

"When, however, the problem is seen in its proper perspective," Marek wrote, "all such artificial difficulties disappear. Since they break the framework of municipal law, the birth, extinction and transformation of States can be made the subject of legal enquiry only by reference to a legal order which is both higher than State law and yet belongs to the same system of norms, on the basis of monism and the primacy of international law."[17] That is, one could not begin with a fundamental dualism between municipal and international law: rather than separate and incommensurable, the two needed to be seen as different levels of a single, unitary legal order, with international law prime and superior.

In this monism, Marek drew explicitly on the international legal theory of Hans Kelsen and the "Vienna School" around him, especially Alfred Verdross and Josef Kunz.[18] Their influential approach to legal philosophy, the "pure theory of law," posited the unity of all law, theoretically understood: such unity was necessary, they argued, to give law any coherence. Integral to this method was the "pyramid of legal order" (*Stufenbau der Rechtsordnung*), a notion first developed by Kelsen's student Adolf Merkl. According to this theory, norms did not exist haphazardly side by side, but in fact formed a single hierarchical, pyramid-like order with the *Grundnorm*, a foundational norm, at its apex. Verdross was the first to argue that the pyramid must extend beyond state law to international law, welding them both into the same chain of norms – a principle which became a precept of the Vienna School in general. With international law at the apex, sovereignty no longer constituted an absolute or unconditional property, but a sphere of relative autonomy under the higher authority of international law.[19]

---

of not being able to tell it at all. One should like to ask: who was the first to have had the brilliant idea of personifying us? But then again the answer could only be 'some other person.' Only someone else could have had that idea." Miguel Tamen, *Friends of Interpretable Objects* (Cambridge, MA: Harvard University Press, 2001), 85–86. Emphasis in original. See generally chapters 4 and 5 on "Persons" and "Rights," respectively.

[17] Marek, *Identity and Continuity of States*, 2.

[18] On which, see Josef L. Kunz, "The 'Vienna School' and International Law," *New York University Law Quarterly Review* 11 (1933): 370–421.

[19] "If one can speak at all of a Kelsenian 'school' of international law," writes Jochen von Bernstoff, "the primacy thesis can be regarded as its shared, central project." Jochen von Bernstorff, *The Public International Law Theory of Hans Kelsen: Believing in Universal Law*

It was only this primacy of international law, Marek argued, that enabled analytical purchase on a state's existence as such. Rather than conceive of international law as *produced by* sovereign consent, sovereignty must instead be seen as derived from a superior, more encompassing, and pre-existing order. That prior, encircling legal order was the logical, jurisdictional "location" of the problem: "the problem of state continuity and identity" could "arise only within the international legal order."[20] As Marek reasoned: "On this clearly correct assumption, a legal evaluation of the birth, death and transformation of States can easily be undertaken from 'without' and from 'above,' by means of a higher legal system whose norms have existed before the formation, and continue to exist after the extinction, of the State in question."[21] For the topic to come into (legal) view, international law needed to be not only *above, without, outside*, and *beyond* the world of states, but also *before* and *after* them. International law had to exist "prior to" the state, as well as "after" it, so that there was an existing legal order in place that could witness and regulate the emergence of a new state or the demise of an old one – an order that was continuous across ruptures of sovereignty.

International law's "priority" was a normative or philosophical proposition rather than a literal historical one. As Kunz explained the point in 1933: "the *logical* and *legal* supraordination of international to municipal law is not to be confused or identified with the quite different problem of *historical priority*."[22] If one was committed to the existence of an international legal order, and if, accordingly, that order needed to be coherent, then such a founding presupposition was necessary. Reasoning juridically about state birth and state death – according to both Marek and the Vienna School – thus required a temporal-logical projection, a theoretical or imagined time travel to a point always prior to sovereignty (and always subsequent to it). Strikingly, international legal reasoning here constructed its own internal, abstract histories, rewriting the sequence of its own origins, projecting itself backward in ways that may have lacked an historical "truth" but could (ostensibly) possess a *normative* truth: a legal fiction or imagined history that made a jurisprudence of state creation and extinction possible.

Marek thereby articulated an international law that was less a subject of study than an *epistemological vantage point*: it was a place from which to

---

(Cambridge University Press, 2010), 93. On Kelsen's deeper intellectual dualism, see Mónica García-Salmones Rovira, *The Project of Positivism in International Law* (Oxford University Press, 2013), 120–56.

[20] Marek, *Identity and Continuity of States*, 3.

[21] Marek, *Identity and Continuity of States*, 2.

[22] Kunz, "The 'Vienna School' and International Law," 402.

reason, indeed the *only* place from which one could grasp and assess the beginnings and ends of state life. In this sense, Marek is not just an "international thinker" in the simple or literal sense that she thought and wrote about international law. More than that, she cultivated the international as a juridical-methodological premise, an epistemological claim. In her hands, international law becomes not just a field of activity and study external to the observer, but the *positionality* of the scholar-jurist, something accruing to them, their *location* vis-à-vis the object of knowledge. When it came to international law, seeing like a state was precisely the problem: one needed to *look from* international law (to states), rather than from states *to* international law; and view states not at eye level, on their terms, from inside their orders, but from over their heads. To borrow a phrase from the literary scholar Pheng Cheah, it was a "specular structure,"[23] one that entailed particular ways of knowing and making knowledge, and opened up a different horizon of the knowable.

This optical-jurisdictional position radically expanded law's world, its "perceptual scope,"[24] pushing back the borderline between law and fact to expand the domain of its knowledge and operation. It turned international law into a complete system. As Marek wrote, this viewpoint from "above" and from "without" left "no legal vacuum in which 'bare facts' could exist and not be subject to legal appraisal."[25] Noteworthy is the way in which this view from outside the world of states was not necessarily a cosmopolitan affect or sentiment (which is the vector along which historians usually investigate internationalism in its various guises), but rather a thoroughly legal-theoretical proposition, a foundational *jurisdictional* premise. Jurisdictional priority was not just a concept to be studied or deployed, but in fact defined the positionality of the scholar herself, the viewing platform that alone enabled the special alchemy of spinning facts into juridical matter.

We might liken the epistemological shift posited here to that entailed in the "Earthrise" moment – so memorably excavated by Benjamin Lazier – in which humankind first sees the earth as a complete sphere, a disc "suspended in the void." If earthbound horizons prevented the perception of the earth as a singular whole, the images beamed back from Apollo 8 transformed the world into "a picture," something graspable,

---

[23] Pheng Cheah, *What Is a World? On Postcolonial Literature as World Literature* (Durham, NC: Duke University Press, 2016), 49.

[24] To think with Duncan Bell's phrasing in: "Making and Taking Worlds," in Samuel Moyn and Andrew Sartori (eds.), *Global Intellectual History* (New York: Columbia University Press, 2013), 257.

[25] Marek, *Identity and Continuity of States*, 3.

an object external to the viewer.[26] Analogously, from the "ground level" of states, the horizons of legal knowledge were too low-set to know anything at all about the state's outer contours, the edges of its life. (At the very most one glimpsed the gentlest curve of a wide ocean horizon that ever so dimly suggested the shape of the whole.) Matthew Craven more recently captured the specular dimension of the problem in writing that historically the "figure of the sovereign state occupied such a central position within the discipline of international law" "that its presence or absence was not something that could be adequately conceptualized internally within the same framework": "their existence or demise could only be presupposed, or appreciated *at some distance* from the everyday discourse of an otherwise relational conception of law."[27] It was only from the distant space deck of international law that one could grasp the state as a picture – could see it as a complete object, its start points and end points, the curled lip of its own existence. In this sense, *Identity and Continuity* augurs a departure in what we might call the history of sovereignty's juridical visibility.

To view states from the outside – can it be irrelevant that this philosophical, jurisdictional departure was composed by a woman, an exile? By someone who could not (in the easy manner of so many men) confuse her own perspective with that of "the state" – could not have the pretension to speak for the state? Someone who did not have the luxury, for most of her life, of the "ground level" of her own state, who could only look at it from a distance and across (an iron) border?[28]

States from the Outside

Krystyna Marek was born in Cracow in the first year of World War I.[29] Her father Zygmunt was a prominent Polish politician and socialist

---

[26] Benjamin Lazier, "Earthrise; or, The Globalization of the World Picture," *American Historical Review* 116.3 (2011): 602–30.

[27] Matthew Craven, "Statehood, Self-Determination, and Recognition," in Malcolm D. Evans (ed.), *International Law*, 3rd edition (Oxford University Press, 2010), 205. Emphasis added.

[28] Methodologically, I am interested in exploring the personal and the intellectual as co-implicated, "parallel" phenomena, as opposed to reducing one to the other in any simplistic sense. I take my inspiration here from Peter Galison's study of the parallel development of Freud's thinking about internal, psychic censorship and his wartime experience of external state censorship. See Peter Galison, "Blacked Out Spaces: Freud, Censorship and the Re-territorialization of Mind," *British Journal of the History of Science* 45.2 (2012): 235–66. Substantively, this approach also echoes Glenda Sluga's arguments about the way in which women and actors from the colonial world often found careers and life avenues in the international world that were closed to them inside their home states.

[29] Much of the following biographical information is taken from the extended CV and dossier (written in part by Pierre Pagneux) contained in map 19 at the Krystyna Marek

member of parliament in the Austro-Hungarian *Reichsrat*. Her mother Ada was a gynaecologist who had studied medicine in Zurich and returned to Cracow to open a landmark women's hospital. The Zurich connection was important: she later sent her daughter Krystyna to finish high school in a girls' school there (Höhere Töchterschule der Stadt Zürich). Marek returned to Cracow to study law at the Jagellonian University in the early 1930s, graduating in 1936. She began work in a barrister's office while developing a doctoral dissertation on penal law. World War II intervened in a number of senses: she fled to Romania, and would not return to the Polish dissertation or the subject of penal law. (Nor, I think, to Poland.) Other questions pressed themselves into the base structure of her life. Communication lines were severed like states themselves: in late 1939, a Zurich school friend of Marek's, Gret Stoll, wrote urgently to Marek's mother Ada in Cracow with the news that Krystyna and her brother had reached Romania and were safe and well. Stoll addressed her postcard to Ada in the "ehemalige Polen" – the former Poland, now legally shrouded by occupation – *the state formerly known as …*[30]

Marek tried to return to Switzerland, but her applications were rejected despite a significant mobilization of her Swiss friends and contacts who wrote multiple letters to the authorities on her behalf.[31] In 1940 she made it to France, where she worked for the Polish Ministry of Social Welfare, before France fell, too. She reached the United Kingdom by way of Spain, French Morocco, Tangiers and Gibraltar early in 1941, where she worked in different capacities for the Polish Government for the rest of the war.[32] She quickly progressed from secretarial and editorial work, passing the diplomatic and consular examination of the Polish Ministry of Foreign Affairs in 1943,[33] and was subsequently formally appointed Attaché of the Polish Embassy in London, where she worked closely with the Ambassador Count Edward Raczyński. The two would

---

Papers, Polish Museum, Rapperswil, Switzerland (hereafter KMP). For a short biographical sketch focused more on her contributions to the Polish community, see Bogumił Termiński, "Krystyna Marek (1914–1993): Polish Lawyer and Patriot," *Revista europea de derecho de la navegación marítima y aeronáutica* (December, 2013), available at: http://rednma.eumed.net/krystyna-marek-1914-1993/ (last accessed September 10, 2018).

[30] Gret Stoll to Frau Dr. Ada Rutkowska, October 21, 1939, KMP, map 57.

[31] An das Eidgen. Justiz- und Polizeidepartement, Abt. Fremdenpolizei, Bern, n.a., n.d., KMP, map 54.

[32] Mrs. A. Deacon, Adminstrative Office (Political Intelligence Department of the Foreign Office) to Krystyna Marek, November 26, 1943, KMP, map 43.

[33] Certification of Marek passing Diplomatic–Consular Examination signed by the Minister Tadeusz Romer, Republic of Poland, Ministry of Foreign Affairs, May 5, 1944, KMP, map 18.

remain close friends for life; he wrote her letters of reference into the late 1960s.

The unorthodoxy of a female diplomat did not pass unnoticed. When the British Foreign Office wrote to the Count to confirm that Marek's name had been duly added to the Diplomatic List, he noted that she would however be unable to attend the the King's Levées, since attendance at such functions was "rigidly confined to men."[34] She could not represent the state seamlessly, or without serration. The shadows hung low, though, not only over the woman diplomat, but over the state itself. This was a Polish government-in-exile, an extraterritorial government, one excised from its state like a brain in a vat, offering only a technical sign of life. The fate of the two were tied together. As the Soviets consolidated control over Polish territory, Britain withdrew recognition from the Polish Government-in-Exile at midnight between July 5 and July 6, 1945, making legal exiles of its erstwhile representatives like Marek. That date is scattered throughout her papers, in both her academic notes and her legal status and documentation. If her life turned on its needle-head, so did the life (and death?) of the state of her youth.

It was only in 1949 that she was able to return to her doctorate, now in international law, at the Graduate Institute of International Studies in Geneva, now under the supervision of Paul Guggenheim. She worked sporadically as a bilingual secretary, translator, and editor at various international organizations to support herself.[35] Her questions were now a world away from penal law, and hardly require contextualizing. How could one tell if a state's international personality was extinguished? What was the legal effect of belligerent occupation, what was the legal meaning of independence, the legal status of a puppet state? Sovereignty in an existential key. The "identity" and "continuity" of a state, she wrote, was also the problem of their "very existence," "another aspect of the problem of State extinction": "To ask whether a State is identical with a State which has preceded it in time [...] is to enquire whether one State has died and another has been born in its place, or whether the old

---

[34] "My dear Ambassador, In your note No. 423/155 of the 16th November you were good enough to inform us of the appointment of Mademoiselle Krystyna Marek as Attaché to the Embassy. We have duly arranged for the inclusion of this lady's name in the Diplomatic List, but I should perhaps observe that she will not be able to go to The King's Levées, since attendance at such functions is rigidly confined to men." R. Dunbar (Foreign Office) to Count Edward Raczyński (Ambassador), December 7, 1944, KMP, map 54.

[35] Université de Genevé, École d'Interprètes, Examens, Diplome, 1949, KMP, map 18; l'Union internationale des télécommunications, Certificate, April 20, 1953, KMP, map 18; World Meteorological Organization, Certificate of Service, June 2, 1954, KMP, map 18.

State continues its unchanged legal personality."[36] William Rappard, erstwhile member of the League of Nations' Permanent Mandates Commission, and the jurist Hans Wehberg, were among the examiners of her thesis, which Guggenheim would describe as in a class of its own.[37]

Reviewers often felt compelled to comment on her intellectual independence. Alfred Verdross offered his praise in "his" journal, the *Österreichische Zeitschrift für öffentliches Recht*. As the "first comprehensive monograph on that so topical problem of the international legal identity and continuity of states," it was already worthy of attention; but beyond that, it was a careful, erudite, and "in many points original work" that widely overstepped "the measure of a dissertation." Marek did not just discuss the positive law, Verdross wrote, but was always at pains to dissect the "theoretical foundations of individual problems." In this connection, she was "substantially influenced by Kelsen and Guggenheim, without being dependent on them, because she also stands with some critical distance to these theories and travels in multiple new directions."[38]

After graduating in 1954, she spent four years in Germany, working the Polish Desk of Radio Free Europe in Munich,[39] and with a research fellowship at the Max Planck Institut für ausländisches öffentliches Recht und Völkerrecht in Heidelberg. Her book circulated. She often received correspondence (whether directly or via her publisher) inquiring about her qualifications. *What was the basis of this lady's authority?* Marek would patiently lay out her experience and degrees in reply.[40] At Guggenheim's invitation, she returned to Geneva as a researcher in 1958, compiling a large compendium on procedure at the International Court of Justice

---

[36] Marek, *Identity and Continuity of States*, 1.

[37] See Raczyński to Malcolm Davis (Dean, Free Europe University in Exile), February 6, 1953, KMP, map 35. The examining committee included William Rappard, of Permanent Mandates Commission fame, alongside Guggenheim and Wehberg. Certification by Rappard, January 21, 1954, KMP, map 16.

[38] Verdross, "Review of *Identity and Continuity of States in Public International Law* by Krystyna Marek," 107–108. "Sehr geehrte Frau Doktor!," he wrote to her that year: "In the coming days I will send you the proofs of a discussion that I have written about your beautiful work for my journal. I am convinced that it will give you great pleasure." Alfred Verdross to Marek, April 30, 1955, KMP, map 43.

[39] See, for example, Radio Free Europe transcript, December 21, 1954, KMP, map 9; Radio Free Europe transcript, June 30, 1956, KMP, map 9.

[40] For example: after her book was acquired by Oregon's Supreme Court library, the Attorney General wrote to her publisher seeking information on the author, "particularly with reference to the author's qualifications as an authority on international law." Marek responded with a full account of her credentials. Robert Y. Thornton (Attorney General), signed by Catherine Zorn (Assistant), to Librairie E. Droz, March 2, 1956, KMP, map 54; Krystyna Marek to Catherine Zorn, March 12, 1956, KMP, map 40.

(ICJ).[41] She was appointed a non-tenured professor (*professeur extraordi-nare*) for public international law there in Geneva in 1964, and as a tenured or full one (*professeur ordinare*) in 1967. In 1979, she was admitted as a member of the Institute de droit international.

Poland runs through this lifework as an absent-present red thread – a home fled, an erstwhile state, a government-in-exile, the reason for refugee status, the destination of radio programs that sent her voice home while leaving her body in Germany. In the last pages of *Identity and Continuity of States*, a streak of emotion rips the otherwise smooth and controlled surface of the text. International law, she had earlier explained, had a general interest in avoiding discontinuities of rights and obligations: it was thus "basically reluctant lightly to admit the extinction of a State," and could preserve the particular "international delimitation" of a state through substantial changes of territory and population, for example, or periods of anarchy and revolution.[42] What about occupied and dominated states? Belligerent occupations did not in themselves affect the continuity of a state's identity. While they remained temporary and unrecognized, occupations created facts but not law, thus leaving the original state legal personality intact. An occupied state could thus re-emerge "as itself" on the other side of illegal domination. If the occupation persisted for a considerable period, however, and commanded a relative stability, then the state would count as a "new" one should it rise again. The question of a state's continued existence – or its eclipse – thus pivoted on the point at which a temporary and provisional occupation sank or settled into the permanent.[43] On this basis, she wrote in the book's conclusion:

There *can still be* a relation of identity and continuity between the independent Baltic States of 1940 and such Baltic States as will recover their effective freedom before an overwhelming normative pressure of facts will have brought about their final extinction; *and there can still be* a relation of identity between the independent Polish Republic of 1939 and a Polish Republic *which will have re-established herself on Polish territory in time to forestall her final extinction by those same overwhelming, law-creating illegal facts.*[44]

International law's view from outside might just have the power to forestall and prevent the juridical death of her homeland. Of course, this

---

[41] *Répertoire des decisions et des documents de la procedure écrite et orale de la Cour permanente de justice internationale et de la Cour internationale de justice:* two volumes appear in 1961 and 1967.

[42] Marek, *Identity and Continuity of States*, 548 and generally.

[43] Marek, *Identity and Continuity of States*, Part I.

[44] Marek, *Identity and Continuity of States*, 581–82. Emphasis added.

fervent, necessary futurism failed to remake the world in its image. Marek had to wait until the very end. Until history ended: the Cold War over, old-new states reappeared on the map where the Soviet Union had stood. As at every other stage, the legal life of these sovereignties tangled through the legal basis of her own life. On July 31, 1992, the Swiss Federal Office for Refugees wrote to Marek seeking confirmation that she was in possession of a Polish passport, and stating that once the reason underpinning refugee status was removed, that status, too, was revoked.[45] Marek replied on August 6, and affirmed that, yes, she would now be taking up her Polish passport once again, with all the consequences of that act, renounced her right of asylum in Switzerland, and thanked them for providing the juridical foundation for her existence over these long decades.[46] She died the following year, having lived Hobsbawm's "short twentieth century" almost to the day, and in more ways than one.

Worlds at Empire's End

From her mid-century world of states occupied and dismembered, dissolved and reborn, Marek opens up the history of law's worldedness not only as an epistemological proposition, but as a geographic one, too – one that allows us to connect the fall (and rise and fall) of Central European empires to the moment of global decolonization that followed on the heels of her book. We might think of Marek's text as an international legal cusp suspended between the history of different imperial formations and their dissolutions, a bridge that ties together intra and extra European histories of sovereignty. I think of her as writing from a crease down the middle of the twentieth-century history of imperial collapse.

Identity and Continuity of States unfolds, first, in the shadow of a different state – the one she was born into, but which ceased to exist already in her infancy. Marek inherited the legal rubble of the Austro-Hungarian Empire in two senses – methodologically and empirically. Firstly, as is clear from my opening discussion, she deployed and

---

[45] Bundesamt für Fluchtlinger to Krystyna Marek, July 31, 1992, KMP, map 42.
[46] "Comme les autres pays de l'Europe centrale et orientale, la Pologne est redevenue en Etat indépendant, en train de se frayer le chemin vers la démocratie. Dans ces conditions, pretender au statute de réfugie serait de ma part incorrect à l'égard des autorités polonaises ainsi que de moi-même. J'ai donc décidé de reprendre le passport polonaise, avec toutes les conséquences que cela comporte, et par là même de renoncer à mon statut de réfugié et à mon droit d'asile en Suisse." Krystyna Marek to Office fédéraldes réfugiés, August 6, 1992, KMP, map 42.

developed further the monist position of the Vienna School of jurists, circling around Hans Kelsen, and writing over the precipice of Austria-Hungary's dissolution in 1918. For her methodological moves, her cues and conversation partners in the text and especially in the footnotes are Kelsen, Adolf Merkl, Fritz Sander, reaching back to the other Austrian Georg Jellinek, with whom I opened, and forward to Josef Kunz and Alfred Verdross. But it is not just the conceptual inheritance from this late imperial world: for her (and for others in this period), all the key examples for these questions – that is, for the birth and death of states – unfolded in Central Europe. When Austria-Hungary collapsed, the status of its successor states raised myriad questions about state identity, continuity, and succession. Were all these states juridically "new"? Were there any lines of legal continuity stretching over the rupture of 1918? The bell-weather case was always Republican Austria and its relationship to the empire; but also Czechoslovakia, and Yugoslavia, whose legal relationship to Serbia proved thorny. After World War II, Nazi occupations and annexations meant Austria and Czechoslovakia were bell-weather cases for a second time in thirty years, joined now by Ethiopia and Albania and the divided and occupied Germany. So if the Vienna School shaped Marek's theoretical perspective, at the level of state practice and empirical test cases, her argument was developed through the lives and deaths of the seam of states between the Habsburg and the National Socialist empires.[47] And in the moment in which she wrote, it was of course a third Central European empire, the Soviet Union, whose power across the states of Eastern Europe pressed legal categories to the edges of their plausibility and into the public discussion. At its foundational moment, this jurisprudence of state identity and continuity is "thinking with the cases"[48] of the Central European states.

The 1950s are perhaps the last moment in which state precarity seemed like a particularly Central European problem. By the 1960s, it was rather the legal status of "new" states the world over that galvanized legal discussion, and a jurisprudence on the status of these decolonizing states exploded. Bound together with the question of self-determination, state succession grew into one of the chief legal flashpoints of decolonization. It cut to the heart of the nature of postcolonial sovereignty and independence: were these states bound by treaties, concessions, and other legal obligations entered into by earlier imperial governments?

---

[47] Roughly half the book devoted to more formal legal argument and the second a kind of empirical tour through all the major cases of the modern period up to that point.

[48] See the posthumously published John Forrester, *Thinking in Cases* (Cambridge: Polity Press, 2017).

Clarification and codification of the law on these questions became a "matter of urgency,"[49] and the topic was taken up by a generation of jurists from the global South.[50] The two chief international legal instruments codifying the law in this area – the 1978 Vienna Convention on State Succession in Respect of Treaties, and the 1983 Vienna Convention on State Succession in Respect of Property, Archives and Debt, "painfully pieced together in the 1960s and 1970s" – documented the imperatives and agendas of the era of decolonization.[51]

It was Marek's fellow Pole, Charles Alexandrowicz, who, in his 1969 article "New and Original States," made famous the argument that states like Sri Lanka were not new arrivals into international law, compelled to accept a (disadvantageous) legal world they had played no role in shaping, but rather old or "original" states returning to the sovereignty they enjoyed prior to European colonization.[52] In this account, the juridical identity of states had the capacity to survive long centuries of imperial rule unscathed. Marek may well be thought of as Alexandrowicz's lesser known, but equally brilliant, twin. Both studied at the Jagellonian University and spent the war years in London. Marek was considerably younger than Alexandrowicz, but came to the topic well before he did. Both were centrally concerned with the capacity of the identity of states to survive imperial rule of different sorts: under what conditions does it buckle and crumble, what is the prose of its survival? A sense of the brittleness of sovereign identity hangs low and heavy in their texts, even as they attribute to the state fantastical powers of duration and persistence.

Telling is the different disciplinary ways that Marek and Alexandrowicz set about founding this sovereign durability and reasoning about "old" and "new" states. In search of a way of measuring and assessing the existence and (dis)continuity of states across time, they both reached toward that wider stream in which states swim: an international law that existed before and after them. Confronted with the same dilemmas of positivist international law, Alexandrowicz tried to solve the problem through a turn to history. Prior to positivist-voluntarist, Eurocentric

---

[49] See "First Report on Succession of States in respect of rights and duties resulting from sources other than treaties, by Mr. Mohammed Bedjaoui, Special Rapporteur," April 5, 1968, Document A/CN.4/204, *Yearbook of the International Law Commission*, vol. 2 (1968), 95 (accessible via the International Law Commission website: www.un.org/law/ilc/index.htm).

[50] See, for example, R. P. Anand, *New States and International Law* (Delhi: Vikas Publishing House, 1972).

[51] See Craven, *The Decolonization of International Law*, 2 and generally.

[52] Charles H. Alexandrowicz, "New and Original States: The Issue of Reversion to Sovereignty," *International Affairs* 45.3 (1969): 465–80.

international law of the nineteenth century, he maintained, there existed a more flexible and porous international legal order characterized by a fluid multi-normativity.[53] In a literal, historical sense, he looked to circumnavigate the current world of states by resurrecting an international law that existed prior to the current order and which in fact already recognized states the world over – including those "new" states now (re)emerging into full life in the postcolonial world. That deep-historical international law already knew these states, and would remember them – welcoming old friends back into the fold. As such, they could possess the status and dignity of pre-existing sovereigns. So where Alexandrowicz dealt with the problem of sequence and priority as a matter of historical fact – obsessively collecting and cataloguing pre-nineteenth-century treaties between European and non-European states that, he argued, showed the latter's full membership in the international legal community – Marek performed a parallel move in an abstract, normative register. She instead sought to circumnavigate positivist sovereignty's traditional priority through a series of formal jurisdictional propositions. Epistemologically, philosophically international law "preceded" and "outlived" states, she argued, and only for that reason could we know if they had died, or if they were still alive. Only the conceptual priority of international law gave us the view from outside.

That philosophical approach was itself in transition as Marek wrote. If a cohort of Weimar intellectuals-turned-refugee-scholars translated their interwar experience of the fragility of (Central European) states into a strident anti-formalism – turning from law and textualism to power and interests, and injecting those values deep into the (American) discipline of International Relations[54] – we might say that Marek doubled down on a certain sort of formalism and an unabashedly philosophical methodology. Here, perhaps, the Central European experience fractures into those (like Hans Morgenthau) thinking "from" large, powerful states such as Germany, and those thinking from the beltway of smaller polities (such as Poland) long wedged on all sides by hungry empires. In Marek we taste the "culture of formalism" that, in Martti Koskenniemi's

---

[53] See C. H. Alexandrowicz, *The Law of Nations in Global History*, ed. David Armitage and Jennifer Pitts (Oxford University Press, 2017), including the introduction by Armitage and Pitts, 1–34.

[54] Martti Koskenniemi, *The Gentle Civilizer of Nations: The Rise and Fall of International Law, 1870–1960* (Cambridge University Press, 2001), chapter 6. This pragmatist turn shaped the declining influence of Kelsen and the Vienna School more broadly. See von Bernstorff, *The Public International Law Theory of Hans Kelsen*.

account, looks to counter brute power by dragging the particularism of individual interests toward the horizon of universality.[55]

As the gravity-point of the jurisprudence on old and new states rapidly shifted south in the years after Marek published her book, the work of these two exiled Poles constitutes one refraction of the nexus between the "second world" and the "third" – one of mobile knowledges moving between, co-constructing, and contesting the world's "peripheries."[56] The story is full of returns, of cycles and circles, as though a narrative formalism should rise to meet its legal cousin. For the worldedness looped back on itself again: in the wake of the Soviet Empire's collapse, the major focus of succession debates returned "from" the global South to Eastern Europe, and protagonists wondered whether the UN conventions, shaped so intimately by decolonization in Africa and Asia, could be useful tools and guides for this post-Soviet moment on the continent.[57] Regional experiences translated into law retranslated into regions retranslated into law retranslated into regions: particular and universal, history and law, inside and outside, shuttling back and forth and back again, not unlike Marek's ideas and identity documents, that record the life and death of states in the most intimate terms – and the most abstract ones – all at once.

---

[55] In the final pages of his landmark book, Koskenniemi celebrates something he calls "the culture of formalism," which "tries to induce every particularity to bring about the universality hidden within it," and argues that it is the only thing that gives the history of international law any "coherence." Koskenniemi, *The Gentle Civilizer of Nations*, 500–509. For a discussion of the critical potential of this renewed formalism, see Justin Desautels-Stein, "Chiastic Law in the Crystal Ball: Exploring Legal Formalism and its Alternatives," *London Review of International Law* 2.2 (2014): 263–96.

[56] A raft of new scholarship explores some of these links: see for example Malgorzata Mazurek, "Polish Economists in Nehru's India: Making Science for the Third World in an Era of De-Stalinization and Decolonization," *Slavic Review* 77.3 (2019): 588–610; Quinn Slobodian, *Globalists: The End of Empire and the Birth of Neoliberalism* (Cambridge, MA: Harvard University Press, 2017) as well as the "Socialism Goes Global" project based at Exeter (http://socialismgoesglobal.exeter.ac.uk/).

[57] Craven, *The Decolonization of International Law*, 2.

Index

Printed in Great Britain
by Amazon

54726635R00214